The Power of the Modern Presidency

The
Power of the
Modern
Presidency

Erwin C. Hargrove

Brown University

Foreword by Harold D. Lasswell

Alfred A. Knopf, Inc. New York

THIS IS A BORZOI BOOK PUBLISHED BY ALFRED A. KNOPF, INC.

First Edition
987654321
Copyright © 1974 by Erwin C. Hargrove

Library of Congress Cataloging in Publication Data

Hargrove, Erwin C
　　The power of the modern Presidency.

　　Bibliography: p.
　　1.　Presidents—United States.　2.　Executive power—United States.　3.
United States—Politics and government—1933–1945.　4.　United States—
Politics and government—1945–　I.　Title.
JK516.H26　　353.03′2　　74–9939
ISBN 0–394–31724–6

Manufactured in the United States of America. Composed by The Haddon
Craftsman Inc., Scranton, Pa. Printed and bound by Halliday Lithograph Corp.,
West Hanover, Mass.

Foreword

Professor Hargrove's examination of the Presidency is no ephemeral potboiler hastily pasted together to take advantage of current headlines. By fortunate coincidence his studies had reached a certain level of completion when the entire complex of developments symbolized by Watergate broke in the news. As a result, we have at hand an impressively thoughtful and scholarly guide for anyone who wants to set his thinking straight about "the wounded Presidency."

The author makes use of modern modes of analyzing personality, politics, and society. He compares recent Presidents with one another, focusing on the role of character. Hargrove offers the striking conclusion that Roosevelt and Kennedy, for example, were "democratic characters who were teaching themselves to be political men," while Lyndon Johnson was an ideological Liberal who was sabotaged from within by an insatiable thirst for power. The author also exhibits the interplay between the Presidency and Congress, Court, bureaucracy, public opinion, ideology, political parties, military, and foreign affairs. The administrations of Eisenhower, Kennedy, Johnson, and Nixon are compared in order to bring out the full significance of motivation and style.

Professor Hargrove handles theory and data with reserve; and this critical attitude saves him from exaggerated claims to superior knowledge, or from proposing inflated prescriptions for reforming the system. Contemporary studies of policy and organization are effectively utilized in assessing the role of various Presidents in the arenas of domestic and foreign affairs. Policy is deftly characterized as "a chain of amended choices" and attention is concentrated on the factors that condition "policy mishap." The analysis shows in detail how personal motivation and style influence both the objects and the means of public action.

Heading the list of conditions that affect mishap is a Presidential style that shuts off debate, thereby narrowing both the range of choice and access to relevant fact and interpretation. Some mishaps result from the distortions produced by "groupthink," which is the tendency to sacrifice realism for a congenial atmosphere in the deciding group. Others are a result of faulty reporting by the bureaucracy to a decision unit. In the case of the former, the character of the President may or may not dispose him to succumb.

The author's analysis of cycles in American politics is especially challenging. The discussion strongly reflects the fluctuating intensity with which component elements of the "Liberal ideology" are held. On the one hand Americans approve of individualism; on the other, we are against extremes of inequality. The great Presidential heroes come at the crest of a cycle generated by an egalitarian demand to curb the excesses of a preceding phase of individual aggrandizement. Professor Hargrove calls attention to the strengthening of trends toward executive authority and control, notably in connection with the continuing crisis of national security since World War II.

In the light of Professor Hargrove's analysis the Watergate affair seems at once more intelligible and more dangerously symptomatic. When things go wrong, the American tradition in politics and business is to fire the manager, reorganize the set-up, or both. Hargrove's diagnosis calls for a much more discriminating approach. The challenge is to support the ideological dispositions and the operating practices that favor both the formation and selection of democratic characters. Hargrove does not, of course, altogether rule out the advantages to be gained from limited changes in structure. He does, however, unsparingly expose the vulnerable features of sweeping proposals, such as adoption of a parliamentary system.

The author makes no claim to have found satisfactory answers to all the questions posed by an ailing ideological outlook, or by malfunctions in the organizational system. His approach to the subject deserves to influence the post-Watergate changes that ought to be made in modifying and updating our form of government. He has prepared a manual that will be of great utility as the nation embarks on the Bicentennial exercise of reviewing and appraising our fundamental perspectives and basic structures. In my view there is too little recognition of promising procedures by which knowledge and power can be more widely, effectively and cumulatively mobilized in the civic as well as the public order. And there is no terse analytic map or model to guide thought about the Presidency in government, society, and the world community. Be that as it may, I believe that the nation is well served by having this comprehensive view of the Presidency available for reading and reflection.

Harold D. Lasswell   July 1974

Preface

As this is being written in February 1974 America is in the midst of a continuing crisis over the Presidency of Richard M. Nixon. It is not immediately clear to what extent it is a crisis of the man or of the institution or of both. The general hope is for a restoration of integrity and constitutional rectitude to the Presidency. This suggests that the crisis is not really deep but will vanish with the man. However, another view would suggest that the Presidency itself has become a kind of republican monarchy by means of which the incumbent President can abuse his powers and be unreachable by any final check short of removal from office. The questions of character and institution thus come together. It is time that we begin to ask fundamental questions about Presidential power as it has developed in midcentury so that we understand the nature of the crisis in which we find ourselves. This is the principal purpose of this book.

Other more strictly professional purposes converge as well. A book is needed that brings together the many different approaches to the study of the Presidency: empirical research by political scientists and historians; memoirs by participants in Presidential government; the work of observant and thoughtful journalists who are direct observors of much of the Presidency; and finally the concepts and theories of the other behavioral sciences that might be brought to bear upon the questions of leadership and authority in the Presidency. This book tries to bring all these approaches together.

Particular attention is given to integrating several relatively new approaches to the study of policy making into the subject of the Presidency: the analysis of leadership that draws upon personality theory and that has of late been directed toward the Presidency;[1] the concern with delineating "good" decision processes to avoid disastrous policy malfunctions, which grows out of the experience with crisis decisions in the 1960s and what seem in retrospect to have been "bad" decisions in regard to Vietnam and other foreign policy questions;[2] the new school of analysis that explains the actions of top policy makers in terms of patterns of "bureaucratic politics" and organizational routines and therefore seems to question the autonomy and rationality of the leaders of government;[3] and finally, an effort has been made to link the abundant literature upon American voting behavior to two other sets of ideas, first the view of American political ideology and culture best expressed by Louis Hartz, and second, descriptions of policymaking patterns as they vary according to electoral trends.[4]

In a sense there is a book within a book here in that I have changed my mind about many aspects of the Presidency in recent years and have used this book as a vehicle to think aloud on those questions. These musings are also addressed to my fellow political scientists, many of whom are increasingly skeptical of the President worship that pervaded our professional literature until recent years.

There is another challenge to political scientists in this study and that is the admonition to take the Presidency seriously as a field for empirical research. For too long many people in our craft have assumed that the institution of the Presidency was only susceptible to broad brush impressionistic and historical treatment by scholars because of the problems of access for conducting detailed empirical studies and because of the discontinuities of the office across time and its great variability in the tides of politics and personality. In contrast, the Congress has afforded a safe and open haven for detailed empirical studies. It is my contention that the same kinds of studies can be done of the Presidency, that problems of access have been exaggerated and that many regular patterns of behavior exist across time that can justify studying the Presidency as an institution. I hope that this book will suggest a broad framework for such inquiries.

It is impossible to write a book without having the selections of theme and the interpretations of material shaped by one's implicit values and perceptions of reality. It might be helpful to the reader to know that a personal view of politics pervades the book and surely shapes the interpretations made and conclusions drawn. The following clues to the author's mode of thought are easily recognized by him as old friends which have, for better or for worse, become one's way of looking at the world. There is first an uneasy but convinced adherence to the general body of ideas that one might call American liberalism. It is a belief in the importance of economic and social reform in the direction of greater equality and scope for living for many who now live poorly in American society and it is, even more fundamentally, an inability to identify with or celebrate the virtues of an American culture of commercialism and acquisitiveness. However, I do not see any viable alternative to incremental reform of our existing society toward unknown ends but by liberal values. There is no convincing radical blueprint for the future. Underlying this liberalism is a Burkean conservative view of man and institutions. Human nature does not change and culture and institutions are extremely difficult to alter in predictable ways. It follows that effective change in the direction of a better society can only be secured through a politics of persuasion. There are no short cuts in history. The view of American governmental institutions that appears is therefore Madisonian in the sense that it presents institutions as only possibilities for the achievement of good. There are no structural or institutional guarantees of private or public virtue. Therefore there is no faith that reforms in the mechanisms of institutions can do much to resolve fundamental ills in their functioning. This is not to say that specific reforms might not meet specific problems. But old habits and folkways are likely to shape such changes back into old paths. It is much more difficult to change the folkways and the underlying ways of thinking and feeling that nourish them. In short, our institutions are manifestations of our culture with all its defects and virtues. As we study the Presidency we find that we come face-to-face with ourselves as Americans, our beliefs, prejudices, and values. We cannot seriously discuss reforms in the Presidency without asking about how the society itself might be changed to sustain reform.

This book could not have been written in its present form without the scholarship of four individuals, all of whom also gave their critical readings and suggestions to the manuscript. Arthur M. Schlesinger, Jr., has a sensible and balanced view of American politics, which never loses sight of the moral purpose of the enterprise. James David Barber has opened up new ways of thought about leadership in his explorations of Presidential character. Thomas E. Cronin was the first among political scientists to shatter the old myths of idealization of the Presidency. And Fred I. Greenstein has provided continual intellectual and personal friendship upon a host of questions dealing with the study of the Presidency and leadership. In a more indirect sense the author acknowledges great intellectual debts to Harold D. Lasswell, Robert F. Lane, Richard E. Neustadt, and Louis Hartz. I also wish to acknowledge the kindness of William Gorham, President of the Urban Institute, who gave me a pleasant place to work and the benefit of his own good counsel.

Other friends and colleagues read parts of the manuscript and gave helpful advice and I wish to thank them now: Stephen Hess,

James Patterson, Elmer Cornwell, and Dennis Kavanaugh. Barry Fetterolf was a very efficient and effective publisher and Anna Marie Muskelly carried the manuscript through the editing process with ease and smoothness. Both were pleasant and helpful, as well as skillful and I thank them. Reba Wilson and Vicky Agee of the Urban Institute were efficient and steadfast with typing and library research respectively and I want to thank them here. All the faults of the book are mine. This book is dedicated to my wife Lynne and to my children, John, Amy, and Sarah, simply because of who they are.

Erwin C. Hargrove   Washington, D.C.
                                                         February 1974

Contents

The Power of the Modern Presidency

1
The Crisis of the Contemporary Presidency

Americans have alternately made heroes and villains of their Presidents, but we have seldom doubted the importance and value of the Presidential office as a force for good in the society and the world. Such doubts are now strong in many sectors of our society, and we are in the midst of a period of disorientation in which many of us have mixed feelings about Presidents and Presidential power. On the one hand, we want to look up to the President as the political key to the improvement of society. On the other hand, we loathe many of the actions of recent Presidents and fear that something inherent in the office and its powers leads to such abuses. We no longer possess a coherent picture of Presidential power and purpose that can be invoked to justify leadership in the White House. There are discontinuities in our perceptions of reality and in that reality itself.

This confusion is found at two levels. The first is in the realm of the symbols, values, and myths of history. The second has to do with the actual constitutional position and institutional power and authority of Presidents. The Presidency is the chief symbol of the nation, and Presidents have been among the primary articulators of the American dream. Therefore, it is difficult for us to really believe that a President or succession of Presidents can do damage to those ideals. We suppress the evidence as it penetrates our consciousness. But, on the second level, once we admit that there have been abuses of power and purpose, the question arises whether anything can be done about them. Although we have a structure of government that does provide checks and balances on the Presidential office, such controls are indirect and difficult to bring to bear. We have seen many examples in the past decade in which Presidents have been able to fight off such efforts at control. Even more importantly, an energetic Presidency seems to be the key to policy and program achievement in our fragmented political system, yet that same energy took us into Vietnam and was responsible for the crimes of Watergate.

There is one school of thought that believes that we have been President worshipers too long, that the fault has been in us and our view of American history and institutions. We have looked to Presidents to solve our problems and therefore deserve to be in our present dilemma. Certainly it is true that most of the articulate national leadership have been supporters of the heroic conception of the Presidency. And this has been most pronounced in the discipline of political science itself. The very models of Presidential leadership that have been dominant among most political scientists and historians are now subject to question in the same quarters, but these models have not yet given way to new ones. Before we explore the new, revisionist ideas let us sketch the model that has dominated scholarly writing on the Presidency for a generation.

HISTORIANS AND THE PRESIDENCY

Due to their progressive interpretation of American history, most modern historians who have written about the Presidency have unquestionably favored and promulgated the liberal, activist image of the office. In 1962 Arthur M. Schlesinger, Sr. asked seventy-five historians to rate the Presidents in terms of their greatness. The results in Table 1 are very close to the same report made of a smaller group in 1948.[1]

The judges in this survey supplied their own criteria, and there was very little dissent within the group about rankings. One of the attributes of greatness was an extraordinary talent at leadership in a period of enormous change in American history to which the leader made a creative contribution. Each of the greats was President at a critical time in history and each came through with a lasting solution. But more than this, each took the side of liberalism and the general welfare against the status quo. Even Washington the Federalist was a republican leader of a newly radical democratic kind of government. Each man had real political abilities, a feel for the mood of the times and the emerging solutions that could be pushed. Each extended and strengthened the powers of the Executive branch. Each was often embroiled in fights with Congress and the Supreme Court. And each had a vision of the potential greatness of the nation that was essentially liberal.

Table 1. HISTORIANS RATE THE PRESIDENTS*

	GREAT	NEAR GREAT	AVERAGE	BELOW AVERAGE	FAILURE
1948	1. Lincoln	7. Theodore Roosevelt	11. John Quincy Adams	22. Tyler	28. Grant
	2. Washington	8. Cleveland	12. Munroe	23. Coolidge	29. Harding
	3. Franklin Roosevelt	9. John Adams	13. Hayes	24. Fillmore	
	4. Wilson	10. Polk	14. Madison	25. Taylor	
	5. Jefferson		15. Van Buren	26. Buchanan	
	6. Jackson		16. Taft	27. Pierce	
			17. Arthur		
			18. McKinley		
			19. Johnson		
			20. Hoover		
			21. Benjamin Harrison		
1962	1. Lincoln	6. Jackson	12. Madison	24. Taylor	30. Grant
	2. Washington	7. Theodore Roosevelt	13. John Quincy Adams	25. Tyler	31. Harding
	3. Franklin Roosevelt	8. Polk	14. Hayes	26. Fillmore	
	4. Wilson	9. Truman	15. McKinley	27. Coolidge	
	5. Jefferson	10. John Adams	16. Taft	28. Pierce	
		11. Cleveland	17. Van Buren	29. Buchanan	
			18. Munroe		
			19. Hoover		
			20. Benjamin Harrison		
			21. Arthur		
			22. Eisenhower		
			23. Johnson		

* William Henry Harrison and Garfield were not included because of their brief time in office.

Three of the five got us involved in our biggest wars. Except for Washington, the other four were elected President after the opposition had been in power for at least eight years and a head of steam had built up for reform. All five began their terms with favorable congressional majorities. Three of the five were martyrs of one sort or another, two dying in office, the third, Wilson, being incapacitated during his tragic defeat over Senate ratification of the League of Nations. All thus had the makings of myth about them. All except Washington were eloquent in their use of language, and their words have been enshrined as an important part of the myths that have grown up around them. Each was savagely abused in partisan rhetoric of his own time but was placed on a pedestal after death. Finally, the great mistakes and blunders that each made in his time are known to historians but are not part of the popular myths that have been carried on.

The near greats were men with the same kinds of aspirations as the greats but either lacked the massive talent of the greats, failed to live in crisis times, or failed of historic creative achievements for a variety of reasons. Nonetheless, in terms of their style and aspirations they rank with the greats. Again, they were overwhelmingly liberal activists.

The conservative Presidents were mostly rated average or below average. The possibilities of skill and achievement here were not even taken into account by the judges. But this is not entirely a matter of subjective bias, for the genuinely great men, persons of great creative powers, seem to have in fact been liberal activists. Washington, who was conservative in comparison with the others, is the one exception. His contribution to the Presidency was in the precedents he set as the first President. In this sense he antedates the alternating spiral of conservatives and liberals.

There are several reasons why a group of prominent historians would have a progressive view of American history and of the role of the Presidency in history. Democrats outnumbered Republicans in the group by two to one.[2] This probably reflects the progressive orientation of leading historians more than anything else. A similar clustering could be expected then and now for any group of prominent historians and social scientists. James M. Burns suggests that modern scholars of American history are the legatees of the nineteenth-century orientations toward history taken from the German methodology in which many historians of that period were educated. This world view emphasized the importance of the state in history and made statesmen the focus of historical study at the expense of less visible institutions. This legacy was certainly compatible with not only American nationalism but the great importance attached to the hero in American history and life.

Less speculative and more easily verified, is the observation that twentieth-century American historians have seen Presidential leadership as the chief engine of progress in our history because the majority of them have been progressives and many were active in the Progressive movement of the first decades of this century. They were representative of professional middle classes who resented the new business elites and the commercialization of American life as well as machine politics. The reforming Presidents were seen as the chief means of fighting such new forces. This would account for the great popularity and close affinity of Theodore Roosevelt and Woodrow Wilson with intellectuals during the Progressive period. During this period there was a symbiotic relationship between liberal, activist Presidents and intellectuals. It reflected the alienation of many academics and intellectuals from the ideals and practices of a capitalist society and the looking to reform Presidents for leadership in behalf of democratic, egalitarian, and nonmaterial values. This has continued under Franklin Roosevelt and the modern Democratic Presidents. This affinity reflects the intellectual's perception of himself as occupying a somewhat marginal status in American life and as being on the defensive against the dominant ethos of a business civilization.[3] It is simply one manifestation of a common phenomenon—the attraction of professional people in highly verbal, relatively nonmaterial fields of endeavor to liberal ideology.[4] Paradoxically, although they feel somewhat separate from other elites in the society, they play the principal role in the political socialization and education of elites by their writing, and it is their ideas that permeate the textbooks.

POLITICAL SCIENTISTS AND THE PRESIDENCY

The discipline of political science developed out of the field of American history, and its practitioners have been much like historians in their beliefs about the Presidency. The office has been presented in the modern writings of political scientists as the key to political reform and policy action in American government and politics. Again, this can be explained by adherence to the progressive interpretation of American history and by personal values of liberalism and desire for reform, which has shaped political scientists much as it has shaped historians. Not all modern political scientists have idealized the Presidency, however. In fact an explicit consideration of the Presidency is absent from the writings of many political scientists who study American politics and government. This is particularly true of the more quantitative and empirical analysts of voting and legislative behavior who have confined their attention to clearly delineated parts of the political system in efforts to discover empirical regularities. These scholars have by and large tried to stay away from explicit normative questions and have not done much to integrate their work into pictures of the larger political system. For example, we now have many detailed empirical studies of committees and subcommittees of Congress, but are not very far along in our understanding of the role of Congress in the larger political system.[5] Political scientists have not thought quantitative research techniques applicable to the study of the Presidency, and it has not been clear that any kind of generalization described as theory about political regularities can be developed from the study of an institution that varies so much according to individual incumbents. Perhaps, too, the study of the Presidency cannot be satisfactorily undertaken without exploring the many relationships in the political system—between the President and Congress, bureaucracy, political parties, and voters. It would hardly be satisfactory to overlook these relationships in the study of the Presidency as they are the heart of what the President does. But a behavioral political scientist who wants to limit the relationships studied, in order to be precise about how they vary, has tended to shy away from such wide, impressionistic assignments.

The chief consequence of this orientation of political scientists to the Presidency is that the studies of the institution have been heavily laced with normative views about the role of the Presidency in American society and history. This is not meant as criticism. Normative perspectives are inherent in this kind of writing and should be present. Values are implicit in all social science research but they have been explicit in writing on the Presidency. The significance of the point is that these writings have had a great influence upon the way that educated Americans have thought about the Presidential office. The writings of Arthur Schlesinger, Jr., an historian who has written many topical works, James Macgregor Burns, Clinton Rossiter, and Richard Neustadt have been more widely read than those of probably any other American political scientist, and their influence upon the thinking of Americans, particularly upon college courses in the Presidency, and other political scientists has surely been important. These views of the office, shaped by the experience of Franklin Roosevelt, took form under the influence of Harry Truman, and were sharpened in criticism of the Presidency of Dwight Eisenhower. John Kennedy entered the Presidency in 1961 armed with a credo of strong Presidential leadership derived not only from the practice of his predecessors but from the writings of these and other political scientists about the Presidency.[6]

This body of accepted ideas on the virtues of strong Presidential leadership is now under challenge and revision by many of the former advocates of that viewpoint. This is to be expected because we have changed as well as history. Historians understand that history must be continually rewritten as perceptions and evaluations of the past change in present time and perspectives. The same is true with the social sciences. We perceive reality selectively according to our modes of thought and values. New events cause us to develop new concerns and see the old reality in new ways with new concerns. And reality itself changes. This stimulates new research and social theory. The picture now portrays the social observer in dynamic interaction with the environment he studies. The model of scientific research by a completely objective observer upon an unchanging environment requires qualification for the study of social reality. The social scientist, then, creates his world out of the mosaic of factors he constructs as his own model of reality. That picture can seldom if ever be completely verified. It is a set of more or less plausible hypotheses that must continually be corrected. This is not to despair of our ever understanding the world; only to admit that we can only understand it imperfectly.

We are in the midst of a time of revisionist thinking about the Presidency—in the aftermath of Lyndon Johnson, Richard Nixon, Vietnam, and Watergate. Not only have we changed, but the office of the Presidency has changed as well. In this respect political science literature will be interesting material for the future intellectual historian. He can chart the revision of old theories and the development of new ones which, while sensitive to new imperatives, are also likely to be bound to time and place and therefore require revision in due time.

Before exploring revisionist thinking, it is necessary to set out in broad outline the accepted views that are now under attack. The following characterizations are broad statements intended to summarize the general lines of thought of those advocates of a powerful Presidency. They are not intended to summarize or accurately depict the thought of any one individual.

THE POLITICAL SCIENTIST'S MODEL OF THE PRESIDENCY

The President is the chief guardian of the national public interest. This is necessarily true in foreign policy, since no one else can speak and act for the nation, and in domestic affairs, because of the structure of government and society. He is one of the two institutions that can speak with a single voice about national problems; the other, the

Supreme Court, cannot mobilize popular support for its policies the way the President can. The President can create popular majorities on overriding national questions. Congress is seen as overrepresenting minorities because congressmen are most likely to look to and be responsive to the organized groups within their constituencies. The President, on the other hand, is seen as having the capability to mobilize the unorganized and the inarticulate and to speak for the people against organized and influential interests.

The Constitution gives the President duties that he cannot delegate or transfer to others. He is commander-in-chief, chief legislator, head of his political party, manager of prosperity, leader of the free world, and much more. In addition, the perennial crisis of our times makes the President an actor on a world stage and a crisis manager to use these constitutional powers.

Although the office has great powers, Presidents are never constitutionally strong enough to accomplish their tasks. Congress can and does reject Presidential initiatives; in fact, the President rarely gets complete compliance from Congress. Great bursts of reform legislation come once a generation and usually take place in one or two congressional sessions of a President's term. The rest of the time the President's lot is to bargain and compromise with Congress.

A President also has great difficulty controlling the bureaucracy of the Executive branch. His appointees are only the top level of a permanent government of civil servants, and the inertia and resistance of bureaucracy are legendary. Civil servants also establish close alliances with congressional committees, and a President may find himself undercut by such unions.

Therefore, because the powers of the office are not sufficient for the duties, Presidents must create power for themselves. The President must be a skillful politician who knows how to maximize personal power in the office in the pursuit of his policy goals. First, he must dramatize himself and issues for the public in such a way as to build up public support for his policies. Second, he must bring this support to bear on Congress and, within the context of that general pressure, engage in bargaining that will result in mutual advantage in order to persuade other power holders that their interests are compatible with his goals. Third, he must organize the advising and implementing tasks in the Executive branch so that his views are protected and his programs are carried out. Skill at perceiving and protecting personal power in the Presidential chair is the only way for the President to close the gap between potential and actual power in the White House.

The implicit model of the skillful President was Franklin Roosevelt; he loved power, knew how to get it, and used it for good ends.

Much criticism was leveled at Dwight Eisenhower, who loved office but not power, who did not see it as his responsibility to be a dynamic power broker for domestic reform, and who adhered to the traditional Whig concept of the Presidency, which included constitutional restraint and a respect for the other branches of government.

Advocates of a powerful, heroic, reforming President were not enamored of this model for its own sake. They were liberals with a progressive interpretation of American history as a perennial battleground between entrenched forces of conservatism and private economic power and the mass of the people in search of greater social, economic, and political equality. Periodic cycles of reform led by heroic Presidents were the chief agencies of social change in American history. Dramatic watershed Presidential elections such as those of 1932 and 1964 were seen as the sources of such creative action. Popular politics and a popular Presidency prevailed. The New Deal experience affirmed this theory of cycles, and the unfinished nature of both the New and Fair Deals stimulated the call in the 1950s for yet a new cycle of reform and a President to lead it.

The same view of history prevailed in foreign affairs. The modern Presidency was seen as the chief force for internationalism, as Franklin Roosevelt cautiously nudged and coaxed an isolationist nation into a broader orbit and prepared it for and led it in war. Harry Truman carried this tradition on by proclaiming an American responsibility to lead the free world, and Eisenhower sought the Presidency in part because he feared the advent of a new isolationism in the Republican party.

Congressional attitudes were often seen as either isolationist or hot-blooded interventionist with a love for military solutions and a contempt for foreigners. It was the post–World War II Presidents who were thought to be directing the nation and public attitudes toward seeking national strength abroad in the defense of freedom in a steady but restrained and responsible way. In order for this to happen, the President required the constitutional latitude to act. Efforts by Congress in the fifties to curb his treaty power or to force weapons systems on him were seen as undue interference with Presidential prerogatives. Likewise Truman's intervention in Korea without seeking congressional approval was interpreted as legitimate. A congressional declaration of war would have prevented the Administration from fighting a strictly limited war.

Implicit in all these attitudes was the assumption that power and morality had to be joined in the service of American ideals. Its adherents saw this as a "tough-minded" liberalism that accepted a secular version of original sin as a fact of life. One had to create dreams out of imperfect men who always acted with mixed motives, and there was no perfection in this world but a moving equilibrium of successive approximations. Arthur M. Schlesinger, Jr. dedicated one of his series of volumes on the New Deal to the Protestant theologian and political theorist Reinhold Niebuhr. Niebuhr's central message had been that in an imperfect world, moral goals cannot be achieved without power; yet power may corrupt men and it must always be judged by higher moral standards.[7] This sense of an imperfect world and fallible men was carried over into postwar pragmatic liberal thought. To some extent it was a reaction against an earlier Wilsonian liberalism, which had sought morality in the world but with little insight into the need for power. In regard to Vietnam, we will later ask if policy makers saw power as an instrument but were insensitive to moral judgment about its use.

This model of the Presidency left little place for either a passive or activist conservative President. The office was seen to exist for a liberal activist. Conservatives were viewed to be less keen for social reform, to be less excited about an active national role abroad, and to resist Presidential power either in terms of political skill or assertion of constitutional prerogatives. Furthermore, they were on the losing end of the progressive interpretation of American history.

This general adulation of the Presidency has not been unique to the politically articulate, and until recently was shared by the great majority of people in the society. Presidential power has been rooted in popular affection and support, and we cannot understand the present crisis of the heroic Presidency unless we see its popular roots.

THE PUBLIC AND THE PRESIDENT

The American people have greatly respected the Presidential office and most of its incumbents. And yet, this has changed in 1973 and 1974 in ways that are not yet fully understood. Part of the declining regard for the office may be due to a general decrease in respect for major institutions—including government—and the actions of Watergate, and the descending popularity of Richard Nixon. One cannot fully estimate the importance of this trend without first looking at the historical background of strong support for Presidents and the institution. One can then estimate the extent of the problem.

Popular attitudes toward the Presidency are largely congruent with those of scholars. This is because both scholars and the public manifest strong beliefs in American political culture. There are also differences between scholarly and popular views. Public opinion seems to have been less ideological in judgments of Presidents than the opinions of scholars. For example, Truman suffered a great fall in popularity in his second term, even though he was generally admired by historians and political scientists. Eisenhower's popularity seldom varied from high support despite the great criticism of him as President by intellectuals. Citizens in general are more likely to judge a given President in terms of felt necessities of the time than they are to invoke ideal standards of performance in the office in terms of theories of the role of the Presidency in American history. They look freshly and realistically at events that face them. On the other hand, the general public is much less likely than the highly educated to take a President to task for violation of moral standards. Bombing in Vietnam in which many civilians, north and south, were killed seemed too remote to many Americans for them to condemn Presidents Johnson and Nixon. It was only when American casualties became increasingly visible in the lives of people at home that the public turned against the war. Many of the sins of Watergate, like wiretapping and plans for surveillance, were too remote from the lives of some ordinary citizens for them to react in the anguished manner of intellectuals who were highly committed to civil liberties. But the revelation that in certain years President Nixon paid less income tax than the poorest citizens brought forth much popular hostility toward the President.

Deference and Support

Before fully exploring recent trends we must lay out the pattern of modern attitudes toward Presidents and the Presidency.

The Presidency is the first part of the political system about which schoolchildren learn and develop feelings.[8] Other executive offices such as mayor and governor also take shape quickly for children. Unlike a legislature or a court, executives are unitary and are easily personalized. Children of course learn personal stories about the Presidents: Washington would not tell a lie; Lincoln split rails and read by firelight; Teddy Roosevelt overcame asthma by becoming a cowboy. Presidents are made to seem good men by teachers and textbooks, and that is the way children learn to perceive them. The office itself is seen as a benevolent one, and being President is regarded as the most important occupation in the country. Long before they know what he does, children regard the President favorably. When they eventually learn political partisanship, they come to see Presidents in a more realistic and more partisan light, but the residue of confidence in the benevolence of the Presidency seems to continue and is a powerful source of support for all incumbent Presidents.

Because of studies of political socialization we know more about the attitudes of children toward the Presidency than we do of adult beliefs. There have been no massive inventories of national popular attitudes toward the Presidency as there have been of voting in Presidential elections. Therefore, we must draw tentative inferences from a few sample surveys of limited scope. However, a fairly coherent picture does appear even from these different studies.

One type of national poll that is taken repeatedly is that which regularly asks citizens their approval or disapproval of the way the incumbent President is doing his job. Assessments of course fluctuate from time to time, but even so, the majority of adults normally have a favorable view of the President's performance. Most people seem to want to like and support the President, even if he is not of their party. The most regular disapprovals come from the most strongly partisan members of the opposition party. There is also a clear tendency for citizen approval of Presidents to rise at times of international crisis when Presidents call upon the nation for support. Even when a President does something that to many knowledgeable observers seems misguided, such as Kennedy's debacle at the Bay of Pigs or Nixon's invasion of Cambodia, popular support rises.[9]

These findings indicate what other more fragmentary studies show, that most people seem to put the highest value on "strength" in a President. People elect Presidents to do things and expect results from them. A President must seem to be coping, to be visibly acting. Often a performance passes for reality, at least in the short run. But voters are descendants of generations of doers, and any action seems better than none at all. If a President does not appear to be a man of action, if he seems more like a philosopher or dreamer, people are unsure of him.

Contrary to journalistic speculation at the time, Eisenhower was not perceived by those who supported him as a man who would give the country a rest. Rather, he was liked because he gave the image of strength and decisiveness. He could end the Korean War, for example. Throughout his term of office, support for Eisenhower declined when people worried that he was not working hard enough and doing too little. One study shows that a small group of adults were worried that he had not done enough to reduce the missile gap with the Soviets. The issue of the missile gap became an important factor in Kennedy's campaign and election.[10]

A study in 1966 showed that a majority of adults polled did, in fact, want a strong President who would be able to implement his policies over the opposition in Congress or any other opponents.[11] Seventy-five percent of the respondents in that year, when the Vietnam War was fully underway, said that the President should send troops abroad if he thought they were needed, in spite of popular opposition. Sixty-one percent said that they thought the President was in a better position than Congress or the people to know what the country needs.

A 1955 Gallup Poll asked a national sample to choose the three greatest Presidents; Franklin Roosevelt led the list, followed closely by Washington and Lincoln.[12] It appears that the judgments of ordinary people about greatness in the past are not much different from those of political scientists and historians.

Several studies, however, also show a fear of excessive Presidential power. For example, people who speak in favor of a strong President also tend to favor the two-term limitation on tenure.[13] This is having one's cake and eating it too, for the limitation of tenure protects the nation from dictatorship. Yet the strong President provides needed action. Such ambivalence about power is very old in America. In all our institutions, public and private, we put our leaders on pedestals and then curb their power. We give them great authority and then worry continually about how they use it. We are individualists who build up individual leaders of whom we make great demands; yet at the same time we criticize them unmercifully and seek to pull them down because we too are all individualists. We admire the pioneer, the inventor, the industrialist, the sports star, the military hero, the Western marshal, the lone hero who gets things done, but all the time we are ambivalent about anyone with power.

We need to know a great deal more than we do about American attitudes toward authority and leadership. Why, for example, do we put tenure limitations on executives, Presidents, governors, and mayors and not on legislatures? Our collective feelings about executives are much stronger. Society-at-large has hardly seemed to care about Congress or state legislatures or city councils. Is this trust or indifference? If one invests strong feelings in an executive, must one also necessarily have mixed feelings about that power? But human feelings are mixed by nature, and one does not feel all one way about anybody or anything. Perhaps the power of the American Presidency to evoke awe also evokes ambivalence and fear of power. Certainly it seems true that the greater the capability of an individual President to evoke strong positive emotions among the public, the stronger the tone of criticism from the public of him. The bland Presidents have evoked little response either way.

There can be no question of the power of the Presidency to evoke strong emotional responses. Whenever a President has died in office, the nation has been in genuine mourning. This has been the case regardless of who the President was. Descriptions of popular emotion at the time of the deaths of Lincoln, Garfield, McKinley, Harding, Roosevelt, and Kennedy are very similar. Comparable feelings in Britain seem to occur only when a monarch dies.[14] The Presidency taps feelings that in Britain are directed toward the king, the symbol of national unity and the repository of collective affections.

Studies of popular reactions to the murder of John Kennedy show that feelings of emotion were evoked on different levels. First, people grieved at the loss of a vibrant person. Many compared it to the death of a friend or relative. Symptoms such as the inability to sleep or eat were common. Interviews conducted during the awful weekend after the assassination revealed that many people had strong personal identifications with Kennedy that reflected their own hopes and worries. They had seen some facet of his Presidency that had encouraged them. The young were entranced by his idealism, blacks by his compassion, and so on.

Second, there was a sense of shock that a blow had been struck against the Presidency and therefore the nation. People were initially concerned that there might be a threat of some kind to the office of President, some concerted effort to do harm to the nation.

Third, perhaps touching the deepest chords of all, was the immediate sense of relief that the transition from one President to another was going to take place smoothly and that the continuity of the nation was to be preserved. The new President was in command and the business of government was going forward. In some murky way, religious and patriotic feelings seemed intermingled here. People went to church in great droves, not only to pray for the slain leader but also to pray for the republic and to reaffirm the bonds of national unity and the importance and value of the American nation. One can recall the atmosphere of sadness, quiet, and yet gentleness in personal relationships that was present everywhere.[15] This phenomenon of identification of God and nation is not fully understood, but it surely is more than superficial. It could be criticized as a debasement of faith into a kind of secularized national religion; however, the depth of feeling shows without question that the Presidency has the power to evoke strong responses in citizens.

It seems probable that people have looked to the Presidency for more than pragmatic, workaday political leadership. They also look for signs that all is going well with the republic. The state of the Presidency is the public's key to the health of our democracy, and they look for cues from the President about the directions the society should be taking. They project their private needs and fears onto him and charge him with a trust. As we will see, the conduct of the Presidency during the Vietnam War and the Watergate affair has poisoned the public atmosphere of American democracy and alienated a great many people from their institutions.

CHANGING PUBLIC ATTITUDES TOWARD THE PRESIDENCY

A number of surveys in recent years have documented a sharp decline of trust and confidence in government and other major American institutions including most leadership groups. In 1964, 76 percent of the American public said that you can trust the government in Washington to do what is right "just about always" or "most of the time." By 1972 this figure had dropped to 53 percent.[16] A survey conducted in November, 1973 by the same group that had recorded the earlier changes, the University of Michigan's Institute for Social Research, reported that 66 percent of those polled felt they could trust the national government only "some of the time." Those choosing that answer were 20 percent more than the respondents to the same question a year earlier during the 1972 election.[17] In 1971 Louis Harris reported on changing public attitudes toward leadership of the Executive branch, Congress, the Supreme Court, and the military between 1966 and 1971.[18] For those who had a "great deal" of confidence the Executive branch dropped from 41 percent to 23 percent, the Supreme Court from 51 percent to 23 percent, Congress from 42 percent to 19 percent, and the military took the steepest drop, from 62 percent to 27 percent. Clearly any change in attitudes toward the Presidency is part of a larger reassessment of American institutions. In 1966 the Michigan Survey Research Center asked a national sample during a mid-term congressional election which occupations they ranked most highly. The President won hands down with 52 percent, whereas U.S. senator got 2 percent and the nearest to the President was "famous doctor" with 14 percent.[19] One study in California in May, 1973 showed a sharp drop. Only 34 percent of the Californians expressed a "lot of confidence" in the Presidential institution and 31 percent said they had "not much confidence."[20] Evidently there was a brief spurt of increased confidence for the Presidency in late 1972 and early 1973 before Watergate broke publicly, which probably signified approval of Presidential achievement of détente with China and the Soviet Union and the successful conclusion of a peace agreement in Vietnam.[21] In this survey the President led both Congress and the Supreme Court in degree of trust.

However, surveys in 1972 and 1973 showed that a majority of the public supported congressional power over Presidential power. Congress was perceived as being the proper agency to act to meet the nation's needs—doing something about economic problems, declaring war, sending troops overseas, and keeping out of war.[22] The Michigan survey taken in November, 1973 recorded that 44 percent said that the President should have less influence over policy and 45 percent saying that the Congress should have more influence. In 1972 in the same survey 41 percent had said they most trusted the President to "do what's right." In November, 1973 the affirmative response to the same question fell to 24 percent.[23]

Many different streams of opinion run through these expressed attitudes. The decline of support for all the institutions of national government clearly antedates Watergate. It could reflect increasing feelings of frustration about the seeming inability of government to end war and prevent inflation and crime. These attitudes have perhaps become stronger in a cumulative, reinforcing way as new problems of energy and food shortages, and simultaneous increases in unemployment and inflation have appeared to explode without any effective governmental response.

But surely Watergate has had its impact and strengthened the increasing distrust of the Presidency. In January, 1974 only 26 percent of a national Gallup sample reported that they approved of the way President Nixon was doing his job.[24] This support figure had been at that approximate level since the late fall of 1973. From the early summer of 1973 until early 1974 large majorities of national samples expressed to pollsters their beliefs that President Nixon was involved in the planning of the break-in at the Watergate and knew about and probably participated in the cover-up and therefore in obstruction of justice. The same surveys, however, never registered a majority of voters favoring impeachment of the President, although by late 1973 those favoring impeachment were a plurality of 4,470.[25] Evidently many citizens viewed impeachment as a blow to the republic. Just as Mr. Nixon had been returned to office in 1972 on the slogan "reelect the President," thus compensating for his lack of personal popularity, so refuge behind the institution of the Presidency in 1974 might save him and keep him in office. This suggests that in fact there is a psychological predisposition in Americans to identify the Presidency with the health of the nation—even in the worst of times. This belief may arise from a fear of political and constitutional instability as much as from any positive identification with the Presidency as a force for good.

In January, 1974 the *Washington Post* sent reporters to a number of House districts to gauge public ideas about Nixon and impeachment. The findings, while impressionistic and drawn from conversations with only 244 voters, confirmed many other reports on the state of public opinion. The voters were described as "unhappy with Nixon, uneasy on impeachment."[26] The balance of opinions about the President, resignation, and impeachment was similar to that described in national surveys. The most interesting finding was a fear that impeachment would somehow dishonor the nation or bring political instability. One Mississippian who disapproved of the President said, "I don't believe he should be impeached. I don't see how that would help the country." Another citizen expressed fear of the adverse effect of impeachment proceedings on the country, adding, "I'm not at all interested in Nixon's future. America is at stake, not Nixon." One congressman remarked that his constituents seemed to regard impeachment "as sort of repealing the Constitution. No one can remember the impeachment of anyone, let alone a President." One lady remarked that impeachment was like overthrowing the government the way Europeans used to do and added, "it's like taking law and order in your own hands." Those who preferred resignation to impeachment often mentioned that this would be better for the country. There seemed to be little concern for the President in such thoughts.

These attitudes suggest that no matter how unhappy people may be at the state of the Presidency, they still place a high value upon the nation and the Constitution. Disillusionment and disapproval of the performance in national institutions of government are not really carried to the conclusion of rejection of the basic institutional system. The November, 1973 Survey Research Center national survey revealed that the proportion of people who wanted to make some change in the form of government dropped from 26 percent a year earlier to 21 percent. Changes in confidence at different levels of government were also recorded. State and local governments received far more confidence than the national government—a reversal of the attitudes of the year before. Trust in Congress remained stable over the year, though not high. But confidence in the Supreme Court rose from 26 percent to 39 percent over the year.[27]

These and previously cited attitudes suggest that people are likely to change their attitudes of approval and disapproval toward specific institutions of government without challenging (in their own minds) the validity of the underlying constitutional system. This is perhaps a highly desirable flexibility within a stable constitutional framework. However, it is cause for distress that levels of confidence in the performance of all institutions are so low. There is a basic alienation in the air. But more effective performance by these institutions could restore popular confidence.

Earlier assertions that a majority of the public is likely to give approval to the incumbent President regardless of the circumstances need further qualification. The earlier conclusion was based upon reactions to Roosevelt, Truman, Eisenhower, and Kennedy. Of these Presidents Truman was the only one to ever register more disapproving than approving citizens and this was due to public unhappiness with the intractability of the Korean conflict. The other three Presidents were extremely popular: Roosevelt as a great crisis leader, Eisenhower, who reigned over a period of good feeling, and Kennedy, a vibrant and appealing young hero who gave the country a sense of dynamism and progress. Political scientists were too quick to cite this regularity of approval for successive Presidents, save Truman, as a manifestation of the deference for the strong symbolic role of the Presidency in the American constitutional system. In fact, these individual Presidents were being approved. This became clear when both Johnson and Nixon duplicated Truman's feat of having a majority of citizens against them for an extended period of time. In each of the three instances the incumbent President was associated with turbulent times and a seeming inability to act to meet the existing problems—Korea, Vietnam, racial strife, crime, Watergate, the energy crisis, and inflation.[28] It may be as well that Truman, Johnson, and Nixon lacked the ability to strengthen themselves with publics by direct personal appeals in comparison to the other three Presidents.

These conclusions suggest that people are able to separate Presidents from the Presidency in their minds and value the institution but not the man. The one exception would be in the extreme case of impeachment in which concern about the institution protects the man.

It is also evident, however, that a succession of poor Presidents can erode the legitimacy of the institution itself. The sharp decline of citizen respect for and confidence in the institutions of American national government has not yet reached the point of criticism of the constitutional system itself, but a continually decreasing degree of support and confidence could have that effect. The legitimacy of a political system to its citizens is perhaps initially built up historically out of that system's effectiveness in meeting national problems. Once established that legitimacy is strong and can survive periods of lack of effectiveness of government. But if effectiveness disappears for too long, legitimacy may begin to decline as well. We have perhaps begun that descent in America.

What can be deduced from the two sets of information about public attitudes toward the President? Before Lyndon Johnson it could be said that there was strong, established support for Presidents and their leadership in the political culture. After Johnson, Nixon, Vietnam, and Watergate, we must modify this conclusion. Presidential performance is fully as important as incumbency to ensure popular support for Presidents. Political scientists carried the deference for Presidents thesis further than it should go. Nonetheless, it appears that Americans do want strong, effective Presidential leadership and that many forces in the political culture will act as resources for Presidents who seem to be providing such leadership. In this sense the original view of public deference for the Presidency, as qualified, is valid. Thus, it is not inappropriate to describe the current decline in confidence in the office as a crisis for the Presidency.

EROSION OF THE HEROIC MODEL

Elite attitudes toward specific institutions of government are as likely to change in terms of degrees of approval and disapproval just as are popular views. Many former celebrants of Presidential power—most often Democrats—are now looking for ways to revive the congressional capacity to check Presidential powers. Such changes lack staying power because they are tied to partisanship, policy and ideology, and reversals in attitude following shifts in power and office.

This is not to say that all changes in elite attitude can be explained in such a way. Expert observers of institutions are more likely to be sensitive to the need for fundamental institutional revision than are publics. Elites watch more closely and think more carefully about the changes in power and the consequences for society and the political system. Publics on the other hand are more likely to hold fast to basic constitutional outlines as a matter of dogma and vary their attitudes to specific institutions according to changing events and conditions. Very few citizens are likely to develop new political theories about whether the balance of power and authority between given institutions should be altered in a given direction as a matter of principle and permanence.

Since 1964 a succession of historical events have been the stimulus for a complete reconsideration of the heroic model of the powerful, virtuous President set out earlier in this chapter. We are now in a period of revisionist thinking by scholars, journalists, and many educated observers of the Presidency on the subject of Presidential power and purpose. Most of these people are former celebrants of the heroic Presidency. Conservatives who were never advocates of Presidential power are not participating in this reexamination to any great extent, and many conservatives find themselves defending the vigorous use of powers by a Republican President. This is politics whether it be a congenial stance to them or not.

Revisionism must be taken seriously because the questions raised go to the heart of the primary functions of our political system. The essential question is whether or not the United States will find itself with a republican monarchy that is able to escape constitutional control in the final analysis. Before posing this question, let us inquire into the historical events that have prompted its asking.

Vietnam War

The Vietnam War contributed in several ways to the decline of the heroic conception of Presidential leadership. First, a powerful, autonomous Presidency in foreign affairs seemed less reassuring if one believed that United States intervention in a civil war in Vietnam was not required by American national interest but was dictated by a mistaken reading of aggression seen in the context of a Cold War rivalry between the United States and China. The doctrine of containment of communism was seen as too rigidly applied. Vietnam was not a test case of United States capacity to resist wars of national liberation but a tragic blunder of a President and his foreign policy advisers. The very same arguments that had been used by liberals to support American intervention in Korea seemed much less convincing to many of the same people fifteen years later.

Second, the manner in which Lyndon Johnson took the nation into the war caused many to question their previous views about the latitude of the Presidency in foreign policymaking. The Gulf of Tonkin resolution was taken to Congress seemingly as a request for limited action but was used as a virtual blank check for unlimited military action by the President. The decision to begin bombing North Vietnam was made without public discussion. Combat ground troops were introduced into South Vietnam by the subterfuge that they were to protect American military posts when in fact they were soon fighting. The nation found itself in a war with little public preparation for the fact. The lack of constraints on the President suddenly did not seem so desirable. People began to talk about the need for Congress to regain possession of some of its abdicated authority in foreign affairs.

Third, Johnson's style of directing the war was as high-handed and secretive as possible and helped create a massive credibility gap between President and press and President and public. Public statements from the President and Administration on the purposes and progress of the war were often at sharp variance with the estimates of knowledgeable experts, whether newsmen or scholars or antiwar activists, and increasingly stirred the fears and conflicted with the intuitions of large portions of the public. Subsequent memoirs on the President's conduct of the war give a picture of an extremely centralized and one-sided system of governance in which the President held all the cards, solicited all the information, scorned and isolated dissenters, and was unreceptive to any criticism of either means or ends. The inner councils of the Administration are now seen as having been composed of extremely self-confident people who were ideologically anticommunist and who possessed a zeal for using American power in the world and a relish for the brandishing of military power. Hubris seemed to be their greatest collective trait.[29] All these things took the halo off the idealization of Presidential power in foreign affairs.

The Great Society

The Great Society programs that flowed from the 1964, 1965, and 1966 sessions of Congress were enacted during one of the three great periods of creative domestic reform in the century, the others having been the New Freedom of Woodrow Wilson and the New Deal of Franklin Roosevelt. John Kennedy had prepared the way by initiating many of the ideas, much as Theodore Roosevelt had done for Wilson. However, in practice the new programs designed to end poverty, improve education, increase racial integration, and bring a larger measure of equality to American life often did not work well.

First, President Johnson and his aides were more interested in legislative victories than in program implementation. The competition of politics drives a President to define achievement as a good legislative boxscore with Congress. All the obstacles to Presidential leadership have been seen to be on the input side, and this is where the energies and the plaudits have gone. This is paralleled by the tendency of political scientists to study the input side of government and pay little attention to the practical application of policy and its effect on people. In fact, experience has shown that many of the legislative programs were poorly conceived in the White House, and that they were pushed through Congress so rapidly that many of their flaws, which might have been discovered in bargaining between President and Congress, were not found until later. For example, the explosive nature of the community action segment of the antipoverty program might have been anticipated.

Second, the Great Society programs were basically different from those of the New Deal. The Roosevelt Administration either distributed money to people, through such means as social security, minimum wages, and farm subsidies, or it provided regulation, such as in labor-management collective bargaining and the selling of common stock. These programs are relatively easy for government to accomplish, for they have precise goals and require only a routine bureaucracy. People did not have to be changed, only served and restrained or curtailed. But many Great Society programs were much more ambitious in that they were directed toward fundamental social change. Experience has proved that it is far more difficult to change human beings than to distribute funds and regulate trade. There are a number of reasons for this. (1) Human nature is not that pliable. (2) We do not know enough about the phenomena of poverty or education to know what action to take in many cases. (3) The federal bureaucracy is an uneven instrument for the achievement of deliberate, controlled social change. Many of the old-line agencies and departments were geared to New Deal programs and staffed by civil servants weaned on such programs. For example, traditional approaches in public housing and social welfare, which were custodial and paternalist, were calculated to destroy new approaches. (4) Programs that emphasized decentralization to the field and delegation to state and local governments encountered the weakness, ineffectiveness, and poor staff resources of those governments. For example, local educational establishments are characteristically status and routine ridden hierarchies that find it very difficult to embrace innovation.

The White House found that it had relatively little control over the administration of federal programs because the permanent bureaucracy was often unresponsive, an old problem, and because it lacked the machinery by which to evaluate the effectiveness of programs in action, a new problem. This compounded the problem of bureaucratic responsiveness to top officials and the lack of knowledge about social phenomena. The federal government has had limited means of estimating the degree of success of social programs.

The upshot of these problems was that many observers began to say that the advocates of the heroic Presidency had been too quick to assume that a creative Presidential legislative role was sufficient for Presidential achievement. This view had been based on the New Deal experience, which subsequent history had shown to be limited. Some drew the conclusion that such heroic stances in the White House were harmful because they dramatized the gap between utopian rhetoric and the actual capacity of government to deliver the goods. Hopes were raised and then dashed down. It followed that reforming Presidents should not be rhetorical and heroic, at least not until they got their own executive houses in order.

Presidential Personality

Lyndon Johnson was a problem in and of himself. He was far too openly and nakedly a man of power to ever be able to establish a rapport with the American people. A man of genuine idealism, he was his own worst enemy because of a compulsive insecurity that caused him to continually take a defensive position against criticism and an offensive position toward associates and friends. All his adult life he had struggled to overcome the label "Texan" and to be accepted as a national leader; he never felt that he had succeeded even as President. In addition, there were deep cravings for power within him that were fed by personal insecurity and that generated a style of leadership that was too often suspicious, bullying, and manipulative. Saddled by his own perceptions of these handicaps, he often acted to assert his power over others when it was not necessary and did him harm. And because this style was so evident, there was a great lack of trust of him throughout the society. The credibility gap was the result.

Other great Presidents of this century shared a psychological need for personal power and developed the skills of power manipulation out of such a need. However, the two Roosevelts and Wilson were able to disguise their liking for power under the veneer of aristocratic public personalities. People could identify with the public parts of their personalities. With Johnson, on the other hand, the insecure private man was continually on public display.

It has been a common belief among students of the Presidency that a successful President must want personal power and enjoy its use. A nonpolitical man is not needed in the White House. The personal drive for power will serve the purposes of public policy. This was certainly the case in Johnson's skillful managing of the Great Society legislation. But the overtones and aftermath of the Johnson style, especially in foreign policy, seemed in many ways to do damage to the man, his policies, and the office of President. It caused students of political personality to reassess the optimistic belief that the strong, personal need for power and its skillful use are always functional for Presidential greatness. In fact, Eisenhower's restrained style of leadership and his refusal to take precipitous action in foreign affairs suddenly looked good by comparison. In 1954 he had refused to intervene militarily in Indochina against the advice of his secretary of state and Joint Chiefs of Staff because Congress and the United Kingdom would not go along.

Richard Nixon's Presidency has reinforced the liberal critique of growing Presidential power; Nixon is a conservative President brandishing the weapons of the office in ways that might have drawn praise had he been a liberal. However, it is not simply a matter of the liberal ox being gored for a change. Nixon's Presidency has affirmed the continuity of trends in the office that are distressing to many liberals and conservatives. His conduct of the war in Vietnam, including the invasion of Cambodia and the bombing of all of Indochina, was carried on without regard for the opinions of Congress and with a maximum assertion of latitude for Presidential war powers. Even after a peace agreement for Vietnam was signed, the United States continued to bomb Cambodia with no legal authorization from Congress and with very little pretense of seeking the need for any such authorization. When, in the spring of 1973, the question of Watergate erupted, it became clear that Nixon had instituted in the White House the most closed, isolated, and centralized government of modern times. To some extent these men saw themselves as on the defensive and besieged by enemies in Congress, the bureaucracy, and the media, and sought to dominate the government without the cooperation of Congress, leaders of public opinion, and the permanent government of the bureaucracy. This kind of thinking led to the pathetic scandals that we call Watergate.

The style of authority that reflected an almost Gaullist view of the Presidency as standing alone ascendant above any other national institutions of government had its origins in a Presidential personality that had contempt for political opponents, often characterized as "enemies," and a self-image of crisis leadership as a time of testing both for the nation and the leader himself. However, in this view of authority there was no place in the short run for accountability to the democratic fact or principle. In President Nixon there seemed to be a mingling of a personal neurosis and a belief in accountability to self and to history but actual contempt for democracy.

Liberal Thought

All these views regarding Presidential leadership were linked with changing ideas in American liberalism about the power of government and the purposes of power. Liberals who were themselves caught up in administering social programs came increasingly to wonder whether government was not too blunt an instrument to achieve social change. Senator Fulbright summed up the thinking of many liberals about foreign policy in the characterization of the American role in the world as the "arrogance of power." George Kennan became the chief spokesman for a view that he had long held, but that had previously been unheeded by others, that moralism was the chief obstacle to a flexible, realistic, and, in fact, moral foreign policy. Kennan, speaking to and for liberals, was actually a classic conservative in his disdain for a popular, militant, chauvinistic foreign policy.[30] In fact, conservative themes of caution, prudence, and a sense of the limits and abuses of power came to the fore in liberal thought during the mid- and late sixties and affected views of the Presidency.

Scholarship was also affected by the development of new themes. First, the idea came into prominence that the President was not the only source of policy innovation in American politics. It was shown that the reform legislation of the sixties was incubated, introduced, and espoused by creative members of Congress in the fifties.[31] Second, studies showed the glaring weaknesses in the administration of Presidential programs.[32] One could forecast a development of a revisionist model of the Presidency that would emphasize the limitations of the office and the contribution of other centers of power in the national system.

This revisionist model was in fact being developed not by conservatives but by disillusioned liberals. It was of a piece with the disenchantment of liberals with aggressive foreign policy and a powerful federal government. The main outline of the model was built around three arguments. First, we must stop making larger-than-life heroes out of our reforming Presidents and assuming that Presidents can work wonders. Thomas Cronin has called this "The Textbook Presidency," referring to the fact that textbooks in high school and college have overemphasized the power and capabilities of Presidents to do good.[33] The textbook model has been a caricature of the modern liberal model. Second, we must recognize that Presidents have the power of life and death for millions of people and that there is very little short-run accountability and control by the other institutions of government and the people over Presidential power. Decisions to bomb North Vietnam, to use military threats in a crisis situation, and to send troops to a danger spot are the President's to make, and we have not worked out institutional means to check him. Perhaps even more forbidding is the fact that the military Presidency has become a gigantic bureaucracy that is now difficult for even the President to control. For example, in the spring of 1972, the air force general in charge of the air war in Vietnam evidently exceeded orders in the bombing forays he ordered, and there is a good indication that the high military command knew the facts although perhaps the President did not. Third, we must recognize that the domestic Presidency has also become a bureaucracy that again the President cannot easily control. If he has difficulty taming it, the link of accountability to the citizen is even weaker.

The revisionist model thus would develop more modest ambitions for the office, would find ways to curb its power in foreign affairs, and would not make such grandiose claims for its potential achievements in domestic affairs. However, this model as it has been expressed is not a viable long-term possibility. It reflects the fact that we are in the aftermath of a period of the excesses of power in which there is a reaction against the uses and misuses of official power. Although we are now discussing the possibilities of governance in modest terms, a time will come when a climate for reform will build up in the society and a heroic President will again come to the fore. The potentiality for heroic political leadership cannot be permanently removed. Therefore, ways must be found, not to scale down the ambitions and powers of the office, but to make it accountable and responsible. Also, future conservative Presidencies will not be the same as those in the past. As the Nixon Administration has shown, there is much in common between his style of governance and that of the previous Democratic Presidents. Finally, the revisionist model will not take root chiefly because it is not compatible with either the political culture or the institutions of government. Presidents have been the chief articulators of the American national myth of liberty and justice for all. There is a dynamic quality in the political culture and the Presidential office that will thrust the expectations of heroic leadership upon Presidents and judge them accordingly. Because of the great pluralism of our society and the fragmented character of political parties and Congress, the great difficulties involved in creating coalitions for constructive action in the society and in government mean that all those who want action will push the President to act. It is not just that Presidents will seek power, but that many others will advocate Presidential power to further their own ends. The important question therefore becomes not one of scaling down the Presidency but one of finding ways to make powerful Presidents politically and constitutionally accountable to other institutions of government and ultimately to the people.

This view rejects the glib assertion that there is nothing wrong with Presidential power so long as preferred goals are being sought. Such a view sees the current dilemma as simply the dissatisfaction of liberals that Presidents Johnson and Nixon have violated liberal values. If that is the case, all that would be needed is the right man in the White House, and we can go back to business as usual without revising our normative models of Presidential leadership. But it is not that simple. In the decades since World War II, fundamental changes have been occurring in the Presidency that should be of concern to liberal and conservative alike who believe in constitutional government and political accountability.

PROBLEMS OF THE HAMILTONIAN PRESIDENCY

James M. Burns has accurately described the contemporary Presidency as Hamiltonian, meaning that the Presidency is close to the semimonarchical power that Alexander Hamilton wished it to be.[34] The office is not directly accountable to others as is the prime ministry of Britain, where the leader of the majority parliamentary party is prime minister. His cabinet, a mechanism for committee rule, is chosen from the leaders of the parliamentary party. These parliamentary leaders are also the executives of government and are able to formally dominate both legislative and executive functions. Ideally this means that there is effective government in the sense that the executive can get what it wants from the legislature but also that it is government by a committee, the cabinet. The prime minister cannot act without the assent of the majority of his close colleagues.

The Hamiltonian Presidency is very different in that the chief executive is not a committee but a single man. In the final analysis all his immediate colleagues must defer to his decisions. President Nixon did not always consult with his secretaries of state or defense when he made crucial Vietnam decisions. Similarly, he secretly tape-recorded all conversations in his personal White House offices over a three-year period with the knowledge of only three White House aides. Certain problems emerge from the singularity of this office.

Personal Qualities

The nation is dependent upon the quality of mind and moral character of the man in the White House. There is not a predictable party ideology and program that an entire governing Cabinet can follow as in a parliamentary system. Nor is a President restrained in any regular and effective ways by his closest associates within the Executive branch. When it comes to a final decision they all defer to him, often against their better judgment. The system thus has the quality of a monarchy in that respect.

Within the White House the semiroyal trappings and excessive deference given a President by his aides can work to preserve the private prejudices of a President and insulate him from the "outside." This is of course common to all organizational hierarchies but it seems to be a particularly acute problem with the Presidency perhaps because of the dignified aspects of the office. Of course there is also the fact that he wields such great power over the careers of his associates and subordinates that the court politics of currying favor is endemic and the courage of facing a President with unpalatable truths is uncommon.[35]

The Invisible Institution

The Presidency is more than a man—it is now an institution of many roles within the White House and the Executive Office of the President. This great proliferation of positions began to develop just before World War II in the form of a modest expansion of Presidential staff. The intention was that the President would have a relatively few personal aides who would be responsible only to him and not actors in their own right. The problem was that with the growth of the Presidential bureaucracy many of these people have became potential actors in causes of their own, free of Presidential supervision and yet politically and constitutionally accountable to no one else. Most of them are not confirmed by Congress, unlike the top officials of the departments, and therefore not required to justify their actions to the public or the legislature. The doctrine of executive privilege is invoked to protect the Presidential right to private advice. Yet many people in these posts exercise greater powers than Cabinet officers and heads of departments. Staff positions have unintentionally become agencies of administrative and political power.

CENTRALIZATION AS A SYMPTOM OF WEAKNESS

The growth of Presidential bureaucracy as a separate institution from civil service and other departments has not really enabled the President to direct those sprawling bureaucracies in an effective way. This, then, is the paradox of the drawing of initiatives and the centers of power into the Presidential orbit. Such action signifies recognition of the great difficulty the President and his aides have in learning about the bureaucractic actions in the implementation of Presidential policies, or in securing responsiveness from the departments and agencies to Presidential directives. The linking mechanisms necessary for program direction and learning about their actual results, which should exist between the White House and the great departments of state, are rudimentary. The result is to compound the draining of power to the center. It is an increasingly enfeebled center, however, since it lacks sufficient "windows on the world" or instruments of command.

Command

Within the strictly Presidential sphere the President possesses powers of command that are virtually unchecked and often lead to actions that are undetected by anyone except a few close aides. The war in Vietnam has shown us the great command powers of the President in military matters. When President Nixon decided the only way to convince the North Vietnamese government to come to an agreement over terms to end the war (late December 1972) was to bomb North Vietnam, he gave the orders and no one could stop him. But this is open and obvious power and it is effective only in wartime. There are much more subtle secret powers that have emerged in the revelations of Watergate.

Americans learned that the President had authorized measures of internal security called the Huston Plan—after their author, a White House lawyer. The plan involved wiretapping, burglary, the opening of mail, and surveillance of supposed subversives. Presidential agents also carried out wiretappings and burglaries, thereby breaking the law. All these acts were justified in the name of national security, but on these occasions they turned inward against uncertain targets of supposed threats to the national security among the citizenry. There were also other tawdry instances of violations of law. The White House "enemies" list, which was to be a guide for the Internal Revenue Service, under White House pressure, to harass political antagonists of the President by auditing their tax returns is an example. These excesses might not have been discovered had it not been for the one discovery of the burglary at the Watergate of the offices of the Democratic National Committee. This great threat to the liberties of Americans revealed that Presidential powers originally invoked in the name of action for national security against foreign enemies had now been turned against American citizens and opponents of the President.

Domestic Weakness

Despite these actions there is still the paradox of the continuing weakness of the Presidency in domestic affairs. Granted the President has to control the budget, particularly in the face of increasing congressional ineffectiveness in influencing budget formulation as an overall matter. This does give him great influence over trends in national life. But he lacks the political and organizational resources to do much that is effective about the deep social and economic problems of American life. Of course all modern democratic governments face the problem of being overwhelmed by domestic problems arising from a rapidly changing technological society, which they neither understand nor can resolve. But the American President is peculiarly alone in this responsibility. He lacks the help of a national political party as an agency of government since parties are primarily electoral organizations. He finds it difficult to carry the Congress with him much of the time because that fragmented and divided body is hard to move in any direction. Public opinion in a pluralistic society is itself uncertain and divided on the nature of problems and their solutions. Publics are also difficult to mobilize for support of decisive governmental action in domestic affairs.

In sum, there is the paradox of a President with far too much power in foreign affairs and far too little influence in domestic policy. It would seem likely that both conditions have been responsible in recent history for growing popular alienation from the Presidency— the first an anger at abuses of power and the second a frustration over problems not met and solved. The imbalance between power and responsibility has somehow got to be brought into a new golden mean in which responsibility and power are joined.

These are the problems that will be addressed in this book. We will begin with the dilemmas of Presidential personality, explore the growth of the institutional Presidency and accompanying problems of accountability and effectiveness, and then turn to foreign and domestic policymaking in those contexts. Finally, we will seek prescriptions for the future.

2
Presidential Personality

Our liberal faith in the inherent union of power and purpose has been shaken by the events of the sixties and seventies. Older literature on the Presidency is filled with litanies to heroic leadership emphasizing the skills of power maximizing, the importance of Presidential autonomy in foreign affairs, and the sure success of Presidential leadership for social change provided that sufficient political power could be amassed in the White House. We had assumed that ideological purpose was sufficient to purify the drive for power, but we forgot the importance of character.

Niebuhr writes of the element of "irony" in history in which a hidden relationship is discovered through experience. Virtue becomes vice through some hidden defect in the virtue. Strength becomes weakness because of the vanity in strength. Wisdom becomes folly because we do not know its limits.[1] He sees American liberal culture as continually overtaken by irony in its pretensions about the relationships between virtue, wisdom, and power. We are blind to the sin of pride in our sense of virtue.

The normative models of the Presidency that have been dominant in political science have manifested an irony of liberalism. They call for a President who can seize personal power in the office and use it for the achievement of liberal policies. But the irony is that the search for power may have unintended consequences not in accordance with our liberal values.

33

CHARACTER

In the heyday of Lyndon Johnson this writer developed the thesis that personal insecurity and political skill were linked. The creative politician was depicted as the man who required attention and needed to dominate and therefore had developed skills of self-dramatization and persuasion that would serve those needs. The thesis was applied to American Presidents. The two Roosevelts and Wilson were pictured as men in need of attention and power, and skill and creativity were related to a perpetual striving to serve these goals. Presidents lacking such needs were also seen as lacking in abilities, for instance, Taft, Hoover, and Eisenhower. They were pictured as almost too healthy to be good leaders.[2]

Richard Neustadt presented the view of the Presidential office and the skills required.[3] The Presidency was seen as institutionally weak in power, and each President had to start anew in developing political resources. A sensitivity to power and power relationships was therefore essential. Conditions of support within and outside of government had to be built up out of the perspectives of others who had power in their own right, independent of the President. My argument went further than Neustadt's in asking what kinds of personalities had such power skills.

This thesis implicitly assumed that Presidents were guided by moral purpose, and it was frankly biased in the direction of the liberal power-maximizing Presidents. It was assumed that purpose would purify power. To be fair to oneself, the argument was made that such power striving, if rooted in personal needs, could lead to self-defeating eruptions of personality such as Theodore Roosevelt tearing his party apart in 1912, Wilson's rigidity in the League fight, and FDR's plan to pack the court. However, it was assumed that institutional checks and balances were sufficient to control such behavior. The price was worth paying because strong, political leadership was required.

Lyndon Johnson seemed the ideal President in this scheme of things in 1965. His voracious needs and insecurities did provide the fuel for his great abilities in the service of genuinely liberal values in which he deeply believed. How much of this position needs to be reevaluated now that we have had a longer and fuller look at LBJ? And does the experience of Richard Nixon, also a power maximizing leader, reinforce a new concern about character and power in the Presidency?

The earlier formulation reflected the liberal optimism of the time that power would be used for the right purposes. Therefore, there was insufficient inquiry into possible variations in the personal needs for attention and dominance of creative leaders. The hypothesis about the relation between needs and skills was taken from Harold Lasswell, but optimistic conclusions were drawn from the inference, something Lasswell did not do. Lasswell drew a distinction between "political man" and "democratic character." The former sought a political life in order to bolster low estimates of the self. Early feelings of deprivation would be overcome by political successes. His prime type of political man was the "agitator," who taught himself to play on the emotions of audiences, whether large or small, and directed their attention and affection toward himself. The democratic character, on the other hand, had successfully passed through the developmental crises of life and had no such insecurities and needs. He had "outgrown" politics, and in a society conducive to the development of democratic character there would be no political men.[4] Lasswell did not solve the problem of what to do about selecting leaders until that ideal time, so this writer adapted the model of political man to the requirements of democratic leadership, aware that a price might have to be paid but not greatly concerned by this. The experience of Johnson and Nixon has increased that concern greatly. The tragedy of each Presidency has been that the basic insecurities of the man, which were one basis for the talent that had been developed, were also the principal reason for failure. The negative effects upon the Presidency of these insecurities have been great.

This chapter will compare Presidents Johnson and Nixon, on the one hand, with Presidents Franklin Roosevelt, Eisenhower, and Kennedy on the other, in terms of the influence of personality upon Presidential style and actions. The comparisons between these men will be marginal so that we may see, for example, the psychological correlates of certain political skills, in one or more men that are missing, along with the skill, in others. The Presidents are grouped in this way because of the conviction that Johnson and Nixon brought destructive personality traits to the office while the other three—in varying degrees—combined political ability with the democratic character required of an American President. After the development of these psychological profiles we will draw together propositions that emerge about personality and leadership style in the Presidency.

THE ANXIOUS LEADER

Lyndon Johnson

In Johnson were combined colossal physical energy, acute intelligence, a generous sympathy for the common man, a potentially explosive insecurity, and a desire for personal power that often confused leadership with absolute dominance. As a young college student he developed a style of influencing others in campus politics that was based upon a one-to-one relationship between himself and the person he wished to influence. He first ingratiated himself with that person by using his acute ability to see the needs and especially the weaknesses of others. He thus found a way to meet those needs or play on the weaknesses; what had been originally a relationship in which he was to serve turned into one in which he became the dominant partner. This was the key to his political style. He thought in dominance-submission terms. The drive to perpetually dominate was fed by powerful inner anxieties. He had to prove his success and thus his inner worth over and over. These inner needs were most clearly revealed in insecurities that emerged in reactions to criticism and perpetual efforts to be loved and appreciated.

In bargaining relationships in which the other person had some independent power, Johnson could in fact bargain in a restrained way, moderating his drive to dominate by realistic perceptions of his own power resources. But when he was clearly in control and the need to bargain was reduced, he overrode subordinates and associates by absolute domination that brooked no criticism or opposition. The first pattern was the dominant one in his Senate years and the second, which always existed in his relations with his staff, increasingly characterized the Presidential years.

Johnson was always at his best in a "closed politics" situation in which he was able to develop one-to-one bargaining relationships with a number of individuals and in an arena in which the principal actions were instrumental and there was not a great deal of value conflict. Emphasis could be put upon the means of action, the practicalities of getting agreement at which he was so skillful. This style found its most constructive expression when he was Senate majority leader. He was able to establish one-to-one relationships with individual senators on a bargaining basis. He found ways to meet the political needs of most members and thus exact a price in support of his measures. His role as broker between the Republican President and liberal and conservative Democratic factions in the Senate expressed his talents well.

All this was congruent with his ideology of consensus politics. His view of the nation had been shaped by a Texas populism that did not really quarrel with the values of American capitalism. The goal was simply to make sure that all people had the good things of life, that material prosperity was common. Thus in the consensus years of the fifties, when the political divisions of the nation were not deep, Johnson in the Senate could concentrate upon reconciling limited disagreements with little concern about the ends at stake.

However, during the Senate years there were portents of his future Presidential style. Johnson was constantly bedeviled by the insecurity of being a provincial political leader with roots only in Texas. He could never quite make the leap to national political figure, and he had few ties to national political constituencies. This was a form of insecurity that continued to bother him for the rest of his political career.

He also showed an acute inability to find and retain capable staff in his Senate posts. He drove his aides so mercilessly and abused them verbally to such an extent that the most able people would not work for him.[5] His relations with the Senate press gallery were good because he could deal with a handful of reporters individually in the same way he did with senators. Even so he showed that critical questions could cause him to fly into a fury. Another sign of his insecurity was his perpetual worry about why people did not love him. For example, in the summer of 1960 he asked a friend: "Just what is it that people like so much in Jack Kennedy?"[6] The real question was: Why do they love Kennedy but not me?

In Johnson's first months as President he had the opportunity to use the positive elements of his style to best advantage. The nation wanted unity and reassurance after an act of horrible violence, and his first actions restored the confidence of people that all was well with their government. He did this superbly by dramatizing the decisiveness with which he took charge, by addressing Congress with a strong plea adapted from John Kennedy's inaugural phrase "let us begin"; it now became "let us continue." Within a few days he had gained the confidence of the nation.

Johnson's dream was to be a great reforming President like his hero FDR, and his strongest thirst was to put his own stamp on the Administration and remove the Kennedy stamp from it. He sought to be a consensus leader of a great majority, and from 1963 until 1965 he achieved this goal. He led Congress to enact the legislative programs of the Great Society, won reelection overwhelmingly, and demonstrated a political skill and artistry that had not been seen since FDR. He saw himself as one of the great Presidents of all time, and this was indeed what many were saying. The liberal model of the Presidency seemed to have emerged incarnate in LBJ. His greatest virtuosity was in the leadership of Congress. It was his home and he understood its members. He had a superb sense of strategy and tactics and knew, as had Wilson and the two Roosevelts, when to push and when to hold back, when to bargain and cajole and when to threaten. Of course, following the 1964 election he had more Democratic votes in Congress and much of his legislative program had finally reached its time for enactment after many years of build-up, but still his skill and forcefulness ensured that the results were unequaled by anything since the one hundred days of the early New Deal.

It is commonly said that there was a limit to the size of the audience with which Johnson could be effective, that his strengths were with individuals and small groups rather than large audiences. This was true in one sense. Uneasy as a national politician, fearing that he would be tagged provincial, he often put a veneer of piety and self-effacement on his public personality that actually concealed the real color and vitality of a rich, expressive personality. It was also a fact that his powers of empathy were best exercised on individuals and not groups. However, he did have considerable skills at self-dramatization and at the heightening of issues through public acts. His dramatic settlement of a railroad strike, the barnstorming through Appalachia proclaiming a Great Society, his exuberant campaigning in 1964—all these actions showed that he did know how to strike a bond between the Presidency and the people. Although he lacked the veneer of the two Roosevelts and Wilson, and the personal appeal of Eisenhower and JFK, he did have the ability to evoke political support for himself and his programs throughout the society. However, there is considerable evidence to show that people did not love him and that many distrusted him as a "politician."[7]

The great insecurity that filled Johnson caused him to act at times to undermine his very support. In May 1965 he ordered the marines to the Dominican Republic in the face of incipient civil war there. His reason was a determination that another Cuba be prevented. But when his action was criticized he created a crisis of credibility for himself by a series of public statements in which he claimed the danger of a communist takeover to be far greater than the evidence warranted. The polls showed that he had majority support but this was not enough. He wanted no criticism at all. Consensus politics had become the politics of unanimity.[8] He was to repeat the pattern with Vietnam in a much more self-destructive way.

Johnson's general style of policy decision and executive rule was to seek unanimity in government and absolute submission to his wishes. Chester Cooper describes how this passion prevented any challenge to his Vietnam policies from within. He ran the war in regular consultation with the secretaries of state and defense, the Chairman of the Joint Chiefs of Staff, the head of the CIA, and his Special Assistant for National Security Affairs. But much of the rest of the government was excluded from policymaking. He had an almost pathological fear of leaks and wanted to keep as many people in the dark for as long as possible. Key officials involved in some phase of the war were often denied information they needed by the White House. In the late summer of 1968 when the President became displeased with the views of the secretary of defense on the bombing, he cut him off from cablegrams from the Paris talks. Cooper adds:

> This compulsive secrecy was not so much a conscious conspiracy as it was a reflection of the President's personal style—a style that favored a "closed" rather than an "open" system of policy making. Nothing pleased him more than to "surprise"; nothing angered him more than to have a "surprise" spoiled by premature disclosure. It was common knowledge that the President would change his mind on a pending policy decision or personnel appointment if there was advance, accurate speculation in the press.[9]

This is not to deny that Johnson attracted able people to government and launched many exciting programs. But in those areas where he took sustained interest he acted to stifle disagreement and dominate unquestionably. This was especially true in foreign policy and particularly in regard to Vietnam.

Johnson's habitual administrative style was compounded by what would seem to be ego defensive behavior in regard to Vietnam. He could not brook criticism within; he did not want to hear unfavorable analyses; he took personal umbrage against dissenters. The result was that it took him three years to learn that he could not win the war.

His belief that the President should be free of partisan attacks in foreign affairs became a rigid and compulsive attempt to deny legitimacy to public critics and antiwar dissenters, and he characterized them as "nervous-nellies" to near traitors who made it more difficult for the United States to persevere in Vietnam by encouraging the enemy to think the public did not support the President. He no longer sought consensus but attacked his critics and showed all his old sensitivity to criticism and his self-pity openly.[10]

Johnson's personal flaws led to the cumulative credibility gap that began with the 1964 campaign and continued with the charge of deceiving the public by his promises that there would be no war. Another source was the Gulf of Tonkin resolution, sent by the President to Congress in August 1964, which gave the Executive a blank check to resist aggression in South Vietnam but which was later used as a justification for a wider war in a completely unanticipated way. The deceptive manner in which combat troops were sent to Vietnam with minimum publicity widened the credibility gap. Another problem was the several elaborate peace offensives and bombing halts that were subsequently revealed as charades designed by the President to convince his critics that the North Vietnamese did not wish to negotiate, when in fact he did not wish to negotiate either.

Lyndon Johnson had taken a war that other Presidents might or might not have become involved in and made it his personal crusade. This was a form of rigidity that was typical of him when he was under attack. He had always placed himself at the center of his political world, for example, referring to the high court as "my Supreme Court," and his strong reaction against criticism of Vietnam was a personal reaction rather than a political one.

All these factors taken together help to explain Johnson's continuation of a policy that could not succeed and his inability to see that fact. In the spring of 1968 the point was reached at which the President was in almost complete physical isolation from the country and there was serious question about whether he could be renominated. It was not until the shock of the New Hampshire primary, the Tet offensive by the North Vietnamese, the request by American field commanders for 200,000 more ground troops, and efforts of his own secretary of defense to reverse the Administration policy that he reluctantly admitted that his policy could no longer be pursued. Whether with this decision to open negotiations and retire from the Presidency he also became convinced of the wrongness of his policy is less likely. Rather, he simply learned that his political capital would not carry him any further in support of his policies.

These character flaws would probably not have damaged Johnson's Presidency seriously had it not been for Vietnam. He would have been an unloved but respected President of great domestic achievement admired for his political skill. But this would have been a Johnson operating in a field of pluralistic, domestic, political constraints. In the Vietnam arena he could impose his will on the government, though not on the society or even on reality, and in the absence of constraints he fell back on the urge to dominate, which when fed by his insecurity in the face of criticism eventually destroyed him.

Richard Nixon

The shock to the contemporary Presidency is that Richard Nixon seems to have many of the same self-defeating traits that plagued Lyndon Johnson. It would not be amiss to claim that the crisis of

Watergate was in essence a crisis of the President's style of authority, isolation, contempt for opponents, encouragement of toughness and vindictiveness, and sense of himself and the White House as besieged by enemies. This style is of course deeply rooted in personality.

Throughout his career there has been a persistent search by observers for the "real" Nixon or the "new" Nixon. This puzzle was based on the fact that Nixon as a congressman, senator, vice president, and Presidential candidate seemed to be a chameleon who took coloration from the immediate political context. Doubt was expressed as to whether the inner man had a core of convictions that guided him, yet he was a hard partisan campaign fighter who had a rhetorical and moralistic style.

Newsmen developed an antipathy to him early in his career because of an almost esthetic dislike of his banal, unctuous, rhetorical style and because of a belief that he lacked convictions and yet was ruthless in his pursuit of opponents. Nixon has always seen himself as beleaguered by enemies, and his habitual response to opposition has been that of counterattack. Therefore since his early career he has been locked in a struggle with most of those who write about politics. This has made it difficult for him to explain himself through the media and has accounted for much of the unflattering caricature of Nixon that has appeared in political journalism.

The man has been much less of an enigma since he became President. The Presidential office engaged a much fuller range of personality and style than did his earlier positions, and general patterns of behavior have emerged about which there is common agreement. We also now have much more information about his early life and career, which adds to the cumulative picture of characteristic ways of feeling and acting. A few scholars have pulled all of this together in attempts at psychologically informed biographies.[11]

In one sense this fuller picture could not have been drawn until after Nixon had been President for a time because the experience of performance was lacking. This was particularly true since he played such a limited role in his eight years as vice president and his congressional career was brief and highly specialized. However, the kernel of the "real" Nixon was present all along had observers thought to look at the man in terms of developmental biography. In fact it probably would have been possible to predict in 1968 a general outline of Nixon's style in the White House, although of course his reaction to specific events could not have been predicted. We could have predicted that he would tend to isolate himself and create a barrier of protective aides. We could have known that he would emphasize public rhetoric and shrink from face-to-face bargaining in government. We could have pointed to his predilection to see the crucial events in which he is involved as personal "crises" and tests of his will and strength. We could have known that he responds to criticism by counterattack. Finally, we could have seen that these characteristic ways of thinking and acting were rooted in a personality that seemed uncertain of its own inner core. Rhetoric, attack, and will were clearly compensations for an inner uncertainty. However, in 1968 this would have had to be balanced with the belief that Nixon out of office for eight years had mellowed and matured into a more relaxed, self-confident man, a "new" Nixon. But if we take the personality theory approach seriously, we should not think that deeply rooted earlier patterns disappear. Although they are usually moderated by growth, the individual is always recognizable.

None of these predictions were made because Nixon was a mystery to many and was described in piecemeal terms. Another way to characterize Nixon is as a Southern Californian who has always distrusted Eastern and liberal "establishments" and who believed in the Horatio Alger story for himself and for America. This subcultural background and conservative ideology leads to Nixon's hostility to the major universities, the national media of communication, the liberal establishment of his own Republican party, much of the federal bureaucracy, and the Congress itself. Nixon sees all these as bound up in protective alliances and policies derived from the New Deal. The result is Richard Nixon the loner and outsider, who, at the elite level as President, seeks to use public rhetoric to forge a new alliance of "middle Americans" against all those elements in the society and government toward which he feels hostile.

An intensive analysis of Nixon in 1968 could have revealed such a pattern. However, it is doubtful whether anything would have come of it. Republican partisans would have seen such a man as a strength. Democrats would have been hostile, and indeed were anyway. Few could have presented an objective picture that would have been influential with anyone. This is very unfortunate because the important question was never asked. Does this man join to his ambition such an inner hurt that he may at a time of crisis act in a way that is destructive both to himself and others? And an equally important question should have been asked. What is the likely effect of Nixon's everyday style of authority upon the office of President? We can now answer these questions from experience, but any such account follows logically from what could have been known about Nixon in 1968.

As a child Nixon was shy and aloof. An old girlfriend remembered that he was "lonely and solemn. He didn't know how to mix." A teacher remembered that he was fastidious: "He wasn't a little boy that you wanted to pick up and hug."[12] One suspects that there were many forces in the immediate Nixon family impeding the development of a sense of confidence and security: the authoritarian father was an economic failure and the family had to struggle for a living; two brothers died in childhood; there was little in the way of established community or subcultural tradition to rely on as a source of personal identity beyond anomic lower-middle-class society.

Despite these factors in his upbringing Nixon had a quick mind and was ambitious. He was continually running for office in high school and college, and his teachers and classmates remember that he was always out front, working and running hard.[13] He was a brute for self-discipline. In college he gradually developed a style of seeking success that turned weaknesses into strengths. He overcame shyness by developing a skill at oratory. Thus, by rhetorical argument, which he developed fully in law school, he compensated for an inner lack of affect and spontaneity. Underneath this ambition, however, was a sense of pessimism and fatalism. He found law school difficult and thought of quitting several times.[14] He was very discouraged at his lack of success as a small-town lawyer before the war.

In 1946 when the opportunity to run for Congress was presented to Nixon, he seized it and developed a recognizable style in that race, a style that he has employed ever since. It was his first independent political success and that success helped him find a way of action that brought together disparate forces in his personality in a unified, constructive way. It was a style that rested upon intensive homework, dependence upon no one, a highly developed skill of rhetoric, and a calculation of timing and issue. Since that time he has seen every major event in his political life as a crisis that he has surmounted in the same way, by combining homework, independence, and rhetoric.[15]

Clearly there is a vein of insecurity that can be seen in his obsession with how well he will meet a crisis. His revealing memoir, *Six Crises*, reveals Nixon's perpetual confusion of political event and personal crisis. Several of the incidents, such as the impromptu kitchen debate with Nikita Khrushchev, seem too trivial to be objective crises. Others, such as the Hiss case or the 1960 Presidential campaign, were important events but not personal crises except insofar as Nixon saw them as such. A politician whose orientation was more outward, toward objective achievement, would not see such events as crises but as opportunities and challenges. However, Nixon laces his book with prescriptions on facing crises that are extraordinarily revealing of inner doubts.

For Nixon the crucial time during a crisis is that of preparation; one must decide how to act and then steel the will to adhere to that decision. He writes:

One of the most trying experiences an individual can go through is the period of doubt, of soul-searching, to determine whether to fight the battle or to fly from it. It is in such a period that almost unbearable tensions build up, tensions that can be relieved only by taking action, one way or the other. . . . A leader is one who has the emotional, mental and physical strength to withstand the pressures and tensions . . . and then, at the critical moment, to make a choice and to act decisively. The men who fail are those who are so overcome by doubts that they either crack under the strain or flee. . . .[16]

These are not the words of a man who is confident that he is in fact a leader. Rather, in each new crisis he must prove it to himself and always face the fear of failing to meet the test.

He describes the preparation for battle, the intense work, the inability to sleep, the great emotional tension. All the key decisions must be taken in isolation. Eventually things become focused, as he writes of the time before the "Checkers" speech of 1952:

Now the emotion, the drive, the intense desire to act and speak decisively which I had kept bottled up inside myself could be released and directed to the single target of winning a victory.[17]

He speaks of the broadcast as the test of whether he would stay on the ticket or not and adds:

This speech was to be the most important of my life. I felt now that it was my battle alone. I had been deserted by so many I had thought were friends but who had panicked in battle when the first shots were fired. . . . I knew I had to go for broke. This broadcast must not be just good. It had to be a smash hit—one that really moved people. . . . I felt I had to launch a political counterattack to rally the millions of voters in my television audience to the support of the Eisenhower ticket.[18]

He remembers that as he talked all the tension drained out of him. But then he warns that there is a great danger of error after the moment of testing when one relaxes. One may lack the "necessary cushion of emotional and mental reserve."[19] These are the words of a man who fears loss of self-control, who does not trust the spontaneity of his inner life but must structure and guide his feelings.

This scenario of crisis has been repeated a number of times in Nixon's career. Three dramatic instances of letdown were his speech denouncing the press after his defeat for governor of California in 1962, his denunciation of student radicals as "bums" after his speech on the Cambodian incursion in 1970, and his attack on the Senate after the defeat of the nomination of Harold Carswell to the Supreme Court in 1970.

Many of his decisions about Vietnam seem to have been made in a self-induced crisis atmosphere, the same pattern as before. He solicited advice and then retired to a remote place to make a decision in isolation. Once he had made up his mind he communicated that intention to very few people but preferred to make a speech on national television, which he wrote himself. Often these speeches went through ten or so drafts and soul-searching rather than through staff work. He had trouble sleeping and worked through the night. And always there was the fear of letdown.

The decision to invade Cambodia in 1970 and 1971 as well as the 1972 decisions to bomb North Vietnam were made in this manner. Surely a great deal more was involved in the President's mind than his preoccupation with his own strength of will. He genuinely believed in the importance of the United States negotiating from a position of strength in Southeast Asia. His ideas are held in common with his advisers and are not unique. But he invests these ideas with a particularly intense personal theme of concern about his own strength and will. This is not a claim that Nixon acts aggressively in foreign policy in order to "test" himself in some psychological sense. It is an expression of concern that he may, in a time of stress, confuse his own inner preoccupations that he be resolute with the requirements of the objective situation. The fact that the possibility exists is disquieting.

We would prefer a leader who is not carrying the load of self-doubt along with the objective problem and who therefore does not personify issues. But President Nixon's remark during his speech, on the Cambodian action, that he would rather do the right thing even if it meant he would be a one-term President shows that the preoccupation with self is just beneath the surface.[20]

A number of the Nixon patterns make sense in terms of what has been said here. He is not comfortable with individuals and small groups but feels at home with crowds. As an insecure man uncertain about his own identity, he finds identity in the many roles he plays. Thus what is often taken to be a lack of conviction is rather an absorption in varied but often contradictory roles of the moment. He surrounds himself with tough men, men like H. R. Haldeman, John Ehrlichman, John Mitchell, John Connally, and Henry Kissinger, who will protect him and strengthen his own resolve. He sees political life as a series of crises and therefore times of personal testing. He is a dirty fighter in politics but actually sees himself as virtuous and, out of his great self-pity, as constantly unfairly attacked by enemies. Therefore he relishes the counterattack. His self-pity and the lack of confidence lead to a kind of self-seeking moralism in his public rhetoric, the Uriah Heep aspect of his character, which is present in most of his dramatic speeches from Checkers to Watergate.

Nixon also has great courage, which is part of his persistence and ambition. All his achievements are cut from the same cloth as his failures. Nixon's strongest drive is not for power but for respect and fame. He wants to be regarded as an event-making man, like Wilson, Churchill, or de Gaulle, whose presence will make a difference in history. He needs deference and respect in order to shore up a weak self-esteem, and the chief vehicle he has chosen for that end is foreign policy. The very same reliance upon unpredictability and surprise and upon the inner self as the source of a novel and dazzling action or policy that has led to events like Cambodia has also led to remarkable achievements like the détentes with China and the U.S.S.R. Here Nixon has made virtues of his desire for fame and his style of authority.

The successful development of new relations with China and the U.S.S.R. was accomplished by Nixon under conditions most favorable to his isolated way of doing things. In Henry Kissinger he had not only a very talented associate but one who would not screen him off from reality. Such basic policy innovations perhaps had to be done in private without congressional obstruction or State Department foot-dragging. Because of the limited number of participants and the relative absence of face-to-face relations, foreign policy is more susceptible to such a closed style of decision. An intelligent national strategy conceived by a few men can carry a long way. Of course there is a price to pay. Such highly personal government can become cut off from knowledge of the domestic implications of acts, as in the Cambodian case. A small White House apparatus can neither make nor implement all foreign policy, and therefore much is done by default by a demoralized State Department. These points will be fully considered later.

Nixon's domestic Presidency and his style of authority in the gamut of Presidential roles also reveal his weak self-esteem and his self-protectiveness. Most outstanding is his preference for personal seclusion and for dealing with others through a few chosen intermediaries. He therefore badly needs the help of staff to counteract his tendency to isolate himself. However, this is precisely what his staff has not given him. Rather, men like Haldeman understood well that the President does not like to deal with people directly, and surely in accordance with his wishes such men were overprotective. The result, particularly during his first term, was a remoteness of the President from government that accounted for many mistakes. Again and again Nixon made decisions on the basis of inadequate consultation with his associates in government whose advice he needed and who were responsible for implementation. For example, the economic policies of his Administration have been made in the most extraordinarily ad hoc ways, with decisive actions being taken in the face of obvious public turmoil because of the President's detachment from everyday government. Contrast this with the careful Presidential supervision of advance planning for the SALT disarmament talks about which he cared greatly. But like the President he most admired, Woodrow Wilson, Nixon seems able to handle only a few important issues at a time and the rest are neglected. The result is a constriction of energy and affect and an absorption in a limited number of matters of heavy personal investment.

No President in recent history has paid so little attention to Congress or failed to open himself up to general political advice from friend or foe as Nixon. He seldom consults outside official circles and is little inclined to bargain or compromise with those whose support he needs to accomplish his purposes. However, having said this, one must point out that the Nixon style oscillates between a kind of quietism and appeal to good will and unity and an activist testing of the opposition. He entered office with the inaugural theme that he would "bring us together." One of his persistent rhetorical themes is that he has helped unify the nation after the times of conflict and disorder of the sixties. He values order and regularity in government. One senses that Nixon has a strong personal desire to be a passive President who would reign over a happy people in a tension-free time when he might receive all the adulation and deference that he conceives as his due. However, he is a pessimist about such a possibility. Such a dream if realized would finally free Richard Nixon from the phantoms that drive him, but it is not about to happen in the real world. Therefore Nixon sees his fate as one of continual struggle, of shoring up self-esteem within and vanquishing enemies without. Every time there is a prediction about a mellowed, relaxed "new" Nixon, he throws down a gauntlet.

There was much speculation after his 1972 victory that Nixon might relax and become a President of national unity. He would never run for office again. The highest prize was his, deservedly. Would not the old resentments and residues of distrust and combativeness recede into a new self-confidence and era of good feeling?

This was wishful thinking. In January 1973 the President gave a most revealing interview to an Associated Press reporter, the title of which was given by Nixon's own words: "The Worst Thing You Can Do in This Job Is Relax." Nixon told the reporter:

> I believe in the battle, whether it's the battle of the campaign or the battle of this office, which is a continuing battle. It's always there wherever you go. I perhaps, carry it more than others because that's my way.

The worst thing you can do in this job is to relax, let up. . . . I find in handling crises that the most important qualities one needs are balance, objectivity, and ability to act coolly. . . .

I'll probably do better in the next four years having gone through a few crises in the White House, having weathered them and learned how to handle them coolly and not subjectively. . . .

When I came into office, I'd been through enough—those shattering defeats in 1960 and 1962 and then those eight years 'in the wilderness' the way De Gaulle and Churchill were.

The result was that I was able to confront tough problems without flagging. . . . An individual tends to go to pieces when he's inexperienced.

Nixon is still protesting too much that he is strong. We suspect that fears abound beneath these words. One of his aides is more revealing in the same interview:

He's a man continually testing himself. Usually that was the next election. Now he's taking on and reorganizing the federal bureaucracy which, of course, needs it. He needs the sense of battle. If it weren't the bureaucracy he'd find a surrogate target.[21]

The new Nixon Administration in the first months of 1973 threw down the gauntlet to both Congress and the bureaucracy. The President resolved to consolidate a number of the Great Society domestic programs into the new form of general and special revenue-sharing with the states. This required congressional approval and reorganization and reorientation in the federal departments and agencies. The President threatened to impound funds that Congress appropriated for the old programs, and in the spring of 1973 Presidential-congressional relations were at a standoff. Likewise, a number of former White House staff members were sent to the departments as top executives with orders to impose the Nixon policies upon recalcitrant civil servants. This was all of a piece with the claim that continued United States bombing in Cambodia despite a withdrawal of American troops from Vietnam was justified by the President's 1972 election "mandate."

These actions showed a determined President who had temporized on domestic policy in his first term but who was now determined to put his ideological stamp upon policy and bureaucracy in a unilateral way outside of the normal canons of political compromise. To question the style however is not to deny that many of the substantive program ideas of the Administration and in fact the efforts to reorganize government were very innovative. A conservative Administration was openly challenging patterns of government that had prevailed since the New Deal, and a great debate was joined.

When the Watergate affair broke openly, the moral authority of this President within the government and polity was perhaps permanently weakened and the dispute with Congress was never joined. Was not Watergate also a manifestation of the style of authority of the President as was widely noted at the time? An isolated President who encourages a ruthless atmosphere of partisanship in his immediate circle was badly served by men who had no higher loyalty than Nixon himself. The fact that the President felt so threatened by potential subversion during his first term that he authorized a number of wiretaps and burglaries in the name of national security reveals a White House seriously out of touch with domestic reality and very much on the defensive and unnecessarily so. The Nixon White House distrusted almost everyone in leading positions in government and society who did not wear its brand. And so, ironically, although they occupied the seat of national power, they felt weak and defensive. This is the atmosphere that Richard Nixon created.

When the total picture is examined and we agree that Nixon's virtues and vices are two aspects of the same personality, we must ask if the accomplishments have been worth the costs. Great political leaders usually bring some destructiveness in their wake. Talent is a dynamic, volatile force. But is Nixon a great political leader or simply a man of modest talent who has worked very hard and had a great deal of luck? If the latter is so, we have paid a price for our failure to scrutinize his character more thoroughly before he became President.

THE SELF-CONFIDENT LEADER

Theodore Roosevelt and Franklin Roosevelt both enjoyed attention and power, and needed office and a full political life to realize themselves. How did they differ from Johnson and Nixon? The answer seems to be that despite their insecurities and strong needs for power and attention these two men sought a life in politics as a self-fulfilling quest. They were not fighting insatiable insecurities. They were at their happiest when in the saddle, and in fact Theodore Roosevelt's aberrations came when he was out of office and desperate to get back in. John Kennedy was similar to these two in the self-affirming character of his leadership, but his needs and drive were not so intense nor were his skills as fully developed.

James David Barber, writing after the experience of Johnson and Nixon, and therefore free of any temptation to idealize the power seeker, has given us a clue to the differences between the two kinds of Presidents.[22] He describes Franklin Roosevelt, Truman, and Kennedy as happy, integrated, self-respecting, and expansive people who were capable of growth and learning. Their energies were directed outward toward achievement, not bound up in defensive postures.

From Barber's viewpoint Johnson and Nixon brought a negative cast to their careers. Ceaseless striving for place, power, and deference could never be satisfied because the lack of self-esteem that needs strengthening was insatiable. Political style takes on a compulsive quality and sharp threats to self-esteem and position are often met in rigid and ego defensive ways. Barber developed a typology of active-positives and active-negatives to encompass these two clusters of Presidents. Both types have energy and drive in common and all are ambitious for office and power. However, where the former lead from self-confidence and high self-esteem, the latter lack these qualities. Nonetheless, not all active-positives are political men in Lasswell's sense. Franklin Roosevelt was both a political man and a democratic character. He had needs for attention and power that stimulated the development of skills of leadership but that were also rooted in a basic self-love and self-confidence. Roosevelt moved out to embrace the world as if it were his right to be loved.

Franklin Roosevelt

Franklin Roosevelt was indeed a "happy warrior" as Al Smith described him, and who, as Neustadt wrote,

> saw the job of being President as being FDR. He wanted mastery, projected that desire on the office, and fulfilled it with every sign of feeling he had come into his own. Self-confidence so based was bound to reinforce his sense of purpose and to guarantee reliance on his sense of power.[23]

The essence of his style of leadership was a reaching out to charm others with his personality, to learn from them about their needs and to act to meet those needs.

The conditions of Roosevelt's childhood fit the standard advice for development of a healthy personality, love from confident parents with the reasons for discipline given in an environment that augments self-esteem. He was an only child, and his young mother and affectionate older father gave him continuous nurture and support. He learned trust and affection and began to develop early in life those skills that would ensure that such affection would always be forthcoming from others. His early social environment among the squirearchy of old families of the Hudson River Valley was stable and serene and gave him a sense of personal social identity that he never lost and that was always a source of strength to him.

Rather than remaining within a comfortable, parochial environment that was extended by his life at Groton and Harvard, Roosevelt chose to extend his adult life beyond that social setting to devote it to reaching and influencing people in new settings. We will never know his exact motivation, for he disguised the inner man behind a mask of geniality that caused many to initially dismiss him as a lightweight. However, beneath the mask was a purposeful striving for power and a compulsion to charm, and beneath the geniality was toughness and strength.

His mature political style became apparent at Harvard where as editor of the *Crimson* one of his coeditors remembered that "in his geniality was a kind of frictionless command."[24] Increasingly the design of his life came to be the drive to influence others. By the time he was assistant secretary of the navy in the Wilson Administration he had developed his mature political style. It was based on his ability to learn from people, mediate between them, and guide them in the directions he wished to go. As the Secretary of War Newton D. Baker commented:

> Young Roosevelt is very promising, but I should think he'd wear himself out in the promiscuous and extended contacts he maintains with people. But as I have observed him, he seems to clarify his ideas and teach himself as he goes along by that very conversational method.[25]

In the Navy Department he showed the ability to get on with all sorts of people, naval officers, labor leaders, and politicians, and he developed his basic style of command, which was to preside over policy experiments while keeping himself at the center of decision and trying one plan after another until something worked. This style reflected not only his compulsion to charm but a mode of thought that was anything but systematic. He thought with his intuitive antennas, learning from people by watching their faces as they spoke together, framing policies by absorbing a number of individual viewpoints, and then developing a solution that somehow reconciled most of them. He never made a final commitment to any person or ideology but soaked up ideas and facts and used them when they were needed.

FDR's paralysis through polio in 1921 reinforced these traits in his personality. His need for contact with people and his sympathy for them were strengthened. As Schlesinger describes:

> They were his vital links with life and his extroverted Rooseveltian sociability was compounded by his invalid's compulsion to charm anyone who came to his bedside. He sought more intensely than ever to know people, to understand them, to win them to him. . . . But the desire to be liked also opened him up to their needs and fears. It explained in great part the genius for assimilation within him which was developing and which was giving him so extraordinary a receptivity.[26]

Illness strengthened his basic optimism and serenity and gave him self-discipline and patience.

Roosevelt's ideology was in accord with the rest of his personality. He had a simple faith in Christian precepts of doing right and believed that the purpose of government was to help people. This was the noblesse oblige of the aristocrat nurtured by the certainties of family and school. Although he had no elaborate public philosophy, as a person he was a natural democrat who genuinely desired to help people.

His political personality was unified through an openness toward people, a reaching out to experiment with ideas and programs, and a desire to serve but with flexibility and self-confidence that he could find the solutions to problems. It is no wonder that his ideal of the Presidency was himself in the White House. His greatest and most enduring political strength was his hold on the people. His leadership of public opinion was based on technique, but much more important was his ability to communicate to people the fact that he really cared about them.

Roosevelt took up the Presidency with the sureness of having been President all his life, and this new sense of strength quickly communicated itself across the country. After he died, John Gunther was told by many people: "I never met him, but I feel as if I had lost my greatest friend."[27] This ability to project a human concern for people, guided by great technical skill, was his chief political resource. For example, he made the radio chat a special art. His talks were filled with the kind of simple appeals that he liked; for example, the justification of Land Lease aid to Britain in the early war years was presented in terms of loaning a garden hose to a neighbor whose house was on fire. Frances Perkins, his secretary of labor, watched him during these talks and noticed that he gestured and smiled as if the radio audience were in front of him. He was thinking of the public as he always did, in terms of individuals whose lives he could visualize. She also noticed that when she sat with people as they listened to these talks that they responded in kind, to Roosevelt as a warm, real person.[28]

In his leadership of public opinion FDR oscillated from the heroic to the cautious. With his sensitivity to public moods, he was forthright as a leader when crisis was high and public sentiment was ripe for heroic leadership. This was the case when he first entered office and embarked on the dramatic legislative leadership of the first hundred days. It was also the case in the 1936 campaign when he proclaimed the need for a new era of reform and in 1941 when the nation entered the war. At other times he was more cautious and gradually prepared the public for a new departure. For example, he held off on social security legislation in order to first educate people that it was not alien to the American tradition of self-reliance. He did this by blending press conferences, a message to Congress, two fireside chats, and a few speeches, in each of which he progressively unfolded his ideas and stressed the soundness and Americanness of the plan. It culminated in a State of the Union message. The main point is that he did this kind of thing with artistry, and the artistry was an extension of his own empathy and ability to act to win others over.

As a legislative leader he used the same skills. Again, he had a variety of styles. He could summon Congress to do its, and his work, with determination and courage if the tide was running in his direction. Throughout his Presidency Roosevelt carefully set up priorities of Administration legislative requests. He thought in terms of Presidential power, and with the knowledge that his political resources with Congress were limited, he would put his reputation on the line only for "must" legislation. Departments and agencies could push bills, but he would personally support only a few. In order to keep his initiative and authority he made sure to keep an overview of all Administration legislative proposals.[29]

FDR made full use of his constitutional power, for example, the veto; drafted legislative measures in the Executive branch; revived the custom of personal appearances before Congress; appealed directly to the people; worked long and hard in face-to-face persuasion with members of Congress; used the various levers of carrot and stick well; and displayed an excellent sense of timing, drama, and political psychology. He never made his methods explicit or used them as formulae, but instead played things by ear, fitting tactics to situation. His method of leadership separated means and ends in a way that never became obvious because he obscured his ways of working. Although he was determined on goals, he was incredibly flexible

about means. Others often judged that what were means to him were
in fact goals. Therefore, people often failed to see which battles he
would fight and which ones he would avoid. He kept his followers
and opponents in a state of uncertainty. At times he seemed vacillat-
ing, even cowardly, when in fact he was pursuing an elaborate
strategy. The idea was to keep everyone off balance in order to strike
at the right time, and to keep everyone uncertain about his final
plans in order to manipulate a solution, the total pattern of which
only he saw.[30]

Congress was made up of veterans to whom no President could
dictate. Roosevelt's achievements were more amazing in light of the
fact that most of the leadership were not New Dealers. He chose to
work through them rather than the progressive rank and file whom
he rather took for granted. Immediate legislative gains were his goal,
and he gave little thought to the creation of an enduring progressive
coalition in Congress. His success with congressional leaders was a
triumph of personal diplomacy. He dealt with them with such skill
that often his personal role made the difference between defeat and
passage of a bill, as this quotation from Burns indicates:

> Roosevelt's leadership talents lay in his ability to shift quickly and grace-
> fully from persuasion to cajolery to flattery to intrigue to diplomacy to
> promises to horse-trading—or to concoct just that formula which his
> superb instincts for personal relations told him would bring around the
> most reluctant Congressmen.[31]

This kind of manipulation through his own personality to win the
acceptance of others was something he had been doing skillfully in
private life since boyhood. During the session of Congress he spent
three or four hours a day either on the telephone or in conference
with members. Once a visitor waiting in the anteroom outside the
Presidential office saw FDR just as he had succeeded in calming
down an angry congressional delegation. Unaware that he was observed, Roosevelt slowly lit a cigarette and leaned back, "a smile of
complete satisfaction spread over his face."[32] He had complete confidence in his ability to win an opponent over by charm.

Once in a while the fox was undone by his own craftiness. Although
this did not happen often, it happened in regard to important matters more than once. The classic instance was Roosevelt's defeat in
his attempt to pack the Supreme Court with pro–New Deal justices
in 1936. Most of the time FDR acted out of a rule of thumb that
people do not like radical change and the leader thus has to guide
them to new directions slowly. However, his overwhelming 1936
election victory when joined to resentment at Court assaults on New

Deal legislation caused him to forget this rule. In fact, for a few months he lost his sense of political reality in regard to this issue.

Roosevelt's strategic and tactical failures during the Court fight were inherent in his habitual political method. He tried to disguise his attempt to pack the Court by pretending to plan to appoint an additional judge for every one over seventy who was still sitting. This was justified as means to greater judicial efficiency. He had decided this approach bore the least political risk. This was his delight in the secret stratagem, the dramatic thrust, the indirect ploy rather than frontal attack. However, in choosing indirectness in this instance he badly miscalculated. The devious method of reform became more a cause célèbre than the substance of his criticism of the Court, which was widely shared by many who opposed his method. He seemed too clever by half, a weakness inherent in his love of process and his vagueness about means and ends. In this case his very flexibility seemed to have doubled back on him.

In the fight with the Congress, which largely took place in the Senate, he made one tactical blunder after another. Most of these can be traced to his overconfidence. FDR had not consulted anyone except his attorney general before suddenly dropping the plan like a bombshell on Congress. The assumption that congressional leaders would do his bidding was so uppermost in his mind that he failed to line up progressive congressional support in advance or to alert interest-group leaders who might have supported the plan in hopes of ending Court obstruction of progressive legislation. Since he had not mentioned the matter in the 1936 election, it came as a great shock to much of the public. His general confidence that the people were with him and that in the end Congress would defer to him caused him to reject the warnings of congressional leaders that he would have to compromise to save part of the legislation. He relied on his personal charm to bring Senate opponents around, a tactic that in fact failed when put to the test. His sense of timing was off, again from overconfidence. Although he failed with Congress he did indirectly convince the Court to support New Deal legislation so he achieved a victory of sorts, but his professional reputation with Congress was never the same again.[33]

Administrative Leader

Roosevelt's experiences in the Navy Department and as governor of New York had convinced him that the chief executive had to be boss and that this took extra effort because of the loosely organized nature of American bureaucracy. He looked on administrative forms with one question: Did they enhance his capacity to rule? He sought to use the Presidential office as a vehicle for his power.[34] His conception of the Presidency demanded that the President make the key decisions, and he deliberately organized his Administration to make sure this happened. His system of command was designed to push the most important decisions to the top. This was accomplished by delegating authority and responsibility in such a fragmented way that competition below would require decision from above. For using such a system he was judged to be a poor administrator because he violated the orthodoxy of the time, which called for the organization chart and regular channels. Roosevelt broke all the rules because of his conception of Presidential power and because of his personality, which enabled him to fulfill his conception. No theorizing on his part was needed; his semiconscious perceptions told him what to do.[35]

Roosevelt did not rely on a single source of information but used both official and unofficial channels and often set them against each other. He was very accessible for a President, and nearly one hundred government officials could get him on a direct line phone. He read a great number of memos, cables, reports, and even the Congressional Record; his unofficial reading consisted of six daily newspapers and a sampling of White House mail. However, his chief source of information, both official and unofficial, was from visitors to his office. He used his cabinet officers and his wife as antennas. Frances Perkins remembered that he could "get" a problem much better when he had a vicarious experience through a vivid description of a typical case.[36] Roosevelt put no trust in abstract rules but acted in terms of concrete people with concrete problems. He pumped cabinet members returning from trips for their observations. This kind of information was necessary, he felt, "to keep his mind fresh and alert about the needs of people."[37]

In his own time FDR was often portrayed as a dictator, but in fact his actual greatest limitation was that he followed more than he led. This was the deficiency of his style of leadership. No great courageous acts were taken to prepare the nation for the advent of World War II; instead he rode the tides of isolationism in hopes that events would educate people, which they eventually did, but at great cost. In spite of this he was convinced that more decisive leadership would have failed. He was never able to actually raise the nation out of the Depression in peacetime in his second term because he could not bring himself to accept any definitive set of economic policies. He could have pursued the new Keynesian theory of priming the pump to restore prosperity, but he would not swear fealty to any one economist or any one theory. Eclecticism, empiricism, and operational flexibility were much more his style than any long-range plan to which he adhered. His political virtues were his policy deficiencies.

The great riddle about Roosevelt is why he was both lion and fox, courageous reform leader at times and crafty and cautious at others. In fact, both styles were rooted in his habit of responding to the dominant tones of his environment. When the climate was ripe for courage he stood forth. When the weather was bad he stayed indoors. Both aspects reflected his love of improvising, his disdain for theories, his responsiveness to the human dimension. On balance he was probably a greater tactician than strategist; a flaw was rooted in his personality and the character of his mind. He also relied upon his own ability to charm more than was warranted and therefore was prone to overreach himself.

Roosevelt's great virtue was his capacity to communicate his courage to others. Robert Sherwood wrote of him:

He was spiritually the healthiest man I have ever known. He was gloriously and happily free of the various forms of psychic maladjustment . . . he was entirely conscious of these extraordinary advantages that he enjoyed and this consciousness gave him the power to soar above circumstances which would have held other men earthbound.[38]

This profile of Roosevelt makes clear that his manipulative and bargaining skills were important to his success. However, by themselves they were nothing; his contagious moral leadership was the key to all his achievements. His second term was really a failure because he lacked intelligent economic policies and could not end the Depression. Nor could he persuade the Congress to support the programs he did present. All his strictly political skills were of little help. If there was a flaw in the political personality it was a tendency to see the world as his personal domain and to permit his strong ego to dim his sense of reality.

It would be an error to idealize Roosevelt and the active-positive type more than is warranted however. FDR himself shows that the active-positive can at times give way to a hubris that reflects an expansive ego. A great many highly skillful political leaders are often a mix of active-positive and active-negative personality characteristics. An ideal type is after all just that and should not be confused with individuals. Certainly Lyndon Johnson had many active-positive traits and Theodore Roosevelt, who would seem to have been predominantly an active-positive, was driven by a compulsive insecurity that caused highly aggressive and self-destructive behavior at times.[39]

It may very well be that manipulative and rhetorical political skills are more often found in the active-negative type because of the greater intensity of the relationship between need and skill. These kinds of people may be favored by our entrepreneurial political system in which the politician who would succeed must develop self-dramatization and power-maximizing skills to a great degree.

We would like to find more active-positives who are also political men. But they probably are not common, at least not in the high development of political needs and skills found in FDR. If this is so, what are we to do about selecting leaders?

Not all persons who have active-positive views about themselves and politics are skillful political leaders. Dwight Eisenhower had a basic self-respect and stability that was a source of strength to him as President, but he lacked the personality needs that might have made him a skillful politician. John Kennedy falls somewhere between the two Roosevelts and Eisenhower on such a need-skill scale.

However, perhaps we have made too much of a sensitivity-to-power relation as the key to success as President. By putting such a high priority on the ability to manipulate others, we make ourselves prey to the active-negatives who are good at this. But as the experiences of Johnson and Nixon have shown, a heightened sensitivity to his personal power position by the President may actually blind him to the kinds of learning and listening required by his official power position.[40] The positive achievements of these Presidents and others, especially the masters of tactics like FDR, were not really based upon tactical skill at manipulating others. Rather, the basis of influence and achievement was the ability to appeal to others in terms of shared values.[41] There are many bases of power and most important among them is the affirmation of life and the possibilities of life in terms of common values. The active-positive leader is more likely to lead in this way, and these are the qualities of leadership that we must look for.

Therefore, since Roosevelts are rare, we would do well to prize character more than skill if a choice must be made. Presidents like Eisenhower and Kennedy should be our models. Neither was a great political craftsman in the skill sense, but they shared self-esteem and the capacity to identify with others. They were not afraid to learn and grow. They were democratic characters who were teaching themselves to be political men.

Dwight Eisenhower

Eisenhower possessed Roosevelt's spiritual health but lacked the political skill of either Roosevelt or Johnson. As a moderate conservative he gave less priority to the achievement of programs and therefore valued activist skills less. Also, he was not a political man in the very fiber of his being the way Roosevelt was.

The young Dwight Eisenhower had a happy, sunny disposition that made him popular. An inner self-confidence joined to an ability for putting himself in the other person's shoes helped to make him an effective leader. However, he did not seek to dominate others and positively resisted developing skills of political manipulation. His standard tools of influence were appeals to reason and good will backed up by the confidence that he was able to inspire in others. This disinclination to run roughshod over other people was motivated in part by a strong normative belief in the importance of the autonomy of persons that was rooted in the Mennonite creed of his youth. He believed that each individual must make up his own mind about right and wrong and that one must take that right as a given in dealing with people. As he told a 1956 press conference in regard to Republican legislators who had not supported his programs: "I am not one of the desk-pounding type that likes to stick out his jaw and look like he is bossing the show."[42]

Thus, although he had greater inner strength and self-confidence he deliberately exercised restraint about the means he used to influence other men. A whole dimension of political tactics and strategy rooted in bargaining and manipulation was foreign to him. The corresponding virtue of his approach was that people trusted him as a man of good will, and once he had won them over they stayed won over.

These predispositions, whatever their genesis, were congruent with a mind that emphasized order and logic and sought to organize the world around him in an orderly manner. His first independent success as an army officer was the great skill he showed during World War I in command of a tank-training battalion. He revealed his ability to create an effectively functioning organization out of nothing and to create high morale in a new unit.[43] In the period between World War I and World War II he developed his organizational skills in the army as a staff officer rather than a unit commander. He had the ability to bring things together for decision.

Eisenhower's skills were not fully recognized until he became Supreme Commander of the Allied Forces in Europe in World War II. There, by his diplomatic skills and organizational abilities, he dominated the largest army ever assembled. Given the difficult task of joining two different national services and different branches of each plus a number of notably prima donna field commanders, Eisenhower was able to create an atmosphere of good will and mutual respect in which Anglo-American unity flourished. He could keep brilliant and often wayward individuals like Montgomery, Patton, and Bradley loyal to him and working fairly smoothly with each other. His method was to give each maximum latitude within his sphere and ensure that the activities of all were coordinated by a larger strategy. Eisenhower was not a strategist himself but a diplomat and organizer who often floundered when he was called upon to exercise a strategic choice between two strongly conflicting points of view. In such situations he would attempt to put together a compromise that would usually not satisfy either side. His conciliating genius had a softness to it that sometimes precluded the taking of hard choices. But he was extremely strong in crisis situations such as the Battle of the Bulge, when all turned to him as a source of strength and hope.

These very same characteristics dominated Eisenhower's Presidency. He became President not because he wanted to be a politician or enjoyed exercising the political arts but because he felt a sense of duty to lead the internationalist wing of the Republican party and preserve the postwar bipartisan foreign policy that he had helped to create. He had originally hoped to be a one-term President who would organize an Administration around correct policy goals and then retire. He believed that Franklin Roosevelt had pushed Presidential power and prerogatives too far vis-à-vis Congress, and he consciously sought to right the balance in terms of an equal partnership of mutual respect. He was fairly conservative in his thinking about domestic policy insofar as he was informed at all, but his very caution meant that he would do little to reverse New Deal programs. Rather, the end result of his two terms was to legitimize such programs for most Republicans.

Given these goals, Eisenhower sought to maximize Presidential rectitude more than power. His conception of the Presidency followed from his great successes in the army: he would be a unifier of government and nation not by assertion of power but by proclamation of virtue. Certainly in this stance Eisenhower appealed to a deep and strong strain in American political life that essentially distrusts politics and calls for men of virtue who will serve in government without compromising themselves by becoming politicians. This impulse is as strong on the left as it is on the right, and it is equally misguided in both cases in its assumption that a nation riven with conflicts of values and power can somehow be governed without the political arts. However, it would be underestimating Eisenhower to cast him entirely in such a role. In fact, he sought to use his personality and skills to bring men together in precise and identifiable ways. His leadership style was not just a rejection of the arts of manipulation; it was an affirmation of the appeal to unity, something in which he excelled.

His playing of Presidential roles fully revealed his political personality. He did not try to develop the skills and virtuosity of a Roosevelt but took a much more restrained stance. Although Eisenhower has been one of the most popular Presidents of the century thus far, he did little in a conscious way to exploit his popularity for policy purposes. He did not even enjoy being so adulated and continually complained when his aides pushed him into speeches and public appearances. His wide popularity, however, was based upon citizens' perceptions of the kind of man he was rather than upon any skills on his part. He was skilled in revealing himself as an honest man who could be trusted. Somehow with Eisenhower in the White House one knew that the government would not take precipitous action, that moderation and balance would prevail. He had been elected President not because people wanted a rest but because he was perceived as a strong leader who would assert himself in government and act to solve problems like the festering and seemingly endless Korean War. When he in fact did not act, his popularity fell; this occurred, for example, during business recessions and after the Russians put a satellite in orbit.[44] However, there is no evidence that he ever indulged in mock action and imagery in order to give the impression of activity, for he simply did not think that way.

The lack of skill he revealed at public leadership must not be confused with his conservatism, which precluded his leading in public on a number of issues. For example, he would not say whether or not he favored the 1954 Supreme Court decision on racial segregation and failed to take the lead in regard to a number of domestic social problems. But even had he been more liberal and committed to speaking out, he would have lacked artistry. Those very intuitive skills that FDR possessed so richly were lacking in Eisenhower. He was a rationalist when it came to persuasion and liked to think that he was popular because of his ideals rather than his personality.

One of Eisenhower's favorite stories was of Lincoln calling on General McClellan at his home and finding him to be out. McClellan knew Lincoln was there, but refused to return. Lincoln's response was to say that he would wait all night if necessary, if it would help win the war. This was the kind of strength in gentleness that Eisenhower admired. He always refused to attack others and sought every means possible to draw opponents to himself.

The positive result of this style was that he was in fact able to create support where it had been absent. This is best illustrated in his relations with Republican legislators during his first term. Many of them were more conservative than he and proposed measures that he was forced to oppose, particularly in foreign affairs. However, he was able to bind Senators Taft and Dirksen and others to him to the point that they and others like them came to support his policy initiatives. He did this by straightforward appeals to their good will and insistence that he needed their help, as he had done with hundreds of men throughout his career. The result was that he stirred very few animosities and made few enemies in the course of a long career.

This style had its negative side in his reluctance to fight. During his first two years in office he permitted the demagogic Senator Joseph McCarthy to trample over and malign many of his associates in the Executive branch with his wild charges about communists in government. One result was a demoralization of the State Department that continues to this day.

The same ambiguity in his style was seen in his legislative achievements. He was able to bring Republican legislators into general support for internationalist policies and domestic reforms of previous Democratic Administrations. In short, he gave the Republicans credibility as a party who would not undo the agreements of the past. But, as in his leadership of public opinion, he lacked the strategic and tactical skills to develop and pursue legislative programs of his own to any great extent. He once undermined his own budget by inviting Congress to cut it. He told a press conference of his doubts about his own civil rights bill and his plan to reorganize the Department of Defense. His greatest effectiveness as a legislative leader came during his last two years in office when he successfully resisted the efforts of a Democratic Congress to add to his budget requests. Here he was in a familiar and congenial role, refusing to be stampeded by those who, in his view, wished to act rashly. Through use of the veto he successfully defended himself. He was not an offensive fighter but he would act to retain his own autonomy and power of decision.

The same blend of looseness and autonomy was manifested in his administrative style. His method with key subordinates was to trust them with great latitude. Thus at times it seemed as if Secretary of State John Foster Dulles was making foreign policy and Secretary of the Treasury George Humphrey was making domestic policy. One was reminded of his generals during the war. This method of decentralizing leadership was often criticized. Quite often his own views seemed at variance with those of his key associates and yet he would defer. However, the positive side of this style was that he had little emotional investment in the commitments of those associates. He kept his autonomy for the most important decisions. For example, he rejected the advice of Dulles and the Chairman of the Joint Chiefs of Staff that the United States intervene militarily in Indochina in 1954 to save the French armies from collapse. His sensitivity to the opposition of Congress and the British government made him rule out action. He would not act unilaterally without the necessary political support. Thus, he was notable for the many things he did not do: he did not misuse power; he avoided unnecessary military adventures. He was insensitive to growing domestic problems of race, poverty, and urban ills but this was primarily due to his conservatism and his unfamiliarity with those spheres of American life. Yet his cautiousness had a strong side to it, for he was able to legitimize New Deal programs with Republicans and begin a period of rapprochement with the Soviet leaders that President Kennedy was to continue.

The structure of the White House in Eisenhower's Administration resembled an army staff system, with a Chief of Staff for domestic affairs, Sherman Adams, who was the President's liaison with all the government beneath. Adams' main job was to protect the President from minor matters so that he might reserve his time, energy, and autonomy for the big decisions. The negative side of this structure was that Eisenhower often did not learn about the bureaucratic politics involved in the big decisions until it was too late. He simply did not have the desire of the thoroughly political man like FDR to understand what was going on at all levels of government in order to protect his own power.

Eisenhower relied on a system that often failed him. In foreign affairs he established an elaborate structure of committees around the National Security Council and insisted that all policy decisions come up through that structure. The common criticism is that he subjected himself to the inevitable compromises of interdepartmental committees before he had an opportunity to see the possible options in terms of his own responsibilities as President. Policy implementation down through a complex network of NSC committees was impeded by bureaucratic politics. However, Eisenhower did not wish to be innovative in either foreign or domestic policy.

Innovative Presidents are likely to prefer more open and fluid staff systems that permit them to personally act as catalysts within the Executive branch, both in a learning and an administrative sense. Consolidating Presidents are more likely to desire stable structures in which routines and continuities of policy will be strong. Organization theory suggests that policy innovation in an organization requires considerable fluidity of structure and that a routine orientation requires a clear and predictable hierarchy. But it is doubtful that Presidents read organization theory. Rather, personality and values shape their administrative style. Roosevelt wanted policy innovation and had a personal sensitivity to his power stakes in the process. Eisenhower sought less innovation and lacked a sensitivity to his personal power in the office.

The same pattern appears over and over in Eisenhower's career.

He was a strong man who deliberately restrained himself in his relationships with others out of conviction. His very technique of leadership, to draw others to him by example and persuasion, was both his
greatest strength and greatest weakness. The positive legacy of this
style was that his inner spiritual force caused all men to trust him.
The negative legacy was that he achieved less than he might have.

John Kennedy

Eisenhower was an active-positive who lacked the needs for attention and power that would give him a high order of political skills.
John Kennedy was in many ways closer to him in this respect than
he was to Roosevelt. He was not a natural political man like FDR.
However, unlike Eisenhower, he entered a political career and
learned political skills and roles. Kennedy is more nearly the kind of
man we can expect and hope to find in the Presidency most of the
time—a democratic character who is a political man by virtue of role
as much as personality.

   John Kennedy is the most difficult of any of the modern Presidents
to analyze and assess. When he was assassinated he had only just
begun his Presidency. It is as if Lincoln had died after Gettysburg.
Because of his untimely death the myth colors the man and makes
it difficult for an objective observer to see the real person. He hid his
inner self in a calm detachment, and it is hard to explain the dualism
of the skeptical, ironic, witty inner self and the often rhetorical and
romantic public man. Finally, it is not entirely clear why he was so
popular. Only after his death have we become fully aware of how he
had touched the lives of many people, and this popular response is
not yet well understood.

   Without retracing the familiar ground of the family life of the
Joseph Kennedys and all the influences that went into the development of the mature man, it can be said that from his beginnings he
brought several characteristics to adult political style. Like all the
Kennedys he had a driving ambition to be first, to win the race, but
in his case it was tempered by wit, a sense of the ironic, and the ability
to laugh at himself. This tempering may have come from the fact that
he was the second son behind a bullying, aggressive older brother.
A history of childhood illness may also have been a factor. Whatever
the cause, the legacy was a refusal to take pomposity seriously and
a touch of fatalism in his ambition and aspirations. Although he received drive and ambition from his family, he got no strong sense of
political purpose. His father was a Democrat but a strongly conservative one. As a child and young man Kennedy lived in a variety of

environments none of which fully put its stamp on him. He was neither a New Englander nor Irish in a conventional sense. His family was cosmopolitan without real roots. He thus entered politics as a pragmatist working within the diffuse tradition of the Democratic party.

The most important thing that he brought from childhood to his political career was his love of life. All the Kennedys devoured experience. They believed that talents were to be used to their fullest. Like his brothers and sisters John had an active-positive view of himself and of human endeavors. This gave the three politicians in the family, John, Robert, and Edward, a great capacity for intellectual and moral growth. All were somewhat conservative at the beginning of their careers, but they were primarily pragmatists who gloried in process. However, each of the three brothers grew in their emotional and moral commitments as they learned from political experience.

This is the chief theme of John Kennedy's Presidency, the tension between a pragmatic restlessness and activism without purpose and a deepening and clarifying sense of historical purpose and policy direction. At the beginning Kennedy's activism and his private skepticism were one; he would embrace no grand design but preferred to take issues as they came, looking at the options and selecting the most realistic course. But as he matured in office the unconnected pieces began to come together in his mind and in his strategies of political leadership. Part of the tragedy was that he was cut off just as he had found himself.

Kennedy was not a natural politician with an intuitive feel for the appeals that will move others. He was shy and in his first campaign for Congress had to force himself to barge up the back stairs of Boston tenements to meet voters. His gifts were those of an analytic mind and an energy for action. He did not enjoy wallowing in the complex richness of the prejudices of others as did both Roosevelt and Johnson. This was one reason that Kennedy was a less effective leader of Congress than either of them. His leadership was too cerebral and did not build on the folkways and perspectives of irregular, individualistic, particularistic legislative minds.

However, Kennedy did have the natural ability to inspire others. In the immediate circle of his associates it was in part due to his decency, good humor, and sense of fun, but it was also because he communicated a respect for brains and ability. He wanted the highest order of achievement by his government and recruited talented men who developed a collective spirit of excellence that he had initially fostered. This led to mutual self-admiration at times and a not uncommon arrogance, much of which survived Kennedy and permeated the government after him. Although his personal wit and skepticism precluded arrogance, most of his associates could not laugh at themselves so easily.

An explanation of Kennedy's ability to inspire people in general is more difficult. Much of his popular appeal was based upon physical attractiveness and clever public relations. But even the superficial bases of appeal were related to the more profound sources. His obvious delight in his family, and in fact in living in the White House and being President, were reminiscent of the national sense of fun at having the Theodore Roosevelt family in the White House. Both Presidents joined to this personal appeal an affirmation of life. Each radiated a sense of excitement and expectation about human possibilities to which people responded with hope. This was primarily an appeal of style rather than policy. It was an affirmation, writ large, of personal qualities, of the sense of activism and achievement. People responded to the enthusiasm of the President that the society could be improved. After his death it was seen that different kinds of people had identified with different facets of John Kennedy, youth with idealism, blacks with compassion, and so forth.[45]

Kennedy had the ability to strike home to individuals so that they felt he cared about them. This was similar to Theodore Roosevelt's remarkable feel and love for the variety and individuality in American life, as seen in the succession of cowboys, naturalists, scholars, and athletes who visited the White House. In both cases this concern for the individual was a democratic style rooted in a semiaristocratic personal background. Democratic manners in Kennedy and the two Roosevelts flowed from a supreme self-confidence that was fostered in an upper-class family tradition. This is not really a paradox. The genuine aristocrat is the true democrat. He has no doubts about himself and therefore is open to the experience of other men.

In domestic affairs he was generally cautious, perhaps even timid. He knew that his narrow election carried little if any policy mandate, and he realized that the votes were not present in Congress to enact the principal pieces of legislation of his New Frontier such as Medicare and federal aid to education. He desisted from rhetorical appeals to the public on such issues because he was skeptical about the likely response.

In foreign affairs, however, his behavior was seemingly very different. The style was one of a heroic, often strident, rhetoric that pictured the United States as the bulwark of freedom in the world and called upon Americans to pay any price to support that historic mission.[46] The theme of his inaugural address was that of a universal American mission to police the world, and from then on he led in foreign affairs in terms of crisis, confrontation, and appeals to the public to rally behind the President.

Kennedy was determined to be tough in the face of a Soviet threat and so we were tough. A Berlin crisis that never materialized saw the call of reserves to active duty and a Presidential speech on the need for fallout shelters that induced a near public panic. He had campaigned on the existence of what turned out to be a nonexistent missile gap and a promise to make American defenses second to none. All this energy and activism and rhetoric went into the definition of foreign policy confrontation and events in military terms, whether the Bay of Pigs or the missile crisis or Vietnam. He also practiced a highly personal diplomacy based on rhetoric. The program of American aid to Latin America, the Alliance for Progress, was very modest but the accompanying language distorted that picture. The effort was made to forge United States relations with the new African nations through Kennedy's personal ties with the leaders of those nations, a transitory and weak instrument for enduring relations between national states.

Although he was so seemingly different in domestic and foreign affairs, the similarities in fact were greater than the differences. In both cases he was the tough-minded pragmatist who faced issues as they came and analyzed the options, choosing the most realistic course. He was cautious in both realms, because the tough, military approach was in fact the cautious approach in foreign affairs. He saw political life as one of continuous flux and struggle and the task of leadership as one of marshalling the resources to solve the problems. In domestic affairs he thought the resources were limited. In foreign affairs they were greater, and he invoked the greater popular support a President has in this area.

Until the last year of his life, however, he lacked an overall political strategy in foreign affairs. Rather, each crisis had to be responded to anew. His lack of a world view and his great caution were evident in regard to Vietnam. He permitted a growing involvement in Vietnam against his better judgment because of caution about challenging what was becoming a military vested interest in South Vietnam for fear of political and especially congressional criticism. He resolved to act to scale down that commitment after a 1964 victory and let it ride in the meantime.[47]

The basic flaw in the Kennedy style of governing, particularly in foreign affairs, was a belief in the importance of analysis and options without any great guidance in the selection of options by a sense of purpose and perspective. The result was endless pragmatic improvisation and activism with the emphasis given to toughness and usually to the selection of the military option. What has since been praised as a Kennedy mastery of command and control over government at the time of the Cuban missile crisis appears in retrospect as a valuable but limited operational skill that focused on means rather than ends. Nonmilitary options were precluded at the outset and the world narrowly escaped a nuclear disaster. Kennedy did refuse to back Khrushchev in a corner and he did control the tempo of escalation superbly. But it is not clear that a military response was even appropriate.[48]

In any event, whatever one's judgment on the missile crisis, Kennedy did fail to grasp the nettle of decision on Vietnam. His great personal physical courage, which he had demonstrated many times in his life, proved unequal to the moral courage necessary on this problem. He temporized.

However, that is not our last word on Kennedy. Had the assassination occurred a year earlier that might be our judgment, but in 1963 he changed as a person and as President. The experience of the missile crisis deepened his belief in the importance of finding a way to live in peace with the U.S.S.R., and in 1963 he gave a remarkable speech at American University calling for an end to the Cold War. At the same time he made a strong commitment to the achievement of a test-ban treaty among the major powers and was prepared to push this measure with public and Congress regardless of criticism and costs to his 1964 reelection effort. Also, during 1963 he made a strong personal and public commitment to the cause of civil rights for blacks. Violence in Birmingham, Alabama, against peaceful protesters and the defiance of federal law by the governors of Mississippi and Alabama changed his lukewarm commitment into a strong, personal conviction. He called on the public to approve and the Congress to pass what became the 1964 Civil Rights Act and was pressing hard despite evidence of a drop in his popularity. Finally, he had decided to go all out for a tax cut in 1964 in order to stimulate the economy and was prepared to do battle for deficit financing because he was now moving toward what was to become the poverty program in which special action for the poor would be joined to economic planning in order to bring the poor into the economy.[49]

John Kennedy had a great capacity for growth and by 1963 was beginning to draw together political strategies for reelection and programmatic strategies for the future. He looked forward to running against Barry Goldwater and expected a decisive victory and the return of increased Democratic votes in Congress to support his programs. He was developing a strong personal, emotional, and moral commitment to a series of related domestic programs, and it seems likely that he would have been a second-term President of great achievement in domestic reform had he been able to sustain strong personal idealism as the chief resource for leadership. Technical legislative skill, or its absence, would not have been as important as personal moral leadership in a new political climate.

In foreign affairs he spoke casually of finding a way to get the United States invited out of Vietnam once the election was over. No one can know what would have actually happened, but Kennedy was not an intellectual prisoner of the intervention and he might not have permitted the commitment to escalate much more. However, the outcome can never be known because Kennedy had not fully blossomed when he was killed.

PREDICTION AND UNDERSTANDING

Can we know in advance what kind of President a given person is likely to be? What seems at first to be a methodological question for scholars is in fact a crucial issue for all of us. The issue of Watergate was in large part the crisis of a Presidential personality. How can we prevent that kind of thing from happening again, or can we?

We know from experience that a person's personality shapes the way he plays the roles of an office like the Presidency. But most observers of the Presidency, whether scholars or journalists, have lacked the knowledge of psychology to make general statements about personality and Presidential behavior. Furthermore, many people are skeptical of such efforts because they seem to be necessarily based upon insufficient information and therefore result in superficial and perhaps misleading conclusions about motivation. Finally, the development of personality theory itself is uneven. More than one model of personality may explain a given action. There is no agreement in personality theory on the inner dynamics of human beings.

The result is that observers of the Presidency fall back upon surface descriptions of motivation and its relation to behavior in explanations of Presidential actions. We piece together explanations of why Presidents do things by drawing on an array of concepts including Presidential role, ideology, conscious political strategies of the President and his advisers, and ad hoc propositions about the importance of Presidential personality. We compare Presidents in these terms, drawing very heavily upon political and social explanations for the differences in Administrations. Everyone knows that Presidential personality is a crucial independent factor, which is clear in the analysis of specific decisions and actions, but few know how to deal with this factor systematically and weigh its effect in relation to other factors.

Clearly there are instances in which individual personal characteristics of a President are not an important factor in a decision or policy.

The increasing American involvement in Vietnam, for example, occurred over the span of several Presidents—from Truman to Johnson. Each of these Presidents, and those who served them, believed in this commitment. One might be able to discern that personality differences shaped the commitment differently; Eisenhower resisted military involvement, while Johnson would not take a seeming defeat and so escalated the war. But the broad sweep of United States policy was set by a climate of opinion shared by most national leaders. However, there is seldom such a predominant official world view in other policy areas and a President has great latitude to shape policy and its execution according to his personal style. In general one can say that personality will be the critical factor in Presidential decision-making when the situation is a) ambiguous, b) when there is great disagreement, c) when there is opportunity for the exercise of personal skill and style, and d) when the feelings and beliefs of a President are likely to be engaged. This covers much of what a President does.

One must distinguish between the different parts of the personality system of an individual in order to understand motivation underlying Presidential behavior. Political scientists who have written psychological biographies of Presidents and other political leaders work from a more or less common framework of psychoanalytic theory but with a strong emphasis upon ego psychology that stresses conscious autonomy and ego independence in the healthy personality.

The basic method of analysis is that of biography. A person's early life is studied for clues as to how he developed habitual adult styles of acting, and the needs and values that seem to be served by such styles are postulated. The central idea is that every human being has a number of developmental crises to pass through in the process of growing up and that out of the solutions to these crises develops a mature style of attitudes toward the self, others, and the world. There is nothing reductionist about such an approach; we do not seek to explain Presidential acts in terms of childhood. But we do suggest that Presidential behavior reflects a man's basic self-esteem or the lack of it, his sense of trust or its absence, his ability to summon aggressive feeling and yet control it, and so on. Of course, such a developmental history must take account of his social environment and the values he learns, appropriates, and creates for himself.

The task of analysis then is to compare Presidents in terms of their basic strategies of coping with forces within the self and with others in interpersonal relations and their basic outlook on the world as it affects their actions. We do this by comparing the way in which different Presidents play common Presidential roles. Personality becomes an independent variable in this sense.

That there will always be gaps in the theory of personality and in our knowledge of the Presidents must be frankly admitted. We must never squeeze men into prearranged theories. But the developmental approach does not require perfect knowledge of either personality in general or the man in particular. Rather, it provides a framework by means of which propositions about the relation of personality to behavior can be developed and evidence for and against cited. The test of any proposition that is used to explain behavior will be the plausibility of the explanation when set against other explanations. Our knowledge of Presidents is thus never complete but is always growing and changing.

The developmental biography approach focuses upon certain key aspects of political personality. These are the needs a man seems to particularly respond to, such as the need for attention or the need for respect. One then asks about the skills that have been developed in tandem with these needs. It does not matter whether the skills were developed to serve the needs or vice versa. There does seem to be a reciprocal relationship. Once this is done the elements of an habitual style of acting usually fall into place. Leaders seek those situations and ways of acting that favor their skills and, beneath the surface, their needs. One must also consider values and purpose and how they direct the use of skills. Finally, one must look at that element in personality, often called the ego, which has the task of holding all the parts together in some coherent way.

This very simple, skeletal model of political personality is not deterministic nor does it reflect any one personality theory. It does posit that individuals have varying degrees of freedom or ego strength. It suggests that men may be very dependent upon serving their needs in the exercise of their skills or that they may be fairly autonomous in their capacity to use skills in instrumental ways without recourse to inner promptings. There is the implication that the degree of autonomy and freedom to act and, correspondingly, the capacity to view the world with a good sense of reality are a result of ego strength. The possibility also exists within the model of discovering, by comparing individuals, that certain needs are often coupled with certain skills. Therefore, if we feel that given political roles require specific skills we may be able to postulate what needs will also be seeking expression and perhaps predict unintended consequences of particular skills for leadership. Any particular theory of personality can be adapted to this model in the case of an individual if it fits the facts of his life. We can thus draw on theory about the compulsive personality or ego defensive mechanisms and join it to our developmental model.

Biographers who are interested in understanding a single individual after the fact can use such a model of personality and fit it together with social and political variables to explain what happened. They can use a general theory of personality only when it seems appropriate to explain a particular case and are not trying to develop general conclusions about political personality. Political scientists, on the other hand, would like to generalize about the relationships between political personality and Presidential role playing and behavior. This is much more difficult than biography. It requires comparing a number of Presidents on the same dimensions and developing general propositions that apply to all of them. Can it be done?

We can follow the method of this chapter and sketch a number of separate profiles of Presidents in terms of the model of political personality and then draw inductive conclusions as best we can. Doing this can uncover certain likely relationships between needs and skills and between degree of ego strength and style of authority. This approach has now been sufficiently developed by political scientists who work in this area that it could be used by all of those who study the Presidency, especially journalists, if they have psychological sensitivity and observational acuteness. If a number of observers of leading politicians do this thoroughly for the main candidates for the Presidency at a given time we would know a lot more than we do now about what kind of a President a given person would be.

As a President assumes office and fleshes out the roles of office we can continue to observe and fill out our theory about the relationship of his personality to how he plays Presidential roles. This method is very good for stating the range of possibilities of style for a given President. We can see that he is going to favor congenial ways of acting. It is fairly good for predicting what an individual will do in certain stock situations. This method can provide hypotheses about what he will do in unique situations like crises, but it is very hard and perhaps not possible to predict behavior for a single case. Thus the greatest strength of the method is in increasing our understanding of how personality shapes the playing of regular Presidential roles and therefore our knowledge of the effect of character upon the Presidential office.

It may be harder to go much further than this for the present. Personality theory has many gaps and contradictions in it. The psychology of political behavior is a particularly underdeveloped field. There are great limitations in our knowledge of Presidents and historical events either after or during a period under study. The personality of each individual is a gestalt, a unique configuration of variables, and there are few general propositions about the links between personality and political style that will apply to a number of people. There will be too many individual variations of complex possibilities. The exploration of these problems of interpretations by scholars has developed a number of rules of thumb for interpretation of Presidential motivation and action.

CONGRUENCE

The stable and recurring leadership styles of a President are likely to take their form from a reinforcing pattern of needs, abilities, values, and beliefs. All the forces that go to make up political style in effective leaders are likely to run in the same direction. Thus, the Presidents in this century who have sought to be strong, creative leaders of great achievement (like the two Roosevelts, Wilson, and Johnson) have simultaneously served deep inner needs for attention and power as well as rhetorical, acting, persuading, and manipulative abilities. These needs and skills were congruent with belief in the importance of extending the role of government in the national life and expanding the influence of the Presidency within the government. The more cautious Presidents of restraint (like Taft, Coolidge, and Eisenhower) have not been men with strong needs for attention and power nor, were they men of great virtuosity in political skill. Rather, the stress was on rectitude and fixed behavior in Presidential roles. This was in keeping with their belief in the appropriateness of limited Presidential power and a modest role for government in the society. This congruence of needs, skills, and beliefs develops in an individual over time. As he develops skills in response to needs, on the one hand, and beliefs and values, on the other hand, there emerges a fairly stable and predictable political style.

Actions Are Multidetermined

Just as political style is rooted in a cluster of characteristics, so motivation for specific actions usually draws upon more than one level of personality. In his acceptance speech to the Republican National Convention in 1968 when Richard Nixon invoked his dream as a lonely boy to be great and famous some day he was drawing upon personal aspirations, but also using the Horatio Alger myth, so dear to Republicans, as a strategy of general political appeal to millions of Americans. Later, as President, he would justify provocative military actions in Vietnam with the argument that the United States must not be regarded by other nations as a "helpless giant," which would not act in behalf of its own interests. This was surely a genuine world view shared by both Nixon and Henry Kissinger that the United States had to maintain a strong posture in Vietnam in order to reach more fundamental agreements with China and the U.S.S.R. Many observers, however, also detected personal undertones of Nixon testing his own toughness and virility by such bold actions as invading Cambodia and bombing Hanoi. This mingling of the highly personal and the manifestly political is probably present in most major Presidential actions. Recognizing that most actions are overdetermined does not make the task of interpreting the relative importance of different motivations any easier. This is a matter for continuing debate between historians and biographers. One's interpretations are usually based on an overall model of the individual personality according to those motivational forces emphasized most. Thus, one might actually emphasize the highly personal element in Nixon's testing of himself, and regard the ideological and political justifications for such actions as secondary to his need to commit provocative actions.

Ego Defensive Behavior

Individuals lacking self-esteem will lash out at opponents and critics in ego defensive ways when they perceive a situation to be threatening. This is what Barber most fears his active-negative type of leader will do when under fire and pressure. The classic case of this kind of action would seem to be Woodrow Wilson who repeated a tragic pattern of stubbornness and rigidity three times in his career. He refused to compromise with the dean of the Princeton Graduate School, a personal foe, on where the new graduate center was to be placed on the campus and subsequently resigned from the presidency of Princeton. When the Republicans gained control of the New Jersey legislature midway in his term as Governor, he refused to submit a program or act as legislative leader in any way. And finally, and most tragically, he turned the dispute with the Senate over ratification of the Versailles Peace Treaty and the League of Nations into a personal vendetta against his enemy Senator Henry Cabot Lodge and thereby suffered an unnecessary defeat.[50] Alexander and Juliette George are the authors of a superb psychological biography on Wilson, which is restrained and yet incisive in its use of personality theory to explain the triggering of rigidity and stubbornness in Wilson when he felt threatened. They have created a model of ego defensive behavior that should guide all subsequent efforts in identifying such behavior in Presidents.

Historical interpretation of motivation of this kind is very difficult.

It runs up against most actions that are motivated by more than one set of forces in personality. Herbert Hoover's rigidity about programs and policies in the face of the Depression may have been a form of ego defensive behavior—a stubbornness under pressure—but it may also have been an ideological rigidity that was always present but was intensified by crisis. The end result was the same, but the source of the behavior in personality would be different. One could maintain that Lyndon Johnson's refusal to face alternatives on Vietnam was not ego defensive action, as suggested earlier, but the style of a political bargainer and compromiser who sought to hew a middle course between inaction and all out escalation. He might have seen himself as balancing these forces, as reflected in domestic opinion, off against each other and thereby keeping some equilibrium and moderation in American war policy. In the new setting and problem, this old style was inappropriate.

The delineation of ego defensive behavior can be tricky. One sign might be Presidential behavior that is judged inappropriate for the situation in which he finds himself. So Wilson could have secured ratification of the treaty, but refused to do so by his rigidity. One person's judgment of inappropriateness, however, might not be another's—since strategies of leadership are so variable and are rooted in subjective perceptions of situations.

Certainly we cannot justifiably infer that a given action was motivated by ego defensive behavior simply because we disapprove of the action. This is an empirical question to be resolved by psychological analysis. Such analysis should not be a pretext for covert political judgment.

Basic Personality Does Not Reflect Total Personality

The risk of using personality theory to write political biography is that aspects of personality that do not fit psychodynamic models will be ignored. The attempt will be made to explain everything about behavior in terms of needs, drives, and coping mechanisms. The existential elements of character, like beliefs and values, will be ignored. One could easily fall into this mistake in an idealization of the happy, well integrated, autonomous active-positive Presidents— Franklin Roosevelt, Truman, and Kennedy. Judgments on the stability of actions must not be confused with evaluations of the substance of actions. Even if one grants that John Kennedy, for example, was an active-positive character, cannot one be highly critical of his militant Cold War nationalism and penchant for taking the nation to the brink of crisis and confrontation over Berlin and Cuba? A revisionist historian would say that no matter how attractive a personality he was, his ideas about the world were in error.[51] Thus it is not sufficient for a President to be an active-positive. We would also like to know something about his values and beliefs.

The term character has many meanings. It can be the index of one's basic orientation toward the self and others. It tells us about self-esteem, ego strength, or their lack. This is an important insight and a key to the difference between the active-positives and active-negatives. However, character can also mean simple old fashioned integrity. But a psychoanalytic model of basic personality would not capture this idea, at least not directly. Yet, much of the pathos of the President's trials in the year of Watergate would seem to stem from deficiencies of character of this kind, particularly in the area of his personal taxes, improvements made upon his two homes with government funds, and allegations concerning the granting of government benefits to interest groups in return for cash contributions to the President's Reelection Fund. Much of Watergate was an abuse of integrity of a different sort—a sin of arrogance of the spirit, a contempt for opponents, and a disrespect for the rights and liberties of others stemming from a lack of character in the fundamental moral sense.

By the same token there would seem to be no reason why an active-negative Presidential personality would not have great capacities for moral leadership of others. Woodrow Wilson probably had the greatest ability to stir people in terms of moral ideals of any President of this century and yet he had an active-negative personality, of a sort.

Political Skill Can Be Destructive

While we praise and call for a high order of political skill in our leaders, we must recognize that the intense needs that generate a high order of skill can also cause unanticipated destructive behavior. This can happen even to active-positive leaders. Franklin Roosevelt grew increasingly willful and domineering as his Presidency came to an end. He seemed to think that he could order the postwar world on the basis of his ability to charm Marshall Stalin. He chose a vice-president in 1944 without serious thought about the man's qualifications to be President. Most political leaders of real stature, like Theodore Roosevelt, David Lloyd George, Winston Churchill, and Charles de Gaulle, have probably been active-positives, but this has not prevented their having so great an intensity of dynamic force and ambition that political institutions were severely strained to contain them. It would appear, then, that we pay a price for greatness and that a democracy might not be able to stand a succession of great, dynamic leaders in too short a period of time.

One cannot just pick out the active-positives from the active-negatives because even the active-positives, if they are highly talented, can be harmful to democratic norms. But this is not to say that an effort should not be made to avoid active-negative leaders.

The situation is made even more complicated by the strong possibility that many very talented political leaders are likely to be a combination of active-positive and active-negative characteristics. Who can deny the great virtues and talents of Woodrow Wilson and Lyndon Johnson? Would the republic have been better off without them? Do we really want to rule out men with deep self-doubt and uncertain egos if they have other redeeming features like high moral purpose and strong minds? Was Abraham Lincoln an active-positive? Probably not, in the strict definition of the typology.

CONCLUSION

Clear and explicit normative models of psychological health against which candidates for the Presidency can be judged should be part of the process of choosing Presidents. But only a relatively small number of people would ever be able to perform this kind of analysis well. There is a risk that the approach could be bastardized into a kind of amateur psychoanalysis. The few people who can do this kind of work should do it, on candidates and incumbent Presidents. But the mass of President watchers, including most citizens, are likely to think of their Presidents in more conventional terms. They will primarily respond to policies and events rather than to style. This provides no defense against destructive forces in Presidential personalities. We, therefore, need to find ways of changing popular perceptions of Presidential qualifications and to take into account the need for a democratic style of authority in the Presidential office. This would be the best defense against an active-negative or destructive personality in the Presidency. This would mean increased emphasis placed on the exploration of the basic style of authority of Presidential candidates. Such analysis can often be more revealing than efforts to predict that a given kind of person will resort to ego defensive behavior under stated conditions. The harmful effects of active-negatives like Johnson and Nixon on the Presidency are most likely seen in the erosion of democratic norms of government and constitutional rectitude, as much as in any specific policy actions.

Personality theory, therefore, should be used to explore style and to suggest what kind of a President a person is likely to be in general.

The criteria for a democratic style of authority will necessarily be general but there are certain minimal qualities that should be looked for in our leaders:

1. They should appear to have an active, affirmative attitude toward themselves, their work, and life. Signs of insecurity and compulsive striving could be potential danger signs. If such signs are noted, compensating strengths of character must be looked for.

2. There should be sufficient evidence that the individual can hold discussions with those who work in his immediate circle, which would reflect democratic norms of essential equality, respect for a diversity of views, and willingness to face unpleasant truths. This may be a more essential fundamental quality than administrative ability. Presidents are not selected for their executive ability and since the Senate appears to be the principal recruitment pool for Presidents, it is not likely that many Presidents will have developed the kind of extensive executive experience that might be wished for in the office. We can, however, assess the degree to which a person has a democratic style of authority by the quality of his relationships.

3. We should require standard political skills of our Presidents— the ability to speak, to persuade, to maneuver and manipulate, to structure situations, and to secure agreement in the face of conflict. Nevertheless, it should be remembered that there are many bases of political influence, and moral character and ability to appeal to shared values and beliefs are a skill and basis for influence by themselves. Manipulative skills without such qualities are likely to be hollow.

We will attempt to construct a fuller normative model of Presidential personality and style in Chapter 9. In the meantime we will observe personality at work in the administrative styles of Presidents, in their ways of structuring decision process, in crisis situations, in the range of available political skill employed, and in the negative sense of unconstitutional and immoral behavior. Following this overview we will try to define more carefully the kind of Presidents we need and suggest how we might better identify them.

3
The
Institutionalized
Presidency

It would be a great mistake to think of the Presidency only in terms of personality. The office is a bureaucracy as well as a man. Indeed, one of the strongest trends since World War II has been the growth of the Executive Office of the President as an organization. Some observers have characterized it as a fourth branch of government—a "Presidential government" that stands apart from the "permanent government" of the departments, agencies, and civil service. The dominant trend of the sixties, which continues today, was the centralization of important governmental functions in the White House and the Executive Office and the draining of initiative away from the departments, including the top levels of Presidential appointees in the Executive branch.

Political scientists have been ambivalent about this trend toward centralization. In general, given a definite preference for continuity and regularity in the bureaucracy, they have seen a strong Presidential institution as necessary for policy innovation. This has been particuarly the case with liberal political scientists who have identified with liberal presidents. Now that a conservative President has accentuated the trend toward centralization even more than his two predecessors one finds liberal political scientists raising questions that might not otherwise be raised about the wisdom of the trend.

These doubts had begun to arise in the Johnson years on the basis of several concerns. First, it became apparent that the White House was designing a great deal of progressive legislation intended to bring about social change without much thought about the feasibility of implementation. Second, the White House seemed to have little control or interest over the way the departments did in fact carry out the new laws. The President seemed very limited in his ability to extend his control despite the great centralization that had taken place. This raised questions about whether a White House that attempts to do everything may in fact fail to achieve anything. Finally, the question arose whether the White House had become a "house without windows"—that is, too much a world unto itself—because of bureaucratization and centralization.

On the one hand, political scientists wanted the Presidency to be a catalyst in the Executive branch. On the other hand, they began to fear that centralization and bureaucratization might in fact fail to achieve that goal by cutting the President off from the departments and bureaucracy and, as some feared, from other parts of government and the political system as well. In order to appraise these questions we will first examine the historical processes of institutionalization and centralization, then inquire into the effects of the Executive Office of the President on those within and without, and finally examine the range of relationships of the Presidency with the rest of the Executive branch.

THE INSTITUTIONALIZED PRESIDENCY

The Presidency, as an institution separate from the Executive branch, is made up of the White House staff and the larger Executive Office of the President, which includes the immediate Presidential staff. The numbers of both groups have increased greatly in the past twenty years. Franklin Roosevelt and Harry Truman each had 10 to 12 assistants in the White House. By 1959 the number of White House aides had grown to 37 under Eisenhower. Kennedy had 23 and Johnson about 20 assistants on their staffs. Nixon brought the figure up to 48 personal assistants in 1973. The total of those in the White House office grew from 226 in 1954 to 583 in 1973. There are indications that a larger number were in fact present but were on loan from departments and were therefore covered in departmental budgets. The Executive Office staff grew from 1,175 in 1954 to 1,664 in 1963 to 5,395 under Nixon in 1971.[1] This figure was reduced by approximately 2,000 when the Office of Economic Opportunity was drastically cut back by President Nixon in 1973 as the first step in its abolition.

In 1973 the Executive Office of the President was composed of the following units: Office of Management and Budget; Domestic Council; National Security Council; Council of Economic Advisers; Council on Economic Policy; Council on Environmental Quality; Office of

Economic Opportunity; Council on International Economic Policy; Office of the Special Representative for Trade Negotiations; Office of Telecommunications Policy; Special Action Office for Drug Abuse Prevention; and the Federal Property Council. With the exception of the Office of Management and Budget, all of the other councils came into being after World War II, at various points in time.[2] The more important groups are supported by professional staff. For example the Council of Economic Advisers has a staff of professional economists of approximately 50 people.

The Presidency has thus become an institution with enduring characteristics that continue across time despite changes in the person of the President. We do not know nearly as much as we should know about the internal workings of this institution. There is a great deal of secrecy in the conduct of business involving national security matters. There, one might expect it. But the formulation of domestic policy based on Presidential initiatives is also closely guarded. Few scholars have the necessary links with a President and his assistants that would allow entry into the White House to study it. Those who leave the government and write memoirs usually deal with history and substance rather than institutional life. Therefore, the history of institutional development and analysis of organizational folkways that follow, are drawn from those few reliable studies that exist but do not purport to explain all the things that we would like to know about life in the White House.

HISTORY OF THE EXECUTIVE OFFICE

When Franklin Roosevelt became President he was authorized by law to employ for his staff only a few personal secretaries. He began the first steps toward institutionalization by initiating the action that led to the Executive Reorganization Act of 1939. This legislation created the Executive Office and authorized the President to staff it with a few aides who he might use for his own purposes. They were not to be subject to the confirmation of Congress. FDR acted upon the formal advice of the Committee on Administrative Management, which was made up of three prominent social scientists who he had selected with a clear eye toward getting the advice he wanted.[3] Two key phrases from their report reveal the fact that they and Roosevelt were of one mind: "The President needs help" and the maxim that a Presidential aide should have a "passion for anonymity."

Roosevelt's guiding principle, as Richard Neustadt describes it, was to make sure that his White House assistants did his work and did not go into business for themselves.[4] Therefore, he would not permit the White House staff to become so large that he could not supervise the daily activities of its members, nor would he permit a chief of the staff to do this for him. For the same reason he seldom gave his aides fixed assignments for fear that they might develop vested interests or positions of their own. They were to be generalists in his behalf. He wished to, and did, use them to check each other. No one except FDR himself was given regular responsibilities in the relations of the White House with members of Congress and with department heads. Although aides were involved in these dealings he did not delegate his major responsibilities. Nor did he rely solely on his aides for his information. He had an elaborate system of intelligence in which he drew on a vast variety of visitors—personal friends, experts inside and outside government, cabinet officers, diplomats abroad, and his wife and other relatives and family. He disliked intensely being tied to any single source of information.

An equally strong principle held by FDR was that he would not do the work of the departments for them. He wished the White House to travel light in its concern with programs and to develop and push only those programs with Congress that were *his* programs and that he identified as vital to his plans. He once informed his cabinet about bills they were sponsoring: "It's all your trouble—not mine."

Roosevelt was also anxious that the departments not send bills to Congress that were contrary to his programs; he therefore acted to ensure that the Bureau of the Budget gave approval to departmental legislative proposals before they could be sent to Congress. Since the creation of the Bureau of the Budget (BOB) in 1921 the departments and agencies had been required to gain Bureau, and thus Presidential, approval of requests for appropriations they wished to make of Congress. FDR broadened this by insisting that departmental legislative plans be approved by the Bureau as well.[5] He wanted to guarantee that departments did not introduce measures that would be contradictory to his own or that might constrain his freedom to maneuver and develop his own legislative strategies.[6]

Through these actions Roosevelt sought to protect his own options and to continue to travel free of departmental demands. But the actual long-run effect was to ensure that departmental demands on the White House would increase and that the President would be more and more involved in judging departmental proposals and departmental conflicts. The requirements of governing during World War II made this fact more apparent. The great bureaucracies became ever more entangled in interdepartmental squabbles about vital policy matters, and the President had to increasingly serve their purposes rather than his own. The White House had to perform many functions for the departments and Congress, such as coordinating budgets, arbitrating disagreements, and sanctioning legislation, so that by the end of the war both the departments and Congress looked to the White House to prepare their agendas for them. This was the seed of a much greater institutionalized Presidency than Roosevelt had intended.

In Neustadt's term, the system of legislative clearance through the President has developed and survived because the "feudalities" at either end of Pennsylvania Avenue find it serves their mutual purposes.[7] Congress is not organized to prepare its own overall agenda but needs external direction. Because many agency proposals conflict Congress needs a cue from the White House on what will be favored. It also needs a certain protection against its own internal conflicts, which would be much stronger if congressmen had to order and rank program requests in terms of priority. The departments also need the White House to obtain their own goals because Presidential support is usually vital to a serious hearing in Congress. The result is that today the President is thoroughly saddled with a massive responsibility for legislative clearance and coordination that goes far beyond Roosevelt's original intention.

These trends took full form during the Truman Administration with the use of the BOB as the President's chief aide in the preparation of his legislative programs. In 1948 the BOB began to supplement negative protection of the President from the bureaucracy by positive help in developing and drafting Presidential proposals.[8] White House teams of experts and BOB teams cooperating with the departments worked out a number of the measures that became the chief themes of the Fair Deal. Some of the resulting legislation was the Housing Act of 1949 and the Social Security Act amendments of 1950. After that time the Bureau increasingly played a role in legislative development along with the departments at the behest of the White House.

The real Roosevelt revolution was that the President became the central and dominant figure in Washington. An increasingly positive and interventionist federal government and an increasingly receptive public had demanded this kind of leadership. Roosevelt held back from many of the implications of institutionalization because of his personal intuitions and style, but in Harry Truman the time and the man converged to give a new spurt to the developing Executive Office.

Truman, faced with overwhelming domestic and foreign problems for which he required much help, had a strong desire for orderly procedure and a very firm belief in the authority and dignity of the Presidency. He also loved to make decisions after hearing arguments on both sides. His habitual decision style was to marshall the experts and then decide for himself in terms of some general principle that he had long held. All these factors caused him to set about to develop mechanisms in the White House by which he could make decisions in an orderly way and enhance Presidential authority. He did not have Roosevelt's feel for the subtleties of one's personal power position, but his reverence for the office ensured that although he would utilize institutional help he would never permit any of it to subvert his authority as President.

He had external help with furthering institutionalization, but not all of it was friendly to his purposes. Both Congress and the Executive departments sought to build up the Executive Office, but their purpose was to better contain and restrain a President rather than to enhance him. They were taking their revenge on FDR by trying to create institutions for the President that they could control. Truman helped in this development but with opposite goals, and it was he that prevailed. Two examples of this point will suffice: the development of the National Security Council and the Council of Economic Advisers.

The National Security Council (NSC) came into being in 1947 as part of the legislation that created the Department of Defense. Truman pressed both measures on Congress out of a conviction that national security policies combined both diplomacy and military matters and that the government needed a coherent center for the continuous consideration of such policies. Roosevelt's highly personal conduct of wartime strategy had convinced many congressmen and State Department and military officials of the same conclusion. For example, the NSC was called "Forrestal's revenge" from its advocacy by the then secretary of the navy James Forrestal's belief that the navy had been pushed into a secondary role in war strategy. Thus, in the first version of the NSC the secretary of the navy had a seat at the table along with the other service secretaries—the new secretary of defense and the secretary of state—and the President. It was "Truman's revenge" that he appointed Forrestal the first secretary of defense.

Both Congress and the departments had hoped that the new NSC would require the President to decide policy in concert with his institutional advisers, but Truman, acting out of his conception of the Presidency, would not permit it. He simply refused to make policy in such an arena and often absented himself from meetings to emphasize that the Council was to bring its thinking to him not to make decisions with him. After the advent of the Korean War he used the Council fully and chaired most of the meetings. Still, his style was to receive a great deal of advice privately from his department heads, particularly Dean Acheson, secretary of state, and he therefore never permitted the NSC to reduce his prerogatives in any way.

The Council of Economic Advisers (CEA) was brought to life by the Employment Act of 1946 in which Congress charged the government with maintaining full employment in the future. It was felt that the President and Congress needed expert economic advice to better meet this goal. Such an act signified the greatly increased confidence of laymen in the science of economics since Keynes and since its demonstrated usefulness in wartime. However, in the creation of the CEA members of Congress also had some revenge on Roosevelt in mind as well. There had been great suspicion in Congress of the Roosevelt brain trust of ad hoc economic advisers during the early New Deal. They gave Roosevelt much of his economic advice but were personal rather than official advisers and were not required to testify before Congress or share information with it. The notion therefore developed that the members of the CEA should be accountable to Congress with confirmation of appointment required and a charge written into law to report regularly to the new Joint Economic Committee of both houses. The CEA was to be in the White House and report to the President primarily, but it was believed by some that by the method of dual accountability Congress could shape the kind of economic advice a President would get from his advisers. This is a further example of the continuous desire of people in government to constrain the President while utilizing the institutional Presidency for their own purposes.[9] This was not the dominant view behind the creation of the CEA but it was present.

The subsequent development of the Council has proved that it is a useful body only when it is used solely as a Presidential instrument. It cannot serve two masters. If it seeks to do so the President simply will not use it. Its economic advice must be meshed into Presidential politics and policy goals. Edwin Nourse, the first chairman of the Council, hoped to pursue a "scientific," nonpartisan role by offering dispassionate, factual advice to both President and Congress. The result was that Truman and Nourse came into open disagreement about policy and procedure and Nourse was succeeded by Leon Keyserling, an economist much more in tune with Presidential policy and purposes.[10]

Another innovation of the Truman years was the creation of a White House congressional liaison staff. This was the beginning of a development of structured specialized roles for White House staff members and a departure from the Roosevelt method of roving generalists. The complexity and press of demands on the White House required such specialized roles and the most obvious need, for legislative liaison, was filled first.

It is really during the Truman Presidency that we can speak of the institutionalized Presidency as a reality. White House staff members grew from 60 to about 200, and observers became aware that authority relations between the President and his staff were important for governing. A new Presidential skill became talked about—the ability to use staff well. Such discussions increased with the coming of Eisenhower since his conception of the office and his personal style seemed such a departure from the spirit of the Roosevelt maxim which Truman followed.

Eisenhower had no feel for or love of the intricate business of conflicts, personalities, and gossip that is the stuff of bureaucratic politics. He was a product of the army staff system in which a staff officer gathers the policy options from unit commanders and formulates a recommendation that the commanding officer either accepts or rejects. He took the National Security Council very seriously and funneled most major national security policy discussions through it. The staff of the NSC prepared national policy papers that were the basis for Presidential decisions. The strength of this approach was that the President received a coherent account of policy options as they were seen below in the government, including an open airing of internal conflicts. The weakness of the method is that such an interdepartmental process of developing policy options may preclude certain alternatives for a President without his being aware of it because of prior interdepartmental compromises.[11]

Eisenhower continued Truman's enlargement of the personal staff by creating an Office of Congressional Relations composed of a head and staff. He also created the post of special assistant to the President for national security affairs, a post subsequently held under other Presidents by McGeorge Bundy, Walt Rostow, and Henry Kissinger. Eisenhower was also the first President to have a special adviser for science, a development that followed from the Russian space shots and led to a formal scientific advisory apparatus under Kennedy.

He also made an abortive attempt to make the cabinet a council of state by giving it a secretariat and holding regular meetings. But the Cabinet meeting never became more than a briefing session for busy people each of whom resented any poaching on his own territory. This innovation did not take root because it went against the grain of Executive politics in which the President's cabinet is not a unified family but a collection of separate fiefdoms with many ties to Congress, bureaucracy, and outside groups.

The common criticism of Eisenhower was that he permitted himself to be smothered by his White House apparatus. Whether true or not, John Kennedy believed it to be so and therefore acted quickly to dismantle much of the Eisenhower machinery. He shared Roosevelt's concern for the personal as well as the institutional Presidency and cut back on bureaucratic forms in the White House. The cabinet secretariat was abolished and no effort was made to use the cabinet as a sounding board. He did away with the NSC bureaucracy of interdepartmental planning and implementation committees. Kennedy was his own chief of staff who wanted his personal staff accountable to him, and in this he was acting on personal predisposition as well as taking Richard Neustadt's advice about the value of the Rooseveltian model.

Kennedy also took advantage of some of Eisenhower's innovations. Lawrence O'Brien built up the Office of Congressional Relations into a strong entity that coordinated all the work of the departmental legislative staffs. The legacy of central legislative clearance had thus eventually resulted in an active White House role in directing departmental legislative proposals.

Kennedy strengthened the position of Special Assistant for National Security Affairs by charging Bundy and his staff with being the central catalyst to make sure that proposals coming from the departments were screened and criticized before coming to the President. He distrusted bureaucracy and wanted a small, highly mobile White House staff to keep a constant eye on it for him. This was particularly the case after the fiasco of the Bay of Pigs invasion in 1961. The President felt in retrospect that there had been too little adversary process brought to bear in White House discussions of the CIA plan. Originally he had hoped to rely on the secretary of state as his chief adviser in foreign affairs and the State Department as the chief source of foreign policy coordination and implementation. However, in a fairly short time he became disillusioned with both possibilities because he found State to be slow to rise to the charge. The central problem is that any strong President is going to be his own secretary of state. Foreign policy cuts across a number of departments, and he cannot rely upon any one, even State, to be his department for foreign policy. Therefore, he needs staff assistance in the White House to take initiatives, clear departmental proposals, coordinate, arbitrate between departments, and ensure that policy gets carried out by the departments. If Bundy had not existed he would have had to be invented and as Kennedy dryly told the press about Bundy's position, "I will continue to have some residual functions."[12]

This institutionalization nonetheless creates very serious problems. Because of the great need of the President for his Special Assistant for National Security such a person tends to be seen as a second secretary of state. This came to its logical culmination with the relationship of President Nixon and Henry Kissinger. Kennedy did not carry the role that far but the problem is inherent in the need for such a role. This is often referred to as the problem of "layering," that is, creating a layer of officials between a President and his departments. One school of thought holds that this is essential if a President is to know what the departments are really doing and to make sure that they carry out his instructions. Another viewpoint is that although this may be so, there is a great danger in a White House bureaucracy that separates the President from the departments. Such machinery tends to signify lack of confidence in the departments and therefore may have the effect of drying up any innovative capacity they might have for program initiation. It also creates a communication barrier between a President and the people in the departments he needs to carry out his programs and advise him as to how they are working. The rejoinder to this is that the people in the departments would be the last to tell the President if their own programs are not working. The problem is a two-edged one: the President needs expert staff in the White House to help him but he does not want to alienate the departments that he needs as well.

Lyndon Johnson retained the Kennedy institutional Presidency much as it had existed but permeated by his own style. His chief contribution to the institutionalization of the Presidency was the use of the task-force device to prepare the legislative programs of the Great Society. The use of the task force came in two waves, 1964 and 1966. The task-force operation was developed in early 1964 because Johnson was a President without a program should he be reelected. He wanted a major legislative program for 1965, especially since he anticipated a landslide victory over his likely opponent, Senator Goldwater. Richard Goodwin, a White House aide, originated the idea of assembling the nation's leading experts on specific problems in small groups and charging them with making specific recommendations for the President's legislative program. Johnson became excited about the idea and put Bill Moyers in charge of recruiting and directing the groups. Moyers mixed government officials with outside academics, professionals, and others, drawing on his allies in the bureaucracy, especially those he thought were innovative. The task forces were chaired in many cases by men who would later enter the Administration, for example, John Gardner, Robert Wood, and Harold Howe. In each task force a Bureau of the Budget representative served as executive secretary. The panels met secretly and reported after the 1964 election. Smaller task forces of cabinet officers, assistant secretaries, BOB experts, and White House staff then culled the recommendations for realistic legislative proposals. Finally, the President brought to bear his political antennas as the key decisions were made.

The task forces produced much creative legislation: Model Cities;

the establishment of the Department of Housing and Urban Development; and many of the education, health, and antipoverty programs of the Great Society. This culminated Roosevelt's initiation of legislative clearance in 1935 and Truman's use of that practice to have the BOB prepare his legislative program in concert with the departments. In this case, however, the President went outside government altogether to strengthen his hand in both the society and the government. He was trying to summon up all possible resources for innovation. It is not yet apparent that the idea as such has been institutionalized and that subsequent Presidents will use it. This may depend upon the desire of the President to innovate as well as his personal style of operating.[13]

Both Kennedy and Johnson used the White House staff to stimulate and monitor the bureaucracy beneath. The central style of Roosevelt was discernible in each. A catalyst was needed but layering was to be avoided. Richard Nixon took the developments of his two predecessors and, out of the predispositions of his own style of authority, layered extensively. The purport was very different from that of Eisenhower, who sought to mesh the White House with the bureaucracy, and from that of Kennedy and Johnson, who sought to balance White House and bureaucracy in creative tension. Nixon almost seemed to be trying to overcome the tension by conducting the main business of government within the White House itself and simply ignoring the departments.

Under Nixon, Henry Kissinger in fact became not a second secretary of state but the de facto secretary who was the President's chief foreign policy adviser and negotiator. He also headed a large staff who did the principal analytic work for the President on foreign policy. John Ehrlichman, counselor to the President, was the first director of the newly created Domestic Council, which is composed of cabinet officers and assistant secretaries of the domestic departments supported by a staff and is intended to be the counterpart of the NSC in the preparation and coordination of Presidential programs.

At the same time that the Domestic Council was created the Bureau of the Budget was changed into the Office of Management and Budget (OMB) with a new emphasis upon central evaluation of the effectiveness of departmental programs and procedures. Policy was thus divorced from administration with the Domestic Council serving the first function and OMB the second.[14]

In the first months of 1973 President Nixon attempted to integrate White House actions with those of the departments by naming Secretary of the Treasury George Schultz an assistant to the President with authority to direct other government officials in matters of economic affairs. The vehicle to accomplish this is the Council on Economic Policy which has a small staff and has become a forum for the exchange of departmental views on economic questions. The President, with the advice of Schultz, is the final arbiter of such disputes. A similar arrangement was created in September 1973 when Henry Kissinger became secretary of state but retained his role as assistant to the President. In this way he might continue to direct and coordinate all national security policy, something one could not do as secretary of state alone. Earlier in the year Nixon had named four department heads as White House counselors with responsibility and authority over other department heads in the areas of economic affairs, human resources, natural resources, and urban affairs. However, these positions were eliminated in the wake of Watergate and a White House concession to the demand for greater direct accessibility to the President by those in his Administration.

The future will tell whether this model of dual roles and a hierarchy within the President's cabinet will become institutionalized. It is not likely that this will happen because some future Presidents will probably prefer a less ordered and more openly pluralistic process of Executive policy discussion and will want to deal directly with a larger number of department heads. Fundamentally different views of political life are involved here. Those who favor centralization think that it is possible and desirable to impose a system of command and control from the top on the Executive branch in terms of the President's priorities. Those who favor pluralism think this is probably not possible because the division in government manifests the pluralism of the society and conflicts that are real will simply emerge in some new way. They see such an effort to control conflict by administrative mechanisms as undesirable.

As this historical survey has demonstrated, one cannot speak for certain about a trend of institutionalization until several Presidents have adopted a given innovation and it has shown itself to fit the recurring needs of all Presidents. Personality is definitely a crucial factor here, and President Nixon's well-known penchant for relative isolation from even his own staff and his preference for dealing with others through a few close aides certainly explains much of the current White House structure.

The long-term trend in institutionalization is clearly toward centralization and strengthening of White House capabilities vis-à-vis the rest of government, but it must be seriously questioned whether this is healthy for the Presidency. If it isolates the Presidents and saps the vitality of the rest of government then it is bad. If it merely provides a catalyst from the White House and creative tension between Presidential and permanent government then it is salutory.

SUMMARY OF INSTITUTIONAL CHARACTERISTICS

Certain features of the White House and the Executive Office remain the same over time regardless of who is President and can be characterized much as one would describe the stable patterns of the House Appropriations Committee or of the State Department.

First, there is a functional compartmentalization of expert staffs into groups each of which interacts more with other parts of the government than it does with its White House counterpart. The groups include legislative liaison staff, expert economic advisers, national security analysts, expert aides in a variety of fields (energy, the environment, science and technology, telecommunications), public relations assistants, and most important, a handful of top political and program advisers who are perhaps the only one of these groups to interact with all of the others.[15]

A typical pattern of interaction would be that of the three members of the Council of Economic Advisers who, with supporting staff, work closely and regularly with officials of the Treasury Department and the Federal Reserve Board as well as with other department officials on economic questions. They are most useful to the President as an analytic check on the advice coming in from the departments, but their influence with him varies greatly according to personality relationships, the kind of advice they give, the current political climate, and the relative influence of other important actors such as the secretary of the treasury. The same pattern holds in national security affairs and all other areas in which staffs of professionals work. Legislative liaison staff and public relations advisers such as the press secretary and speech writers speak to the President from the perspective of their different constituencies, respectively Congress and the media.

Second, there is a continual rivalry between these functional staff groups for the attention of the President. These rivalries can often be humorous, as in competition for office space and the important matter of whether one's office is actually in the White House or across the street in the Executive Office Building. Since these groups come at the President as they do from a variety of perspectives, they must compete for attention and influence. For example, the legislative staff is likely to favor political accommodation with Congress on certain matters, whereas the President's program advisers may favor putting greater pressure on Congress in order to enhance the reputation of the President. An economic adviser may favor a reduction in the budget, while national security aides will simultaneously wish an increase in expenditures for defense.

Third, a hierarchy of staff exists in terms of the degree of closeness to the President. The composition of the group will vary according to Presidential taste, but each President will usually have four or five closest advisers whom he will see regularly although not always together. A department head or two is usually included as well. John Kennedy worked most closely with McGeorge Bundy, his national security adviser; Theodore Sorensen, his chief domestic aide; Walter Heller, chairman of the Council of Economic Advisers; his brother Robert, attorney general; and Robert McNamara, secretary of defense. Lyndon Johnson chiefly relied upon Walt Rostow, who succeeded Bundy; Kermit Gordon, the director of the Bureau of the Budget; and Joseph Califano, Bill Moyers, Dean Rusk, and Robert McNamara. President Nixon relied during his first term primarily upon H. R. Haldeman, his chief of staff; John Ehrlichman, his chief domestic adviser; Henry Kissinger, his national security adviser; and increasingly upon George Schultz, John Connally, and John Mitchell, three strong department secretaries.

This inner circle of advisers is made up of the people who are responsible for those policy matters that most engage the President, primarily national security questions and key domestic issues, especially those having to do with the management of the economy and domestic program formulation. Such men are literally assistant Presidents who have authority in the Administration beyond their official responsibilities.

Fourth, there is perennial and unavoidable tension between White House staff and the departments because each has different perspectives and responsibilities. This is the case in regard to both program development and implementation. The White House finds it difficult to draw ideas from the departments, which are either new or innovative. Policy-inventing work must be done for the President in the White House to a large extent. White House resources for observation of how well the departments are carrying out programs are slender, however, and lead to frustrated efforts to direct programs from the Executive Office itself. This problem will be dealt with in detail throughout this chapter.

Fifth, the institutional development of the Executive Office, including the White House itself, occurs in response to those needs of the Presidency that are stronger than the particular demands of any one President. For example, the increasing diversification of expert staff units meets Presidential requirements, but the use made of these bodies varies according to Presidential style. Therefore, there is flexibility in the institutionalized Presidency.

PAST LEGACIES AND PRESENT PROBLEMS

As the Presidency has become less a one-man operation with a few helpers and has grown into a large institution, a question has arisen of whether, without quite intending to, we have created a king and his court. The office of President is after all something of a republican monarch in the great symbolic power residing in it and the deference accorded the person of its incumbent. Few people ever call him by his first name and his physical presence seems to carry an aura with it of the kind that attaches to the Pope, to monarchs in the past, and to other powerful heads of state. Court politics in such a setting takes the form of currying favor and an exaggerated deference to a President that may insulate him from the harshness of reality.

George Reedy, at one time Johnson's press secretary, advanced the thesis that the White House had become a sealed-off place in which there was far too much deference to the President and in which views of the world outside the White House were manufactured within to suit the Presidential mood.[16] Reedy sees the institution of the Presidency as a kind of monarchy in which the rituals and realities of power reinforce the natural tendency of subordinates to tell the man in charge what he wants to hear. His argument is that there is no one in the White House who will tell the President to "go soak his head." This is even more true if the President is "stronger" and more activist because he must dominate his staff in order to dominate the government. The result is that the President becomes the prisoner of his own illusions about reality, and everything in the structure and atmosphere of the White House, in which his will is paramount, acts to reinforce this fact. Therefore, according to Reedy, no one is in a position to stop the President from making a terrible blunder; everyone who serves him is afraid of him.

Certainly Reedy has hit upon an enduring reality in power relationships. Albert Speer describes how Hitler's inner circle agreed with his increasingly illusory ideas right up until disaster came because of his ability to play on their desires to be close to the man of power and their fear of him.[17] Anyone in a position of executive power, even in a democracy, can draw on such deference. Robert Kennedy remembered a high Presidential adviser who strongly advocated one position before a meeting with the President and then changed his view completely and advocated the opposite argument when he discovered in the meeting with the President that John Kennedy had accepted a position different from his own original one.[18] This kind of behavior exhibits a mixture of ambition and fear on the part of subordinates who dare not offend the leader for fear they might fall from favor if they advance views contrary to his.

Therefore it is common for the advisers of executives in any organization to suppress their real views if the executive telegraphs his. Chester Cooper describes how Johnson would poll his principal foreign policy advisers one at a time on questions to do with the conduct of war. He would go around the table and elicit an "I agree Mr. President" from each one. Cooper developed a fantasy in which he stood up and announced with a flourish, "Mr. President, gentlemen, I most definitely do not agree." But when the time came for him to speak he always heard himself saying, "Yes, Mr. President, I agree."[19]

The stronger, more dynamic, and more magnetic a President the greater the danger of this kind of deference. A President who would learn from his advisers must continually guard against destroying their independence. On the other hand, he must also make sure of their loyalty. The line between these two tendencies is not an easy one to walk especially for a President determined to dominate the governmental process. John Kennedy kept the balance fairly well largely because of the skepticism, humor, and sense of irony about the pretensions of men that were part of his personality. Johnson did not know how to keep any such delicate balance, and Reedy's description of the White House is in large part a description of Johnson's Presidency. Reedy identifies tendencies that are present in all centers of executive power, public or private, but he forgets the crucial importance of the personality of the President as the key variable. If a President wants to create an atmosphere of openness and adversary argument within a common framework of loyalty he can do it. However, it will not develop by itself because all logic of the situation is against it.

The very malleability and limited institutionalization of the White House are both a blessing and a danger. The positive features are that the White House is staffed primarily by professionals who have a high regard for knowledge and objective analysis and share professional habits of free discussion of ideas. In this sense the hierarchy is basically flat, and the people who work there are inclined to resist stratification and rank, and to want to have a high level of communication with others. Most organizations staffed primarily by professionals, like hospitals and universities, are likely to have such characteristics as opposed to highly formalized, hierarchical bureaucracies.[20] This looseness is a resource for a President who would promote widespread discussion within the White House and use his staff for listening and learning about what is going on elsewhere. However, because of the intrusion of power and status relationships there is no such thing as a pure model of organization based solely upon the free exchange of information. The very business of government, with its conflicting goals and the insecurity of staff vis-à-vis each other in their claims upon the President's time and decisions, makes for counter-processes of secrecy, game playing, and efforts to cut the President off from potential sources of advice. Once again a President must be aware of this and, by means of his own personal style of authority, act to counteract such possibilities.

Staff are divided into functional groups that do not communicate across group lines often enough. Each group, and often individuals within groups, has a one-to-one relationship with the President. It would take a courageous individual to tell the President of the United States the unvarnished truth in a face-to-face meeting if the facts are in any way unpalatable or do not reflect credit on him or you. It is much easier to sense what Presidents want to hear and to tell them this in order to ingratiate oneself. The lack of spontaneous collegial discussion across functional lines limits the existence of multiple advocacy.

Any President creates a hierarchy among his staff, which results in a small inner circle around him that may seal him off from the outside unless he takes great precautions to maintain independent channels. Many of these men lack governmental experience and do not know how to deal with either Congress or the bureaucracy. They openly show their negative attitudes toward the governmental folkways of Washington, all of which does the President more harm than good. They bring to government the self-confidence of the successful in American life, which can act to create an aura of arrogance in the White House in its dealings with others. Although there were real drawbacks to Lyndon Johnson's bullying of his aides, they were in fact much less likely to go into business on their own than either the Kennedy or Nixon White House staffs who often overstepped the staff role to become assistant Presidents.

All White House aides lack bases of political power and constituencies of their own and identify with the President as the one source of policies for the public interest. But unlike Congress and the bureaucracy they have short political memories and few communication links with groups in the society who are affected by the programs they invent. They may easily come to confuse their own preferences with the public interest.

These problems can lead to excessive deference to the President within the White House and exaggerated service to his supposed interests outside of it. The results can be far-reaching—anger in Congress and demoralization throughout the Executive branch. In the end it is the President who suffers and he therefore must seek protection from his own aides.

The revelations about life in the White House that emerged during the hearings of the Senate Select Committee on Campaign Practices (the Ervin Committee) in 1973 show the institution at its worst, but not all the problems can be blamed upon institutional structure as such. Rather, the institutional norms and atmosphere that developed took their character from the President's own preference for seclusion and isolation and his contempt for most people and institutions outside the White House. Also contributing heavily to this was the extraordinary degree to which the top White House staff men, particularly H. R. Haldeman and John Ehrlichman, shared these views. Many of the tendencies implicit in the institution of the White House were reinforced: isolation of subgroups and filtering of information through staff hierarchy; hostility to outsiders; and Presidential will seen as the prime goal of government.

This atmosphere produced inept congressional relations, a massive deterioration of morale in the bureaucracy, and efforts to subvert units of the bureaucracy from their missions into unlawful acts. For example, the CIA was asked to participate in the Watergate cover-up, the Internal Revenue Service was to be used to harass Presidential "enemies," and the FBI was to do illegal burglaries and maintain surveillance of domestic disrupters. The resistance of these agencies to being used led to the White House assuming such roles itself, as witnessed by the burglary by a White House team of the office of the psychiatrist of Daniel Ellsberg, the man who released the Pentagon Papers to the press. Presidential wishes took precedence over the law and Constitution.

Nixon would have been better advised to have staffed the White House with politically experienced people who knew how to get along with Congress, the press, and the bureaucracy, while maintaining a sensitivity to public opinion and political currents. He did bring Bryce Harlow and Melvin Laird—experienced political men—onto his personal staff after Haldeman and Ehrlichman retired. Both Harlow and Laird contributed a good deal to opening lines of communication with Congress, press, and public. In order to break down the image and reality of the White House as a closed bastion, Laird consciously and deliberately tried to encourage open debate among Administration officials. The system of four super-secretaries who would direct other department heads in a dual capacity as counselors to the President was dismantled at Laird's insistence.[21]

In the ensuing months, as the possibility of impeachment grew stronger, the President reverted to old habits—relying primarily upon nonpolitical technicians (General Alexander Haig, who succeeded Haldeman as White House chief of staff and Ron Ziegler, the press secretary who was promoted to assistant to the President with unspecified duties) for consultation about general political matters, including his own self-defense. In the final analysis, it would appear that Nixon did not appreciate the advice of political men like Laird, and the former secretary of defense left the White House staff in early 1974. Nixon's persistence in a style of authority that was completely discredited by the disclosures surrounding Watergate illustrates that a President cannot easily change his habitual ways of doing business and that his style is the most single crucial factor in shaping organizational life in the White House.

WHITE HOUSE AND THE GOVERNMENT

To conclude that a President should try to create a White House atmosphere of openness, freedom, listening, and learning, and that his chief staff aides should be people of political experience and sensitivity is adequate as a general statement. But it does not speak to difficult questions of the proper relationships of such assistants to the rest of the Executive branch. The most prominent prescriptions are general and perhaps necessarily so. It is accepted that the President needs a specialized staff that can also be used as catalyst to stimulate the departments and as monitors to follow up upon the administration of programs. The excessive layering of White House staff between the President and the rest of government is a mistake, however, because it cuts him off from people he needs to see and hear from. Again these are general prescriptions that do not speak to specific questions such as whether the assistant to the President for national security affairs should be the President's principal adviser for foreign affairs as opposed to the secretary of state, or whether the Domestic Council is the proper place for developing domestic policy. There are many unresolved questions of this type that are answered by practice in successive administrations without any pretense at a final institutional form. This is as it should be, for each President must be free to shape staff relationships and White House links with the rest of government in ways that match his personal style of authority, the kinds of people he has in his government, and the problems that he faces.

4
The President, Public Opinion, and Foreign Policy

Democratic theory has been ambivalent toward the proper relationship of public opinion and government leadership, ranging from elitist notions on the desirability of leader autonomy to populist ideas on the importance of public opinion as the chief factor in policy. The same tension has been present in democratic practice throughout the history of the republic. The authors of the Constitution preferred a strong, independent executive who could act swiftly, conduct secret diplomacy, and be free of volatile mass opinion. The modern progressive tradition, however, has distrusted executive power in foreign policy because of a conviction that the power of the state would be so enhanced by war that democratic control would be seriously weakened. Many American progressives were opposed to the entry of the United States into World War I for this same reason. This was the cause of the dramatic filibuster in the Senate by Senator Robert LaFollette, Sr. and others to prevent United States aid to England before entry into the war itself. They feared it was a step toward war. Some conservatives, such as Senator Robert A. Taft, expressed similar views in Congress at the time the Truman Administration requested American troops to be a part of the NATO military establishment. Taft felt this was a commitment toward future military action that could be too easily triggered without public or congressional assent. He was acting from the same democratic concerns as the progressives in World War I.

In the 1950s and 1960s, however, a strong coalition of liberals and conservatives in Congress and throughout the country supported the autonomy and prerogatives of the Presidency and the Executive in foreign policymaking and execution. They did so in the belief that America was caught in a dangerous Cold War with the Soviet Union and China, which had twice developed into a shooting war—in Korea and Vietnam. It was felt that the Executive could best act to deal with the continuous government by crisis brought on by the Cold War.

The reaction of many liberals against the use of Presidential power in regard to Vietnam, and the acquiescence by many conservatives in President Nixon's rapprochement with China and the U.S.S.R., thus seemingly easing the Cold War, may have broken the spell of Executive dominance, which once prevailed. New kinds of problems —arms control, energy needs, monetary systems—invite a larger congressional role in Executive decisions and presumably a greater voice for the public. As yet, such roles have not been established. The Executive overwhelmingly dominates foreign policy, although in less dramatic fashion than during war. The very structure of foreign policymaking and implementation is elitist. The everyday business of policy is too remote from the lives of most citizens for them to relate to the issues at stake, even if they are informed about them—which is uncommon. Few domestic interest groups impinge upon the foreign policy decision process, at least in comparison to domestic policy. Those strong interests that do, such as the oil industry, tend to work closely with top levels of government in symbiotic relationships so that it is hard to tell one from the other. The nature of policy problems, including the frequency of crisis, favors action by the Executive rather than widespread deliberation by the public before decisions are made. For these reasons and more, the Presidential role has thirst for autonomy in foreign policymaking built into it.

In this chapter we will, first, consider the perspectives of office that push a President toward desire for autonomy in the foreign policy sphere—especially in regard to national security policy. We will then explore the resources and constraints that public opinion might put upon Presidential power in this area. In the next chapter, we will ask the same questions in relation to the President, Congress, and the rest of the Executive establishment. These two chapters, then, form an integral whole directed toward the age-old question of democratic theory—how much power should the Executive have in matters of foreign policy and war?

PRESIDENTIAL PERSPECTIVES ON FOREIGN POLICY

World View

Each President will have a world view derived from his personal history and experience that is not likely to change greatly once he enters the White House. For better or worse, his preexisting world view is the intellectual capital on which he will draw as President, and most of the expert advice and intelligence he receives will be filtered through that world view. This is not to deny that individual Presidents will show an ability to grow and learn in their understanding of the world. Franklin Roosevelt came to office with limited experience or understanding of foreign nations and paid little attention to foreign policy until forced to do so by events in Europe. However, the great responsibilities of leadership in World War II educated him in an extraordinary way, and he did grow in his understanding. It is noteworthy, however, that many of his ideas were drawn from his pre-Presidential experience. For example, his deep affinity for China and unjustified belief that he understood that country were based on the background of his family in the China trade. His negative views about the British and French empires were also old attitudes. Woodrow Wilson, on the other hand, never really understood other nations and made little effort to do so. As part of his ideology he created an imaginary world that he adhered to until the final, tragic defeat of his hopes for American leadership in the League of Nations.

John Kennedy came to office a militant Cold War warrior but gradually moderated his zeal and began to move toward a rapprochement with the Soviet Union as a result of the near nuclear confrontation of the Cuban missile crisis. Lyndon Johnson was not prepared for leadership in foreign affairs and his responses to events that he did not fully understand were by and large visceral.

President Nixon seems, however, to have come to office with a coherent and systematic set of goals for the relations between the major powers, and he and his chief adviser Henry Kissinger have been most systematic about pursuing the highly intellectual vision in specific policies that they share. Nixon has in fact seldom deviated from his prime goals. For example, at the time of the brief war between India and Pakistan in 1972, most articulate opinion in America called upon the President to support the Indians in their resistance to Pakistani efforts to put down the rebellion in East Pakistan. But Nixon was determined to achieve a rapprochement with China, an ally of Pakistan, and permitted no moral considerations to interfere with his larger vision of realpolitik. By the same token, he persisted in a policy of continued support for the South Vietnamese regime from the view that rapprochement with both China and the Soviet Union was to be guaranteed only by their knowledge that the United States would not permit itself to be driven into a position of weakness in Southeast Asia.

The point is not that a President will be necessarily impervious to the opinions of others. Rather, he must have some ballast and coherence to his views in order to be able to function in policy decisions and he is not likely to be able to get this overriding world view from others. There will be too many competing presumptions and assumptions thrust at him. Therefore, because events move so quickly and there is little time to read, learn, and reflect once he is in office, a President is very dependent upon the intellectual capital he brings into office with him. In most cases he will cling to it because he lacks any alternative. He cannot develop a new world view once the pressures of events are upon him no matter how important his critics think it for him to do so.

Greater Political Capital from Foreign Policy

The President is much more likely to strengthen his domestic political position through his foreign policy rather than his domestic policy. The former tends to unify the country and strike the chords of popular nationalism while almost any domestic policy will anger someone and continuous action causes gradual erosion of support. But decisive Presidential action in foreign policy crises spaced over time can keep a President high in public esteem.

A President soon learns that he enjoys institutional and constitutional prerogatives and autonomy in foreign policy that are simply not present in domestic matters. There are fewer people to influence and diplomacy is sometimes a more reliable and controllable instrument than, for example, government action to promote domestic social change. It is difficult for any President to resist the appeal of attempting one or more dramatic diplomatic solutions to longstanding problems. Success ensures a place for a President in world history. Also, the overriding importance of foreign policy, particularly questions of war or peace, guarantees that a President will spend much of his time in this sphere and attach the greatest importance to it. This is also a means of political capital which Presidents often use very cleverly when domestic troubles increase and, for this reason, they try to keep as much autonomy as possible in foreign policy. And even if the substantive intent of the action fails, publics do not always realize this because it is often very difficult to distinguish image from substance in foreign policy. Public opinion is quite often prepared to accept the image as token for substance, and Presidents soon learn this.

Any person, though, will find his perspective changed by the fact that he is President. He will feel a responsibility for guarding the national interest as he sees it, and of course different Presidents will see it differently. This sense of responsibility may override every other consideration in his actions, including those of domestic politics. The fact that four successive Presidents have felt that Southeast Asia, and specifically South Vietnam, should not be lost to the communists has surely been influenced by domestic politics. But probably of greater importance in the thinking of these Presidents has been a sense of responsibility to do nothing that might in any way weaken the American power position in the world. Presidents are therefore likely to emphasize actions that guard their perception of that power position and shy away from actions that seem to hurt it.

This bias, which may be inherent in the Presidential role, seems to favor military solutions to foreign policy problems. It may also predispose Presidents to try to do more than their knowledge or resources will in fact permit. Our ignorance of foreign nations is in fact very great, but American Presidents have been prone to assume that we could manipulate the affairs and governments of other nations as we wish. This has often led to terrible miscalculations.

Confusion of Rhetoric with Reality

In the leadership of any organization, including a government, it is tempting and easy to confuse one's aspirations with actual achievements. It may be necessary to do this in a world of uncertainty, and one cannot always be open to new information about how badly things are going. A leader can get so caught up in his purposes that he confuses intensity of commitment and effort with actual results. The process of trying becomes the important thing to him and not the end result.

This can lead to credibility gaps between official words and the perceptions of others. The most dramatic recent instance was seen in the first years of American involvement in Vietnam. It was not so much that Presidents and others in high places in government were deliberately lying that the war was going well for the Americans and South Vietnamese when it demonstrably was not, but it was more the case that Presidents and their aides *had to* believe it was going well. Their investment in the event was too great for anything else to be the case. This can lead to a confusion of self-induced images with actual policy. Thus when Presidents seem to lie it is often not deliberate lying but self-deception projected outwards. It is based on uncertainty and insecurity and is reinforced by the closed atmosphere of the White House bureaucracy.

It takes great courage for a President to be willing and able to push his government to face the truth in difficult foreign policy questions. When he does succeed, and all the forces of bureaucracy are against him, he nullifies the arguments of all these propositions that a President seeks autonomy. For in order to learn and separate rhetoric from reality he must sacrifice some of his autonomy by incorporating the perspectives of others. Not all Presidents are endowed with sufficient moral courage or intellectual self-confidence to do this well.

Taken together, all these predispositions of the Presidential role mean that a President will seek maximum autonomy to act abroad as he thinks right. He will resist control at home in the name of his responsibilities abroad.

Much of this chapter and the next will be spent seeking to achieve a balanced conclusion about the domestic resources for and constraints on a President's autonomy of action in foreign affairs. The attitudes and emotions of publics, patterns of partisan political competition, congressional politics, and the complex Executive foreign affairs bureaucracy all provide both resources and constraints for Presidential action. The conclusion will be that a President's resources are greater than his constraints, but it does not follow that his ability to mold the world as he might wish is equally great. In fact, reality imposes very severe constraints on Presidential efforts to enact foreign policy. Thus we have the paradox of a giant at home in foreign policymaking who cannot really be a giant abroad no matter how he tries.

THE PRESIDENT AND PUBLIC OPINION

Is there a dynamic relationship between the thinking and actions of a President and changing states of public opinion as he perceives them or anticipates them? Democratic theory guides us to ask about such links of responsiveness and leadership. Unfortunately the evidence is not good, and considerable inferences must be made from sketchy data. There has been a great deal of speculative writing about the role of public opinion in foreign policy formulation and from that literature we can develop three general theories.

Theory of Popular Mood

One view sees the public as directly and emotionally involved in policy in the form of communicating strong preferences that policymakers dare ignore only at their peril. This has been seen as a bad state of affairs. According to Walter Lippmann, the chief proponent of this view,[1] a democracy is bad for foreign policymaking because public opinion is not only uninformed but also irregular, spasmodic, and emotional. Public involvement obstructs the continuity and decisive action required in foreign policy, and the public therefore should play only a limited role through voting approval or disapproval of leaders in elections. Lippmann was influenced by the events before and after two world wars. The American public, in his view, was at first isolationist and difficult to educate about the importance of an American role in World War I. Then, once at war, Americans became crusaders bent on unconditional surrender and extinction of the enemy. Crisis is necessary to arouse publics but once aroused it is very difficult to moderate popular passions. This proposition was originally formulated by Alexis de Tocqueville as a characteristic of Americans that might become true of all mass democracies.

Lippmann's writing was very much influenced by the disillusionment of liberal internationalists with the defeat of Woodrow Wilson and the failure of the United States to join the League of Nations. He saw foreign policy as properly and necessarily made by an Executive elite with only periodic checks by the public. However, he does not specify the range of public involvement in foreign policy nor the mechanisms of linkage between the people and government. He seems to see an all-pervasive public mood, a spirit of the times and even of the moment, as infecting policymakers in ways that hobble them improperly.

Gabriel Almond developed a more sophisticated and empirically based statement of this position that seems to have been informed by the same liberal, internationalist concern about the dangers of oscillation in the popular mood between isolationism and aggressive interventionism. Because he first presented this view in 1950, he lacked the benefit of actual postwar experience with the Korean War and a continuing Cold War.[2] He describes the orientation of most Americans to foreign policy as one of radically shifting attitudes in response to events, and he thinks that these changes manifest paired opposites which are deeply rooted in the American character. For example, we move sharply between the urge to withdraw from the world and the desire to overwhelm and dominate it. Both stances reflect a disdain and low tolerance of international power politics.

The American approach to foreign policy at any given time is seen as a cluster of attitudes derived from formative historical events. Just before World War II, the pattern was a blend of the withdrawal impulse, cynicism about power politics, intolerance of foreign peoples, and pessimism about the prospects for an idealistic internationalism. The events after Pearl Harbor are said to have created an interventionist consensus characterized by tolerance of allies, idealistic aspirations, and optimistic expectations about peace after the war. With the coming of the Cold War optimism gave way to pessimism, idealist internationalism became security realism, and impatience and intolerance emerged. One might have mentioned the phenomena of witch hunts for traitors and McCarthyism as symptoms of public intolerance for the ambiguities of power politics.

It is Almond's view that the public is basically fickle; support for intervention often conceals an impulse for withdrawal and idealism mutes but does not vanquish cynicism. Publics cannot really know much about foreign policy so they project their emotional hopes and fears onto leaders about whom they are also fickle. Since publics are ill informed they should take their cues about events from leaders. It is here that Almond joins Lippmann in an elitist model of democracy. A disciplined elite and a broad attentive public, as distinct from a mass public, may be well informed about foreign policy and have stable and sound views of the world. If this elite gives the mass public its cues and wins support from attentive publics, then the worst excesses of swings in mass mood can be prevented. The elite will be a filter for mass emotion and many questions will not be raised at all by responsible leaders for public attention.

Almond documents his case about changing public moods by the use of Gallup surveys. For example, polls from 1935 through 1949 showed wide variations in popular attitudes about issues in response to the changing international situation. From this he develops a theory of popular mood that any President must understand and anticipate if he is to act effectively in foreign policy. The mood is seen as a constraint far more often than as a resource for Presidents presumably because, to Almond and others of this school of thought, it is likely to be illiberal and present problems for a liberal, internationalist President.

After looking at the experience of the 1950s, Almond returned to his thesis ten years later and revised it.[3] He reports that surveys showed far greater stability and continuity of public attitudes than in the previous decade and concludes that a better educated and informed public has become more mature. There was still a paucity of public knowledge and a danger of popular eruptions, but Almond takes heart that surveys consistently show the American people are prepared to bear the burdens of higher taxation and other sacrifices in order to sustain a more effective national effort, for example, in space exploration and in military preparedness. Despite this, he concludes that the quality of American foreign policy depends upon leaders not followers. Publics are essentially supportive. Lippmann's fears are groundless so long as elites are sophisticated.

Survey data from the 1950s and 1960s in fact show that public moods and attitudes about the Cold War and international politics were very stable. The mood theory of wild oscillations was not empirically accurate, and the evidence shows strong popular support for an active United States role in the world. The policies for which there have been constant support include Cold War policies such as military preparedness and willingness for the United States to intervene militarily abroad in order to stem a communist act of aggression. The evidence is that so-called attentive publics, the 10 percent who are best informed, are not more concerned about international matters than the rest of the population. One could in fact conclude that American public opinion on foreign policy is characterized by a strong and stable permissive mood toward international involvement.[4] However, having said this we suddenly find ourselves with a much different dilemma from that of those who feared the public as a "great beast." Are not the American people in fact too permissive and deferential to their leaders and has not this encouraged foreign adventures such as Vietnam for which leaders are not held to account? In short, are there drawbacks to Almond's elitist democracy that were not foreseen when it was assumed that so long as leaders were liberal internationalists all would be well? An answer is given by the second theory.

Theory of Supportive Constraints

The second theory of public opinion in a democracy we shall call the theory of supportive constraints. This view grows out of the post-World War II experience after Almond first wrote and accounts for the great stability of opinion after that time. It posits that public opinion is characterized by a consensus of beliefs and attitudes which have been formed by historical events and which persist until events force changes and the development of a new popular consensus. This prevailing world view is widely shared in the society and there are limits to what policymakers may do which are set by the consensus. These dikes set implicit constraints upon the actions of leaders. In this sense elected leaders are and must be responsive to the limits of the world view. Within the dikes, however, publics leave leaders great latitude to act freely in regard to means of implementing the goals and values of the consensus. Public opinion is primarily supportive and permissive, but it does set implicit limits and constraints on what leaders may do.[5]

This national consensus and outlook is seen as based on loyalty to the nation and hostility to those who threaten the nation, and includes a belief about the broad stance the nation should take in the world. After World War II this consensus shifted from isolationism to internationalism and has continued in this vein. Most of the time, it is believed, there is no conflict between public attitudes and elite actions because they are in accord with each other. Publics may not know what their leaders are doing in regard to particular events, but they would approve if they knew. The actions of government fall within the dikes. However, the problems of leaders become more difficult if they are faced with novel situations requiring adaptations in public attitudes. If publics are not prepared for innovation, or are thought by leaders not to be ready for change, then leaders may temporize and delay action. Leaders must then decide whether to try to educate and change public opinion in line with the new directions required. This is seen as an inherent problem of democratic leadership.

The general view of this theory is that publics are supportive of leadership and give it great latitude, but the opposite side of the coin is the view that if leaders violate given limits they may be in trouble. Elites need public opinion in order to undertake radical new ventures. For example, President Kennedy took the issue of the nuclear test-ban treaty to the public and sought widespread support at a time when he was also asking the Senate to ratify the measure. It is simply assumed by adherents of this view that Presidents cannot prevail or make any kind of innovative policy unless they persuade sizeable portions of the public to agree. It follows from this argument that public opinion does not develop by itself, but requires education from political leaders and especially the President.[6]

This theory requires active Presidential leadership of public opinion. It assumes that Presidents will seek to mobilize public opinion as a resource for support for Presidential measures in other governmental arenas such as Congress. In so doing, Presidents not only seek popular support for specific measures but also invoke the chords of the prevailing general consensus and tie the two together. Of course this is not necessary on most foreign policy questions. The public plays no part and has few opinions about complex international monetary questions or the distribution of military aid programs across the world. Nonetheless, the achievement of détente with China is an issue on which a President would not want to move without evidence of great popular support and relatively little opposition. Thus the question of how much latitude a President has beyond the dikes is an empirical one for observers and for Presidents.

The chief problem with this theory is that there is very little evidence that it is true across a wide range of cases. In fact, it may simply be an idealistic construction of what ought to be derived from democratic theory and ideas about the need for leaders to be responsive to publics in a democracy. The actual links between public opinion and the actions of Presidents have not been shown, and most of what has been written about the impact of public opinion on foreign policymaking is not backed by evidence.[7]

The frequently made statement that policies depend for their effectiveness upon public support may or may not be true and may vary according to policy. For example, President Kennedy directed his appeal on the test-ban treaty to the public, but it was the Senate that seemed to have been most concerned that the President's case be supported by evidence that national security would not be harmed by a limitation on testing. It is doubtful that much of the public was informed or even cared a great deal about this, or that members of the Senate looked to public opinion. On the other hand, an unpopular war can no longer be fought if public support erodes. But this case may be the exception that proves the rule that publics are seldom involved in foreign policies. Support may in fact be so latent as to be nonexistent.

One also finds contradictions that make it hard to characterize the relations of leaders and publics as responsive. Why do Presidents seem to defer to what they perceive as public attitudes at some times and clearly and consciously go against such expressions in other instances? Perhaps there are other considerations that move Presidents and conditions under which they can safely ignore publics.

The notion of dikes that form a consensus in public opinion that leaders dare not overstep may be valid, but at present it suffers from a lack of empirical verification. We do not know whether such dikes exist or what their limits are if they do exist. And if we are this ignorant, how can politicians know enough not to overstep these limits? The limits beyond which a President chooses not to go may be inherent in the situation. Most Presidents, once committed to Vietnam, would have preferred not to widen the war and yet not to abandon the effort in a rout. In this sense leaders and publics may perceive the limits on action in the reality of the situation and agree.

However, if Presidents and politicians behave as if public sentiment sets limits to what they can hope to do, then the idea of dikes becomes useful because it affects behavior. It is useful even if the dikes do not in fact exist in the public mind. This does suggest that something exists in public attitudes that leads leaders to try to anticipate what the likely reaction of groups in the public will be to a possible action. This political intuition at the top may be based on a memory of public reactions to similar actions of leadership in the past.

It would not be good to completely rule out the notion of implicit resources and constraints in public opinion upon Presidential actions.

They may in fact exist to be activated by events. When President Nixon talked of "peace with honor" in Vietnam, he was appealing to a very strong strain of American nationalism that is deeply imbedded in popular thinking. Americans will support a negotiated peace and the absence of victory in Vietnam, but they will not support a hasty departure that looks like an American defeat. This attitude may reflect a strong nationalism that was perhaps at the root of the initial involvement and that is shared by both leaders and publics. There are many persistent nationalistic themes running through American foreign policy throughout the history of the republic.[8] We seem to see ourselves as a special people who made a fresh start in history and who are therefore a beacon to the world. This leads to the generosity of Wilsonian idealism and the unselfishness of programs like the Marshall Plan and foreign aid. It may also be one of the roots of our self-appointed role as the guardians of freedom wherever it is seemingly threatened and may therefore help account for our somewhat rigid anticommunism during the post-World War II period. A balance of power contest was transformed into a crusade. These general statements among publics are also shared by elites and can be triggered by leadership during times of decision and crisis. While these stock ideas may indeed be dikes or constraints, perhaps more importantly they are habitual themes of action to which both leaders and public respond.

We should not rule out the kinds of popular passion that are the focus of the first theory nor the concept of prevailing ideas that are both resources and constraints for leaders. Nonetheless we need to shift the emphasis of both theories away from the idea of publics setting constraints upon leaders. The limited evidence suggests that the balance is more in the direction of leaders evoking themes and seeking support from publics. There surely are dynamic relationships between leaders and publics, but the range of possible combinations and links between leaders and publics is not accounted for by the two theories discussed thus far.

Theory of Deference to Presidents

The central tenet of the third theory is that the opinions of many diverse publics are shaped in response to the words and acts of Presidents and other leaders who are behaving in terms of political strategies. Leaders may decide that they need a popular response on a given question and do something to evoke it. Or they may decide that any stirring up of the people would do more harm than good to their objectives and they refrain from such an action. In either case, there is no massive public opinion pressing itself upon leaders nor is there even an implicit consensus. There are, rather, specific and perhaps temporary popular responses to the acts of leaders.[9]

We lack empirically based propositions about the dynamic relationships between Presidential words and actions and public responses across a broad range of policy possibilities. Still, what is known can be pulled together to suggest that the third theory has a great deal of plausibility if the kernels of truth in the first and second models are joined to it.

"RALLY ROUND THE FLAG" Presidents can almost always command the support of a majority of citizens for their actions at a time of international crisis when high stakes are riding for the United States and the issues are dramatic if they are seen to be acting in a decisive manner. John Mueller calls this the "rally round the flag" dimension of popular support for Presidents.[10] There are times when citizens stand behind the President as the symbol and leader of the nation. The kinds of events that correlate with sharp increases in support for the President are American military interventions, such as the Bay of Pigs invasion in 1961 or the sending of marines to the Dominican Republic in 1965; important military events in ongoing wars, such as the Gulf of Tonkin episode in 1964 or the extension or intensification of American bombing of North Vietnam; major diplomatic developments, such as the Cuban missile crisis, recurrent Berlin crises, or the successful conclusion of Vietnam peace negotiations; dramatic technological developments, such as moonshots; and highly visible meetings of heads of state, such as President Nixon's visits in 1972 to China and the Soviet Union. These kinds of events generate a strong surge of popular support for the President. The support seems to reflect at least two things. First, the President is seen as acting decisively and, as we saw in Chapter 1, this is very important for citizens. The President should be on top of his job. Second, it is a way for citizens to stand behind the nation. Thus, even when many people disapprove of what was done they will stand behind the President, as in the case of the Bay of Pigs.

One study in 1966 found that 75 percent of a sample of citizens were willing to say that the President should send United States troops to fight abroad if he thought it important for the nation even if most Americans were opposed.[11] This deference to the President seemed to be based upon a belief by the public that they were ill informed and incompetent to know what was best. There was trust the President would not abuse his power. The same question in regard to domestic affairs produced a sharp reduction in assent to Presidential wishes; however, it was not below 50 percent. Just above half wanted domestic leadership to rest with the President rather than with Congress and the people.[12] It is generally the case that domestic crises such as urban riots and civil rights demonstrations do not cause people to rally around the President but in fact divide popular opinion and thereby dilute support for Presidents who act decisively. In foreign affairs, on the other hand, Presidents have the unity of the nation and the emotion of nationalism to exploit as a resource. The great and strong recognition of the Presidency as the chief symbol of the nation surely is manifested here.

Mueller also finds that a large and important group of citizens whom he calls "followers" will rally to the support of the President in foreign policy, no matter what he does.[13] Followers see the President as the embodiment of the nation. Thus, for example, when the President publicly reverses an official policy followers who had supported that policy reverse themselves. Mueller's analysis showed a dramatic shift in 1966 from a majority opposing the bombing of Hanoi because the President was opposed to it to a majority favoring the act after the President initiated it and spoke for it.[14]

The most surprising finding is that followers are likely to be among the best-educated members of the electorate.[15] This group has been the most consistent supporter of the wars in Korea and Vietnam. They have the strongest identification with the nation of any social group and are well informed about its role in international affairs and the problems of its leaders. They are thus very susceptible to leadership in foreign policy. They usually know what present policy is and are likely to support it. These are the liberal internationalists who identify the Presidency with the American role in the world.

This finding suggests that at least part of the explanation for the rally round the flag factor, aside from the President as the symbol of national unity, is an ideological dimension. It is the most educated people who have been in favor of the positive postwar United States role in the world. They are the legatees of the tradition of liberal internationalism. A close examination of the main instances of the rally round the flag phenomenon in the fifties and sixties shows that eleven of the instances deal with United States actions in the Cold War.[16] In short, in addition to deference to the President as symbol we also have the Presidential invocation of the postwar national consensus on liberal internationalism. Better educated people are more likely to be articulate about and responsive to such themes than less educated people.

There is ambiguity in these data, however. Can a President achieve a rally round the flag effect with the public if he deliberately uses restraint in a situation of potential international conflict and therefore appears to be not acting rather than acting decisively?

Eisenhower refused the urgings of his advisers to commit American air power in defense of French armies at Dien Bien Phu in Indochina in 1954. The events in Indochina and his decision regarding them probably did not permeate to the mass public, but had they done so could he have achieved an increase of support by forbearance? The example may not be a good one, since the connection with the American national interest was not obvious to many Americans, although polls at the time did show a majority of the samples willing to have the United States intervene to stop communist aggression.[17] However, because one can assume that many Americans knew nothing about Indochina at that time and cared less, the finding is dubious. Still, the question remains. If a President can do something dramatic for peace like a summit meeting and get a crescendo of popular support, can he forbear in a dramatic situation and get the same result? We do not know in part because there are so few examples.

PRESIDENTIAL LATITUDE Presidents have great latitude in setting foreign policy when public opinion is divided and perhaps confused and ambiguous, and when there are no clear clues for Presidents to follow. The vote in the 1964 election could have told Lyndon Johnson anything he cared to believe about various war options. He received 62 percent of the vote of those favoring pulling out of Vietnam, 82 percent of the vote of those favoring keeping soldiers in Vietnam but trying to end the fighting, and 52 percent of the vote of those who wanted to escalate the war, including those who favored invading North Vietnam.[18] Johnson may have violated his own campaign pledges, but he did not go against public opinion because it was so divided and because he had support from all camps.

Public attitudes seldom give clear directions to a President even if he wanted to follow them. For example, in 1968 a national sample of respondents were asked by the Survey Research Center if the commitment in Vietnam had been a mistake and which of three courses should be pursued: pulling out, preserving the status quo, or escalating. Those who favored the intervention tended to favor stronger measures to win than those who opposed the war. But among those who saw the war as a mistake almost as many favored escalation as were for withdrawal.[19]

Sometimes a President who recognizes such a disparate cluster of attitudes can play on separate themes in order to create a coherent strategy. For example, at the end of 1969 President Nixon was aligned with several majorities: those regretting the American role, those wanting to reduce our commitment there, and the large majority rejecting withdrawal as an alternative.[20] Since none of these clusters of opinion dictated any particular course of action to him in disengaging, he had great latitude. This fact together with the rally round the flag factor and the idea of standing behind the President as a source of support permitted him to both negotiate and bomb simultaneously so long as people were persuaded that his actions were disengaging Americans from the war.

In such situations either majorities among both publics and elites support the President or opinion at both levels is divided, but in either case there is no clear majority against him. In the case of fragmented opinion, a Presidential governing coalition, supported by substantial numbers in the public, is usually strong enough to prevail and dominate policy. A President in such circumstances cannot successfully be challenged unless his governing coalition breaks apart. When this happens he has probably suffered great defections in public support as well.

Presidential latitude is inherent in the fact of governing. Publics cannot govern and seldom even give clear signals about policy. The disagreements and confusions that one finds at elite levels are also present at popular levels. In this sense our government is inherently representative, but the checks are imperfect and indirect.

One can illustrate these points with Lyndon Johnson and Richard Nixon on Vietnam. Johnson began the United States intervention with a high degree of public and elite support primarily based upon rallying round the flag. During the midyears of the American involvement intense dissent developed at both popular and elite levels. In spite of this, he felt free to ignore that dissent because he felt that intellectuals, college students, and a few early doves in the Senate were not strong enough to challenge him. Even when very large portions of the electorate showed their disenchantment Johnson persisted in his policy. There was nothing that could be done to check him at either popular or institutional levels. However, a combination of events in 1968 broke his own government wide open and suggested that he would not be able to keep a strong governing coalition together throughout 1968 to sustain his policies. The January Tet offensive, the Presidential candidacies of Senators Eugene McCarthy and Robert Kennedy, and the open opposition of many of his own advisers to his policies finally brought the President around. The movements against prevailing policies in both mass and elite opinion were parallel. Both were important and perhaps no President could have withstood either for long. But had opinion remained divided and had Johnson's government and party held firm, he might have persisted in his policy.

Complaints in the sixties and seventies that the President could not be controlled in his military and foreign policy actions miss the point that it is usually only dissenting minorities who want to reverse existing policy. It is very hard to develop a popular and elite majority against Presidential foreign policy. President Nixon had this kind of latitude in his first term about Vietnam. It was clear from surveys and the 1968 election that the American people wanted our role in Vietnam ended, but it was also clear that both publics and elites were very divided about how this might best be done. Therefore the President had latitude to end the war as he thought best.

POLITICAL OPPOSITION Presidents will perform acts of commission or omission rather than permit their political opponents to make political capital with publics against them. For example, Presidents in the past have acted aggressively in foreign affairs for fear of being labeled "soft" on communism. John Kennedy said after the Cuban missile crisis that he would have been "impeached" if he had not gotten the Russian missiles out of Cuba. The crisis occurred in the midst of a midterm congressional election, and Kennedy was seriously worried that his failure to act decisively and quickly might cause many Republican votes in the election. Certainly the fact that he precluded a nonmilitary response from the outset was influenced by these domestic political considerations. Republican senators had been pressuring him on Cuba and charging that the Soviets were building missiles there. He had been publicly denying it and his first response when he learned of their existence was the "He [Khrushchev] can't do that to me."[21] Clearly it would have been politically intolerable for an American President to have permitted Russian missiles to remain in Cuba even if the actual military threat to American security was not that much greater than before. Secretary McNamara had originally suggested that the military danger had not increased that much and that a United States military response therefore was not warranted. But it is fair to say that democratic politics would not permit the missiles to stay. Their continuance would have been a festering sore in the side of any President because his political opposition would never let him forget it. Kennedy had exactly the same problem with the Republicans over the mere existence of the Castro regime. The Soviet government felt no such internal pressure about the existence of American missiles in Turkey on Soviet borders. This entire story could be read as an instance of how democratic governments overreact to supposed threats to national security, perhaps necessarily so, given the dynamics of domestic politics.

Lyndon Johnson sent marines to the Dominican Republic when civil conflict broke out there because he did not want to take any chance of another Cuban-type communist coup occurring in the

Caribbean. The fear was a domestic political one and not a concern about what such a regime might do. Democratic Presidents since Harry Truman have had to face the danger of partisan attacks from Republicans that they were responsible for the United States "loss" of some piece of real estate in the world. The root cause of this fear was the poisonous domestic politics that resulted in the late 1940s and early 1950s over the loss of China. Lyndon Johnson never forgot what happened to Harry Truman's domestic legislative program in Congress as a result of such partisan clashes, and when he was faced with difficult decisions about Vietnam in early 1965 his first concern was what the effects would be on his Great Society legislative proposals.[22] Such considerations were surely involved in the determination not to lose South Vietnam to the communists.

These kinds of political calculations follow from the logic and structure of partisan political competition in America. It is not the fear of direct reactions from public opinion that inhibits leaders so much as it is the fear of what the political opposition will do to stir up opinion and perhaps affect elections. This certainly makes life more difficult in governing and makes it harder to lead in new directions. Political rhetoric can paralyze the taking of initiatives and can limit the options that one can safely consider. Such political competition takes its form and substance from the ideological competition of the opposing camps.

Since the 1940s there have been constraints on Presidents that they must appear tough vis-à-vis communist nations. This has been a particular problem for Democratic Presidents, who have been saddled by Republican rhetoric with the loss of China and softness on communism. Republican Presidents have ironically been much freer to be moderate in the Cold War than Democrats because Republican political rhetoric has had more of a claim on patriotism and anticommunism and because the vocal Republican right wing is more neutralized when the Republicans are in the White House. It may be that only Republican Presidents could have successfully negotiated the conclusion of the wars of Korea and Vietnam and have made those policies acceptable to broad segments of the American people.

Lyndon Johnson did not want to discuss Vietnam in the 1964 election campaign. He did not wish to either escalate or pull out, and therefore the policy was not examined within the Administration. All had to wait until after he had won in 1964. However, the Gulf of Tonkin resolution of August 1964, in which Congress gave the President carte blanche to resist attacks on American troops in Vietnam and resist communist aggression, was in part used by the President as an electoral weapon against Senator Goldwater. Johnson could prove that he too was tough and therefore hope to nullify the senator's charges. Of course, this action hastened the momentum toward a more active United States role, which was at that time building up and which was intensified by the failure of the government to consider its policies and options during that fall and winter.

The climate of public opinion and patterns of partisan politics have changed a great deal since the 1960s, and now a Republican President must be on the defensive against political opposition that is quick to charge abuse of Presidential war powers in military actions, such as the Christmas 1972 bombing of North Vietnam when the Paris peace talks were stalled. However, President Nixon persisted in his actions, just as he had persisted despite popular and partisan outcry over the earlier invasions of Cambodia and Laos. This suggests that Nixon felt he had public support in the main, but it also suggests that a President is guided by his own ideology and strategy so long as he feels that opinion is supportive in a diffuse way even if there is great disagreement about particular Presidential actions.

It is something of a puzzle that Presidents have deferred more to hawkish than to dovish opinion. In part this is because successive Presidents have helped to create a climate of opinion of anticommunism to justify a number of official policies, beginning with aid to Greece and Turkey, the Marshall Plan, NATO, and foreign aid and continuing to the development of the missile program and the drive to land a man on the moon. They have therefore become prisoners of their own rhetoric.

On the other hand, it is also probably true that the emotional theme of anticommunism has become part of the public consciousness and that it has therefore been difficult for Presidents to go against it. Certainly they have been faced with much elite opposition when they have seemed to do so. This suggests that despite the great latitude afforded to Presidents it might have been hard for John Kennedy, who had serious doubts about the Vietnam commitment, to do anything decisive to reverse this commitment in 1963. In fact, he was waiting for a victory in the 1964 election in order that he might have the political resources to end the commitment. By the same token, by the time Lyndon Johnson faced up to the issue of what to do about Vietnam in 1965 the position of the South Vietnamese armies and regime had so gravely deteriorated that, despite his huge victory in 1964, it might have been politically very difficult for him to simply withdraw and let South Vietnam go communist. Thus the bias of postwar political party competition has been in hawkish rather than dovish directions and Presidents have been aware of this fact.

Major departures in foreign policy that go against the grain of existing or past policy require not only public support but the support, whether tacit or active, of wide sections of the political elite, including a President's opposition. Franklin Roosevelt gave his famous speech about the need for democracies to "quarantine" the dictators in 1937 as a trial balloon in the face of isolationist opinion. It is popularly supposed that the public response was negative. In fact, that response seems to have been very favorable, but Roosevelt found little support at elite and especially congressional levels for a change in policy and therefore held back and trimmed until events were to give him a firmer handle for making changes.[23] This finally happened with the plight of Britain and the invention of Lend Lease.

President Truman's success in moving the country toward a permanently internationalist foreign policy in the late 1940s in response to Soviet actions has been presented as a successful mobilization of public opinion. Senator Vandenberg is said to have told the President that the Congress would not support the Marshall Plan unless the President went to the country and explained the communist threat to Western Europe. In fact, Truman's triumph was in his persuasion of a Republican Congress and its leaders, men like Vandenberg, to support his policies. The public responded to the message the President sent, but the important relationship was between the President and his opposition at the elite level. Agreement at this level prevented the public from being bombarded by conflicting messages. The role of the public was passive and responsive rather than active.

John Kennedy saw his speech at American University in 1963 calling for a winding down of the Cold War as the beginning of a reversal of many of his own and past foreign policies. This belief was a result of his learning experiences in office, particularly in the aftermath of the Cuban missile crisis. The speech seems to have had little effect at the time, and of course he did not live to continue his strategy of change, which included a 1964 election victory and perhaps a withdrawal from Vietnam. No one can say whether he would have been successful.

The question still remains, however, of whether a President can invoke the emotional power of his office and the rally round the flag factor, not for a peace initiative, because it is clear that he can, but for an act of forbearance in the face of an enemy threat. Could Kennedy have pursued the course of diplomatic negotiation to get the Soviet missiles out of Cuba, or would domestic politics have created a storm that would have hurt him badly if he had attempted it? Could Kennedy in 1963 or Johnson in 1965 have withdrawn American troops from Vietnam with "honor" and have rallied popular support at home for it? (De Gaulle achieved such a reversal in withdrawing France from Algeria, but the circumstances were unusual and involved filling a political vacuum with a new regime and Republic to which there seemed no alternative.) One small clue can be found in the form of a question: Why in the United States is the national anthem regularly played only prior to one kind of event, contests of sport? Do we unconsciously identify patriotism with aggression, combat, and masculinity? There is surely no simple answer but the intriguing thought is left dangling.

POLITICAL COMPETITION A new President will also enter office with a set of foreign policy goals derived from the recent period of partisan political competition. These goals will have been developed by the Presidential candidate and leaders of his party and in the case of the out-party candidates will in large part have been derived from a competitive effort to differentiate their positions from that of the party in the White House. There will also be convergence of positions of Presidential candidates toward what they see as the center of opinion on salient issues. For example, in 1968 most voters could not tell the Nixon and Humphrey positions apart on Vietnam and therefore that issue played less importance in the vote than it might have.[24] But Nixon was clearly pledged to end an unpopular war begun by the previous administration.

An example of Presidential policy being set by patterns of political competition is seen in the criticisms by Democrats in the 1950s of the Eisenhower policy of concentration on a military strategy of "massive retaliation" by nuclear weapons and avoidance of limited wars. This downgrading of ground forces and of alternative military strategies brought the Democratic charge that the nation was in no position to fight limited wars like the Korean conflict should the need arise and that a strategy of nuclear deterrence actually would leave us without an effective response in minor conflicts. These arguments entered the rhetoric of political competition and there was a convergence of the arguments of Democratic politicians and Presidential aspirants with those of unhappy army leaders such as Generals Ridgeway, Gavin, and Taylor, all of whom wrote books to this effect. John Kennedy was, therefore, committed to creating the capability to fight limited wars and a more flexible set of strategic options in general. This commitment coincided in time with Soviet statements about the virtue of wars of national liberation and caused the Kennedy Administration to respond with plans for developing capabilities at counterinsurgency warfare. Such capabilities were never developed to any extent, but in the minds of top policy makers these past and present factors converged to help explain some of the attitudes toward Vietnam as a test case of a war of national liberation. The logic of political competition rooted in the world situation, but also shaped by party predispositions, thus also explains Presidential commitments upon entering office.

REVERSAL OF PRESIDENTIAL FOREIGN POLICY There are three ways by which a reversal of basic Presidential foreign policy comes about. First, a President gradually moves both elite and public opinion in new directions. This is usually only possible when he can dramatize the need for new departures through events. Two instances are the leadership of Franklin Roosevelt away from isolationism and toward United States involvement in World War II and Harry Truman's leadership in the development of United States Cold War policies.

Second, when Presidential foreign policies are so obviously unsuccessful, that widespread public dissatisfaction is expressed in a Presidential election in which the incumbent loses the White House. This was clearly true in 1952 with the election of Dwight Eisenhower. A majority of the public had turned against President Truman's handling of the Korean War. It was less true in 1968 because both candidates, Nixon and Humphrey, promised to end the war; however, they did so under the stimulus of the election and the clear changes in public opinion.

This factor should not be overestimated. Foreign policy issues seldom present themselves dramatically in elections. Partisan identifications of voters are not based on foreign policy stances. A multiplicity of issues are involved in a vote, not just a single question. The competing parties often converge on foreign policy thus directing the voter's attention in other directions.

The steady erosion of popular support for the Korean and Vietnam wars over time finally did work itself into electoral politics, though to critics of the prevailing policies it seemed a maddeningly slow process. In both cases the public overwhelmingly supported the original Presidential decision to intervene. Surveys showed that this was a compound of two factors, first, rally round the flag support for the President as such and, second, support for the idea of resisting communist aggression.[25] When respondents were asked if either war was justified in terms of preserving self-government in South Korea and South Vietnam the expressions of support fell sharply. Both wars were therefore seen by the public as American wars in the national interest.

Both Presidents Truman and Johnson kept that support for a long time, but gradually after prolonged conflicts that seemed endless and fruitless, public support fell. It fell below 50 percent on Vietnam presumably because the war lasted longer and the casualties were greater and perhaps more visible to the American people.[26]

The chief reason for decline of support in both cases was that people lost confidence in the capacity of their leaders to find a way out of a bottomless pit. Kenneth Waltz suggests that President Truman and his advisers badly erred in sending allied troops north beyond the thirty-eighth parallel to unify North and South Korea because in so doing they rashly ignored Chinese signals that such a move would bring their intervention. Once the Chinese came in the war, it was a long, costly, and frustrating stalemate for the United States.[27] This decision says more about the hubris of American leaders than it does about the American people.[28] It was a fatal misstep, the result of which was that the public increasingly lost confidence in Truman's management of the war and eventually supported in large numbers the candidacy of Eisenhower, who was seen as a man of stature who could find a way out of the war. There is no question that many of the crossovers of Democrats to the Republican Presidential column in 1952 reflected this frustration about the war and confidence in Eisenhower.[29] However, it does not follow that the public did not support the original objective of the war or that it wanted an elegant withdrawal. By 1953 large majorities were in favor of negotiation to end the war but opposed either escalation or withdrawal.

In Vietnam it is harder to point to a fatal Presidential mistake that led to public disillusionment with the war. However, what became increasingly clear across time was that public support was falling away and support for negotiation was growing.[30] The pattern of Korea reappeared. Moreover, by 1968 a majority of the public had come to doubt the value of the initial commitment. Everything we know about support for Presidential crisis actions suggests that Johnson could have had majority support for negotiation sooner, had he wanted it. His refusal to negotiate did, in fact, mean a continuing decline in popular support for the war.

Clearly in both cases a majority of the electorate would follow a Presidential lead to enter such a war and, after a time of fighting, to negotiate an end to the war if it could be done without either further escalation or retreat and withdrawal in a way that would humiliate America. These changes in popular opinion over time were paralleled by changes in elite opinion. For example, one survey of congressional opinion in 1966 revealed almost the same distribution of attitudes as in a concurrent public survey.[31]

Public opinion, or elite opinion for that matter, did not give clear cues to Presidents on what to do, and Presidents had latitude to act. But over the long run, there was a clear popular displeasure about the inability of Presidents to bring both wars to an end. It seems very likely that the fault in both cases rests with the two Presidents. They deserved to be judged. Truman and his advisers were carried away with euphoria in their drive to unite all Korea. Johnson rigidly refused to negotiate and insisted upon North Vietnamese acquiescence in United States war objectives. Both paid a political price. The possibility of running for reelection was foreclosed.

Third, a major policy failure produces such a convulsion in the society at all levels of participation that a governing coalition falls apart, public disaffection from policy is widespread, and political elites begin to question the world view that they have held. That world view is suddenly called into question for its accuracy. When this happens political elites gradually develop a new world view that then becomes the new conventional wisdom. In time it trickles down to the public and becomes the basis for a new foreign policy consensus for both publics and leaders.[32]

This happened in the transition from isolationism to internationalism before and after World War II. It is probably happening again now as a result of Vietnam, although it is not clear what the new consensus is. These changes come from the concern of leaders that they can no longer cope with their problems using the old postures and perspectives. The widespread disaffection may even call the legitimacy of the government into question and stimulate a search for more viable approaches to governing. So each new generation challenges the conventional wisdom of the past generation because it is forced to do so by events.

CONCLUSION

The crucial problem of Presidential foreign policy is perhaps not so much control of arbitrary Presidential action as it is the problem of how to bring "enlightenment" to Presidential policymaking in foreign affairs. Here it would seem that public opinion has little to contribute; it reacts and responds rather than creates. Enlightenment must come from ferment at elite levels to ensure that elite world views correspond with reality.

We therefore conclude that the key to understanding foreign policy at a given time is to be found in an understanding of, first, the prevailing ideological consensus at both popular and elite levels and, second, the patterns of partisan political competition within that consensus. In the postwar period the consensus has been one of a defensive and national security outlook fueled by American nationalism. This has put the burden of proof upon those who would go against that prevailing attitude. Patterns of competition for the Presidency have reflected the same themes.

However, this consensus and the patterns of political competition are changing in the 1970s as a consequence of Vietnam. In the future the burden of proof may be put upon those who wish to act in aggressive military ways. The emphasis upon national security and military responses to foreign policy crises and challenges may be giving way to an emphasis upon political and diplomatic responses to those international challenges that are seen as essentially political rather than threats to national security.

The key to the kind of foreign policy America has is to be found in the intellectual and moral character of its political elites. What kinds of questions do they raise or fail to raise for public discussion? Publics follow elite opinion much more than they influence it.

To return to our original question about the responsiveness of Presidents and political leaders to public opinion in a democracy, we are regretfully forced to conclude that Presidents and others in high national office are primarily responsive to the mass opinion that they themselves have created. Leaders use events to teach publics the appropriate responses over time until widespread mental sets exist. Then when they wish to act, leaders send messages to the public and receive the responses that they want. This seems inevitable in a situation in which real autonomy seems virtually impossible for the masses of citizens in matters of foreign affairs. They respond largely to an ethos of ideas created by elites.

Some scholars have taken refuge in the hope that attentive elites who are not political leaders can exercise constraints and bring enlightenment to public policymaking in foreign affairs.[33] However, it is not evident that such people are really much better informed than general publics, and it is certainly not the case that their stock responses and ideologies are any different from those in the prevailing public and elite ethos.

By and large, then, we must look for the sources of constraints on Presidential power in foreign policymaking at the elite levels of government. Are there characteristics of the governmental process that will ensure that the foreign policies of Presidents will be carefully scrutinized and openly debated before they are implemented?

5
The President
and
Foreign
Policymaking

THE PRESIDENT AND THE EXECUTIVE BRANCH

Within the Executive bureaucracy one finds a great deal of closed politics, that is, competition for power and influence among small groups of policymakers, advisers, and bureaucrats without direct reference to any larger political arena. Closed politics, which exists in all organizations, is very different from the influences on the Executive arising from open electoral and legislative politics. Although a great deal of what goes on in the Executive cannot be explained by closed politics because these external factors are taken into account in the calculations of Executive actors, much can be explained by developing models of Executive behavior as such. The task of explanation involves bringing together external and internal influences to provide convincing reasons to account for the actions of Presidents and those close to them.

Political science is just beginning to develop crude models of policymaking processes in government organizations. These models are simplified versions of what is thought to go on in a given kind of organizational process. The key is to identify the important variables and then suggest possible relationships between them and likely consequences for policymaking. A model is a guide to theory, but no model by itself is theory. Only an imaginative observer can generate theoretical propositions using the bare bones of models. Models are no sure path to explanation of specific historical events but are guides to possible explanations. Every case is a different combination of factors and thus no model will automatically explain a case. Nor is any one model adequate to explain all elements of any single complex case. Several models may be required. Models have to be used selectively, as sources of hypotheses, about what actually happened and why.

In the final analysis there will always be imponderables because the models we are going to use to help explain Executive behavior rely heavily upon inferences about the subjective motivations of the policymakers. We can infer causal links between actions and probable motivations, but there will always be a reservoir of factors that are unknown and indeterminate to both the actors themselves and observers. For this reason the systematic study of policymaking has not been able to move beyond the methodological problem of the historian who knows that human behavior is shaped by many factors, both within and without the individual, and that he can never, in the end, weigh and measure these factors in any scientific manner. However, our models do give us an analytic perspective that the historian, concerned to write narrative and explain specific events without drawing general conclusions about political behavior, may lack. If we use models carefully we may be able to develop generalizations about governmental processes to which the historian does not aspire.

We will present three models each of which can be used to explain one aspect of policymaking in the Executive. But these models will have to be joined to explanations of Presidential actions and integrated with explanations from external causes such as electoral and legislative politics.

BUREAUCRATIC ROUTINE AND MOMENTUM[1]

Government leaders sit on top of a conglomerate of bureaucratic organizations each of which has folkways of its own, an organizational culture that reflects concern with certain kinds of policy problems to the exclusion of others, the possession of habitual strategies for dealing with problems, and stock solutions. The chief problem for the top policymaker is that the organization develops a life of its own that is difficult for him to alter should he seek to do so. This internal culture is reinforced by selective recruitment and socialization of members. The organization equates its own health with the pursuit of organizational goals rather than with Administration goals, and thus develops vested interest in its own programs. Such organizations can handle routine problems well but are often at a loss in crisis or unprecedented situations where they then offer inappropriate responses.

It follows that the President is confronted with a variety of organizational responses to his requests or initiatives, and he must approach each with wariness. For example, a Presidential proposal to cut back a missile system may be seen by the Defense Department controller and the Office of Management and the Budget as a budgetary matter. The air force would see it as a threat to its organizational mission. The other services would be anxious to fill the vacuum with systems of their own. The secretary of defense would have to work out a position that would keep each of the services happy and yet serve his overall strategic objectives. The State Department would ask about the diplomatic effects; if, for example, the missile system were to be sold to allies of the United States it might be opposed for political reasons.

The President would have to move carefully between these protagonists, each of whom would be actively engaged in trying to get his ear, nor is it immediately clear that he could have his way either. He might feel it unwise to challenge opposition within a closed bureaucratic setting for fear that a dissatisfied opponent would carry the issue to an open setting where the President might have a harder time winning. Successive Presidents have been very leery of rallying all the members of the Joint Chiefs of Staff against them because of the strong ties between the Chiefs and the leaders of the Armed Services Committees in Congress. On the other hand, the State Department has fewer allies in Congress and little political influence over a President. His problems there are ones of getting control over a set of rigid bureaucratic norms that are seldom responsive to Presidential wishes. Long before the Cuban missile crisis John Kennedy had ordered that obsolete American missiles be removed from Turkey. However, out of deference to the Turkish government, the State Department never pursued the matter to any degree, and Kennedy was astounded to discover during the missile crisis that the Soviets were able to use the missiles in Turkey as a lever against the United States. Bureaucratic style had frustrated a President.

One could develop innumerable propositions about the kinds of problems that organizations within the government pose for Presidents, but a few will illustrate the point.

Biased Information

Once an organization receives responsibility for implementing a policy the full development of that policy becomes a definition of organizational health and therefore a source of pressure on the President. The army was not greatly involved in the decisions that led to United States intervention in Vietnam, but once the army and the other services were given a central role in South Vietnam their organizational stakes in the success of the United States commitment increased greatly. A number of army officers had been skeptical and remembered the lesson of Korea to never get involved in a land war in Asia; however, the more positive minded in Washington and Saigon came to the fore, and the President found himself under unceasing pressure to fully honor the commitment. Larger appropriations and combat experience for the officer corps come from such an involvement and careers are thereby enhanced. At this point it becomes very difficult to get any rational appraisal of the merits of the policy within the organization.

This clearly affects the President, for he is thereby subject to biased reporting up through the channels of the organization. Once the army began to dominate official reporting from South Vietnam, thereby displacing the embassy, information was structured in ways congenial to the army's own view of its mission. Accurate reports on Viet Cong strength and North Vietnamese infiltration were diluted in order that the Army might show Washington that it was successfully doing the job required. When setbacks came that was simply an argument for reinforcements.[2] Dissenters to this policy within the top commands were ruthlessly weeded out and silenced.[3]

The situation can lead to outright though disguised disobedience to Presidential orders, as when the top air force commander in Vietnam deliberately falsified reports on bombing of the North to the President in order to exceed his orders on targets. Loyalty is not to the President but to the uniform, the service, and perhaps to one's career. The massive cover-up after the Mylai massacre was a frantic effort on the part of individuals to protect their careers.

A good deal of the time the reporting is simply the standard view of reality within the organization, derived from its experience. Having been previously embarrassed by Castro and Cuba, the State Department's Latin American desk at the time of the 1965 civil conflict in the Dominican Republic was very sensitive about communist insurgency in the Caribbean area and therefore the department reported the risk of a communist coup to the President.

However, to be effective, such information usually has to square with a President's view of the situation, so it is easy to overdo the argument that the bureaucracy unduly influences Presidents by what is reported. Presidents are just as often likely to ignore the reporting of intelligence from below if it does not square with their biases or with existing policy.[4] One of the intriguing discoveries to be found in the Pentagon Papers is that the CIA consistently reported to two Presidents that the military effort was not going well in South Vietnam and that the conflict was essentially a political one requiring political measures.[5] But this information, although known at the top, was ignored because the political commitment to the successive South Vietnamese regimes was too great to permit honesty in Washington about what a weak reed was being leaned on. The same kind of skeptical CIA reporting about the limited value of bombing the North was also ignored.[6] There was too much military organizational momentum and Presidential investment wrapped up in the bombing.

Limited Organizational Repertoire

The President is limited by bureaucratic routines in the range of policies for which he can require implementation. Although the Vietnam War was clearly a political guerrilla war and there had been much talk in Washington about developing special counterinsurgency techniques of warfare, the army fought the war in a conventional manner. The strategy of using large units of troops, protected by armored divisions and air power, to search and destroy was derived from World War II. This was the only scenario in the organizational repertoire. The army had very limited capability of fighting a guerrilla war.

The effort to set up a program-budgeting system in the State Department that would have permitted ambassadors to evaluate and compare the costs and benefits of various United States programs under their responsibility failed because the mode of thought and professional role orientation of most senior Foreign Service Officers, including ambassadors, did not include such quantitative and management skills. They saw themselves as political reporters in a qualitative sense and certainly not program managers.[7]

The bias of the Agency for International Development has been that of the economist rather than of the anthropologist or political scientist, with the result that problems of economic development have been viewed primarily from one partial perspective, perhaps a too optimistic one.[8]

The real problem is that Presidents are often not aware of these organizational predispositions when they develop policy. This is what one observer has called the "missing link" between analysis and execution.[9] Presidents need help in estimating the actual bureaucratic capability to carry out a policy.

Bureaucracy as a Window on Government

The effort by a President to escape bureaucratic pathologies may lead to undesirable unanticipated results. By using White House experts, Richard Nixon has tried to do without a foreign affairs bureaucracy. However, this attempt may have some of the same drawbacks that come from a Presidential effort to ignore Congress in a given matter and to have a minimum of face-to-face dealings with congressmen and senators. Political reality is more than logical arguments and position papers. The rich variety and fragmentation in Congress and the bureaucracy may be essential sources of social intelligence about reality for a President, which he should not ignore.[10] Executive agencies, despite the distortions of reporting to which they are prone, may be much more in touch with problems in the field than White House experts. The very clash of argument between Executive agencies is something to which a President should be directly exposed in order to get a feel for prevailing governmental views, different slices of reality, and the problems and prospects for policy implementation. One has to see the "flesh and bones" in order to do this. Such a process of argument and clash is a fine stimulus to vigorous discussion at the top. Otherwise, the White House is living in a world of its own making and preferences.

In the main a President cannot avoid dealing with the bureaucracy. He needs it and must find ways to make it work for him. He must also respect its integrity and independence and be guided by the multifaceted views of reality it presents to him. Mechanisms must be found to stimulate it to report to him and others accurately and to carry out assignments effectively. This kind of organization and momentum comes from the President, not from within the bureaucracy itself.

Bureaucracy and Policy

One can seldom, if ever, explain major policies merely by recourse to bureaucratic influence or momentum. Bureaucracy is most useful to help explain the kinds of information that come to top decision makers and the process of policy implementation that follows decision. However, the motivations and actions of the very top decision makers can never be fully explained by propositions about bureaucracies beneath. Certainly, policy makers take departments and agencies into account in their calculations just as they do Congress and public opinion, but autonomy at the top still exists.[11]

One can go further. The very patterns of bureaucratic reporting and policy implementation are, by design or default, a reflection in large part of the style of authority of a President and his beliefs about organization within government. Only the President can set up checking and multiple reporting mechanisms and make sure that he hears face-to-face adversary debates and that he is aware of the problems of policy enactment in the face of bureaucratic routine. No President can cause deep-rooted bureaucratic patterns to disappear, but every President has latitude to do something about them and must if he would govern effectively.

HIGH BUREAUCRATIC POLITICS[12]

The leaders on top of a government are never monolithic in their unity. They differ as individuals in their values and ways of looking at the world. Also, they have quite different skills that will predispose them to different kinds of methods for solving policy problems. Each will have somewhat different, and limited, information. Thus they need each other for the things they want to do. Because of this need they must persuade each other and not command. Even the President can seldom command his top associates. He must usually support them against subordinates, which puts him in their power to a certain extent. In order to show confidence in them he must at times defer to their judgment and views, even if they go against his own. Moreover some of a President's top associates may have influence with power holders outside the circle of Executive politics, which is another reason for him to defer to them. However, the other side of the coin is that a top policy maker's influence with other actors is based to a great extent upon their perception of his closeness to and influence with the President. People go up and down in favor. Power relationships between a President and his top officials are thus reciprocal.

A great deal of policy at the top can be explained in terms of bargaining games between a President and his associates and between the associates themselves. Each actor must continually calculate the kinds of resources he has to influence the others. Resources in this sense are a combination of personal reputation for having influence, the allies one can count on throughout government, the personal skill that one brings to the task of persuasion, and the institutional advantage that may come from being in a particular position. No individual has perfect resources and therefore each must calculate how far and hard to push on a given question in terms of the effects on other disputes and discussions going on simultaneously.

Although we do not understand a great deal about high governmental politics in any systematic fashion, a few general characterizations of the process, which has many more variations, can be developed.

Dangers of Agreement

There is often too much consensus between a President and his top policy advisers. This may occur because they defer to him and fail to use their critical faculties, or because they have coalesced behind agreed positions that serve the interests of each but may not serve the interests of the President or of solving a policy problem. There are many different variations here.[13]

Sometimes the options are deliberately kept narrow by advisers because they have coalesced behind one option and wish to structure the decision in this way. Lyndon Johnson was not seriously advised to leave South Vietnam in 1965 when it looked like the regime might collapse. Rather, his advisers presented a limited range of options, all of which involved a United States military effort. The three options were to continue the existing policy of limited aid, to escalate into a total war against North Vietnam, and to escalate in the air and on the ground to a sufficient degree to save the regime and discourage the enemy. It was clear that all had coalesced around the third and seemingly most moderate alternative. No one suggested giving up a bad job, in part because of their convictions, but also because this was what they thought the President wanted to hear. He may have cued them to give the advice he wanted.

There are many other variations on this theme. The advisers fail to tell a President hard truths. The assumptions of a plan are evaluated only by its advocates. The President does not sufficiently analyze minority views. In every case, there may be a coalition of advisers to structure reality in a given way for a President and the ironic twist is that he may wish it that way.

Bargaining Games

Policy is sometimes the result of implicit or explicit bargaining games between a President and his top associates, with the actual outcome something that no one planned. From the beginning there were two camps in Washington on South Vietnam, those who saw the war as a political struggle and those who would have subordinated the political to the military effort.[14] The former were mostly civilians in the State Department and the Pentagon, and the latter were White House officials and the military. The American military was wedded to the belief that the war had to be won with arms and that pacification and other political methods were less important. Secretary of State Rusk saw Vietnam as a military problem and kept the State Department out of it. Secretary of Defense McNamara and General Maxwell Taylor, the chairman of the Joint Chiefs of Staff, urged

President Kennedy to give priority to the military effort.

Kennedy was always skeptical of the military approach, feeling that the South Vietnamese regime had to be politically viable before it could defend itself. He was fearful that the Joint Chiefs of Staff, working through allies in Congress and the press, might cause an open breach within his Administration on Vietnam strategy. He relied on McNamara to control the Chiefs and thereby had to defer to him on the war. This meant permitting McNamara and General Taylor to issue statements that the war was going well militarily, something they believed but the President did not.[15] A price was later paid for this compromise because the expectation was raised that the war could be won.

The immediate result of this compromise was that coordination of the political and military aspects of the war was never very great. The military was not guided in the field by political objectives. The President felt that his hands were tied, and the mute quality of the State Department on the question meant that he had little help. State should have supplied the political perspective.

Kennedy always thought about the war politically and denied the military a number of requests for additional United States military advisers in South Vietnam, but he had difficulty imposing his ideas on his own government. One problem was getting reliable information from Saigon and reliable advisers. Although he felt constrained to act in any way except to muddle along, it was not solely bureaucratic politics that constrained him. He could have acted decisively toward the South Vietnamese regime and demanded political reform or withdrawn United States support. He did not take this action for domestic political reasons. He was waiting until after the 1964 Presidential election when, after a victory, he could act quickly to liquidate the commitment and withdraw the United States. In the meantime he drifted, and the momentum of bureaucratic politics, powered by the Pentagon, moved in the direction of military intervention. Bureaucratic politics was important to explain the balance of power within the government but does not fully explain what the President did or failed to do. External politics also figured importantly.

Incrementalism

Issues and decisions come in bits and pieces, and it is very difficult to get coherent policies because different combinations of actors, each seeking specific, limited goals, are involved in each decision. Policy is thus a chain of amended choices.

There was always great difficulty coordinating peace offensives during the Vietnam War with plans for bombing the North, and once a peace and a bombing offensive took place at the same time.[16] This occurred because different sets of actors were involved in two different channels of access to the President and no one, except the President, had the resources to coordinate the policy. He did not choose to do so for whatever reason.

Secretary McNamara was determined to reduce the reliance of America upon nuclear weapons; however, by arguing against them, he was required to argue for a need to increase conventional capability and thus produced, unwittingly, a rationale for their use in Vietnam. He was also opposed to the biological warfare programs of the army, but he had so many conflicts with the Joint Chiefs of Staff that he did not see this question as worth an all-out fight. The navy and air force had no interest in the army's biological warfare program but as a general rule they preferred to bargain with their sister service in terms of each protecting the programs of the other.[17]

President Johnson's advisers converged behind support for the bombing of North Vietnam in early 1965 on the theory that this would stop the war in the South quickly. No one stopped to ask what would happen if this did not prove to be true. There was no plan for the use of ground troops nor was the possibility ever discussed.[18] Policy emerges in an incremental way out of such temporary coalitions.

This is not to say that such an incremental process is always bad. In fact, it is probably inevitable. Policy seldom, if ever, emerges in a complete, coherent fashion from the minds of policy makers after an exercise of rational debate. Rather, it proceeds by fits and starts as policy makers continually amend their past choices as they learn from experience. We never know enough about the consequences of our decisions to really predict what the effects of our actions will be and therefore the most rational method of improvement is the incremental one of amending past decisions and then watching the effect of the change. Just as the American role in the Vietnam War began and was accelerated through incremental processes, so was it ended in the same way. A change in the secretary of defense, the increasing disaffection of high civilians in the Pentagon from the war, and the gradual introduction of the war into the race for the Democratic presidential nomination in 1968 all gradually came to a head with a cumulative effect. But it took another four years and a continuing incremental process to end the United States role in the war. This suggests that the incremental process of decisionmaking does not automatically guarantee anything about the quality of policy decisions. People who, from their viewpoint, want good decisions have to learn how to make that process work for them. The control of any participant over so much is always very limited.[19]

Power Imbalances

There is a "mobilization of bias" within the Executive in the form of an imbalance of influence among holders of different positions. John Kennedy wanted to be his own secretary of state so he chose a relatively weak man for the post of secretary. One unanticipated result was that when questions of the use of military force rose in the government the advocates of force were always better organized, more numerous, and more vocal. The President had little help from the political side, the State Department, against the Defense Department.

This was in part due to Rusk's passive and reticent style. He seldom spoke in meetings but saved his advice for private conversations with the President. Thus he was of no help to a President who wanted vigorous debate. The cause of the mobilization of bias in favor of the military ran deeper than this, however. Since the late 1940s there had been an implicit pact between the State and Defense Departments that each would stay out of the affairs of the other. This was desired by State to protect what was seen as its traditional diplomatic function. But in an era of national security policy it meant that the military were inevitably involved in every problem of international politics. As the prime example, State often held back on becoming involved with Vietnam policy. This pattern was reinforced by the strong personality of Secretary of Defense Robert McNamara, who became the virtual secretary of state to fill a vacuum but who always held a bias toward military solutions to political problems.[20]

Under such circumstances the main actors will seek to structure the rules of the game and the pattern of information in line with the mobilization of bias. For example, McNamara was adamant that the State Department not challenge the figures of the military on the actual progress of the war in Vietnam.[21] After a particularly explosive meeting in which Assistant Secretary of State Roger Hilsman had made such an effort, McNamara got Dean Rusk to promise that it would never happen again The ironic result was that he was deliberately blocking from discussion the kind of information that he would later need and want when he began to doubt the merits of the United States role. The President may be one or more steps removed from such questions and disputes, but the information he eventually receives is affected by these processes below, often without his knowledge.

Presidential Autonomy

Presidential style of authority is the most important independent variable shaping the patterns of bureaucratic politics at the top level of the Executive. It simply is not accurate to depict the President as a prisoner of processes of bureaucratic politics that he cannot control. As the previous instances have shown, he must always face the realities of bureaucratic politics and develop strategies for coping with them, although he may feel constrained at times as a result. This, however, is not being a prisoner. Political scientists who try to explain major foreign policy decisions by recourse to models of bureaucratic routine or bureaucratic politics leave out the key explanatory variable, the President. These models are most helpful for explaining middle-level decisions, routine decisions, and organizational processes with which the President must cope, particularly in getting information and implementing decisions. By definition they will not explain policy actions that stem from Presidential ideology or world view.

Presidential perception of an international situation in which the constraints on action are seen as precluding a wide range of options or, perhaps not paradoxically, requiring drastic innovation cannot be explained by factors within the government. President Nixon's overture to China was developed within the White House and deliberately excluded the bureaucracy. Bureaucratic politics cannot account for factors in American politics that stimulate or guide or constrain a President. The determination of four successive Presidents not to lose Southeast Asia to the communists is surely better explained by either ideology or domestic politics than by processes internal to the government. Another factor that gives a President an autonomy vis-à-vis the bureaucracy is his own conception of his role as originator of American foreign policy. This institutional role is a reality and it separates a President somewhat, not only from public and Congress, but from his own bureaucracy as well. Their perspectives cannot be completely his perspectives if he is to be true to the fullness of his own constitutional and institutional role.

The model of bureaucratic politics also gives us caricatures of the motives and perspectives of Presidential associates and advisers. They are pictured as strictly instrumental actors always in pursuit of short-term strategic and tactical advantages over each other in games of bureaucratic maneuver. Policy, in this view, becomes almost a means to success at winning bureaucratic games and influencing the President rather than an end for which the game is played. One would not want to deny that this process of inversion does take place nor that personal ambition and careerism are powerful motors in the advocacy of policy positions, but a better balance is to see human beings as moral and purposive creatures who are trying to achieve policy goals and who act out bureaucratic games to achieve those goals. This view makes the model of bureaucratic politics incomplete, for it makes no provision for elite ideology as a factor to explain behavior.

Finally, because the relationships are difficult to untangle it is difficult to draw causal conclusions about how much bureaucratic politics constrains a President. For example, we do know that Lyndon Johnson imposed a very closed, secretive, and highly selective pattern of decisionmaking upon the conduct of the Vietnam War. Only a handful of people were regularly consulted on major decisions, and quite often those who had to implement decisions were in the dark about the actual policy and its purposes. He was determined that there be no leaks and no dissension within his government on Vietnam. But it is not immediately obvious that this closed arena was a cause of the content of Presidential policy decisions, as some have claimed. This may be the case, but it is as plausible to suggest that Presidential policy preceded specific decisions and was guided by a personal determination to see the United States effort through. He then imposed a lid on internal debate. These causal threads are difficult to untangle. The following section illustrates how one might go about untangling them in order to develop prescriptive statements about policy-making processes.

EVALUATION OF PRESIDENTIAL DECISION PROCESSES

Foreign policy crisis decisions of the past two decades have stimulated a scholarly literature on crisis management that, with modifications, can also be applied to crucial decisions that do not take the shape of dramatic crises. This research has emerged out of a concern with detecting the elements of a governmental decision process that may cause faulty decisions and policy mishaps. The tragic experience of Vietnam is surely the chief cause of this concern, but there are other instances, for example, the American sponsorship of the abortive Bay of Pigs invasion of Cuba in 1961 and the sending of the marines to the Dominican Republic in 1965. These authors believe that, other things being equal, a "good" decision process is more likely to produce a "good" decision than a faulty decision process. This is a reasonable view, but it does not immediately tell us what a "good" decision process is or how to show the consequences of any decision process for policy. By "good" we do not mean a normative standard of right or wrong policy but an instrumental evaluation of whether the decision process was so structured as to permit the chief actors to have a realistic view of their problems and to make decisions that had a likely possibility of achieving their goals. If the subsequent policy implementation that follows from a decision goes seriously awry we may want to try to reconstruct the decision process to see if part of the cause of the mishap can be found there. The mistaken view of reality that led to an erroneous decision may have been nourished in a faulty policymaking process.

One cannot fully judge the merits of a policymaking process by criteria inherent within it without looking at the actual consequences of policy. However, this is not entirely the case because there are criteria of normative democratic theory about how power should be distributed and organized that do not depend upon an assessment of policy results for their invocation. One can simply believe that it is good for leaders to consult widely without worrying about whether it is a method that always produces good decisions. In the long run if it did not lead to good decisions much of the time, consultation might cease to be valued so highly even by its advocates. By the same token, a judgment about the link between a good decision process and a good decision is not in the first instance a normative judgment. It is an instrumental evaluation that the process permitted the policy makers to achieve their objectives. One can then back off and normatively criticize those goals. But that is a different process of judgment.

We are here concerned with instrumental rather than normative judgments and want to try to link decision process to outcome in terms of the perspectives of the participants themselves. The goal is to be able to tell policy makers how to organize themselves to improve their decision capabilities. The purpose is to avoid policy malfunctions. What factors in a decision process are conducive to an accurate picture of the world? What factors take account of the attainability of the objectives chosen, whether it be problems of bureaucratic implementation or political feasibility? These are the kinds of questions that one asks of a decision process, and unfortunately we usually only ask them after a policy fiasco, not before.

This is a scientific effort that attempts to link process variables to outcome variables. But there are many other key factors that are not taken into account in this formulation. The world view of the policy makers is not fully explained by the governmental processes leading to decision, and there are many contingent and uncontrollable events and circumstances that always intervene between a decision and the final outcome that could not have been foreseen at the time of decision. Nonetheless, it is important to try to identify the main variables in crucial Presidential decision processes in order to ask how such processes might be improved in the light of policy goals.

Crisis Decisions

Glenn Paige was one of the first scholars to attempt to derive propositions about the effects of a decision process on policy output in his study of the Korean intervention decision of 1950.[22] He develops a number of propositions about crisis decisionmaking. A crisis decision in foreign policy is defined as an unexpected occasion for decision thrust from outside upon the organization and society in which important goals are threatened and a quick response is necessary. The most important stage of the response is the first perception of the situation and the problem by decision makers. Their collective response follows from that first look. His key propositions are important for subsequent discussion:

1. The decision unit is a relatively small, ad hoc group assembled by the President.
2. There is strong emphasis in the decision unit on group solidarity and support for the President.
3. The decision unit seeks new information about the problem, but the greater the crisis the greater the reliance upon central themes in previously existing information.
4. The decision unit will generalize its decision not in terms of the specific case but in terms of general national goals.
5. The decision unit will seek support outside itself from friend and foe and pay little attention to critics. It is cut off from normal political constraints.
6. The stronger the Presidential leadership of the group, the clearer the President's own position, the more homogeneous the group, and the less tolerable the decision delay, it follows that there will be less variety of information and values supplied from within the decision unit, less articulation of alternative courses of action, and a greater probability of selection of a single course of action that is in accordance with the group's perception of Presidential wishes.

Paige describes this as a "high consensus" decision. This is a predictive proposition about the effect on policy of a given decision process. However, he then draws instrumental-normative prescriptive propositions from the case. He sees potential defects in the decision process. There may be so great an emphasis upon conformity and unanimity in such a cohesive group that the existing stock of information coming from the bureaucracy, which may be erroneous, will not be challenged. Secondly, critics outside the group may have important messages to convey but will be ignored. Therefore, Paige urges that adversary reporting be built into staff work at top levels so that official reports can be challenged and that members of decision units pay special attention to friendly critics.

Paige does not demonstrate that such bad consequences could follow from the actual process he describes. To do so he would have to show that the Korean decision itself put too great a priority on a single response without sufficient debate. For example, perhaps someone should have raised the question of whether the conflict was a civil war rather than overt aggression and that it perhaps might not involve American national interests or world peace in the short or long run. Such questions were not raised and the evidence suggests that had they been raised they would have been put down because of the group atmosphere.

The implications of different ways for a President to structure a decision group that emerge from the Bay of Pigs and Cuban missile crisis experiences are clearly found in Paige's embryo theory. The clue to the different decision processes was in the change in style of John Kennedy. In the Bay of Pigs instance, Kennedy did not encourage those in the decision group to challenge the information and assumptions supplied by the CIA nor did he support the efforts of Fulbright and Schlesinger to challenge the consensus. Kennedy and his associates closed ranks behind a decision that was poorly presented and inadequately scrutinized. The execution of the decision proved this to be so. Simple things went wrong that could have been foreseen had the decision makers asked hard questions of the advocates of the plan.[23] The CIA had told the President that their intelligence showed Castro to be very unpopular with his people. The State Department in fact had better information that showed this to be erroneous, as later events proved. The CIA had reported that even if the attack should fail the invaders could take refuge in nearby mountains to mount a guerrilla war much like that originally begun by Castro. But no one ever thought to point out that the original claim of a retreat possibility was ruled out by a change in the invasion site and that now there was a jungle and swamp between that beach and the mountains. These kinds of silly and inexcusable errors were legion in the operation and it was the President's fault that they were not exposed. He and his new team of fresh associates were perhaps unsure of their hold on the government and therefore not disposed to challenge what they were being told by the CIA and the Joint Chiefs of Staff. But that very newness should have made them extra skeptical; they were gullible.

In the missile crisis case, Kennedy acted out of the experience of the Bay of Pigs fiasco. He had already changed decision styles within his government to favor adversary debate and the introduction of outside opinion and special expertise; he had developed procedures of debate within groups by dividing them in half and forcing debate, charging McGeorge Bundy, Theodore Sorensen, and Robert Kennedy with being devil's advocates. He communicated this to his colleagues by his own searching style of interrogation of advocates of positions. All this came to fruition in the missile crisis when he charged the small executive decision group with developing and debating the maximum number of options and deliberately pushed for adversary debating procedures and painful confrontations within the group. The result was a high consensus decision but one at a higher level of synthesis than the Korean decision. The final consensus had emerged from a much more intense series of disagreements and was therefore achieved by debate that systematically criticized the empirical assumptions of alternative policies rather than by conformity.[24]

The implication from these three cases is that Presidents should always act as Kennedy did in the Cuban missile crisis. The more the leader structures adversary debate the better his information and the wider his range of options. However, this would seem to be more true of the cases where things go awry. One can say with conviction that the failures of the decision group during the Bay of Pigs did lead to a gigantic policy failure, but we do not necessarily know from the missile case that the decision procedures produced a "good" decision. It is much easier to see a negative link between process and decision than a positive link. One could say that the decision processes in the missile crisis produced the moderate decision for a blockade that was the middle way between inaction and use of weapons. Furthermore, it worked in permitting the Soviets a graceful way out of the impasse. But the same decision process almost produced agreement on a pinpoint surgical air strike. Had the air force not given the President an erroneous report that a surgical air strike of missile sites was impossible the tale might have been different. The only available air force plan provided for a total attack on Cuba. Had they been more astute and given a surgical strike plan the moral argument against it made by Robert Kennedy might not have been able to prevail. Would we think the decision so good in that event? It probably depends upon the subsequent events. But so does our afterglow approval of the blockade option.

Furthermore, all the adversary debate in the world does not seem to have been able to shake the world view of Cold War rivalry held by the members of the decision group, especially given domestic politics. The debate was instrumental and basic premises were not examined. Secretary McNamara came close to examining such premises in initially suggesting that a missile was a missile no matter where it was and that the United States do nothing because the missiles in

Cuba were no greater threat than missiles in Moscow, but he got nowhere with this and shifted his ground after two days. Adlai Stevenson later challenged a Cold War world view when he suggested trading American missiles in Turkey for Soviet ones in Cuba. This option raised too great a challenge to the crisis emphasis upon the virtue of the United States in the situation and had to be brushed aside. It also clashed with Kennedy's image of Presidential strength in a crisis.

Thus we have a refinement of Paige's prescriptive proposition. Presidential style to stimulate adversary debate within the decision group can widen the range of options considered but is not likely to permit the examination of the basic world view of decision makers. Nor can we say that an open, adversary process necessarily produces "good" decisions.

Dialogue and Conformity

Joseph De Rivera and Irving Janis make an effort to give psychological roots to the dynamics of group decision described by Paige and, in the case of Janis, of the two Kennedy episodes. Their insights are taken from small-group laboratory experiments. De Rivera posits that individuals and groups screen most information through predispositions and learn new ways of looking at reality most often through shock or crisis. There is thus a strong tendency toward working conformity in small groups. Most groups lack mechanisms for challenging unexamined premises. Small groups will tend to reject deviants from the group norm and follow the leader under conditions of stress requiring quick decision.[25]

Janis develops these ideas into a formal theory of "Group think," which is defined as a process in which such a high priority is placed by members of the group upon getting along together in a comfortable atmosphere that shared illusions and misjudgments about reality prevent good decisions from emerging.[26] What seems like vigorous debate actually is not so. The psychological hypothesis of the explanation is that uncertainty, heavy pressure to decide, and doubt and anxiety about the rightness of options cause individuals to seek reassurance in Group think. The characteristics of Group think are described in a number of historical cases, the failure to anticipate attack at Pearl Harbor, the decision to unify Korea, the Bay of Pigs, and Vietnam intervention. The positive cases where Group think was avoided were the development of the Marshall Plan and the missile crisis. The characteristics of Group think are an illusion of invulnerability in the group, blocks against negative information and feedback, belief in the inherent morality of the group, stereotyped view of opponents, direct pressure against dissenters to fall into line, minimizing of doubts by individuals, a shared illusion of unanimity, and emergence of self-appointed mind guards within the group who protect the leader and members from information or viewpoints that might challenge the consensus. The chief consequences are that the group considers fewer alternatives than it might, does not probe for positive aspects of minority views, fails to consider negative aspects of the dominant view, absorbs factual information with selective bias, seeks little outside advice or expertise, and devotes little attention to problems of implementation of the chosen policy. All this is in Paige in embryo form. The key is in the style of the chief executive. He must build in adversary processes.

Janis's prototype solutions are found in Kennedy's policies after the Bay of Pigs, which were fulfilled in the missile crisis. However, he carries the problem further than Paige by pointing out that there may be undesirable and unintended side effects from such a leadership style. Prolonged debates can lead to disintegration of a group in a crisis situation and the inability to make a decision. Or the leader may find his playing an initially open-minded role puts him at odds with his group if they select an option he cannot support. Such procedures may also create a greater opportunity for intraorganizational rivalries to flare up thus intensifying the struggle for power, putting clamps upon the open use of information, and lowering the quality of decisions. Janis relies on the leader to be shrewd, quick, and skillful enough to overcome these negative side effects. He must know how to catalyze a group to be open and yet be able to hold it together.

Following from Paige and De Rivera, Janis gives us richer and fuller propositions about the dynamics of decision than either, but he is more convincing on the negative cases than the positive ones. It is much clearer that we should avoid doing certain things but he cannot promise positive results.

One flaw in the De Rivera–Janis approach is the imposition of a hypothesis about psychological motivation on overt behavior. This gives their interpretations a quality of uncertainty. One wonders if the psychological interpretations are forced, especially when there is no interview material.

Finally, it is difficult to integrate the Group think hypothesis with alternative explanations and give relative weight to each. But there is no inherent obstacle to such interweaving. The problem of the historian is to give weight to different factors in explanation drawing on hypotheses about human motivation. The psychological hypothesis of Group think simply adds important factors that might be present.

The most arresting quality of the Janis cases is that they show history repeating itself. Flaws in a policy process at one time that cause mishaps do the same thing when repeated much later. One can find many similar features in the 1950 decision to escalate the war in Korea with the 1965 decision to do so in Vietnam. After the initial successes of United Nations troops in driving the North Korean forces out of South Korea in the summer of 1950 a decision was taken in Washington to drive north and unify the country. This decision brought Chinese armies into the war and proved disastrous for the men who had made it. The rest of the war was a holding operation and stalemate and caused the defeat of the Democratic Administration in 1952. This choice was made in a state of euphoria in which the clear Chinese warning of intervention should the United States go north was dismissed as a bluff. American policy makers had stereotypes of the Chinese as puppets of the Russians, and it was felt that the Russians did not want a wider war and therefore the Chinese would not. This was a serious miscalculation, and in making it the men in Washington became prisoners of General MacArthur's military adventurism in Korea. Their awe of him may have been a factor in the decision but that in itself should have been examined. George Kennan, at the time a high State Department official, made an accurate prediction that the Chinese would come in if American troops crossed the thirty-eighth parallel. But Dean Acheson, the secretary of state, kept Kennan and his aides out of top Administrative discussions. No one wanted to spoil the euphoria by asking hard questions. It would have been too painful to develop new strategic thinking under the pressure of events.[27]

Once the Chinese entered the war and President Truman saw that he was faced with a disaster he did not look for flaws within his own house but sought external scapegoats. He publicly attacked the press for dividing the nation by criticizing his actions and thereby encouraging the enemy, and he lashed out at his Republican critics.

One determinant of this decision was Truman's leadership style. He set the tone of an aggressive American response to problems at all meetings. But the dynamics of the group also helps explain what happened. Truman was always willing to accept opposition from his advisers and could often be persuaded to change his mind. For example, he was persuaded by the group not to send Chinese Nationalist soldiers from Formosa to Korea as he had originally intended. But they were all trapped in the momentary exultation of success in the decision to go North. In the process we see many features that were to recur in 1965: an excessive risk-taking based upon a shared illusion of invulnerability, a false stereotype of the Asian enemy, and the exclusion of experts who saw the pitfalls in what was about to be done and who might have questioned the group's unwarranted assumptions.

Executive Branch Politics

Roger Hilsman gives us a picture of bureaucratic politics in operation from which one can develop propositions about the potentiality for policy mishaps that are inherent in the dynamics of the process.[28] It is a view of strong-minded men with passionate convictions seeking to move each other toward vague and uncertain goals with highly imperfect knowledge. In such processes there is a very strong strain toward agreement and consensus because each participant needs most of the others to achieve his goals. A great deal of communicating, persuading, and educating is always at work. Paradoxically, such a need also creates an impetus to oversimplify and oversell, particularly as the circle of participants widens. There is an incentive not to communicate effectively, to be fuzzy about articulating policy and its possible outcomes, because one hopes that different actors and groups will climb aboard a particular policy for different, perhaps incompatible, reasons but with the consensus fuzzed over by general ambiguity. Policy thus proceeds by incremental zigs and zags with each actor thinking of his influence stakes in a given short-term decision more than in terms of achieving long-range objectives. The tendency in this process is for consensus decisions to be put together by minimal agreement of all concerned and for there to be great pressure that such decisions or policies not come unstuck. The threat of dissolution of consensus is a threat to the influence stakes over agreed policy of each actor. Such agreements are often set by crisis decisions and come unstuck only during a subsequent crisis when they again take a new rigidity that lasts for a time. One could read successive decisions on Vietnam intervention in this way with the basic underlying policy being reversed in 1968 only with great difficulty and in the face of obvious failure.

The chief potential for policy mishaps that observers see in this process is a kind of Group think on a much larger scale than the small decision unit. The entire top reaches of government become prisoners of a consensus that is steeped in vagueness and ambiguity but seems necessary in order to carry on the business of government. The potentiality for mishap is that it is very hard to change the prevailing consensus without a crisis that shakes such agreement. Misperceptions of the world and even disastrously mistaken policies can go on because there is little leverage to change them. Often such consensus embraces incompatible policies under a common umbrella because of the need for bureaucratic alliances. Such bargaining games are inherent in government because of uncertain values and imperfect knowledge. Men will differ on what is right and wrong and be unable to reconcile their disagreements by reason. The only alternative is bargaining. This process has great advantages for good policymaking when the competing groups of advocates are knowledgeable about the problem, when attentive publics are well informed, and when those who must carry out the policy are persuaded by the decision. A more open decision is likely to be a better decision because the opportunities for new information are better and so are the chances for the entering wedge of policy innovation. Whether such prescriptions are applicable to crisis decisions that must be decided quickly and secretly is doubtful.

Thus, the pluralism, fragmentation, and fluidity of the policymaking process is two-sided. Such a process can generate artificial and rigid consensus often on mistaken policy, but it can also permit flexibility, creativity, and new policy departures. The conditions for the latter would seem to be actor knowledgeability and relative openness of debate.

Multiple Advocacy

The literature gives us few clues on how to promote genuine intellectual dialogue in a process of internal personal and policy competition and bureaucratic politics. Alexander George takes up this challenge in a direct and innovative manner by pursuing the insight that Presidential will is the key to openness and dialogue and prevention of policy mishaps due to excessive closure.[29] George is critical of Charles E. Lindblom and others who assume that bargaining games will more likely than not produce an equilibrium of interests and perspectives in which every relevant point of view will be represented.[30] He maintains that this is simply not so because of the imbalance of power, influence, and information among actors in such processes. Thus George asks a President to promote "multiple advocacy" by securing a greater distribution of the resources of power, competence, information, and bargaining skills. The weaker parties must be strengthened so that all can be heard.

He develops a list of nine kinds of policy malfunctions that can arise in the absence of multiple advocacy: when a President and his advisers agree too readily on the nature of a problem, when advisers develop too limited a range of options, when there is no advocate for an unpopular option, when a President is confronted with a unanimous recommendation, when advisers fail to tell a President what he needs to know, when a President is dependent upon a single channel of information, when a plan is evaluated only by its advocates, and when a President fails to follow up negative views or find out how firm a consensus is.

He calls upon the President to appoint a "custodian" as his staff assistant who would guard against such malfunctions by ensuring that the conditions for multiple advocacy were present. Such a person must not be a policy advocate or spokesman or implementator. These roles would interfere with his objectivity. Nor must he be a guardian of the President's personal power. Such a posture could act to hinder multiple advocacy. His tasks must be to ensure that all key actors have the resources to play their full potential role and that all viewpoints are heard. But George's very language illustrates the difficulty of this task, for example, "by balancing actor resources when necessary by strengthening weaker advocates."[31] In fact such imbalances are deeply rooted in the structure of government. The chronic weakness of the State Department at the policy table cannot be easily adjusted overnight.

A second criticism is that whereas George sees that the President must want such a system, he perhaps fails to see that only a President can play the custodian role. He will need staff aides to assist him but only a President can call in outside advisers, restructure the membership of meetings, insist on devil's advocates. George knows this but he gives us a picture of a President as magistrate who relies on the custodian to do these things. In fact a President must do them for himself. We are much more dependent upon the personality and style of the President than George admits. He seems to hope that a multiple advocacy system can exist somewhat separately from a President, though with his blessing. Because the theory depends so much upon personality it is hard to institutionalize. All of John Kennedy's decision rules, developed out of the Bay of Pigs and missile crises, vanished from government with him. Lyndon Johnson imposed a very different style of authority and set of decision rules on the same people who had worked with Kennedy. Group culture seems to follow from the leader more than it shapes him.

This analysis has uncovered a number of different conditions for policy mishaps. The basic cause of a policy mishap is the failure to learn about the environment during a crisis or time of crucial decision. The conditions for a policy mishap are:

1. A tight-fisted Presidential style of decision that closes off debate and discussion within the decision unit and throughout the government.
2. The stress toward Group think within the decision unit.
3. Faulty reporting of bureaucratic organizations to the decision unit.
4. A high priority assigned to consensus in intragovernmental bargaining games at top decision levels.

The key to avoidance of policy mishaps is a Presidential style of authority that structures interpersonal relations of multiple advocacy at every level of government and in all decision units and is yet able to keep the government together behind firm decisions. Only the President can set the rules of the game for decision.

However, there is one limitation to this prescription. There is no evidence presented by any of the cases considered that even the most open, catalytic, creative President can push decision units or entire top levels of his associates in government to reexamine their basic views of the world of political reality and their basic philosophies of international politics and American foreign policy. These are too deeply rooted to be reexamined by busy, harassed officials who are struggling to make day-to-day decisions. Thus mistaken world views and political philosophies may be the greatest single source of policy failures.

THE VIETNAM EXPERIENCE

Was the United States decision to take an active military role in Vietnam a policy mishap that can be related to any of the foregoing propositions? I would contend that it was a policy mishap in two senses. First, the decision makers saw the conflict between North and South Vietnam as an instance of the supposed global rivalry of the free world and international communism. This was a misperception of reality. Second, the decision makers did not see that the struggle in Vietnam was essentially political rather than military and that United States military efforts were therefore in vain. Of course these are my interpretations. To be valid they must not be based simply on my dislike of the policy. Rather, one has to demonstrate that in fact the world view of policy makers was mistaken and that decision-making processes distorted an accurate view of what was going on in Vietnam. This cannot be done here. Instead, I will present a thesis that connects Vietnam policymaking with the ideas already developed and the reader can draw his own conclusions as to its plausibility.

The argument is based on four hypotheses. First, that the ideological legacy of the Cold War explains the increasingly active United States role in Vietnam until 1964. Second, that this legacy was reinforced by processes of Group think at the top decision levels of the Johnson Administration in the winter of 1964–1965. Third, that the personal style of authority of Lyndon Johnson from 1965 to 1968 virtually precluded a reexamination of the premises and means of policy until crisis intervened in the spring of 1968, and that even then the continuity of policy was more evident than any reversal because the President remained in charge. Fourth, that once ground troops were sent to Vietnam to fight the morass of United States commitment was very difficult to reverse even by the most astute Presidential leadership.

The historical legacy has four components. First was the general Cold War ideology. The ideological themes of government memos written in the late 1940s and in the early and mid-1960s, as collected in the Pentagon Papers, are identical. Second was the successful experience of fighting a limited war in Korea. This was seen as successful in the eyes of top officials of the Kennedy-Johnson Administrations, many of whom had served in the Truman Administration. This was the antidote to the appeasement memory of Munich and to the Republican belief in total victory. Third was the commitment of Democratic political rhetoric in 1950s to the need to develop conventional warfare capability in order to fight successful limited wars; this was in opposition to the Eisenhower massive retaliation strategy. Fourth was what one might call the "Stillwell dilemma" after the problem was posed by Barbara Tuchman.[32] Franklin Roosevelt knew that Chiang Kai-shek was a weak ally who would not fight and who barely controlled his country. But because he saw no alternative government and because he wished to shore up China for a postwar role, he supported and gave considerable aid to Chiang, even to the extent of sacrificing General Stillwell who opposed the policy. The same drama was repeated in the increasing American commitment to South Vietnam's Diem, a leader who could not govern and who the United States urged to broaden and reform his government but who would not do so. Thus, there was an ever deepening Stillwell dilemma for the United States in supporting a regime over which it had little influence.

The Kennedy team acted on this legacy when they came to office. They gave a special intensity to Cold War views with their activism, self-confidence, and hubris. They tried to build up conventional warfare capability in response to the fear of wars of national liberation. They sunk deeper and deeper into the Stillwell dilemma in their love-hate affair with Diem. They failed to develop a fully adequate view of Vietnam in political terms and permitted the military strategists to dominate Administration councils. Most important, the basic premises of the world view, which saw the conflict in Vietnam in Cold War rivalry terms, were never challenged.

The winter of intervention of 1964–1965 saw the advent of Group think within the key decision unit of top administration officials. The danger of an actual "loss" of South Vietnam to the North and the need for an immediate American decision hardened and reinforced the historical legacy and the momentum of commitments. There was the illusion of invulnerability and of the inherent morality of the ingroup. W. W. Rostow wrote that "we are the greatest power in the world—if we behave like it."[33] Negative warnings were shunned about the futility of bombing and about the essentially political nature of the conflict. There was pressure on dissenters to come into line and in fact deviants like undersecretary of state George Ball and Vice President Hubert Humphrey were isolated and tolerated at the same time. Ball was the institutionalized devil's advocate whom Johnson would listen to in high-level discussions but whom he would never heed. However, actually listening to a critic of prevailing policy can convince a President that he knows what his critics are saying and free his mind from any concern that he is not listening to diverse points of view. Whether he seriously entertains such criticisms is a different matter. Humphrey was treated differently. He was simply frozen out of policy discussions so long as he expressed doubts about the validity of the American role in the war. He was brought back into the inner circle only when he showed his repentance by making public speeches in behalf of Administration policies. There was a stereotyped view of the enemy—"a raggedy ass little third rate country" Lyndon Johnson called it. It was inconceivable that the United States could lose a war to such an enemy. But perhaps as important as all these things, despite any doubts that were expressed, was the fact that the top policy makers held a view of the world that required them to send American forces to save South Vietnam. The result seems to have been that they failed to fully consider the possible flaws in their world view and that they excluded experts who might have challenged their premises and analysis. A basic flaw was the weakness of the State Department and its failure to present political views of the world as an antidote to the military strategy that was created incrementally over time.

The conduct of the war entrapped us even more deeply into the Stillwell dilemma. We were not winning and the successive South Vietnamese regimes were not capable of winning or even fighting for themselves, but no alternative seemed possible given basic American premises about the stakes. At this point the style of authority of Lyndon Johnson became the crucial variable. Chester Cooper describes this style vividly. Johnson drew on a small group of advisers at the top, Rusk, McNamara, Wheeler, and with them the President set policy and ran the war. The concentric circles of actors around this inner group were often in the dark as to policy, information, and the President's mind. There was anything but a multiple advocacy system of decision. Johnson repeated the same cycle seen in the

Dominican Republic intervention. Having been misled by the bureaucracy about the actual situation he found himself unable to extricate the United States from a situation in which we could not win but dared not lose. Thus, as in the earlier instance, he reverted to his legislative style and tried to square all the interests through manipulating an artificial consensus. He failed.

It took the crisis of the Tet offensive, coupled with the New Hampshire primary, for the Vietnam dissidents within the government to bring the President around to a change in policy. It is not even clear that Johnson actually changed his policy. His restriction of the bombing of the North and his offer to negotiate may have been efforts to assert the continuity of policy and the strength of the United States commitment rather than a reversal. The President, even in the face of political defeat, held the cards.

What conclusions do we draw in terms of our models and propositions about policy mishaps? First, the most important cause of the policy mishap was the world view of top decision makers. Second, it is not apparent that lively multiple advocacy within the Kennedy Administration was able to reverse the momentum of commitment. Third, the style of authority of President Johnson when combined with the crisis atmosphere of 1964–1965 created a process of Groupthink at the top decision level. Fourth, this personal style of the President made it very difficult for internal critics of the policy to get it reassessed until another crisis came along. One can speculate that had Kennedy lived and fostered a more open, multiple advocacy style that the United States government might have learned more quickly about its mistakes and fought a different kind of war or found a way to pull back and perhaps out through negotiation. But that is speculation.

We also see the operation of organizational process and bureaucratic politics. The model of organizational process helps explain why top decision levels had a faulty view of reality before and during the American intervention. Bureaucratic reporting was too heavily weighted in military directions, and a great deal of the conduct of military operations was based on false reporting from the field. However, this model does not explain the political perspectives of decision makers that stimulated intervention. It seems most useful for explaining information going to the decision unit and the implementation of decision but not the decision itself. The model of bureaucratic politics helps explain the search for consensus at the top reaches of government and the great difficulty of getting such a consensus opened up for reexamination. But there can be more than one version of the model, and Lyndon Johnson's version was much more closed and tight-fisted than John Kennedy's. Johnson did not use the dynamics of bureaucratic politics to learn about reality. Rather, he jealously guarded his Presidential and personal power in a narrow sense by a posture of secrecy and distrust, even of his own associates, and failed to learn about his own policies.

We could conclude that another President than Johnson might have run the war differently. But this begs the question of whether any President, no matter how committed to multiple advocacy, could have reversed the momentum to intervention from 1961 to 1965 by causing a reexamination of the dominant American world view about the Cold War. It is unfair to ask in retrospect more than was possible of the decision makers on Vietnam at the time. One may feel that their view of the world was disastrously wrong, but most of us have come to this belief only after the actual shock and horror of the war. The flaw in our ideologies usually emerges into consciousness only with harsh experience.

The strongest cure for major policy mishaps therefore is a tragedy like Vietnam, which may point broad American policy in a new direction for a generation until that world view too suffers shock and gives way to a new path. Vietnam was for Americans the culmination of a post–World War II policy that had developed out of the experience of appeasement of the 1930s. It was a sound policy in most instances but it was carried on too long and it was too little examined in the society at large.

The predominant world view about foreign affairs among the elites of American society, however one characterizes such groups, is probably the chief intellectual and moral resource for a President and also the primary source of constraints upon his actions, not in the sense of sanctions but in his internalizing of the prevailing ideas. However, the several dimensions of this phenomenon can each explain things independently.

Certainly the personal world view of a President, while drawn from the experience of his generation, cannot be explained in social terms alone. In the final analysis, after all discussion and debate, the personality of the President *is* the decision system in crucial foreign policy decisions. Hugh Sidey describes how Richard Nixon decided to respond to the North Vietnamese offensive in South Vietnam in the spring of 1972 by mining the harbors of the North and ordering all-out bombing.

> Nixon had wanted out of Vietnam. He was the one who had withdrawn half a million men and sought a final resolution to the lingering tragedy. But he could not bring himself to accept the final enemy demand to abandon the South Vietnamese government. What hardened in Nixon's mind was the conviction that North Vietnam no longer

was interested in any kind of reasonable solution. What they sought was a total military victory. For the man who admired the way John Kennedy stood up ten years ago at the Cuban missile crisis, the man who felt the honor of his Presidency was threatened, the man who had lived his entire life as a battle to be fought unrelentingly, there was only one answer.

Early in his deliberations, he decided that he would not raise a challenge gradually, the way Lyndon Johnson had escalated the war. That, in Nixon's mind, was Johnson's downfall. The Nixon move would come all at once—not only harbors mined but bombing greater than any yet seen in this world, bombing of any and all military targets, bombing of rail lines and the destruction of any airlifts mounted by Russia. But along with it would come the most generous offer yet for a ceasefire and a complete American withdrawal.[34]

Nixon carried out the same strategy when the Paris peace talks came close to collapse at Christmas time in 1972. He and his advisers were convinced that it was the savage punishment that North Vietnam took in the Christmas bombing that brought them back to the conference table and achieved a peace agreement. This cannot be known. But the important point for us is that no President will abdicate his world view in such situations in the face of criticism, no matter how widespread. He may in fact be right and his critics wrong about both strategy and immediate tactics, but such judgments require historical perspective.

There is a strong dynamic in the Presidential office to cause a President to think in terms of his obligations to American history and national purposes. Short-run public criticism will not likely deter him. These Presidential perspectives are likely to be widely shared by his associates and usually by elites throughout the society, but the President will always weave a personal perspective. When this perspective comes to bear on a decision is difficult to analyze, perhaps even to himself; furthermore, nothing can be done about it, for better or for worse, by others. Such autonomy is inherent in the Presidential office. The same issue of *Life* that carried Hugh Sidey's description of the bombing of the North also shows a picture of the President entering the cabinet room after his television speech to the nation; all the members of the cabinet are standing and applauding him with broad smiles of respect and deference. Thus, all the psychological structures of the office reinforce his autonomy.

A second dimension to prevailing elite world views is the cluster of modes of thought and values that characterize the top echelons of Presidential advisers. The model of bureaucratic politics does not fully encompass this dimension. We do not understand much about how a President and his key associates interact in terms of such modes of thought and values but the relationship seems an important one. David Halberstam, for example, finds a tough-minded "machismo" ethos among the Kennedy and Johnson advisers that made them celebrate their successful management of the threat of nuclear terror at the time of the Cuban missile crisis and see such command and control as an ability to turn up and tone down threats and actual use of force as the blueprint for success in Vietnam. This tough-mindedness made them scorn and ridicule the "tender-minded" among them like Adlai Stevenson and Chester Bowles, who advocated diplomacy rather than force in such crises. This kind of tough-mindedness may be endemic in highly successful American men, and there may be little that can be done about it. Each successive White House, no matter who the President is, seems to be populated by arrogant, careerist, and often ignorant men, who do their President more harm than good in their relations with others and their advice to him. But the headiness of power is intoxicating.

Of course such cadre characteristics change across time and any Administration will have crosscurrents within it. Henry Kissinger has written about the inherent pragmatism of lawyers and businessmen who came from private life to serve Presidents in foreign affairs and of the consequent inability of such practical men to think of foreign policy in terms of ultimate policy ends. Rather, in their professional lives, they had been accustomed to developing their instrumental skills, whether writing contracts or negotiating business mergers, and this kind of virtuousity promotes a belief that most problems can be squared through negotiation and bargaining. Ultimate questions get buried in such an atmosphere and basic policies roll on and are seldom questioned.[35] Vietnam intervention could be explained as a surfeit of pragmatism, a belief that American military techniques and coercive diplomacy could carry the day without any serious thought being given to ultimate purpose, either political or moral.

A third variation on this theme of ideology is our actual state of knowledge about the world. Policy makers often substitute ideology for knowledge in their perceptions and appraisals of foreign nations without being aware of it. Secretary of State Rusk would often tell those State Department colleagues who argued that the North Vietnamese were much tougher than Americans and could outlast and wear down United States power that this was a "man from Mars" argument, which made the North Vietnamese out to be superhuman. In fact, Rusk admitted years later that he and his colleagues had seriously underestimated the resilience of the North Vietnamese. This had been easy to do because they had lacked the advice of experts on Southeast Asia. These advisers were few and they were not in government. Career government people on Asia had not been of high quality or forthrightness since the troubles over China in the 1950s. The result was policymaking at the top in a vacuum of ignorance surrounded by a host of American prejudices about superior American power and the weakness of a peasant people.

Richard Neustadt has shown how the United States and Great Britain, its closest ally, failed to understand each other at crucial times, specifically the Suez issue in 1956 and the Skybolt question in 1962.[36] The action of Kennedy in the latter incident in offering Polaris missiles to both Britain and France but in a context that made both seemingly dependent upon the United States showed a basic lack of understanding of the British situation vis-à-vis General de Gaulle as well as little comprehension of de Gaulle's determination to free France from such dependent alliances in NATO. It also precipitated the French rejection of British membership in the Common Market. If an intelligent President with able advisers can make such a blunder, this suggests that there are very great limitations upon the ability of the United States or any other major power to influence the actions of other nations, even those we understand fairly well. There are only a handful of the nations of the world about which American policy makers have any real understanding. Within the scholarly fraternity detailed knowledge of the many nations abroad is spread quite thin. How many American experts are there on South Africa, Laos, even Japan? There are not many, and yet American foreign policy is conducted as if we had great knowledge of these places. In fact, elite ideology is often invoked as a substitute for knowledge, whether it be the conventional wisdom of the State Department or the application of quantitative models of the systems analyst or the raw, untutored perspectives of the top decision makers themselves.

In the face of this situation the best that one can hope for is a high quality of intelligence and general education in top elites backed by a great deal of personal experience and thus considerable empiricist wisdom about life and politics and the relations of nations. These commodities are usually very uneven at the top and even the most talented and experienced of men are capable of the greatest blunders. Furthermore, it is not a good thing to have a high elite all with the same world view because such homogeneity inhibits the possibilities of multiple advocacy. Almost any elite world view will have serious deficiencies for some purpose. The separation of George Kennan from both Harry Truman and Dean Acheson and their immediate successors, Dwight Eisenhower and John Foster Dulles, was a separation over interpretation of the nature of the Cold War. Kennan, a diplomat and classical conservative realist, saw the United States rupture with the Soviet Union as an inevitable conflict between two great powers that could be moderated and contained by expert diplomacy and firm resolution of national determination. He did not see it as a holy war and resisted the Truman Administration's appeal to Congress and the public in terms of an anticommunist crusade, a posture that was followed by the succeeding Republicans. In retrospect Kennan's classic manner of restraint is very appealing.[37] But we cannot foresee a whole generation of conservative realists like Kennan in top governmental positions, and if it did happen these people would not be able to cope with the irrationalities of democratic politics. Kennan himself resigned as ambassador to Yugoslavia after returning to government because of his incomprehension of congressional attacks on United States aid to that country.

Our best hope therefore is for a multiplicity of elites and elite modes of thought and value perspectives that an intelligent President can draw on to fashion policies that are fairly close to the realities of the world. But the quality of elite values and perspectives is to a large extent a manifestation of the quality of life of the educated classes in American society. We are unlikely to have a great deal of American military adventurism abroad for a generation not because of institutional structures and restraints but because of the effect of Vietnam upon present and future Presidents and their associates. In this sense the President is guided and constrained by the national experience. Presidents in the sixties could brandish military power abroad as if there were no constraints on the effectiveness of that power, though in fact there were many. Today Presidents are conscious of the constraints. Just as we see the Presidency differently across time the behavior of Presidents reflects the same cyclic ebb and flow. Revisionist theories and revisionist Presidents go together.

PRESIDENT AND CONGRESS

The Constitution gives the President the chief role in making and executing foreign policy, but Congress has the constitutional authority to make the laws, appropriate money, and declare war. However, in each instance the President has the initiative to set options, make proposals, and execute policy.

There are a number of other reasons why the Executive dominates foreign policy that are congruent with the constitutional prescription and reinforce it. The main one is the nature of foreign policy itself. The policies of one nation about its relations with other nations do not have to be absolutely coherent and consistent, and usually are not, but a minimal kind of continuity and coordination in both policy formation and execution is required that Executives and not legislatures can provide. This is much less true in domestic policy areas with a few exceptions such as national economic policy. The organization of Executive bureaucracy provides the division of labor, the expert specialization, the capacity to develop information, and the vantage point of day-to-day proximity to policy decisions and implementation that the decentralized and much less bureaucratized and specialized legislature cannot rival. Congress is organized and predisposed to react to Executive proposals and to do little initiating on its own in foreign policy.

There is no question that Congress has leverage over the Executive, however. The President is free to set the major directions of policy but he does need congressional assent to programs and budgets implementing those policies. Congressional hearings and investigations can prod, stimulate, embarrass, and at times constrain the Executive from doing what it might otherwise do as well as persuade it to move in directions desired by Congress. Once again the role is reactive rather than initiatory.

The variety of types of relationships between President and Congress is very great and the balance of influence over policy varies widely among different types of issues. An important variable is the political cast of the times. Congress may be in a mood to openly challenge and frustrate the President at one time in history and be extraordinarily supportive at another time. This variation depends upon the nature of the world problems confronting the nation, the political response to those problems, and the policies of the Executive. One cannot therefore speak in certain generalizations about the balance of influence between President and Congress over foreign policy without specifying the type of issue and the political context of the issue. Let us now attempt a few propositions about general relationships that will illustrate the risky status of generalizations.

Crisis Leadership

The President easily dominates and carries Congress with him at a time of crisis when a unified national response can be evoked. The scenario is always the same. Headlines erupt and special emergency meetings are held at the White House to which the President invites the leaders of both congressional parties. These men, who are usually not specialists in foreign policy, approach the meeting after a day of discussing farm price supports or public housing, matters on which they are knowledgeable. The President presents the "facts" in the form of intelligence reports, and Administration experts put the facts in context, making clear that the United States did not seek the crisis but that firm action is now required. The President points out that the Executive is prepared with contingency plans and that quick action is imperative. All this puts congressional leaders at a great disadvantage since they lack the information or the leverage to ask hard questions or dissent from the Presidential lead. It has been made clear to them that the country must act in a unified way. Thus, when the President asks them for the one thing he wants, their endorsement, either informally as a group or formally from the Congress, they cannot deny him that support. It would be unpatriotic to do so nor are they in a position to suggest or carry out an alternative policy. If they discover later that what they were told was only part of the story and if events go awry, they can only conclude that they should be more cautious next time. But, as events have shown, next time will not be different. Their greatest helplessness comes from the fact that the President does not want their endorsement of his actions to legitimize him at home so much as to strengthen him abroad with his antagonists, and it is hard to deny him this.[38]

This theme varies when the congressional leaders are more belligerent than the President. This happened during the Cuban missile crisis when President Kennedy told the leadership that he had decided upon a blockade rather than harsher military action.[39] Their response was critical and aggressive and in support of a military strike against the missiles or an invasion of Cuba. Coming in cold and untutored, without the benefit of the previous days of debate between the President and his advisers, their visceral response was not surprising. Nor was it surprising that the President ignored them and expressed disgust with what he saw as an emotional posture. This is, of course, an example of why Presidents are often loathe to seriously consult with Congress in crucial matters. But the case simply illustrates the futility of consultation and mutual discussion when one party is prepared and the other is not.

Presidential Initiative

The President seems to have the power to carry the nation into war on his own initiative and to conduct the war much as he pleases without serious challenge from Congress. In this case war is a prolonged crisis in which the President can invoke rally round the flag support from the public for the initial actions and in which the Congress is reluctant to deny him the appropriations needed to fight the war or to interfere in military strategy.

This proposition is superficially plausible in the aftermath of the

Vietnam experience but it needs immediate qualification. The use of the war powers of the President depends upon the dominant moods of national ideology and politics far more than it does upon Presidential authority. It does not seem likely that a President in the near future will involve the nation in a limited war such as Vietnam regardless of his power to do so because both popular and congressional opposition, plus the lessons of bitter experience for Presidents, would be too great. The inhibitions would be political and experiential rather than constitutional or even legislative. In fact, one can imagine a future situation in which a President would believe that military forces should be used abroad but would feel constrained from acting by memories of Vietnam and probable criticism.

On the other hand, in most postwar instances of Presidential intervention in conflicts abroad Congress was enthusiastically behind the actions. The Gulf of Tonkin resolution of 1964, which authorized the President to use American troops to resist "aggression" in Vietnam, had only two dissenting votes in the Senate. Subsequent dissent and turmoil about Vietnam in Congress and the series of challenges to Presidential authority of various resolutions and committee hearings and investigations failed, for the most part, to have a direct effect upon the President because his critics could not summon enough votes in both houses to actually constrain Presidential actions. There is no constitutional barrier to Congress setting constraints on a President even in wartime. Had the votes been present, constraining action could have been taken against Presidents Johnson and Nixon on Vietnam. However, Congress was itself politically and ideologically divided, much as was the country, and it was this division that gave the President latitude. Many members of Congress do not want to be put in a position of jeopardizing the lives of American soldiers abroad by withholding funds for their support as a means of reversing Presidential policy. But Congress could pass a joint resolution of both houses, with the force of law, to require a President to stop a policy and proceed in new directions. This could have been done with Vietnam. The lever would have been a threat to withhold budgetary support at some future date unless policy were changed. But the constraints here are political, not constitutional or institutional.

The War Powers Act which passed in November 1973 is well intentioned but beside the point. The law, which passed over President Nixon's veto, requires congressional approval after sixty days if the President has committed troops abroad.[40] The Congress may end the action by joint resolution at any prior time. One suspects that the actual actions taken by Congress would have little to do with its constitutional authority.

During the Vietnam War there was no instance in which Congress directed the President not to do something and he refused. On a number of occasions President Nixon said that he would refuse to obey a proposed congressional resolution that the United States leave Vietnam by a given date or desist from bombing the North. But the actual impasse did not take place. The House was not as antagonistic as the Senate to Vietnam policies, and there was little in law to constrain a President. However, there is a very serious question about what would happen if a President should defy the Congress on such a matter. There is no Presidential authority to use military forces in Indochina since the withdrawal of American troops. President Nixon has publicly threatened the North Vietnamese that he will do so if the truce is not observed by them. Such action on his part could cause a constitutional crisis at home and open warfare with Congress. There seems to be no solution to this problem except a constitutional crisis, appeal to the courts, and perhaps eventual impeachment of the President.

In less dramatic fashion a great deal of Presidential foreign policy never comes to the Congress for legislative review because it is composed of clusters of concrete Presidential actions that do not require legislation but are the result of the President acting and reacting as the leader of the nation in regard to other nations. For example, President Nixon's desire to give American support to Pakistan in the brief 1972 military clash between India and Pakistan was an autonomous move about which Congress could do little. It was a correlate of his efforts at rapprochement with China, for Pakistan has been the Chinese favorite in the perennial conflict of the Indian subcontinent. Détente itself lay almost entirely within Presidential initiative. Any constraints that might have existed would have been political, and they had pretty well vanished, especially for a Republican President. The Nixon search for a general understanding with the two great communist powers and the achievement of a stable balance of power in the world are again beyond the competence of Congress to challenge. The policies of any President in the Middle East, particularly in regard to Arab-Israeli conflicts, may be politically sensitive to a degree, but they involve diplomacy and not legislation and Congress can have little effect except to advise.

Need for Consent

In time, Presidential policies require support for programs to be enacted into law and sustained by appropriations. It is here that the influence of Congress can be very great. For example, the SALT talks with the Soviet Union on arms limitation in 1972 required the assent of the Senate to the treaty, and a good deal of bargaining resulted because of the concern of key Senate Democrats about the effect of the agreement on American military strength. The real point is that the President usually gets his way on essential points in matters of overriding national importance.[41] However, one must not deny that a great amount of bargaining takes place and that a President must at times give way.

The continuing story of revision of reciprocal trade legislation illustrates how Congress has handed over much authority to the Executive as well as how it takes it back in piecemeal fashion when legislation is required.[42] Congress would rather not have responsibility for setting specific tariff levels because the flood of demands for individual industrial areas would be far too intense. Therefore, it has allowed the Executive to set such levels within parameters set by Congress. This permits members of Congress to make their requests in behalf of constituency interests and still permit the President do what is needed for a national position on international trade.

The kind of intelligence a Presidents gets from taking such legislation to Congress is very valuable to him. Members of Congress think of questions like trade in specific terms, seeing particular plants and groups of workers, perhaps even individuals, who may be put out of work by lower tariffs. To them this is not pursuing a special or local interest against the "general" interest. Rather, it is speaking for the needs of their people, who are Americans and human beings. The kinds of people who write trade legislation in the State Department and the White House are likely to think in terms of abstract general rules about trade flows and balance of payments problems and to leave out the human dimension. It does such people good to know there is unemployment in Rhode Island or North Carolina from textile competition. This kind of bargaining is absolutely essential for Presidential learning, and of course Congress learns too. The parties meet half way and some kind of rough consensus is formed, of necessity temporarily, because the law will have been written as a compromise so that those who lost did not lose completely and can return to the fight again. This is parliamentary wisdom, the understanding that no question can ever be completely resolved and that respect for one's opponent requires that this be so. Congressional politicians can teach a President a great deal about democratic norms in such a process.

Sometimes the fights between President and Congress are open and rough. The debate about whether the ABM defensive missile should be built, which President Nixon barely won in 1969, is a very good illustration of Congress forcing the President to persuade its members of the correctness of his views about a matter on which there was deep disagreement. An arranged bipartisan agreement in which doubts were held but not expressed would have been a lot less honest and would have harmed the spirit of dissent and challenge. In a similar incident Congress denied the President the option of developing the supersonic airplane (the SST). In this debate all the mixed and complex concerns about the environment, the national economy, national priorities, and much else combined to focus popular attention upon a question of wide ramifications.

If one looks at postwar history, almost three-quarters of Presidential legislative proposals to Congress in the area of foreign affairs have been approved and passed into law, which shows that Presidents do get their way on most major foreign policy questions with Congress. The congressional defiance of the early Nixon years was in large part due to frustrations about the inability to do anything to curb the President on Vietnam and the determination of Democrats, particularly in the Senate, to strike and wound the President. The interesting fact is that they succeeded so little in terms of the efforts made.

Congress therefore must defer to the President on major legislative proposals most of the time for the same reasons that it must defer on crisis management and major foreign policy initiatives. Congress is neither organized nor specialized to be a policy formulating rival. Moreover, the bargaining that goes with assent and perhaps modification of Presidential proposals varies in strength over time with political currents and cannot be explained by the institutional relationship.

Congress is not organized to take a coherent overview of Administrative foreign policies because of the decentralization and fragmentation of the leadership and committee systems in both houses, although this defect has an opposite virtue too. Congressional committees and subcommittees, which are specialized to the task, can subject Administration legislation to detailed scrutiny, insist on modifications, and hold hearings and investigations that dramatize problems with Administration foreign policies.[43]

The Foreign Affairs Committees and Armed Services Committees in both the House and Senate do not examine national security policies by combining diplomatic and military matters as a whole but divide the labor between them. Furthermore, program budgets must pass through still a third arena, the Appropriations Committees, which are not composed of policy experts. Policy is thus funded without being assessed in a substantive way. Many foreign policy questions are scattered across an even wider spectrum of committees concerning foreign trade, international monetary questions, agriculture, foreign aid, and cultural exchange. Each committee acts on its own and each house is inclined to accept the recommendations of each particular committee, so that congressional overview of programs from a coherent vantage point is rare. Quite often committees prefer to push aside the foreign policy implications of a measure and fasten on the familiar and perhaps more pressing domestic implications.

It would be extremely difficult to impose a central overview in either house over Administration foreign policy as an ongoing matter for a number of reasons. One logical way to do this would be to join policy overview with budgetary controls, but the folkways of the Appropriations Committees are contrary to any such fusion. Those folkways are based upon the great deference each house gives to its Appropriations Committees, which make incremental decisions about funding countless programs without taking any central overview or ranking program priorities. Rather, every effort is made to avoid any such ranking or overview of program trade-offs because to make such an effort would raise the level of conflict in Congress considerably. The system of decentralization of decisions in the specialized Appropriations subcommittees and the deference of each house to those subcommittees permits continuity of domestic programs as manifested in the legislative process. In addition, this system of decision protects the existing balance of rank-and-file pressures for programs, especially domestic programs, that are tied to the political careers of members of Congress. Therefore, any attempt to tie budgeting to program assessment is a threat to this legislative system.[44]

Another important obstacle to a stronger central overview in Congress of Administration foreign policy is the perennial inability of congressional party leaders to exercise authority over their own committee leaders and even over the rank and file. Of course, there are likely to be policy splits within each party on any controversial foreign or domestic policy. Legislative leaders lack the sanctions over committee chairmen and party caucuses that would somehow bring together unified party positions on foreign policy questions.

The last strong Senate and House leaders who came close to having such authority were Lyndon Johnson and Sam Rayburn, but their strength rested primarily upon unusual force of personality and legislative skill. Even then their great energies were directed toward compromise and consensus policies not only within their party but with the Republican President as well. The legislative and Executive branches are both decentralized, fragmented, and full of conflicting units; however, the Executive branch has the President to pull it together, whereas Congress lacks any comparable unifying agency.

Those committees that do frontally face major Administration proposals are severely handicapped. For example, there is no source of intelligence information for Congress comparable to what the President receives from the CIA in both raw data and expert interpretation. Congressmen have difficulty informing themselves on foreign policy questions in the course of their daily work in a way that is natural to the domestic part of their jobs where they can talk with citizens, interest groups, and middle-level bureaucrats without the veil of Executive secrecy that is thrown over questions of foreign policy. When a committee like Armed Services or Foreign Affairs is faced with an open conflict within the Executive such as a difference in estimates of the Soviet missile threat between the CIA and the Pentagon its members are likely to lack the expertise to resolve the dispute.

When the Administration comes to a congressional committee with an important program proposal the committee does not explore all the alternative options that were considered in the phase of policy development with an analysis of the costs and benefits of each. This process of policy development within the Administration may not have been so "rational" to begin with, but even if it were it is the habit of the Executive to come at Congress forcibly behind one proposal. Any dispassionate discussion of policy options would open the door to congressional probing about lack of agreement within the Executive; therefore, it is not surprising that this is one of the favorite congressional pastimes. Still, congressional committees lack the staff, expertise, and information resources to really know what to do with the policy options that are developed. In fact, any effort to use a congressional information procedure to systematically explore policy options would raise so many incipient conflicts within Congress that it would not last long. If Congress is to oppose the Executive it must do so not by trying to make foreign policy itself by considering a large number of options and then deciding but by focusing on single issues. Thus we get the dramatic debates over ABM and resolutions on Vietnam of which many examples can be cited stretching back into the fifties: disputes over Sputnik and United States missile strength, foreign aid controversies, aid to the countries of Eastern Europe, and in fact the establishment of the keystone postwar foreign policies of the country. All were debated and resolved, usually in favor of the Administration, by simple pro and con votes.

This very same fragmentation and decentralization of the structure of Congress is a strength in two respects. It means that congressional subcommittees can look closely at details of Administration foreign policy programs and can raise difficult and embarrassing questions if they wish. In the absence of the ability of Congress to take a central overview of policies, as a whole this power over detail, in regard to both legislation and appropriations, is vital for congressional supervision of foreign policy and its implementation. The chief limitation on a more active congressional role here is not structure but the lack of political will on the part of committee and subcommittee chairmen.

If Congress wishes to it can investigate the Executive through its committees. The Senate Armed Services subcommittee chaired by Senator Stuart Symington uncovered a great deal of previously unknown information about the activities of the CIA and military in Laos during the 1960s that contravened the general agreement of the Geneva accords of 1961 on Laos to which the United States was a party.[45] The hearings of the Senate Foreign Relations Committee on Vietnam in February 1966 were held before television cameras and brought the first serious questions of dissent into American homes. One wonders what the effect on subsequent American policy would have been had Senator Fulbright scheduled such hearings, as Senator Wayne Morse had asked him to do, at the time the President sent the Gulf of Tonkin resolution to the Senate. However, this was politically unfeasible. Fulbright was a supporter of a strong Presidency in foreign affairs, and in his role as Chairman of the Foreign Relations Committee he saw himself as the President's man in the Senate.[46] Lyndon Johnson was about to begin a reelection campaign against Barry Goldwater, who many Senate Democrats thought was extreme and dangerous, particularly on Vietnam. No Senate leader was going to embarrass his President at that point. One can only wonder what the effect on policy might have been had a Senate subcommittee been closely monitoring events in Vietnam since 1961 and subjecting Administration actions there to scrutiny and criticism. However, it seems unlikely that a Democratic Senate committee would have looked that closely into Administration activities, particularly if the President made known that he would prefer they not do so. One could reverse the argument and suggest that a beleaguered President Kennedy might have actually preferred such publicity as a search for a way out of a nonviable situation, although his negative response to the press in Vietnam, which was telling the truth about a hopeless situation, suggests he would not have seen it that way.

Deference to Presidents

Much of this passivity can be explained by a postwar tradition of deference of congressional leaders to Presidents, which is explainable for many reasons. Congressional leaders and Presidents have shared the same world view in which communism was the enemy and the role of America in the world was to check the enemy by the use of national power. The President has been seen as the agent of this power, although, if anything, congressional leaders were more hard line than Presidents at times, as JFK learned at the time of the missile crisis. Many congressional leaders have had close relationships with the military over the years and have identified closely with military values and a military definition of international problems. This again has meant a supportive rather than a challenging attitude. In fact, one of the chief problems for Presidents has been a concern that the high military would carry dissent within the Executive to the Congress. Such dissent has however seldom been over policy so much as it has been about options in weapons development. Successive Presidents have had to persuade Armed Services Committee chairmen that a particular bomber or aircraft carrier should not be funded. This is the kind of check on the Executive that is not really a check, for it reinforces the generally supportive congressional attitude for Cold War policies.

The dominant theme in Congress has been an attitude of self-restraint on the part of the leadership that the President knows better than they and that the nation must speak with only one voice. This is a patriotic sentiment. One could see it in Senator Richard Russell, chairman of the Armed Services Committee during the fifties and sixties. In 1954 he told an emissary of President Eisenhower that it was a "terrible mistake" to send military advisers to South Vietnam, but "I will never raise my voice against it."[47] In August 1965 he told a CBS interviewer: "I guess I must be an isolationist. I don't think you ought to pick up 100,000 or 200,000 or 500,000 American boys and ship them off somewhere to fight and get killed in a war as remotely connected with our interests as this one is."[48] At the same time he was telling President Johnson not to escalate. He felt intuitively, he said, that it was wrong. But he also said he would "support the flag."[49] This is a deep patriotism very common to an older generation of senators and congressmen that does not permit an open challenge to Presidential action in behalf of the nation. Certainly this attitude was not the dominant one in the Congress before World War II, nor does it seem the dominant one today. It is a phenomenon of the postwar Cold War era and is actually a manifestation of the rally round the flag response. President Nixon complained bitterly in a 1972 campaign speech to relatives of prisoners of war that the national establishment of leaders, presumably including Congress, did not rush to support him when he found it necessary to bomb North Vietnam in May of 1972. This was a response out of the past on the part of a President, and it is something that his predecessors had learned to expect. But this kind of automatic deference is now much weaker.

The experience of Vietnam and particularly the strong feeling in Congress that it was deceived by the President in the Gulf of Tonkin resolution have brought a complete reversal of this habitual deference to the President. But there were other causes as well. Senator Fulbright, a Democrat, openly broke with the President of his own party in a 1965 Senate speech accusing Johnson of a lack of candor as to the real reasons for sending marines to the Dominican Republic.[50] The turning point for many dissenters came in 1965 and 1966 with a full-scale United States intervention in Vietnam, and the dissent has continued to the present day in almost open warfare between a Democratic Congress and a Republican President. However, it is not clear that such warfare provides for constructive congressional contributions to Presidential policy. It may simply strengthen the determination of a President to pursue his policies without congressional support if need be. There is always enough support for existing programs, particularly if troops are in the field, and Congress is usually sufficiently split in its attitudes toward the President and his policies that a President can follow through on the policies that he wants in most instances.

CONCLUSIONS AND PRESCRIPTIONS

The general principle which must guide all prescriptions for the relationships of President and Congress is that those ties are ultimately political rather than legal. The Constitution established separate institutions with shared powers and responsibilities but constitutional principles do not resolve the question of who should prevail in given instances. The beginning of wisdom is the recognition that the two institutions cannot function well if either attempts to overwhelm the other or to act in isolation asserting its autonomy.

A second principle is that it would be a mistake to assert the inherent virtue or merit of Congress over the President or vice versa. People's views on such questions almost always depend upon a judgment about the implications for policy of a given balance; and the views of the same individuals often change over time. The strong protagonists of Presidential power among liberals in recent years have commonly become champions of congressional checks upon the Executive in response to Vietnam, President Nixon, and a growing concern about the national security state. But the day may come for these people to reverse themselves when a President whom they favor sits in the White House and comes into conflict with congressional opponents.

There is no guarantee that the winds of politics will keep President and Congress in any kind of optimal balance of power, however one may define that situation. Congress kept the Presidency from acting boldly to help Britain and her allies against Germany after the outbreak of war in 1939. Congressmen tried to make American foreign policy by holding the Executive to a policy of strict neutrality in the war and impeding American preparations for the eventuality of war. A one-year renewal of the military draft passed in the House by one vote in 1941. This record, of which few in Congress and the country were proud once war began, was a strong contribution to the postwar acquiescence of Congress as a whole to Presidential dominance in development of foreign policy as the Cold War progressed. Anyone who would romanticize the potential contributions of Congress to foreign policymaking should remember the Congress of the 1930s and the strains of witch hunting that stained parts of Congress in the brief reign of Senator Joseph McCarthy in the early 1950s. The State Department was said to be filled with spies and communists and a generation of Foreign Service officers was intimidated. Congress in those years was if anything more virulently and fanatically anti-communist than the Executive and much of the popular fever about the Soviet threat to American security that was stimulated by Presidents Truman and Eisenhower was initiated in efforts to keep Congress under control and establish the right of the Executive to make foreign policy. A generation of Presidential foreign policy aides from Dean Acheson to Dean Rusk firmly believed that the President should make foreign policy because Congress was fundamentally irresponsible in this regard. This was the political background for the gradual assumption of Presidential claims to virtual autonomy in foreign and military policymaking. When President Truman decided not to ask Congress for its approval of his decision to commit American forces to Korea in 1950, liberals, whether scholars, journalists, or members of Congress, applauded.[51] But the result was that the prevailing patterns of politics swung in the direction opposite to that of the 1930s and, as we saw in Chapter 4, the Presidency became supreme in foreign policy. This led to the excesses of assertion of Presidential autonomy seen in the Bay of Pigs, the Dominican intervention, the missile crisis, and, finally and most crucially, Vietnam.

In the aftermath of Vietnam the politics of foreign policymaking have come close to a point of balance between Congress and the President; but that may be a fragile equilibrium. It is a good time, however, to take stock and ask what general prescriptions might be invoked to describe a good state of affairs in the policymaking relationships of President and Congress.

Open Politics Is Better Than Closed

As a general rule the claims that superior policy emerges from decisionmaking by a small, secretive elite group do not bear up well under the inspection of historical cases. The Bay of Pigs and Vietnam intervention are examples in point. One could go back to an analysis of the appeasement policies of Neville Chamberlain in Britain in the 1930s or the disastrous British decision to invade Egypt in 1956 after the Egyptians nationalized the Suez canal. In both cases policy decisions were taken by a small inner group within the British Cabinet without consultation with the rest of the Cabinet, much less the House of Commons.[52] Presidents and prime ministers who are prudent will soon learn that the best resource for firm acceptance of policy is the favorable opinion of those in government whose assent is needed step by step as policy develops. Presidents should look on Congress as a resource by means of which Presidential policies can be given solid footing. But in order for this to be so Presidents must be willing to persuade, to make a public case, and to suffer defeat in some respects. Policy that prevails in this way is incorporated into the prevailing opinion of national leadership and actually strengthens a President when he needs support. Other things being equal it is also likely to be better policy if it has been subjected to a process of debate and criticism.[53] A President in a democracy must be required to go through the exercise of persuading other power holders to accept his views or else we have no democracy. This process of persuasion and bargaining keeps democratic norms alive. If a President is free to do as he wishes, in what sense can we say that we have a democracy, and why will a President be concerned at all about his accountability for what he does?

Therefore, it follows that congressmen have two absolutely essential roles in foreign policymaking. First, they must speak regularly to the President about the merits of his policies. Second, they must require him to justify his policies in an open forum. All judgments about the role of Congress in foreign affairs follow from those two yardsticks. It is perfectly clear that Congress cannot and should not displace the President and make foreign policy, but it must hold him accountable for what he does. This need not be in behalf of public opinion necessarily. Congress can simply exercise its constitutional prerogatives in our representative form of government to hold the President responsible.

It is important that Presidential foreign policymaking be "political" in the sense of taking soundings across a broad spectrum of opinion and that it not just be based upon expert analytic advice about the costs and benefits of policy options given within the Executive. Such advice is unlikely to include analysis of the political costs and benefits. Here one quickly gets a feel for conflicts of preferences and intensity of opinion. If the nation is divided or united so is Congress likely to be. Long-term trouble for a President can thus be avoided if he listens to Congress. Of course, this is not always the case. Lyndon Johnson manipulated the Senate in securing approval of the Gulf of Tonkin resolution, but it is likely that even had he admitted that the attacks on American ships were occasioned by secret American military strikes against North Vietnam the Senate would have supported the resolution. Subsequent defection and eventual repeal of the resolution could not have been predicted. So Congress is not always a sure guide to the future.

But this is simply an argument for so organizing and leading a legislature that it resists the impulse of a ruler to guide the mass of the people to "right" policy decisions. Only Congress can call such arrogance into question. Rule by a single chief executive is an ancient, rather than a modern, idea. Rule with the consent of legislatures is in fact a modern idea despite what is said about the inevitable decline of legislatures.

If we look at the question from the viewpoint of the President, we see that he must learn that whereas he does not need widespread support for every major foreign policy action, he does need it over time for the general direction of his policies. We know the importance of such support when it is withdrawn. The most dramatic examples are those of Woodrow Wilson and the League, Harry Truman and Korea, and Lyndon Johnson and Vietnam. Truman, Eisenhower, and Kennedy had such support for most major policies however, and Nixon presents an instance of mixed support and opposition on very divisive questions but an absence of massive withdrawal of support. When we speak of withdrawal we mean a wave of opinion, whether fast or slow, that cuts across both mass and attentive publics and elite opinion including Congress. The President needs to appeal to all three simultaneously. We do not want to exaggerate the importance of Congress here. A President may be able to appeal directly to mass publics and ignore Congress, but he may also pay a price if he ever needs anything from Congress. The chief argument is that a President should be seeking to maximize his support in all quarters. Viable long-term policy requires it. Therefore, it is simple political expediency for a President to persuade Congress of the rightness of his policies unless he is persuaded that they will be adamant against him. The matching proposition is that Congress should always press the President to explain himself.

It cannot be argued that Congress speaks for public opinion any more than the President does. In fact, what little we know about how congressmen and senators cope with the conflicting currents of opinion in their constituencies shows a strategy similar to the President's. Insofar as there are opinions, and often there are not, they identify with congenial groups and publics that are part of their electoral coalition and seek to stimulate such support. Contrary views are ignored. And of course many groups and voters will forget a disagreement with the representative on one issue if they have general confidence in him or others.[54]

However, it can be argued that the members of Congress are likely to be a microcosm of the broad diversity of public views on any highly salient question. In this sense Congress is full of "representatives." In addition, the members of Congress unconsciously manifest many traits of American political culture, as do members of the Executive, and it is good to air these for examination and criticism. Both President and Congress are responsible to history for facing up to cultural biases and seeking to overcome them. For example, we have a strong liking for asserting our own moral purity in international affairs and seeing the mote only in the eye of the opponent. It is all right for us to have missiles in Turkey because we are peace-loving, but it is not all right for the Soviets to have them in Cuba. We condemn the increased sending of men and materials from north to south in Vietnam in violation of the truce, but we were blind to our massive build up of the same war-making force in the south just before the truce. This kind of moralism is a very deep trait found in publics and elites that, like most culture traits, is not eradicated but recurs and must be beaten down time and time again. Open adversary debate in Congress is one way to do it. Too often Presidents have taken the easy way out and appealed to Congress and public for support in terms of such cultural blindness, and undoubtedly that will happen again. So debate is no panacea.

Above all the principle of political responsibility must be affirmed. The President must be accountable and responsible for what he does and Congress is the best forum and check available. Presidential elections provide very vague mandates, if any. Voter responses on foreign policy questions in elections are likely to be a choice between personalities. Who can best stand up to the Russians? Who can best be trusted with the nuclear trigger? These are important judgments of character and voters are often very discerning. But judgments on personality are not judgments on policy. Here Presidential elections play a minor role and the political process needs supplementing. Unless Congress plays an active role in foreign policy formulation everything is left to a closed Executive and the preferences of a relatively small number of people. Unless Congress plays a role there is no way to engage the interest and participation of well-informed attentive publics and elites outside government. There must be a discussion process for them to focus on.

The great danger that must be prevented is one that may already be upon us. That is a kind of Presidential constitutional dictatorship in which the President can, by crisis management and skillful use of the media, mobilize public support to short circuit any checks at the elite level at all and govern with free rein. If Administration leaders feel they know what the realities are and doubt the capacities of publics and congressmen to develop the same sophistication, there is a very strong impulse to resort to tricks and devices to gain autonomy. The illusion of democracy is maintained because the electorate believes that their leaders are articulating public preferences, whereas leaders are manipulating information and symbols to force their preferences on the citizenry. This is an easy alternative in a crisis world but it violates democratic values.

PRESIDENTIAL PREROGATIVE

The occasion may arise in which the crisis facing the nation is so great that the President may feel that he has to take extra-constitutional action in order to protect the very existence of the Constitution and the nation. The actions of Abraham Lincoln in 1861 and Franklin Roosevelt in 1940 were two such occasions. Lincoln was faced with a rebellion backed by military force and action. He felt that he had to act in order to put the Union on a war footing and before it is was possible to ask the approval of Congress. Therefore he initiated a number of measures such as suspension of habeas corpus, proclamation of martial law behind the military lines, and the seizure of property of rebel sympathizers. However, he reported all of these actions to the Congress and the public and spoke of their extraordinary nature. He also asked for support for these actions. No claim was made that the President had any right to so act except in the most serious emergency which threatened the nation itself.[55] Roosevelt faced a situation in 1940 in which Britain was about to fall to a German invader and the Congress would not permit direct American aid to Britain because it violated neutrality laws. Yet he knew the fall of Britain would create a serious military security problem for the United States. Under this kind of pressure he conceived a plan to loan destroyers to Britain under an Executive agreement, rather than a treaty, which would require Senate ratification. He secured an opinion from his attorney general that such action was constitutional because it was a one-time-only agreement rather than a treaty. Like

Lincoln, he was acting for what he thought was the greater good of the Constitution and the nation. However, like Lincoln, he kept his political fences mended all along the way. He thought of acting in this way at all only after the Republican candidates for President and Vice President indicated that they would raise no objections; and he consulted with congressional leaders at every step. Roosevelt also announced his actions publicly and called for general support, which he received. This was a politically feasible way to aid Britain without violating the congressional adherence to the neutrality laws.[56]

The general principle here is that if a President faces such an acute emergency he may have to act in the name of the nation even if he is unsure of his constitutional right to do so. But he should act openly and ask Congress and the public for support. Lincoln and Roosevelt adhered to this general rule. Compare this with President Nixon's illegal and secret bombing in Cambodia in 1969 and 1970, contrary to what he told the American public and without the knowledge of Congress or the relevant committees. The Nixon official after-the-facts justification was that the Cambodian government supported but could not publicly admit the bombing for fear of having to ask the United States to stop it, for domestic political reasons. Therefore no one, except the North Vietnamese and the Cambodian people, should know of it. This was a flimsy justification. The United States was neither at war nor allied with Cambodia. It was never clear that the bombing of North Vietnamese sanctuaries in Cambodia had any salutary effect on the ending of the war in South Vietnam. In this instance the President was simply asserting a prerogative to wage war secretly without consulting either Congress or the public; and there is no such right. It is clear that the real reasons for the President's order of secrecy in the matter was fear of stirring up antiwar sentiment at home caused by concern about his own political position.[57]

The President Has No Right to Start a War

The American founding fathers were clear in their debates that a war could be begun constitutionally only by the joint concurrence of President and Congress. They construed the title Commander-in-Chief to mean simply director of the armed forces during wartime. There was no mention of any implicit prerogative of Presidential power to order troops into combat without the assent of Congress. When Presidents feel that they must act to assert their powers in an unconstitutional way in national emergencies it is not valid for them to claim that they are exercising an implicit prerogative given them by the Constitution. Unfortunately, Presidents since Truman have at times asserted such a prerogative. Truman claimed the right to involve the nation in a police action in Korea without a congressional resolution of support or a declaration of war. Eisenhower asked Congress on several occasions for resolutions of support for military action should it become necessary in a future emergency; but this was seen by him as politically prudent and simply a confirmation of his inherent war powers. President Johnson firmly believed that the President had the right and the power to safeguard the national interest and security as he saw it by taking unilateral military action, which he did in Vietnam in 1965. And President Nixon carried these claims to an extreme degree by his assertion that he had a right to continue military action in Indochina after the conclusion of a truce agreement with the North Vietnamese if he judged it necessary to the preservation of American war aims. This was said in defiance of congressional statements that the American military role in Indochina had ended. All of these claims are wrong, historically and constitutionally. They refer to Presidential prerogatives that do not exist except in the limited sense of those rights invoked by Lincoln and Roosevelt in national emergencies.[58]

The National Security State as the Root of the Problem

The chief cause of this aggrandizement of Presidential power has been the post World War II American commitment to keeping the peace of the world through the use of American military power. We have been almost continuously at war somewhere in the world since 1950—in the name of peace. Since the Cold War began successive Presidents have worked in an atmosphere, largely self-induced, of intense concern for the national security. This has meant a bias toward the use of military power and an emphasis upon secrecy within the Executive. This simultaneous commitment to a world wide policeman's role for the nation and to tight secrecy and rule by a small executive group at home has put great strain upon the principle of constitutional sharing of powers and the possibilities of open government.

The assertion of Presidential prerogatives to do what seems best for the nation is inevitable in such a situation. There is not much difference between such claims and the 1970–1971 actions of President Nixon—wiretapping members of the National Security Council staff in a search for news leaks, wiretapping the telephones of reporters, developing an elaborate plan for surveillance, burglary, and interception of communications against so-called disruptive forces who were seen as threats to internal security. Presidential war power claims, which had been directed toward action abroad, were now being turned and used against domestic dissenters at home. It was not much different from President Truman claiming the right to seize the steel mills in order to prevent a strike during the Korean War in the name of national security except that Nixon, unlike Truman, acted in secrecy.[59]

The best cure for exaggerated claims to Presidential power would be an end to the Cold War and an international politics of continuous crisis and confrontation. Although détente with China and the U.S.S.R. did seem to have eased things in 1974 one could not be certain what the future holds. Certainly new kinds of policy problems are emerging such as world economic problems, foreign trade, and energy shortages that are not susceptible to military solutions or Presidential assertion of prerogative. Rather, such problems require diplomacy and a great deal of political persuasion by the leaders of nations, of each other, and of their peoples and governments, including legislatures. This is the most promising development away from a politics of plebiscitary leadership.

The world of power politics, however, has not gone away. There will be conflicts between nations that will require national strength and resolve and perhaps even military capability as a bargaining resource. The task ahead is for democracies like the United States to learn to live with power politics without turning national security into a crusade. The new conditions require respect for democratic politics and shared powers of government on the part of political executives. And legislatures in turn must learn that their principal role is not to make foreign policy but to ensure that executives are pursuing generally accepted goals and that the means to action, which are inseparable from ends, are continually scrutinized and debated.

POWER TO CHECK A PRESIDENT

There is little that a President's associates and subordinates within the Executive branch can do to check him if he acts in ways they feel are contrary to the Constitution, law, or good policy. But Congress can so act to check a President if it has the will. We are not entirely dependent upon the good character of a President for guarantees against the abuse of power. However, the Constitution does not enforce itself even if we supposedly do have a government of laws. If a President chooses to defy the Congress and the Constitution in his assertion of Executive prerogatives to use military force, send troops, conduct Executive agreements, police internal security, or whatever else, the only effective checks upon his actions must come from the willingness of Congress to act to restrain him; whether by resolutions with the force of law, budgetary restraints, statutes, or impeachment. Such action is never automatic but depends upon favorable political conditions. The situation is currently favorable toward the use of such restraints but it may not always remain so. This leaves us with a dilemma that is inherent in the structure of the Constitution. The President has institutional powers that he can exercise in defiance of those who are not willing to oppose him. This means that there are no constitutional or organizational mechanisms that can ensure a good balance of power between President and Congress. These questions must be left to the uncertainties of politics.

At the conclusion of Chapter 4 we resolved that the President is very much dependent upon the quality of world views among different circles of national leadership. If that thought is sophisticated in its view of the world and sensitive to ethical values, a President is likely to be responsive to these views. Likewise, if dominant elite views and values are crude, nationalistic, and arrogant he is likely to manifest this fact. The same propositions apply to the effects of politics upon the exercise of Presidential powers. If democratic politics pursue phantoms of national pride and power and seek scapegoats for national mistakes Presidents will use their power wrongly without restraint. But if democratic politics accepts the world as an imperfect place which can only be incrementally changed and accepts that America must preserve its power but not at the expense of its morality and without claims to being a nation of special virtue then Presidential powers are likely to be moderately used within a field of restraints.

In the final analysis the best balance between President and Congress comes when each respects the other. We need Presidents who respect the Constitution and value democratic politics as the most effective means of persuading others to follow them. We need congressional politicians who will not frustrate the efforts of such Presidents for political ends of their own but will realize that the best politics is open discussion, debate, and resolution of disagreement, which permits the President to lead but requires him to lead democratically.

6
Politics
and
Policy

THE TWO PRESIDENCIES

We really have two Presidencies rather than one in the sense that the conditions that make for Presidential dominance in foreign affairs are not present in domestic policy matters.[1] A President cannot invoke his office as the chief symbol of the nation in a rally round the flag way in a domestic crisis to support decisive action without dividing the society. He lacks the constitutional and Executive power to act independently of Congress in domestic affairs that he has in foreign affairs. Furthermore, the elite ideological consensus of Cold War perspectives that has been predominant in Congress is certainly not present for domestic matters. Whether liberal or conservative, the President is likely to face a splintering of views on domestic problems and their solutions. In short, pluralist politics intrudes into the domestic arena to a much greater extent.

Domestic Malaise

We expect and welcome a process of conflict and its resolution through politics. But the critical question about domestic politics and policymaking is whether the President has enough political resources to lead at all. We may be going from one extreme to the other as we move from foreign to domestic matters, from dictatorship to impotence. There seems to be a serious lag in American society and its polity between the time that social problems reach a critical stage and the time that a policy response is developed, agreed upon, and implemented. The United States was the last of the Western industrial nations to enact minimal social welfare programs in response to the costs of industrialism: social security, publicly supported medical care, and minimum wage laws came late, and we still lag behind in other areas such as public transportation in comparison to the European democracies. We have been incredibly slow to give social justice to the heirs of slavery, and at this writing there are over 5 million officially poor families in the nation with no solution to that problem in sight. Furthermore, we seem to have a prolonged malaise of the institutions that deliver services to our citizens. Educational bureaucracy is tradition bound; health care services are a tangled mess; our transit systems are pathetically inadequate for our spreading cities; pollution threatens our health; we have a serious national shortage of housing, especially for low income groups; and finally, our state and local governments, with a few exceptions, seem to be bureaucratic and unresponsive to the real needs of citizens. Something is wrong with our society and we are not at all sure what it is. For the first time in their lives many Americans are beginning to doubt whether the nation can solve its problems. To cease to believe this is to cease to be an American in a fundamental sense.

One would not necessarily expect the President to find solutions for all these problems. Nevertheless, such solutions must come through politics in a free, pluralistic society, and there does seem to be a problem of mobilizing enough political resources to meet these unsolved difficulties. Clearly the Presidency is of key importance here. How do we judge that it is serving us? We may find that politics or the structure of government is not the problem but that our ills go much deeper, into the very values of our society. In order to evaluate the numerous proposals for reform that are current, such as the reorganization of Congress or the ideological realignment of the political parties, we must go into the fundamental causes of our dilemma.

Each President enters office with three political resources: a general set of ideological values and goals, more or less well defined, an electoral base of social groups, and a greater or lesser electoral victory. He must use these resources as fully as he can in leading public opinion and Congress. We want to consider each in turn and develop a comprehensive picture of the power of the domestic Presidency insofar as it is grounded in politics.

THE AMERICAN LIBERAL IDEOLOGY

Americans believe in equality of opportunity but not equality of condition. We venerate the Horatio Alger story but also supported the New Deal that called on government to cope with a depression brought on by a generation of Horatio Alger heroes in business and industry. According to Louis Hartz there is an ideology that permeates the culture that keeps individualism on the one hand and equality on the other in a state of uneasy balance. This ideology, which we might call "liberalism," emerged out of the American historical experience as beliefs brought from England were adapted to that experience.[2] The expanding American frontier was hospitable to the ideas of English middle-class liberalism but not to either hierarchical conservatism or radical egalitarianism. The social conditions necessary to support an aristocracy and European conservatism emphasizing rank, title, and noblesse oblige or a proletariat that might be converted to revolutionary ideologies simply did not exist. All men had hope that they too might rise. The result is that our conservatives are optimists and rationalists who hope for a productive economy and believe in the free enterprise system to create opportunities for all. And our progressives are reformers who accept capitalism and seek governmental action and social reform only against its excesses. Both operate within a basically liberal framework.

Politics Within the American Idelogy

Several consequences for American politics and government follow. In the first place, political conflicts are both horizontal and vertical. They are horizontal because of the absence of deep ideological cleavages between groups in the population such as social classes. Of course, the facts of material abundance, a frontier for settlement, and high social mobility are congruent with liberal ideology. As a result American politics have historically been about conflicts between sections of the country and social and economic groups on horizontal lines. However, a vertical division and potential conflict between "haves" and "have nots" were also present in the ideology itself as well as in social conditions. It is the tension between individualism and equality. Satisfied groups have invoked the conservative half of the national ideology to support minimal action by government in behalf of social reform. And dissident groups have evoked the progressive half of this cluster of beliefs to call for action in the name of equality, or at least equality of opportunity. The groups on either side of the vertical alignment have changed over time as has the actual degree of conflict over such questions, but the theme has always been present as an overlay of our horizontal conflicts. It is implicit in the ambiguity of liberalism.

Second, there has been an absence of higher normative standards of community to appeal to for the resolution of either horizontal or vertical conflicts. This is inherent in an ideology of individualistic egoism. One could trace the dilemma back to the political theory of John Locke, the first articulator of Anglo-American liberalism. The only "public interest" in Locke's ideal polity is the sum of the individual interests of all its citizens. The notion of government is essentially negative. It must safeguard the rights of individuals, for higher standards of choice are lacking when these rights conflict. This is a very real problem for contemporary American society. We do not know where to turn when pollution conflicts with the need for energy supplies or when urban sprawl cannot be corrected because of the invocation of property rights. Political decision makers lack the resource of implicit cultural beliefs about the priority of values in a community seen as a "good society." Bargaining thereby replaces judgment, and we idealize the politics of pluralism. We do employ a vocabulary that admits of a "public interest" against "special interests" but these terms lack definition. The Presidency has been the institution of our national polity that is most often seen as serving the public interest as opposed to the particularism of Congress. However, the Presidency is in fact allied with some group coalitions rather than others and whether this represents the public interest or not depends upon one's views of that portion of values of the liberal ideology that is being served by such representation.

Third, political leaders, and especially Presidents, have to take account of coalitions of interests and social groups as they lead. However, such a cluster will not be sufficient to define a Presidency for candidates and incumbents. The very act of becoming President causes the incumbent and those who help him to try to define a larger sense of purpose in line with national ideas. We think of ourselves as pragmatists, but there is a strong rhetorical strain in our political thinking that is heavily infused with nationalist sentiments. This sense of national purpose is a very strong factor in the motivation of Presidents, however, and is not just rhetoric. Presidents are likely to identify themselves with and invoke one-half of the national liberal ideology as a basis of political appeals to a diverse coalition and the development of programs. Such idealism is obviously tempered by the realities of group politics, but these two factors usually reinforce each other. In the twentieth century there has been a clear competition between conservative and progressive conceptions of Presidential purpose that has been a very important but not the sole element in the competition of the two major parties.

Presidents of Action and Restraint

The liberal ideology sets the context for this competition and provides resources and constraints for Presidents. The progressive reformers see the logic of American history as favoring them. Each such President wishes to push the spiral of reform one step further. They invoke the potential resources of the office much more fully than the conservative Presidents because they want action. Publics must be mobilized, the gap between ideal and reality must be dramatized, legislators must be persuaded, and the bureaucracy must be galvanized to act. Progressive Presidents seek to be heroes; they want to walk in the footsteps of the two Roosevelts and Wilson. They have a clear and explicit model of Presidential power and skill that they invoke as a litany.

The spiral of change does favor the progressives in the sense that the increasing role of the federal government in domestic and foreign policy, economic management, and social reform cannot be avoided. But in that fact there is an irony. American progressives have spent great energies trying to win popular and elite support for economic and social programs that were introduced much more easily and earlier in the other great democracies. Americans are behind—in management of the economy, in provision of basic social services like health. Only in public education do we lead the other democracies in investment, and this is because of our ethic of equality of opportunity. But that very ethic, which is different from belief in equality of condition, often gives us a blind spot to the real social and economic inequalities.

Coupled with this ethic has been a very real fear of government and centralized public power among Americans. Progressives are always on the defensive in their efforts to extend the reach and power of government, particularly the federal government. We are an individualistic people who like to build protective islands around ourselves and defy others to enter our space. Government is seen as antithetical to the liberty of the individual. Therefore, the progressive who would use government to promote equality must take great pains to prove that such action will not harm liberty and is in fact a pursuit of liberty. For example social security was presented in this way by Franklin Roosevelt, not as a welfare state action but as the government helping people to help themselves, a new version of an old self-reliance. The result is that American progressives and their Presidents have in fact been cautious and incrementalist in what they have pressed on the nation. A careful look at the content of the reform ideologies of the Progressive movement, the New Freedom, the New Deal, and the Great Society makes clear that the stated goal is to find ways to return the society to a time when all individuals were free.[3] The great reformers in modern American life have not been radicals or collectivists but individualists who have wished to use limited governmental power to protect the individual citizen against concentrations of private power.

The conservative tradition in the Presidency makes fewer demands on government. The Presidents of consolidation and restraint are required almost by definition to praise not the role of government in society but the dynamism of the private sector. Conservative Presidents are placed in the position of being almost nonpolitical. They have sought to equate existing conditions with American ideals and to manage things rather than create new ideas or programs.

One reason for this is that conservative ideology in America has been far too rigid, far too much in defense of an idealized laissez faire that never existed, far too fearful of governmental power. This is in contrast to conservatism in either Britain or Canada where established conservative parties and leaders are identified with the exercise of state power and the rule of establishments and governing classes.[4] The English Tory believes that he has a God-given right to govern and a natural ability to do so. He speaks from the long experience of a governing class that has changed its social composition across time but has never lost the will to power. He also speaks from an aristocratic tradition of noblesse oblige and concern for community that is older than the laissez faire, individualist ideology of nineteenth-century liberalism, which contested the power of government that is more characteristic of American conservatism. The English Tory will use the power of government in behalf of community and the needs of people so long as social inequality is not threatened. The American conservative is more like the English nineteenth-century liberal. He is a middle-class man who exalts the private sphere and fears government. In our society many working-class people are middle class in their ideology and conservative in their politics.

Thus the modern conservative Presidents have lacked the sense of public purpose and the tradition of enjoyment of the skill of power and political leadership that the progressives have had. This is unfortunate because they play an absolutely essential role in the cycles of political competition. It has been the acceptance of reform measures by conservative Presidents in periods of consolidation that has legitimized those programs for many Americans. The conservative impulse to social unity can reunite the nation after the divisiveness of reform periods. The greater sense of restraint of conservative Presidents has sometimes disentangled the nation from foreign problems into which the activism of progressive Administrations had involved it.

One of the strong and distinguishing marks of conservatives is that they like to make things work. Progressives like to create things but conservatives are more interested in their functioning well. The mark of a truly sophisticated conservative Administration would be its ability to take programs developed by progressives in all their creative, inchoate state of incompleteness and make them work administratively. This was a great challenge to the Nixon Administration in the aftermath of the Great Society, which put many programs into operation but gave very little thought to their organizational and social feasibility.

The nation badly needs a sophisticated, politically skillful conservative tradition in the Presidency to make constructive use of the waiting periods between the cycles of reform. This tradition will always have as its characteristic limitation an insensitivity to the development of new social problem areas, and eventually it will be displaced by a new period of movement. This is true of most conservative parties and leaders in the democracies. The conspicuous deficiency of leaders of the American conservative tradition has been their lack of public purpose and political skill. They have not had the tradition of a governing class to draw on.

Thus we do not have a fully complementary fit between tendencies in political competition. The progressive Presidents can make greater use of the resources of the Presidential office, but they are held back by popular beliefs. They must be heroic incrementalists. The conservative Presidents have been able to make political capital from the perceived excesses of progressive Presidents, but they have not been able to fully develop a tradition of will and skill for themselves in the Presidential office.

However, for better or for worse, the result of this competitive pattern is a politics and policymaking process hovering around the middle of the ideological spectrum, though antagonists will seek to move the center slightly to the right or left. In fact, the ideological center always keeps moving to the left because government must respond to the conditions generated by an incredibly dynamic society. The crucial question is whether the response is ever sufficient to cope with the problems.

The Public and Its Beliefs

Presidents draw ideological resources from the culture and are constrained in different ways by the same source. But a culture is only embodied in people. Can it be shown that the American people respond to politics and policy in part in terms of a national ideology?

It would be my contention that almost all Americans do so at all social levels, from elite to mass, and that these predispositions are inter-laced in complex ways with all the other factors that go into politics, such as groups, regions, occupations, religion, ethnicity, and much else.

It has been the conventional wisdom of political science that the great majority of Americans do not think about politics in ideological terms but rather in terms of more immediate identification and in-terests.[5] This argument has been far overstated. First, the voting studies on which such conclusions were based were conducted dur-ing the 1950s when American Presidential politics was upon dead center and there were few divisive issues. Second, the conceptions of ideology used in such studies were overly intellectual and not put in terms of the frames of reference of citizens. Third, subsequent voting studies make very clear that most people can think about politics in ideological terms, which they themselves set, and that these ideas are a clear link between citizens and their political lead-ers. Greater divisiveness of issues in a changing society since 1960 have shown citizens responding in kind. Popular ideologies have been sharpened.

Furthermore, there is evidence that the national liberal ideology is the dominant world view among Americans. Two national surveys taken during the 1964 Presidential election found that a majority of Americans are "conservative" at the ideological level but accept "practical liberalism" at the programmatic level.[6] The surveys and other data cited by the authors show overwhelming popular support for the Great Society social programs from 1964 to 1966, and the 1964 studies find that two-thirds of the sample were "operational liberals" in this sense.[7] However, when questions concerned ideolog-ical matters such as the proper role of government in relation to individual freedom were asked in abstract form, half of the respon-dents took conservative positions and another third were in the mid-dle of the road.[8] For example, a great majority felt that the poor were to blame for their own condition. A great many operational liberals are also ideological conservatives. Very few ideological conservatives are in fact operational conservatives. This has profound implications for American politics. It means that the trend of progressive pro-grams extending from the New Deal to the Great Society has had insecure ideological foundations. Only 16 percent of the sample were both ideological and operational liberals, a very limited base for a sustained reform politics.[9] So long as three-fourths of the public be-lieve that any able-bodied person can find a job and earn a living, there simply is no solid support for a "war on poverty" or for reforms of the welfare system in the direction of a guaranteed minimum income.

It is clear that operational liberals will support government actions to meet their own personal economic needs, whereas operational conservatives are much more likely to be ideological conservatives who are concerned about principles. The match between ideological and operational consistency is much higher as the level of education and social status rises. Once again this suggests that whereas the great majority of the people are operational liberals in regard to their own interests as they perceive them, they are likely to be suspicious of any program that seems to be outside those interests and to run counter to the ideological conservatism that they also embrace. In this sense the New Deal, which benefited millions of people in ways they could see in their personal lives, surely had deeper popular support than the Great Society, so much of which was directed toward helping the minorities of our society. Also, such operational liberal programs seem to be accepted by publics after the fact, once they have been in operation. If they seem to conflict with conservative ideology, there are difficulties in gaining initial support. This ambivalence about reform can be seen in regard to the responses on civil rights where a majority supported the legislation of 1964 but were fearful of moving too far, too fast.[10] One could see this as a case of ideological liberalism and operational conservatism in tandem, and that may be the case on this issue. Halley Cantril and Lloyd Free have only caught this mix of predispositions at one period, and surely there are changes and different combinations over time.

The conclusion for political leadership is clear. The national ideology of liberalism is ambivalent about the tensions between individualism and equality, so that although this provides resources it also sets constraints upon leaders. For example, a President who articulates a progressive position in both ideological and operational terms will often find great public ambivalence if such ideas seem to threaten popular understanding of what the society is about. Such a President must be cautious and patient, spelling out to people the means he proposes to use to attain his goals and showing these goals to be realistic and not inconsistent with their basic ideological assumptions. On the other side, a conservative President may be able to win elections by talking a good ideological game as a conservative but, if he wishes to survive, he dare not turn away from liberal programs. Free and Cantril conclude that Democratic leaders are in the programmatic mainstreams of American history but lack ideological legitimacy. Republican leaders, on the other hand, have an acceptable political philosophy but no plausible programs in the face of the operational liberal expectations of the majority of the people.

Cantril and Free find this situation incongruous and call for a restatement of American ideology more in conformity with operational, pragmatic liberalism, which is the reality.[11] We will return to this theme again. But clearly this is not an easy thing to do in the face of a deeply rooted set of cultural beliefs.

Political Coalitions

This may seem to be an overly ideological interpretation of American politics, but it is intended to be selective and does not discount the fact that the basic structure of American competitive party politics is not organized along ideological lines. American parties as organizations have been decentralized as state parties along the lines of the federal system and dominated by cadres with predominantly local orientations since the time of Andrew Jackson. They have been vehicles of integration and representation at the national level and umbrella organizations that have helped to contain the sectional, religious, ethnic, and class conflicts.[12] These functions and the diversity of social bases in each party have precluded clear ideological alignments and prevented parties as such from being oriented toward linking ideology and public policy. The very fact that the key question in American politics and government has been over the proper degree of "minimum government intervention" because of the national ideology precludes parties from developing sharp ideological distinctions.[13]

One must not stop there as is so often done. The ideological impetus in American politics and government is injected by Presidential core parties, which are made up of floating bands of Presidential candidates, intellectuals and academics, journalists, and political activists throughout the country. These are people who seek to capture a national party organization in behalf of a Presidential candidate and then win an election and staff and run the Executive at the top level. Their primary motivations are more likely to be ideological in the sense of having broad policy objectives for the nation. This has been the national pattern certainly since the New Deal, and all trends favor its strengthening.

One cannot precisely define the characteristics or limits of a core Presidential party. When a party does not control the White House the Presidential wing is less important, and the national party is dominated by congressional and state and local leaders. When it controls the White House the Presidential core party staffs the upper reaches of the Executive. The Nixon Administration, for example, has tended to draw its top officials from the West and the South, from business and the professions, with less representation of academics, particularly from Eastern universities, or of minorities or the labor movement. Its members reflect a conscious effort to move the axis of the Republican party away from the "Eastern Establishment" and toward new national elites of new wealth and Western and Southern perspectives. This is an operation heavily infused with conservative ideology.

Since Dwight Eisenhower entered politics in 1952 the Presidential candidates of both parties have increasingly created temporary national organizations to elect themselves independently of the formal national and state parties. The trend was dramatic in 1972 when the Committee to Reelect the President (Nixon) was run by former White House staff members, some of whom had never run for office and who had spent no time or money helping to elect Republican candidates to Congress or any other office. The McGovern nomination was secured by a virtual takeover of state party organizations by a new generation of activists.

This heightening of the trend illustrates the problem that ideological Presidential partisans may become far too divorced not only from the regular party organization but from the popular bases of the party that the regulars represent better than they do. The Goldwater or McGovern candidacies illustrate this myopia of the activist.

However, this trend of Presidential parties powered by ideological activists is likely to increase. The long-term trend seems to be toward the weakening of party bonds even with a countertrend toward the nationalization of party politics in terms of issues. A politics of public relations is displacing the politics of organization.[14]

The trend of the sixties was very striking in the increase of the number of Independents, particularly among youth, and the widespread popular disaffection from party identification and labels.[15] Much of this was the revulsion of the morally sensitive against the war in Vietnam, a revulsion from which neither party could benefit. But it is not clear those voters will ever embrace a party.

Despite this, it does not follow that Presidential candidates can be elected by virtue of ideological appeals. There is no potential for such a possibility in the electorate. The disaffection of blue-collar Democrats from Senator McGovern because he was perceived as too radical on questions of welfare and race and the high support that blacks gave him because they saw the national Democrats as the party of civil rights illustrate this dilemma. It is a continuing dilemma for future Democratic Presidential candidates. They need both groups. They must face the question whether to seek to patch together the old coalition of labor, blacks, and Southern Populists and combine it with new constituencies among the ideological upper-middle and professional strata. The incongruousness of Edward Kennedy and George Wallace on the same platform in Alabama in the summer of 1973 is a sign of the seriousness with which such a goal is taken.

The point for our purposes is that Presidential parties, electoral appeals, and subsequent public policy efforts rest upon bases of electoral resources in which ideological and group interest appeals are intertwined in the most complex and subtle ways. A President needs both kinds of support and he needs it fused in reinforcing ways as much as possible. But there will be inherent conflicts in those bases between groups that are a part of a constituency. For example, it is not at all clear that decisive action can be taken by a future Democratic President to increase racial integration in Northern suburbs without a revolt of white working-class supporters of that party. At least this is a great challenge in policy invention that will join effectiveness of program and political acceptability. However, the success of President Nixon in wooing such working people into his orbit by appeals to patriotism in war, law and order, and attacks on welfare is not likely to be long lasting because of the economic policies of his government, which seem to have hurt working people in much more direct ways.

There simply is no mass base for an ideological competition between two national parties that could provide unambiguous mandates for victorious Presidents as party leaders. Ideology and interest are both crucial dimensions of Presidential appeals and support, and the task of putting together such a majority coalition as a basis for governing is very difficult. It is important to understand that the formulation of public policy in the White House is heavily and continually influenced by such considerations. A President must always have his diverse, conflicting, and yet joined constituencies in mind and be seeking formulas in public policy that will strengthen him with those constituencies.

CYCLES OF GOVERNMENT

The third political resource of a President is the type of electoral victory that brings him into power. In this century there have been three complete cycles of the rise and fall of reform politics. Each cycle contains three types of Presidencies according to a different phase of the cycle. Each type of Presidency reflects different political conditions in the country, and therefore Presidential goals, styles, and strategy are likely to differ accordingly. Table 2 gives the three cycles with identification of types within them.

The cycle normally has three stages: a period of preparation; a burst of activism and reform; a time of reaction against the previous stage and therefore of consolidation and conservation. During the

Table 2 TWENTIETH-CENTURY PRESIDENTIAL CYCLES

I PREPARATION	II ACHIEVEMENT OF REFORM	III CONSOLIDATION
Theodore Roosevelt	Woodrow Wilson	Warren Harding
William Howard Taft		Calvin Coolidge
		Herbert Hoover
	Franklin Roosevelt	Dwight Eisenhower
	Harry Truman	
John Kennedy	Lyndon Johnson	Richard Nixon

third period new social problems emerge to which the Administration is insensitive and the cycle begins again. However, even though the party of reform wins the Presidency in the first stage of the cycle, it usually lacks the political resources to carry through the reforms it seeks. In this sense the Presidencies of Theodore Roosevelt and John Kennedy had much in common as periods of education and articulation from which Wilson and Johnson respectively benefited.

There was no preparatory period before FDR because the suddenness of the Depression made it unnecessary. Taft and Truman were special cases. Taft was in the shadow of Theodore Roosevelt and suffered from the fact. Truman caught the tail end of the New Deal after the momentum was gone, but he was also a premature harbinger of the New Frontier and Great Society.

One can draw no firm conclusions from the model about whether the normal or dominant pattern of American politics is progressive or conservative. But clearly the ultimate direction is progressive, or perhaps one should say activist and interventionist however belated in accomplishment.

The impetus that brings a President of the first type to office builds up out of a variety of social demands during an Administration of the third type. The Populist and Progressive movements developed during the Presidency of William McKinley. Senator Robert La Follette, running for President as leader of the Progressive party in 1924, and even Al Smith in 1928 articulated much of the social discontent of the time. Much of what eventually became the legislative programs of the New Deal was germinating among progressives in Congress during the 1920s. Adlai Stevenson as Presidential candidate and party leader gave John Kennedy the themes for his New Frontier during the fifties. And almost all of the social programs of the Great Society were incubating in Congress during the Eisenhower years.

Eventually enough social discontents rise to visibility to cast an Administration from office, but the election mandate of the President of the first stage is incomplete and uncertain. Large supporting congressional majorities do not exist and the legislative accomplishments of the Administration will be modest. There will be something of a standoff with Congress and publics will seem to provide no great support for either side. Presidents during this phase would like to be heroic reformers and their public rhetoric is likely to have such a ring. But their chief contribution is to articulate issues for later resolution. Of course, a President of the first type can move into the second phase with a new electoral majority, as John Kennedy might have done after 1964 had he lived and been reelected.

The second phase begins after an overwhelming election victory for the party of reform. Even here the popular mandate is very general, but there is clearly widespread support for governmental action in a number of areas. Large congressional majorities favorable to action are elected, and the hallmark of the Administration is a great burst of legislative victories, drawing upon the ideas developed during the periods of incubation and articulation. However this period of legislative achievement is relatively brief, often lasting only two years. The electoral coalition that elected the Administration begins to crack as demands are met. Moral fervor lapses. Congress senses the new wind and rebels.

The very activism of the government in the second phase eventually does it in. Often, it is due to a combination of attempting to achieve social change through government more rapidly than is possible and the precipitation of a war out of activism. All four wars in this century have been begun by Democratic Administrations and, with the exception of World War II, the political fruits have gone to the Republicans. After a time voters want a rest and stability. They do not necessarily want inaction or lack of strength in government. Certainly a strong popular theme in the elections of Eisenhower and Nixon was the hope of a strong President who might impose order in a reaction against dissension, conflict, and activist policies that were failing and yet were being continued.

The election mandate that opens up the third period is therefore primarily negative, and the people who lead such a government are consolidators rather than innovators. The Administration comes into office with few well-formulated policies because in opposition, as a latent Presidential party, it has been opposing rather than inventing. This is a fundamental difference between Republicans and Democrats. The latter are continually at work in opposition developing a new program because they firmly believe that history is on their side. The Republicans, on the other hand, believe that virtue is on their side. They merely need to *be* in office in order to be justified.

The legislative achievements during the third phase are modest even when the Congress is supportive because the goals are limited.

Presidential style is much less engaged in seeking support through-out the government. Progressive Presidents need support—from congressmen, from bureaucrats, and from the press—in order to make the kinds of bargains out of which policy is made. Conservative Presidents want less, need less support, and therefore need to reach out to bargain less. They create more autonomous and separate Presidencies. This type of Administration usually sets limits, consolidates, and legitimizes the achievements of the previous period of reform. However, in time they lose an election because they do not develop solutions for new problems nor meet new demands. They are prisoners of their very coalition of political resources.

The following section is an analysis of the most recent cycle from the last years of the Eisenhower Presidency until the present. Voting trends, issue development, and policy enactment are linked together in terms of the general propositions about American ideology, party competition, and Presidential perspectives developed earlier.

Eisenhower to Nixon: A Full Cycle

In 1956 President Eisenhower soundly defeated Adlai Stevenson on the theme of "peace and prosperity." Stevenson attempted to arouse voters to national deficiencies in education and health and the general quality of the society requiring a federal role but the appeals aroused little response in a time of calm and affluence. Studies of voters found that 10 percent at most viewed the parties in ideological terms, that parties were not seen as differing greatly on issues, and that links between issue preference and party choice were weak.[16] The election was interpreted as a mark of satisfaction providing no mandate beyond the status quo.

However, after that election two simultaneous trends began that have continued until the present. First, voters increasingly perceived the two parties as taking distinctly different issue positions in ways that might be characterized as liberal for the Democrats and conservative for the Republicans. Second, there was an increase of public support, up to majority levels in the mid-sixties, for most of the leading domestic reform policies of the day, such as federal aid to education, medicare, and civil rights measures. These trends continued after 1968 but the turmoil of war, social disorder, and racial conflict introduced new concerns among the voters that were stronger than the earlier progressive trend and moved the polity in a stabilizing direction.

Surveys show that from 1956 to 1968 the Democrats were increasingly seen as the more liberal party on domestic social questions.[17]

In 1960, when John Kennedy was elected President, the link between party and issues was only a bit clearer in the public mind than in 1956. But the 1964 election was a critical one in driving home this point because the Republican Presidential candidate, Barry Goldwater, made it an ideological contest. By so doing he stimulated ideological thinking in the electorate though not in his favor. By 1968 a majority of voters, both Democratic and Republican, saw the Democratic party as the liberal party.[18] The most striking change had occurred on racial issues. In 1956 the voters did not see any difference between the parties on civil rights questions, but by 1968 the Democrats were clearly seen as more liberal, not in terms of an ideological label but because of issue positions identified with the party.

This change in public attitudes cannot be attributed to an increase in young people in the electorate because the young shared only a slightly greater ideological awareness than others. There were group differences. Southern whites did not change much in their perceptions except to identify Democrats with civil rights action. And blacks changed drastically in their increased perception of the Democrats as liberal on civil rights.

The most plausible explanation for these changes is that the historical events and the political campaigns from 1958 to 1964 presented politics to the voter in terms of alternatives between liberal and conservative issue positions and the voters responded in kind.[19] This was the chief difference from the fifties, in which leaders did not present issues in polar terms nor had many of the problems emerged strikingly. But the dramatic events and increasing problems of the sixties—race, poverty, education, and health—all pushed politics in a more ideologically competitive direction. The social environment was ripe for new definitions of problems, but the more important fact is that Presidential candidates from 1960 on, and especially in 1964, provided a powerful influence on public attitudes. This suggests that the pattern of competition for the Presidency is a key factor in structuring how voters see the society. Therefore American Presidential competition alternates between periods of consensus and the "end of ideology" when conflict and choices are muted and periods of ferment and conflict when choices are more sharply drawn. The independent variables are the actual policy purposes and electoral strategies of Presidential candidates. However, social conditions have to be congenial to a departure from consensus politics for the dramatization of new, divisive issues to be successful. Politics and social change interact in a spiral.

Along with the growing ideological divisions over time there was increasing support for liberal policy positions so that the major measures of the Great Society had majority support by the time of passage.[20] How were these changing attitudes related to electoral and governmental patterns?

In the late 1950s congressional Democrats, especially in the Senate, developed a number of policy initiatives that were to be later taken over by the Kennedy Administration. Medicare, federal aid to education, and early environmental protection measures were among these initiatives. This was a kind of policy entrepreneurship by liberal legislators working through their committees with outside help from interest groups and academic advisers. For example, in 1958 and 1959 the Joint Economic Committee of the Congress held hearings organized by a temporary staff of Harvard economists, which, in a 1959 report, called for stimulation of economic growth and reduction of unemployment by a planned tax cut and deficit financing.[21] This incorporated Keynesian economics into Democratic policy thinking and was taken over by President Kennedy and the Chairman of his Council of Economic Advisers, Walter Heller, in the tax-cut proposal that became law in 1964.

At the same time public opinion was showing growing support for Democratic positions on such issues throughout the late fifties. The greatest ambiguity was in regard to civil rights legislation. There was support for the idea of general reform but much less for specific measures like school desegregation.[22]

James Sundquist has shown a strong relationship between voting for Democratic congressional candidates in 1958 and 1960, and the Presidential candidate in 1960, and dissatisfaction about economic conditions, particularly unemployment.[23] The 1958 congressional elections, held in the midst of a recession, brought in a large increase of Democrats and a number of individual senators such as Edmund Muskie who were to remain in national politics thereafter.

John Kennedy's clearest signal from the voters in 1960 was to do something about the economy. Surveys taken during his Presidency also showed popular majorities in favor of most of the key New Frontier legislative proposals such as medicare and federal aid to education.[24] However, these public attitudes were not sufficient to sway the Congress to support the President's program. The main reason was that Kennedy did not bring in enough liberal Democrats. The Democrats had twenty-one fewer House seats in 1961 than before because of voter defections in the North and West due to Kennedy's Catholicism. The formal Democratic majorities concealed ideological opposition to the President's programs and this fact, combined with well-organized and adamant Republican opposition, made his problems difficult. Furthermore, many liberal Democrats in Congress said at the time that they sensed no great sense of public imperative that New Frontier programs be passed.

In fact, there seemed to be very little public support for the taxes that would be required to pay for these programs. Public opinion is spongy. People will give assent to general principles or even to particular measures when asked, but they may feel no particular urgency and even see the question in a negative light if they are told there will be substantial costs. The early sixties were good times of social contentment. Kennedy had excited the nation in a general way and a perception of new social needs was gradually emerging, although it had not yet come to a head. Nor was there any clear crisis that the President could take advantage of as FDR had in 1933.

As we saw in Chapter 2, President Kennedy went all out in the summer of 1963 in civil rights, the tax cut, and the test-ban treaty. He was looking forward to a big electoral victory over Barry Goldwater in 1964 and in getting the votes in Congress to pass his program. Certainly he saw himself passing from the stage of public education to one of accomplishment. The irony is that his death provided the crisis and catharsis that permitted a great public awareness of and support for his programs. President Johnson pleaded for passage of the civil rights bill and tax cut in the name of the fallen President and in 1964 accomplished the victory, which permitted the third great burst of legislative action for social reform in this century.

These three periods of accomplishment were brief: 1913–1915, with a renewed burst in 1917 for Wilson; 1933–1936 for FDR; and the congressional sessions of 1965 and 1966 for Johnson. We will look at Johnson's legislative leadership in detail later, but aside from his own great skill, his success with Congress was due to the fact that the Goldwater debacle permitted the election of a large increase of Northern Democrats to Congress whose political future was tied to the President and his programs. The votes were there and the leaders of Congress, who had resisted Kennedy, knew it and acted accordingly. Johnson had campaigned on a consensus mandate and pictured New Frontier and Great Society programs as middle of the road and accepted by all Americans, compared to the desire of Goldwater to abolish social security and dismantle TVA. Johnson's achievement from 1964 to 1966 was to legitimize the items on the liberal agenda and make them "safe" for Americans. Medicare, federal aid to education, and even a war on poverty passed from the stage of innovative ideas to that of established programs. It was not long before the Congress that had resisted them began to guard such programs in practice as part of its standard network of alliances. Protective groups grew up to defend the programs, join such alliances, and resist the efforts of the Nixon Administration to cut them back. Such is the story of progressive reform in America. It creates a left-right dichotomy for the public but succeeds by picturing the left position as actually in the center. The programs that are established then become part of the expectations of people and cannot therefore be revoked. But the process is a powerful constraint on any kind of radicalism.

There is a puzzle about this pattern that we will try to resolve later. Why is it that Congress resists a progressive President during the first phase of the cycle even on matters for which there is overwhelming public support? A progressive President seems to need an extra large majority to be successful with Congress, as Johnson was after 1964. An illustration would be federal health insurance, which Franklin Roosevelt avoided because of the opposition of the American Medical Association and its influence in Congress, and on which Harry Truman was defeated in Congress because of AMA opposition to "socialized medicine."[25] Yet surveys show that two-thirds of the public supported various forms of government-supported health insurance from 1946 to the enactment of medicare in 1965. Gradually the legislation was tailored by the Truman and then the Kennedy Administrations to aid for the elderly on the grounds of greatest need and therefore political acceptability. However, the congressional-AMA opposition stood firm until the 1964 election brought the necessary support to Congress. Even then the resultant legislation was timid by European standards and covered a minority of the population.

The key question is whether we attribute this slow and cautious process to the difficulty of building up popular support for this and other progressive programs given the kind of ideological constraints described earlier or whether the answer might not be found in an important missing link in the congressional system of representation. There are many intervening factors between popular attitudes and government action that explain what government does without resort to political culture and ideology as explanation. It is not even clear that strong Presidential election victories provide much in the way of policy mandates. An election like 1964 opens the way for action by government in terms of majority support for a general tone and direction to government. But the intellectual and moral traditions of the two Presidential parties at elite levels tell us a great deal more about the actual legislation that is proposed. And, of course, the process of Presidential congressional relations explains the final outcome. Thus, these three electoral cycles only set the backdrop for policy. They do not set policy itself in any but the most general way.

By 1968 Johnson's consensus had vanished as a President was elected who sought to put the government on a new course, and we entered the third phase of the cycle. There is no evidence of a popular shift against the programs of the Great Society. Rather, there was a colossal vote of no confidence in the way the Johnson Administration was handling what were seen to be the three greatest problems: the war, crime, and race.[26] We saw the effect of the war in Chapter 5. A public inability to perceive any difference between candidates Nixon and Humphrey on Vietnam permitted other concerns to shape the election despite the fact that Vietnam was the greatest single concern. There was a very great vote defection among Democrats who had voted for LBJ but who now felt that the Democratic Administration had been ineffective in dealing with racial violence and crime in the cities. The classic dove/radical pattern was very limited, confined to highly educated whites.

Throughout the broad American public there was a strong sense of breakdown in authority and a fear that society was coming apart at the seams. The Democratic Administration took the blame but this was not a rejection of liberalism. In fact, a majority of Wallace voters surveyed designated themselves as liberals.[27] Yet they were the strongest manifestation of the new "social issue" cutting across the electorate. The great majority of the voters stayed with party identification, regardless of issue, in the 1968 election, but a key minority of the unhappy set the tone and decided the election on the issues of race and crime. These were the changes from 1964 to 1968. Clearly these were not the Goldwater conservatives of 1964 who had been upper-middle-class ideologues. These were ordinary working people who were frightened of many forces in the society they did not understand and could not control. Somehow the progressive achievements of the 1960s had gone sour. People did not turn against medicare or federal aid to schools. But civil rights and antipoverty measures, though not radical, had perhaps created such turmoil in their implementation that large numbers of Americans sought a period of respite, if not reaction.

The Nixon Administration, as we have seen, had great latitude with the public in achieving a Vietnam peace settlement, but there was little if any mandate in domestic affairs. The Administration took victory to mean an opportunity to construct a new long-lasting electoral coalition of conservative forces, a new Republican majority of white Southerners, white ethnic groups, and union workers, plus a traditional rural, small-town, and solid middle class following. Much of this was done by symbolic appeals: for example, a Presidential letter to Cardinal Cooke condemning abortion, and a go slow Administration attitude on school desegregation not only in the South but in regard to de facto segregation in the North, with busing the principal issue and the President openly opposed to it.

Much of the Nixon domestic program was not derived from any

election mandate and reflects the ideology of high officials of the Administration. The critical assessment of the operation of many Great Society programs, the effect to cut down their cost, the desire to eliminate many separate categorical programs as such and have them administered by the states and localities—all this has its origin in the managerial style of the Republicans in charge. They think they can make the machinery of government work better to achieve social objectives. But it is not clear that many people in the electorate have ever shared these views. We see the latitude that an election victory gives the government of the day.

The 1972 election illustrated the impossibility of pure ideological party politics in America, as had the 1964 election, and in this sense the McGovern and Goldwater candidates were mirror images of each other. In 1964 Lyndon Johnson had played beautifully on the moderate-to-liberal tendencies of American ideology, and Richard Nixon emphasized the moderate-to-conservative element of that same set of tendencies just as skillfully.

Nixon received 61 percent of the vote, which included 94 percent of the Republicans, 66 percent of the Independents, and 42 percent of the Democrats. The chief reason for the election of the President of a minority party was the large defection of nominally Democratic voters from the candidate of their party. There were striking ideological differences between those Democrats who stayed with McGovern and those who left; the former were much more liberal in their attitudes on the war, the economy, social questions like welfare, cultural questions like amnesty for those who refused to serve in Vietnam, and permissive laws on abortion and marijuana. Even though surveys showed that the electorate as a whole had grown more liberal in four years, particularly in the direction of favoring action toward racial justice, it was clear that a majority of the voters perceived their positions to be closer to those of Nixon than McGovern.[28]

The election results showed a close tie between voter issue stands and the voting decision. This factor and attitudes toward the Presidential candidates were the two most important determinants of the vote, far more important than party. It seems likely that the two dimensions of issues and candidates came together in the minds of many voters.

George McGovern, like Barry Goldwater, was seen by a majority of the public as being on the wrong side of a number of articles of faith of the American creed, from which the President automatically benefited. This prevented specific issues from being discussed or considered in the campaign. Walter Dean Burnham has cited a number of basic tenets that McGovern violated.[29] First, he tried to make

Americans feel guilty and responsible for an aggressive war and an unjust social system. This kind of collective conscience is beyond the ken of most people, who simply do not feel responsible for a situation they did not create. Nor do people apply standards of morality to foreign policy, not because they are amoral but because the only standard that rings true to them is American self-interest. Therefore, a majority of Americans continued to believe that the country has a free, democratic political system, that the free enterprise economy works in their favor, that the poor and rich alike get what they deserve, and that no one, including blacks and the poor, are entitled to special considerations. In foreign affairs the President's definition of the national interest is accepted and public perception of an honest effort by him to end the war was all that was required. Given this perception, the raining of bombs on Hanoi was really irrelevant to people and not seen as a moral question. The moral dimension was blocked out by the legitimacy of the Presidential quest for peace.

Second, McGovern's attacks on the tax system, plans for a new welfare scheme of direct payments to the poor, and the spectacle of a Democratic National Convention dominated by officially set quotas of minorities, youth, and women all went against the deeply held conservative symbolic and rhetorical values of the American myth. Goldwater had invoked such symbolic values, although he had gone blatantly and openly against the concrete achievements of the liberal half of the American myth. Failure in both cases was easily predicted.

The 1972 election revealed new dimensions of the tension between the two halves of the American liberal ideology. The emphasis shifted from controversy over the role of government in the economic lives of citizens, one of the chief themes of the 1964 election, and raised new questions about the proper role of government in matters of social control. Here one saw a reversal of the two ideological tendencies. Those on the more conservative end of the scale favored government action for social control, for example in the matter of drugs, amnesty, and law and order. This would seem to put such people at variance with the traditional emphasis of American self-styled conservatives on economic individualism and a limited role for government. Those on the more liberal end of the spectrum, who continued to favor a strong role for government in economic matters, for example the McGovern hopes for revision of the tax laws for greater equity, took positions friendly to greater individual freedom on the social control issues. Again, one could ask if this was a departure from the progressive ideology of the past. In both cases the seeming differences between attitudes toward the role of government within each camp were really not conflicts. Rather, the traditionalists in American life have long favored a limited role for government in economic matters and a high rhetorical commitment to economic individualism along with a negative view of cultural and social individualism that departed from the implicit conformity required by both Protestant and Catholic puritanism. Progressives on the other hand have presented limited challenges to the traditional conservative ethic of limited government, economic individualism, and social conformity. This division within the broad American liberal ideology is thus more complex than a simple split over the role of government in the economy. These several facets of ideological difference are introduced into electoral politics and influence outcomes and politics that follow.

Gerald Pomper suggests that electoral trends since 1956 have created the conditions for a "responsible party system" in which voters would choose between parties on the basis of ideological-issue alternatives. There has been a decline of one-party sectionalism, interest groups are increasingly tied to parties in left and right ideological identification, and a number of dramatic crossovers of party affiliation such as John Lindsay and John Connally have taken place in conformity with ideology.[30] President Nixon has pursued this objective with his hope of a new middle American electoral majority and the virtual jettisoning of liberal Republicans from Administration ranks and graces. The McGovern movement complemented this potential alignment with its own reading for a top-bottom coalition of the disaffected, idealistic professional upper classes, and the poor and minorities. The problem was that this left the bulk of the traditional working-class constituency to the Republicans.

A number of trends run counter to the responsible party model. The parties seem to be disintegrating as organizations. The old machines lack purpose and power and new cadres of activists lack staying power between elections. This is matched by a declining party identification among voters. A new kind of Independent, who is well informed and issue-oriented but who feels no identification with either party, is becoming very common and obviously very important. Finally, the development of social movement parties such as the Wallace phenomenon, which appeals to voters from both traditional camps and which reflects genuine discontents in the society, is a further force to weaken the party system.

In fact neither party seems able to put together a stable electoral coalition. The Democratic potential majority is deeply divided on the issue of race, and it is not at all clear that party leaders or Presidents can bring black and white together on the integration of schools and housing and the amelioration of poverty. But it is equally unclear that the Republicans can keep the blue-collar support they garnered on social questions like law and order and appeals to patriotism in the use of national power abroad when it comes to the rising cost of living. The increasingly ideological cadre of the Republican party is just not sympathetic to the material claims of labor.

The present period bears the marks of a time of party realignment as the old parties weaken and new movements outside the parties grow and manifest a closeness to popular consensus that the old parties seem to lack. These are the hallmarks of the break-up of one party system and the formation of another.[31]

The two most recent party systems have been the Republican majority of 1896 to 1932 and the subsequent Democratic dominance, the New Deal Coalition, which seems to be crumbling. Each such dissolution and realignment in American history has come about because the old alignment has ceased to be relevant for new social tensions and demands, and because political leaders pick up the new questions and fashion a new majority, usually in a dramatic Presidential election such as 1932. New, stable party identifications are created that last for a generation, and the new electoral coalition majority is the basis for a general style and philosophy of government by the majority party. The minority party may win the White House in a "deviating" election but this is usually followed by a "reinstating election."

However, the present period is one of great confusion in which no clear pattern for the future has emerged. It would come in creative actions by a Presidential candidate, if it comes at all. We may be entering a time of troubles in which neither major party can lay claim to a strong electoral coalition of support and therefore a period in which the political resources of future Presidents will be limited and the consequences for policy will be inaction, indecision, and uncertainty. Social change has been so rapid and the old political alignments seem so irrelevant to it that most political leaders, and most of the rest of us, lack conceptual categories to cope with new developments. We can neither diagnose what is happening to our society nor propose solutions.[32] For example, we used to have faith that technology was a beneficent force for a better, more comfortable society. Now we increasingly feel like prisoners in a technological nightmare but lack understanding of our dilemma.

Those who look forward to the desirability of a realignment that pits a Democratic top-bottom coalition against a Republican silent majority of solid working-class and middle-class whites might reflect on the actual consequences. It would range black against white; the peripheral regions of the country against the urban centers; parochials against cosmopolitans; blue-collar whites against both blacks and affluent liberals; middle Americans against intellectuals, students, and many of the professional classes. These would be much more open and divisive cleavages than in any previous party system.[33] Rather than leading to an increase in political resources for Presidents, such changes might bring a paralysis in government caused by intensified social conflict.

Such a realignment is not likely to happen in so stark a form, at least not in the near future. Rather, efforts will be made to create a new Republican majority while the old Democratic coalition will be held together, imperfectly, with bailing wire. In neither case will there be strong political resources for governing. Furthermore, there will be a great temptation for leaders to appeal to the worst elements of political and social resentment, especially in regard to the frustrations caused by race, for short-run political advantage. For example, both Republican and Democratic Presidential candidates will compete for the Wallace following, and it will be difficult to do this without serious moral sacrifice of programs for racial equality unless Wallace changes his appeals.

A progressive solution to these problems would find a way to appeal to lower- and working-class blacks and whites in terms of social programs that would unite their common interests while at the same time appealing to the idealism of the educated and professional classes and their desire for a qualitatively better society. This would involve a great deal of hard thinking and policy invention to devise programs that could serve both black and white without being tokenism for the former and threatening to the latter. The task may be too difficult. However, if it is not done an alternative majority in behalf of public and private order may then form that would simply repress the problems and further polarize the society. There is also the possibility of a new conservative majority that would find a way to release the economic capacities of our productive systems to end poverty and bring together black and white in countless spontaneous, unplanned ways.

This is a discussion of future conditions on one dimension only, that of questions of social justice. Several other kinds of questions must also be faced, such as the entire matter of national response to despoliation of the urban and natural environment by economic and technological forces.

The Presidency is a place for the creative fashioning of these different dimensions of politics into stable alignments that can provide the resources for policy responses. It is obvious how difficult this is to do well. Few Presidents come into office with strong, clear support in specific directions on a number of dimensions at once. Rather they must cope with crosspressures in their own constituencies that severely limit their political resources. There simply is no ready-made ideological alignment for a President nor can one be created.

There are too many dimensions of conflict. Still, the dynamics of American history and culture impel Presidents to extract national moral purpose from these chaotic raw materials.

Presidents are more than broker politicians. They are limited by the moral perspectives of the society at a given time, but almost all Presidents feel an obligation, by virtue of the office, to act in terms of those perspectives and to try to enlarge support for them. So the question of leadership in the Presidency becomes very much a question of the moral quality of American society as it affects Presidents and as they influence that quality.

7

The
President,
Congress,
and
Domestic
Policymaking

We have been pursuing parallel themes in regard to policymaking in foreign and domestic affairs. In post–World War II history Presidents have been able to expect substantial public and congressional support for their foreign policies. When large portions of the electorate have turned against those policies, as in the cases of the Korean and Vietnam wars, the controversy has been resolved through the politics of Presidential elections. Congress has played a relatively limited role in either challenging these Presidential policies or in influencing him to reverse them. In matters of domestic policy both public and Congress have been able to place constraints upon a President and influence his strategies of leadership and policies. As we saw in Chapter 6 the electorate can create general constraints upon a President in domestic policy because of the pluralism of beliefs, values, and interests in domestic matters. The Congress, because it manifests these pluralistic divisions and has sanctions, is able to impose specific constraints upon Presidential action. Congress therefore serves as an agency of representation in domestic policy far more than it does in foreign affairs. This role is enhanced by the organization of Congress into a high degree of division of labor along the lines of domestic policy, something that is much less well developed for foreign policy.

The relationships between the Presidency and the Congress in domestic policy are shaped by two sets of forces—institutional and political—each influencing the other. The institutional forces are fairly constant. There is a separation of powers, modified by checks and balances. Each body is responsive to somewhat different electorates in regard to time of election and social composition. Either body can virtually bring government to a halt by defying the other. Neither institution can freely do its work without the cooperation of the other.

The political forces at work in the society permit and even force a great deal of variation over time in the relation of President and Congress. For the past generation or more, since 1936, a particular political configuration in the country has set its mark on the national government. The chief characteristic of that configuration is the nominal domination of Congress by the Democratic party. The Republicans have controlled Congress for only four years, on two separate occasions, since 1936. By 1976 the Democrats will have held the White House for twenty-four of the forty years since 1936. Therefore for much of that time we have had responsible party government in which President and Congress were linked in a common political accountability.

However, one of the strongest themes in political discussion during that period has been the inability of Democratic Presidents to carry Congress with them in domestic reform proposals. Franklin Roosevelt lost control of Congress after the 1936 election and never really regained it until the war. Harry Truman's Fair Deal was more effective as a campaign theme than as a legislative program. In Chapter 6 we saw how Lyndon Johnson had to amass extraordinary congressional majorities in order to carry the programs of John Kennedy, and even Johnson lost his hold over Congress after 1966.

Two patterns of Democratic rule emerge: rare bursts of activity and continuous stalemate. A third pattern is the configuration that emerges when the President is a Republican. The pattern again is stalemate but not in the resistance of Congress to a liberal, activist President. Rather, the activists and liberals came forward into positions of leadership against a President who wishes to scale down past programs.

This last pattern becomes even more significant when we realize that Republicans will have held the White House for sixteen of the twenty-eight years between 1948 and 1976. What first appears to be a long period of Democratic rule of both White House and Congress from 1936 to 1976 becomes Democratic dominance of only Congress with the Presidency alternating regularly. The result of these patterns is a system of governmental inaction. Democratic Presidents can only rarely achieve results in Congress with party government. Republican Presidents have even less success with virtually the same kinds of Congresses.

POLITICS AND THE COMPOSITION OF CONGRESS

A number of forces have converged to produce this stable pattern.[1] The Republican party continues to be a minority party that is outnumbered not only by Democrats but by those voters calling themselves Independents. This continuing minority status is a great obstacle to the election of a Republican Congress. Voters will clearly support a Republican for President but split their ticket and vote for Democrats for Congress. Traditional party identification, which favors the Democrats, seems to hold for congressional voting. This is seen in the fact that Richard Nixon has not carried a Republican Congress into office with him and Dwight Eisenhower did it only once, in 1952.

There has been a great increase in voter ticket-splitting in recent years. According to Richard Boyd this is a result of the declining strength of party identification among voters.[2] It is not clear whether this decline has extended to congressional candidates. Clearly it does include the Presidency. If the decline does affect voting for Congress it will take away the chief cue to citizens for their vote, since most voters have a limited perception of the actual behavior of their representatives in Congress. Boyd postulates that the combined effect of a decline in party identification and the increase in ticket-splitting has been the increased staying power of incumbent members of Congress. Ninety percent of incumbent members of the House are regularly reelected. Senate incumbents won eighty percent of their reelection bids from 1946 to 1970. The implication is that voters are sticking with the familiar. This has favored Democrats in Congress, and traditional party identification, though declining, is congruent with the trend of support for incumbents.

There has also been an increasing insulation of congressional races from the Presidential contest.[3] This is seen in the great stability of House membership despite the fact of changes in party control of the Presidency. The older patterns of an increase of seats for the party of the Presidential winner in a Presidential election has become less marked as has the accompanying regular loss of seats for that party in the next midterm election. In 1968 Nixon gained only 4 seats in the House. In 1970 he lost only 12 and in 1972 he gained back only 11. This meant that the composition of the House was almost unchanged over three elections, including a Presidential landslide victory in 1972.

In 1968 the composition of the House changed hardly at all. Three hundred and ninety-four incumbents were reelected: 173 Republicans and 221 Democrats. Ten Republicans succeeded Republicans who were not running for reelection, and 16 Democrats succeeded

Democrats. Of the 435 House seats, 420 did not change party hands in 1968.[4] This pattern did not begin just with Nixon but has been increasing since the 1940s. We might conclude that there is too little real political competition for House seats throughout the country and that therefore the balance of political forces in the House is relatively unchanged over time. The structure of competition for House seats favors incumbents. State legislatures do their best to draw constituency lines for the House in such a way that either one party or the other, depending upon who controls the legislature, has an electoral advantage from the social composition of the district. Also, the districts of representatives are coterminous with no other electoral district so that House members are required to develop a personal electoral machine over time that is hard to compete against. The challenger has not had the same time to build a counter-organization. These factors work to divorce House members from national competitive party politics.

Presidential candidates have themselves been instrumental in the divorce of Presidential and congressional politics. The 1972 Nixon victory was a personal one in which the President worked through a reelection committee separate from the Republican National Committee and did little to help other Republican candidates. This pattern is more likely in the candidate of the minority party, who needs many more votes than the party can provide. However, Lyndon Johnson ran as a nonpartisan candidate in 1964. It may very well be that many voters are coming to see the Presidential office as above partisan politics. Perhaps the Presidency is becoming a plebiscitary office. The same trend is seen in regard to Congress with the increasing emphasis upon personal view or issue rather than party appeals. And therefore, candidates for President and Congress know that they do not particularly need each other at election time.

The national political party is still required to nominate a Presidential candidate, but he captures the party machinery and owes it very little afterwards. He wins an election by virtue of his personal appeal and his own national organization of volunteers independent of the regular party structures. This was the character of the McGovern candidacy. Gerald Pomper suggests that the nomination of a President may soon become a nonparty matter, at least for the Democrats. Proposals for change in the party charter to permit much more direct choice of the Presidential candidate by self-styled party members may democratize the party in a formal sense and take it away from the "regular," but it may also subject the party to the control of ideological activists to whom principle is much more important than party and thereby increase the divorce of Presidential candidates from the rest of the party organization and mass supporters.[5]

The sum total of all these trends is the great likelihood that alternating Democratic and Republican Presidents will face similar Congresses. There is the further probability of stalemate and conflict between President and Congress. Liberal Democratic Presidents will be unable to move the Congress to the left except during infrequent reform periods and Republican Presidents, who are likely to be more conservative, will face a Congress controlled by the opposition party that has few incentives to cooperate. We will look at Presidential leadership of Congress since 1960 in this way.

Progressive Presidents and Congress

The Kennedy Presidency permits us to take a clear look at the problems with the Congress that plagued FDR after 1936, Truman after 1948, and Kennedy during his entire tenure. They are problems unique to liberal Democratic Presidents that have provided the central puzzle of modern American politics. How is it that a Democratic President has so much difficulty carrying a Democratic Congress with him in support of his program? What happens to finally permit action? Before we look at the Kennedy and Johnson periods as a case study, let us consider a number of hypotheses that have been put forward to answer the question.

A combination of the rules of the two Houses of Congress and the importance of Southern Democrats in the congressional Democratic party is said to present roadblocks to the enactment of the President's programs. The absence of party competition in congressional politics and the consequent dominance of safe Senate and House seats by conservative Southern Democratics is said to be reinforced by the fact of seniority in awarding committee chairmanships in both houses. A Democratic President thus faces the obstacle of unfriendly committee chairmen. For example, in the Democratic-controlled Ninetieth Congress (1966–1968) there were no Senate committee chairmen from any of the ten largest Northern states and nine of the sixteen chairmanships were held by Southerners. A tenth chairmanship was held by a senator from Oklahoma and other chairmen were men with long seniority from places like New Mexico, Arizona, and Nevada. In the House four of the twenty chairmen did come from Northern urban districts. But nine of the remaining committees, including the powerful Rules Committee that controls the House agenda, were chaired by Southerners.[6]

The very fact that these are figures from 1966 to 1968 suggests the weakness of the thesis, for these sessions occurred after Congress had passed the Great Society legislation. These chairmen were not able to prevent that from happening. Such people did give John Kennedy a difficult time of it, but after the 1964 election Johnson had enough Northern Democratic floor votes to pass his legislation, which, from 1961 to 1963, Kennedy had not had. Committee chairmen adapted their behavior accordingly in the two situations. A prime example was Wilbur Mills, the chairman of the House Ways and Means Committee, who reversed his opposition to medicare after 1964 and led the fight for the measure in the House.

So although rules about chairmanship can be a problem, the more essential concern for Democratic Presidents is to get the rank-and-file votes. If a Democratic President can win a majority, or great plurality, of national popular votes why is this fact not reflected in Congress?

One argument has been that the President represents a different electorate than the Congress. The necessity of winning a majority of the votes in the electoral college directs him to the Northern urbanized, industrial states for his campaign appeals, whereas Congress, with two senators for each state and much rural overrepresentation in the House because of malapportionment of seats, represents a very different electorate. This argument may have been correct at one time in the form given above, but court-ordered reapportionment of House seats has reduced rural representation and increased suburban electoral strength. A two-party system is developing in the South in which liberal Democrats are beginning to compete against conservative Republicans. Finally, the Senate has become a relatively liberal cosmopolitan body primarily because of the great urbanization of all areas of the nation. Most senators must represent cosmopolitan urban populations, even from small states; in fact, the Senate has been much more supportive of liberal legislation than the House in the sixties and seventies. The senatorial electorate is very much like that of the President.

Once again the House is the key to an answer. Reapportionment eliminated a number of strictly rural seats, but the central cities were also losing population and seats. The suburbs have gained political strength, but this does not necessarily benefit liberal Presidents.

There are several hypotheses that are used to explain a general lack of rapport between a liberal President and Congress as a whole. One of these is the argument that Congress represents the more organized parts of the society and the President represents the relatively unorganized larger population. Grant McConnell argues that oligarchy follows from simplicity in that the more homogeneity and the less diversity there is to a political community, the more likely it is that it will be dominated by the organized dominant interests within it.[7] There will not be a sufficient pluralism for competing organized groups to develop. Members of Congress are likely to come from such settings and be responsive to the dominant organizations within their constituencies. It might also be argued that not as many people vote in congressional elections as in Presidential ones and that congressmen are therefore responsive to a smaller, more stable, better organized, and probably more satisfied electorate than the President, who seeks to mobilize numbers of people largely untouched by politics.

There is plausibility to this thesis and it is probably true in many cases. But there seems to be a variety of strategies of representation at work. Lewis Dexter has shown that a member of Congress has great latitude in fashioning a coalition of support in his constituency and that it is largely a manifestation of his own goals and purposes.[8] How else can we explain the actions and survival of a liberal senator like Frank Church from a conservative state like Idaho or the fact that senators of very different ideologies will long coexist in representing one state, for example, the liberal Paul Douglas and the conservative Everett Dirksen, both from Illinois?

There is a variation on this hypothesis, which is that members of Congress are responsive to the particular needs of their constituents in a way that makes them oppose some Presidential plans. For example, a liberal, dovish senator may want very much to scale down American military forces but he comes from a state with large naval installations. Therefore, he calls for strengthening the navy as a purely defensive force and recommends reductions in the missile program. Civilian jobs are at stake in his state that he should concern himself with. Who else will represent his constituents if he does not? This presents problems for a President of his party who wishes to reduce naval expenditures and installations. Examples of such potential conflicts in all policy areas are countless.

However, in practice, liberal Presidents seem to resolve such problems by combining appeals to particular and general interests. They give way on the particular in order to have the general. In one sense, the Great Society programs were one enormous pork barrel that created new vested interests in every state and community, and Democratic congressmen are now zealously guarding them against the hatchet of an economizing Republican President.

Another theory maintains that the President necessarily articulates a conception of the public interest as a vision and a goal that, in fact, goes beyond the actual election mandate that he received. We know such mandates are ambiguous and often contradictory. Presidents must preach high aspirations, but members of Congress see a different facet of the electorate. Public opinion surveys may show majority support for liberal Presidential programs, but congressmen also notice that people are reluctant to approve of any increase in taxes for such programs. The support is thus soft and not worth taking a risk on for a cautious member of Congress.

Harry McPherson, an assistant to President Johnson, remembers the diverse responses of the White House and Congress to the riots of blacks in American cities in the mid-sixties. The Executive wanted costly new programs for delivery of services to the poor. The President and his aides were looking for an immediate solution. However, members of Congress, who saw the budget running a heavy deficit from the Vietnam War, had angry constituents demanding law and order and were not sure hastily concocted programs would work after the very mixed experience with the poverty programs.[9] There is much validity to this picture. A liberal President is pushed into the advocacy position and Congress as a whole is pushed toward caution. Their roles are different.

This suggests that the problems of getting the votes to carry liberal programs in the Congress are in large part intrinsic in the system of representation. This is particularly a problem in the House. The very diversity of the country may preclude a uniform system of party competition throughout and in every House district. However, the separate existence of a Congress and a President, each with different roles, may also be an important reason why the Congress resists Presidential innovations.[10] The highly productive Congresses of Franklin Roosevelt and Lyndon Johnson were heavily weighted in favor of the President's party, and the electoral tide that will bring such a result is rare.

Another important impediment to action is the complexity of legislative problems. Both President and Congress may be unclear about what to do or how to do it intelligently, or there may be disagreement that is not easily resolved. There may also be a very intense minority that opposes action to which the Congress as a whole is responsive, whether it be senators from agricultural states or Southern congressmen or Catholics opposed to federal aid to education that does not include aid to parochial schools. Finally, there is the question of leadership commitment, whether Presidential or congressional. A President may decide to hold back on innovation in one area in order to get support for action elsewhere. He may lack personal commitment on certain questions himself. Congressional leaders may have problems stemming from the internal politics of Congress that make it difficult for them to push a President's program.

The point of reciting these possible causes of the failure of a Democratic President and Congress to act is to affirm the existence of an existential political factor that is highly intangible and variable but that makes it difficult to harness and hold any congressional majority for very long, even one that is responsive to a reforming President. This means that the relationships of Presidents with Congress are dominated by unknowns, unpredictables, and widely oscillating changes over time. We will develop some ideas about variations in congressional response to a President's key program proposals and the reasons for these variations in the case studies that follow.

It is useful to compare Presidents in this regard in order to assess the relative importance of different variables. It is too easy to personalize the office and explain outcomes favorable to Presidents as due to the superior skill of a given President. In 1964 when Lyndon Johnson succeeded in winning the passage of previously stalled Kennedy bills, such as the tax cut and the public accommodations bill, was it Johnson's superior legislative skill or the fact of Kennedy's violent death or some combination of these two and other factors?

A comparison of the three most recent Presidents will permit us to estimate the relative importance of Presidential values, skill, and action or outcomes against the background of political forces. The comparison will follow the model of the three-phase cycle and suggest that Presidential legislative achievement is set by the constraints and resources peculiar to each period.

This suggests that it is possible to predict the gross patterns of Executive-legislative politics for a given phase so long as the patterns of politics that have prevailed in the country since 1936 continue. Should there be a partisan realignment, patterns of government might change greatly. However, within the constraints of each phase, there is room for variability according to Presidential personality. Presidential strategies and styles of leadership are not dictated entirely by the logic of a situation but follow from the predispositions of Presidents.

THE KENNEDY PRESIDENCY: PREPARATION AND FRUSTRATION

As a congressman and senator John Kennedy was not a particularly liberal or crusading legislator in domestic matters. However, as a candidate for first the Presidential nomination and then the Presidency he consciously took over the liberal issue positions that had been germinating in Congress and among intellectual and activist Democrats. In the summer of 1960, before he was nominated, he told Arthur Schlesinger, Jr. that he needed a "political identity" in order to get the nomination, and he subsequently drew on a Schlesinger memo calling for a time of forward movement that in turn cited

Arthur Schlesinger, Sr.'s theory of alternating cycles of progressive and consolidating movement in Presidential politics.[11] Both Kennedy and Schlesinger were influenced by the public words of Adlai Stevenson throughout the 1950s, which had subtly shifted liberal Democratic rhetoric away from the material needs and goals of the New Deal and toward a concern with quality of life issues like health and education. However, as we saw in Chapter 5, public acceptance of these positions was developing only slowly and had not become firm by 1960. The result was an absence of great or divisive themes in Kennedy's 1960 campaign, which was reinforced by his own instrumental attitude toward domestic reform issues. He used the rhetoric of liberalism, and he certainly believed it, but his style was rather detached from conventional issue positions of any kind, whether those of the business ethos or of fervent liberalism. His primary interests were in foreign affairs, and he brought no great depth of concern or experience to domestic policy leadership.

The election of 1960 did not give him a domestic policy mandate for social reforms either. A majority in most categories of voters had not supported him—whites, Protestants, college graduates, women, farmers, businessmen, and professional men—and his support was equally diverse, ranging from blacks to white Southerners to Catholics and blue-collar workers.

The result was a match of personality and situation in which a realistic, cautious man chose a strategy of safety in his dealings with Congress. This was the only approach consistent with his pragmatic approach to issue leadership. He wanted to be effective and not launch losing battles. The line up of votes in both the Eighty-seventh and Eighty-eighth Congresses did not seem to favor any alternative strategy. On paper the Democrats had large majorities in both chambers, but in fact the two Congresses were very closely split between liberals and conservatives, because there were more conservative Democrats than liberal Republicans, and the latter were not regular supporters of the President. The 217 to 212 vote in favor of enlarging the House Rules Committee to permit Administration measures to get to the floor is a good index of the uncertain nature of every key vote.[12]

Kennedy therefore resolved to play down any issue that would break apart his Democratic majority and to work very hard on keeping it together. For example, this meant scuttling legislative proposals on civil rights and concentrating on Administrative remedies in that area. He was particularly concerned to keep the Southerners in his camp.

In this light his initial requests of Congress were not startling but had been in the congressional hopper for years. Except for a few key proposals the New Frontier was a new wrapping on an old package. The response of Congress over three sessions was predictable. They passed most of the noncontroversial measures and failed to act on the few controversial ones. On the whole the President's record was a good one in the former category. His White House legislative liaison team, headed by Lawrence O'Brien, was skillful and experienced and the Democratic leaders of the two houses were cooperative. The following measures indicate the kinds of important domestic legislation the President could win approval for: 1961—area redevelopment for depressed areas, minimum wage increases, public housing programs, community health facilities; 1962—a farm price-support bill, the trade expansion act, a public works program, manpower development and training; 1963—accelerated public works appropriation, mental health centers. But the measures that the President had flagged as most important failed to pass; 1961—aid for elementary and secondary schools, aid for college construction; 1962—medical care for the aged, a Department of Urban Affairs; 1963—medicare, aid to elementary and secondary schools, civil rights legislation.[13]

On most of these issues the Democratic majority fell apart and the Republicans provided little or no support. But these measures were widely controversial issues about which there was much division in the Congress and the society, and Congress is not likely to produce majorities on such questions. Rather, it waits for a sense of consensus to develop.

A typical instance would be the failure of proposals for federal aid to education. The President did not submit anything very innovative in 1961 but called for aid for school construction and teacher's salaries. The sticking point was that he explicitly excluded Catholic schools from the bill on constitutional grounds. This was in part because he, as a Catholic, did not wish to appear as a partisan in that regard. But he did support the subsequent adding of an amendment permitting federal loans to Catholic schools.

The measure immediately ran into trouble from the open opposition of the national Catholic hierarchy and the objection of secular educational interest groups to any aid for Catholic schools at all. The Senate passed the bill with the controversial loan provision in it. Senators seem to have found compromise within themselves as individuals since they represented both Protestants and Catholics and wished to be responsive to both. But the greater homogeneity of House districts created problems. Compromises had to be between individual representatives and this meant conflict over the religious question in a way that could not be easily resolved. The Rules Committee settled the matter by refusing to send the measure to the floor and the negative majority on the committee reflected a strange combination of Catholics, who wanted more, and Southern conservatives, who wanted less. Observers agree that the same counter-pressures existed in the House and doomed any legislation.

The President did not fight very hard for this proposal nor for a 1962 plan for federal aid to higher education that floundered along the same lines. Kennedy was simply not prepared to go to the wall in a politically self-defeating way. The logic of legislative politics suggested Presidential arrangement of a compromise on aid for private schools. But, as the first Catholic President, who knew of many Democratic voter defections in 1960 because of his religion, Kennedy was not willing to risk a 1964 election by fighting hard for such a divisive measure for which there seemed to be no groundswell of popular support.

Nor should one fault the role of Congress here. They ventilated the issue and pointed out problems that the Presidency had not recognized. The Administration's original program reflected the traditional demands of the National Education Association without too much reflection. But it was Congress that raised the constitutional questions about separation of church and state and the further viability of parochial school systems. Congress has difficulty integrating support for measures by itself. It must take its cues from the environment and these signals were very mixed. There was no coalition of support for innovation nor had the President tried to create one.[14]

Although this is only one case it catches the essence of Kennedy's problem. Many of the factors we have cited converged here. The nature of representation in the House made agreement difficult. The conservative coalition of Southern Democrats and Republicans was a thorn. Then was no clear public support to override such factors, and the President felt inhibited from boldness by the fragile character of his electoral plurality.

Kennedy had a coherent strategy, which was to submit controversial legislation to Congress with accompanying messages as a form of public education. He did not expect them to pass. His eyes were on 1964 and the creation of an electoral majority for himself that would also give him the increased congressional votes that he needed. This was the choice of a man who was good at electoral politics, who did not like to make rhetorical appeals to publics on issues for which he felt there was uncertain support, and who did not enjoy the atmosphere and requirements of congressional bargaining. Kennedy was not a good legislative politician and never felt entirely comfortable as one of the "boys" in the cloakroom. In spite of his great popular appeal he was not a good dramatizer of specific issues on the stump. His public style in such situations was contrived and mechanical.

Therefore, he emphasized those strengths that projected a diffuse popular image and the fashioning of an electoral organization and coalition. Through these means he was relying on success in 1964 to give him the support in Congress that he sought.

Kennedy was neither a moral leader flaming with rhetoric nor an intuitive politician with a feel for legislative folkways. It is doubtful that either a more rhetorical or a more skillful legislative style would have made much difference in success with Congress during that period. The political conditions were not favorable to action, and Presidential style and skill may have been an irrelevant variable. Had he lived to run in 1964 and achieved the kind of victory that Johnson did, his style and skill of legislative leadership would have been important for achievement or its absence. We cannot say what that might have been, but an analysis of Johnson will show the importance of Presidential skill when conditions are favorable.

LYNDON JOHNSON: FULFILLMENT AND DEFEAT

John Kennedy was influenced in an academic way by the examples of previous Democratic Presidents, but Lyndon Johnson drew strength from an intimate personal tie to Franklin Roosevelt. FDR had consciously been his model of a heroic President ever since Roosevelt had taken a personal interest in the young congressman, and as President Johnson wanted to be another FDR. He was determined to be one of the "great" Presidents. In a conversation with Theodore White in 1968 he compared his achievements to those of FDR, who he said had been his guiding star, and slighted the Kennedy record in passing.[15]

When he became President, Johnson realized that he lacked a coherent philosophy of purpose for domestic policy. He had been a legislative broker in the Senate, responding to tactical requirements, and was not a well-read or reflective man to begin with. Eric Goldman describes how the President responded enthusiastically to a Goldman memo describing American liberalism as the new consensus. The memo pictured the President as the steward of the national interest and the federal government as the agency chiefly responsible for the general welfare. It described the division between liberalism, which called on Presidential and federal power, and conversatism, which resisted it, but suggested that in recent years the line had been blurring. Conservatism had come to realize the importance of government action and the way had been prepared for a new consensus on liberalism. The memo concluded: "Today, in a very real sense, almost all of us are liberals, almost all of us are conservatives —and we are all moving toward a new American consensus."[16]

The memo strongly affected LBJ because it articulated his basic intuition. Two things in Johnson came together here, his genuine Texas populism, which sought social reform but accepted the goodness of American society with the hope of more of the good things in life for all, and his impulse to dominate. As Goldman put it: "Of course I had my concern. It was not possible to hear Lyndon Johnson talking consensus without visions of a relentless pursuit of that last possible vote down that farthest creek bottom."[17] This combination of idealism and ambition was to bring Johnson down in the end because he pursued it so relentlessly.

The Presidency propels an incumbent to search for a grand theme that may be proclaimed; for Johnson it was the Great Society, a phrase devised by Goldman and a White House speech writer, Richard Goodwin. As expressed in a Presidential speech at the University of Michigan on May 22, 1964, the phrase called for a solution to all of American material problems and for an increase in the quality of life enjoyed by Americans. White House aides feared it was too utopian and perhaps a bit ridiculous, but Goldman realized that it was "as Johnsonian as a roar down an eight-lane highway."[18]

These ideas are important in understanding Johnson's Presidency because they indicate a style of leadership. Following the model of FDR, his interpretation of Presidential success was victory over Congress, not for its own sake but for the enactment of programs. It is often said that because he was a former senator who had spent his career in the legislature, Johnson focused almost exclusively upon the legislative side of government and paid little attention to program design or implementation aside from the political implications. This forgets that the theory of Presidential greatness that Johnson embraced also emphasized legislative achievement and Presidential mastery of Congress. Many of the strengths and weaknesses of the Johnson Presidency can be seen here. He would seek great victories and enact new programs in the interest of his values and his place in history. But there would be too little attention to whether the program could work. There was often a missing link of concern about implementation in program formulation.[19] This problem followed, in part, from the exaggerated emphasis of the President and his aides upon legislative enactment as the key to achievement and greatness.

Of course, we seek to use our better skills rather than our weaker ones, and Johnson did know how to move legislators. He knew the people, folkways, and structures of Congress well and shaped his legislative strategies in that knowledge. To strategy he joined his own great persuasive powers, which were based upon an empathy for what would move congressional politicians. His style of legislative leadership, therefore, combined intensive cultivation of individual personalities, great attention to strategic details, and relentless pressure for action. In fact, he sought to dominate the Congress in the same way as he ran the war in Vietnam. Evans and Novak describe the Johnson style in the 1964 dispute with Panama over the Canal Zone as a portent for Vietnam: "an insistence on deciding every detail for himself, a tendency to encourage the most frantic mood of emergency in the government and a willingness to employ massive American power to the fullest."[20]

Johnson knew that Congress would ultimately take his measure, that there would be a reaction against him, as with every strong President. This does explain his haste for achievement, for he knew his time was short.

We thus see that Johnson brought skills, determination, and purpose to legislative leadership to a far greater degree than Kennedy did. If Kennedy's style was cerebral Johnson's was visceral. He drew on his entire personality for leadership. The major pieces of legislation that passed were inspired by a genuine personal passion in Johnson for the goals themselves and for greatness as President. The interesting question is whether personality and style made any difference in the outcome. Would Kennedy with the same majorities, but with less skill and commitment, have been able to extract the voting rights act, federal aid to schools, the war on poverty, and medicare from Congress? A look at these four cases may provide a speculative answer.

As a Southerner LBJ had always been cautious on civil rights, but his deep sympathies had been with the downtrodden ever since he had taught Mexican-American children in school. Becoming President freed him from any Southern role and, as a Democratic President, required him to affirm his large black and liberal constituency. Opportunism and sentiment merged. In 1964 he was bound to call for the passage of Kennedy's civil rights bill, the Public Accommodations Act, as Kennedy's heir and as leader of the party of reform. The growing acceptance of the civil rights movement and the warm memories of Kennedy assured passage. Johnson also wanted an opportunity to show Congress who was master, so in this opportune case he took an advanced position and built support for it. It became clear that he would not be defied easily.[21]

It was in the passage of the Voting Rights Act of 1965 that LBJ showed his virtuosity. Action was triggered by the beating of people marching in Selma, Alabama, to register to vote in the face of official hostility. The brutal action of the state troopers was seen on national television, and Johnson seized the opportunity to bring a voting rights bill to Congress in a prime time television speech. The word was passed around high circles in Washington that this speech was not to be missed, and it was in fact an instance of a single man having a direct impact in history by the sheer force of personality. As Goldman put it:

> It was the nature of Lyndon Johnson that once he made a decision, it became an all-encompassing one. People spoke of his sense of political timing. But there was also a kind of inner timing, the process by which something happened inside the man to pull together all sorts of connections, political considerations and personal likes and dislikes into a consuming composite of thought and action. . . . his conception of the role of President, his impatience with the politics of "nigra, nigra," and the political needs and opportunities presented by Selma rushed to the fore, and all complexities merged into a simple sharp issue to which a son of Johnson City easily responded: the right of American citizens to vote. . . . suddenly Lyndon Johnson resolved that he would not only send a voting rights bill to Congress; he would envelope the black revolution and stand forth as what he had always wanted so much to be, the President of all the people.[22]

John Kennedy had undergone a similar deepening of commitment in the summer of 1963. This was a natural occurrence for any morally sensitive man who was the leader of a liberal coalition. But Kennedy could not bring the force of personal presence to a congressional speech like Johnson. Johnson proclaimed the right to vote as basic to the American creed, incorporated the civil rights movement into that creed by using its slogan "we shall overcome" with maximum dramatic effect, and concluded with a story of how he had never dreamed as a young teacher that he might be in a position to help his Mexican-American students—"but now I do have that chance—and I'll let you in on a secret—I mean to use it. And I hope you will use it with me."[23]

The President had exercised such overwhelming moral leadership that it could hardly be resisted. His skillful use of legislative tactics during the passage of the bill was secondary in importance to that moral momentum. He cultivated the support of Senate Republicans, permitted Southerners to have their way in a filibuster before calling for an end to debate, and counteracted House criticism of his own civil rights record by admitting in a press conference that he had much to regret and was now trying to make up for it. Kennedy might have done it successfully also, but it is doubtful he could have generated the personal impact on members of Congress to the same degree as Johnson. Personality was a critical factor.

Aid to education and medicare were ideas with great popular

support after 1964, and the votes were now there for their passage. Aid to education was still controversial but Johnson was able to link it to his theme of a Great Society by adopting a Presidential task-force idea that federal aid be directed toward low-income school districts and thus joined to the war on poverty. A related idea was the provision that Catholic schools be given federal aid in the indirect form of participation in neutral educational centers for special subjects in which public and parochial students would share.[24]

LBJ had created a larger supportive context for social action in his rhetoric against poverty and for a Great Society that made support of federal aid for education much more likely than before. In fact all the principal interest groups, secular and Catholic, that had been carefully cultivated by Johnson were now strongly behind the bill. Congress could see a consensus that had not existed before and it acted. Johnson does not deserve all the credit. Opinion had grown more favorable. But he took advantage of the fact and joined moral pressure to a sustained insistence that Congress enact the bill without major change. He rode hard on the leadership for this goal in order to prevent a resumption of church-state disputes. A less forceful President might have lost control.

The passage of medicare was more certain after the 1964 election because of the larger number of Northern Democrats in the House. Johnson wisely left leadership in the House to Wilbur Mills, chairman of the Ways and Means Committee, who sensed the trend and decided to lead what he had earlier thought was a losing cause.[25] When faced with a series of undesirable amendments in the Senate Finance Committee Johnson called the individual members to his office and worked on them using a blend of persuasion and pressure. As one senator described it: "Well, the President told me how he understood all my problems. Then in the nicest way—he was passing me a soft drink—he suggested what more problems, and damn practical ones I must say, I would face if I didn't see the light."[26] Neither Kennedy nor Nixon had that kind of face-to-face presence and power with congressmen. It was another instance of the force of personality and will as an instrument of leadership.

The passage of the antipoverty bill was the purest form of the Johnson style. Kennedy had initiated the ideas of an antipoverty program and the economic advisers who brought the original idea to Johnson in 1963 suggested an experimental pilot plan approach in a few cities since little was known about the cures for poverty. The President would have none of it. Congress would only buy a national plan with fruits for all, he said. Besides, there was a chance to erase the Kennedy stamp and replace it with his own in time for the 1964 election. A national war on poverty would become the hallmark of his Administration and would win him the votes of blacks, working-class and low-income people, and progressives. He took little interest in the actual design of the bill or in possible problems of implementation. His emphasis was on a moral crusade to end poverty in America. This theme was evident in his evangelical rhetoric as he spoke to numerous groups around the country. This was also the tone among members of Congress regarding passage. Democrats were ready to give their new President what he asked for, particularly as 1964 election ammunition for him and themselves, and they acquiesced in Presidential pressure to pass the bill without revision. The few hard questions were raised by Republicans, which were ignored. Congress therefore played little constructive role. Unlike the voting rights act, federal aid to education, and medicare there was no history of congressional evolution of a position. Therefore members of Congress felt no particular stake in the program in later years when it revealed so many problems. It was Johnson's achievement alone; John Kennedy could never have done it in 1964.

Johnson's success nevertheless returned to haunt him. The program was never properly financed and raised popular expectations it could not meet. Community action organizations came into conflict with Democratic mayors, and Congress eventually acted to curb community action. All the events showed a flaw in the Johnson style when not checked by a constructive congressional role in legislation. He was so intent on Presidential achievement and glory that he would run roughshod over Congress, if permitted, and produce a faulty program because of the ignoring of implementation concerns. Presidential ambition and politics were the worst enemy of ultimate Presidential effectiveness in policy. This was much less the case with medicare, aid to education, and civil rights because Congress had a history of concern and knew what it was doing. However, Congress would never have acted in those cases without a strong Presidential lead.[27]

By the fall of 1965 Johnson was beginning to lose his influence with Congress. There was great resentment about his intense pressure, his reluctance to accept amendments and revisions, and his claims of congressional subordination. After he kept Congress in session until midnight on the environmental beautification bill in which his wife was so interested, feelings on the Hill were never the same.[28] But no President could have expected to keep up such a pace, and the 1966 election loss of many of the House seats won in 1964 brought an end to domestic reform.

This, however, was not the tragedy of Lyndon Johnson's Presidency. Such an erosion of power was normal. The tragedy was that his desire to create and dominate a national consensus had forced him to push too hard and claim too much and that the inevitable counteraction occurred. One of the principal reasons that Johnson had decided to increase the United States military intervention in Vietnam in 1965 was his desire to continue the foreign policy consensus then existing. He feared that a failure to act would break apart that consensus. He remembered the political poison that followed the loss of China in the Truman Administration and was afraid that a repetition would destroy his plans for domestic reform. Moreover, he deliberately misled Congress and the public about the seriousness of the Vietnam intervention in 1965 because he thought it would be brief and did not want to imperil his legislative program. He feared that realization of war would turn attention and concern away from reform.[29]

What occurred was that the consensus leader who wanted to have it all was overreaching himself. At the same time that the impact of Vietnam was turning on him and reducing his popularity as well as his support in Congress, unforeseen consequences of the Great Society were also erupting. Resistance to the war and the spread of the civil rights movement to the North, aided by the catalyst of the poverty program, generated a new kind of politics of direct action that was hostile to authority and to the traditional compromises of politics. A President bent on dominance of a national consensus was helpless in the face of dissent that did not accept his premises. The only response possible for him was to deny the validity of their claims. He was President of all the people and expected the public to respond in kind. The consequence was rigidity in the President and an increase in the volume of protest in the society. Johnson had placed himself in this dilemma because he had tried to govern without making choices. He wanted both war and reform. He sought the support of both liberals and conservatives, hawks and doves. He wanted liberalism to be the new consensus about which one could be conservative. He claimed too much and lost it all. The sheer velocity and power and ambition of his leadership unleashed forces he could not control. Any President would have suffered from Vietnam, and the expectations raised in the Great Society, particularly the poverty programs, would have intensified a new populist activism. But Johnson's simultaneous action in both directions unleashed forces that were too strong even for him.[30]

RICHARD NIXON: THE SEARCH FOR AUTONOMY

President Nixon has always run for office in Democratic constituencies, whether his original congressional seat in California or in the United States of America. He has become an expert in detaching voters from a majority Democratic coalition by divisive rhetoric. Consequently he has primarily thrived on negative appeals. He was elected to the Presidency in 1968 with promises to end the war in Vietnam, reduce crime, and stop inflation at home; in short, he was the beneficiary of popular unhappiness with Democratic activism. This gave him latitude to develop domestic programs but without any clear cues at to what the electorate wanted beyond the restoration of order. He conceived foreign policy as his forte and had few if any ideas about what to do in domestic policy.

Conservative parties in any democracy are seldom elected to power on the basis of positive domestic ideas. The triple appeals of candidate, foreign policy issues that cut across conventional partisan alignments, and popular reaction against unanticipated consequences of the domestic programs of progressive governments are much more likely to explain conservative political success. This means that conservatives give a high priority to symbolic appeals. They promise to stop the "welfare chiseler" or bring about "law and order" or stop the "busing" of school children. But there is seldom a positive response to the underlying domestic problem if fundamental social reform is required.

Conservative governments and leaders necessarily speak for all those groups in the society who do not favor progressive social reform. Conservative governments can, however, play a most constructive role in rationalizing, consolidating, and to some extent legitimizing the programs of progressive governments. For example, by 1968 it was painfully clear to adherents of the Great Society that many of its programs had been badly designed and were not meeting the early hopes. Much of the problem was a belated admission of ignorance of the problems. Concentration on legislative enactment also meant a failure to see in advance the potential bureaucratic snarls of administration. For example, many educational and antipoverty policies were formulated as categorical programs designed and funded for specific purposes but without regard for their relationship to other similar programs. The result was a multitude of specific programs fragmented across a number of departments and agencies and bound to strict limits by the laws written by Congress. This created problems of administrative coordination among federal agencies in Washington and the field and compounded the problems of state and local governments in applying for federal grants to attack such problems. The problems were unitary but the federal programs were not. Congress likes to fund programs in this way since it can keep tabs on their specificity and the discretion of federal and local bureaucrats is limited. Also, in time, supporting coalitions in constituencies develop behind such programs and members of Congress necessarily defend their continuation.

After a time the way is clear for a government of rationalizing disposition to reorder such programs, eliminate those that do not work, and consolidate others to permit program planning and coordination at all levels of government. These are the kinds of things a conservative government of managerial orientation could do well. Tough-minded policy analysis that really asks if programs are working is much more likely in such an Administration than in a progressive government that is concentrating on developing the collective political will to pass programs in the first place.

Given the logic of this situation one scenario for the Nixon Administration was set from the outset. The President and a number of his appointees brought a managerial style to government. They did not formally reject the purpose of the Great Society programs but began to search for ways to make them work better. This eventually resulted in Administration plans for general and special revenue-sharing with the states and localities. The idea was to eliminate specific categorial programs and consolidate them in block grants to lower levels of government, which would have discretion about allocation of funds according to local needs. The federal role would become increasingly one of supervising, monitoring, and research and experimentation.

However, by assuming this position the President immediately put his Administration at loggerheads with a Democratic Congress, which was protective of the programs it had enacted. Much of the Great Society had become the status quo and the President was challenging an entire ethos of government involving alliances of mutual interest between congressional committees, Executive agencies, and the organized beneficiaries of programs. In the third phase of the cycle the dialogue between President and Congress shifts from a concern with policy innovation to debate about program administration. This dispute is intensified by the differences between liberal and conservative views about government spending and the subsequent efforts of the Administration to pare down programs, thereby reducing inflation and encouraging the growth of the private sector of the economy.

This is one important theme of the Nixon Administration and in large part it follows from the logic of political competition. It appeals to an orderly, managerial side of the President himself and is manifested in a typical kind of knowledgeable, programmatic, managerial official found throughout the Adminstration, men like Charles Schultz, John Connally, Elliot Richardson, Caspar Weinberger, and Roy Ash.

However, there is another side to the Nixon Administration, to the President himself, and to most conservative governments, and that is a kind of primitive populism. This is the side of the President that unleashed Vice-President Agnew for attacks on the press, the universities, and liberal intellectuals; that attacked welfare and celebrated the "work ethic"; that invited hard hat union leaders to the White House after a group of construction workers in New York beat up some antiwar protestors; that played on the fear of working-class whites about school busing of blacks; and that often identified the political opposition with long-haired protestors and dissenters who were unpopular with most citizens.

There is a sense in which conservative parties and leaders are required to play on the non-economic emotions of people in order to be popular. Disraeli, the Tory democrat, built up the Empire and Queen Victoria as an electoral weapon. Charles de Gaulle glorified French nationalism. Managerial effectiveness is not sufficient to win elections. However, there are great variations between conservative governments in the types of appeals employed. English conservatism is likely to draw on a combination of traditional themes like national unity and patriotism with appeals to material self-interest. The two most recent Republican administrations have proclaimed "peace and prosperity." This was all that President Eisenhower had to do. He delivered on his promise, and this plus his great personal popularity established a bland rectitude as the popular basis of his government. Nixon, however, has not been able to draw on his public personality as a political resource. He has relied largely on rhetoric and symbolic appeals and actions.

There is a third dimension to Presidential leadership in addition to the managerial and the rhetorical. It is the ability of a President to influence the political professionals in Washington.[31] These professionals include members of Congress, the reporters and columnists of press and television and, to some extent, the top ranks of the permanent civil service. These groups watch a President closely to assess his influence with opinion in the country. They shape their actions toward him according to their estimate of his political strength. But they must also be dealt with by a President in their own terms. He must find ways to appeal to them according to their political and institutional interests as they see them. Since they are independent power holders in their own right every President needs the support of this community of Washington professionals. Democratic Presidents seek a variety of modes of accommodation with these professionals because they want positive action from the other parts of government outside the White House. They become experts at political accommodation and bargaining. Republican Presidents, particularly if they are conservative in domestic matters, are much less likely to pursue this strategy. They want less from Congress, are likely to see the working press as unfriendly, and distrust the top ranks of the civil service. Washington has been a Democratic city, in terms of the values of this community of professionals since the time of Franklin Roosevelt, and Republican Presidents know this.

Dwight Eisenhower was able to use the political capital of his popularity to induce the Democratic leaders of Congress—specifically Lyndon Johnson, the Senate majority leader and Sam Rayburn, the Speaker of the House—to meet him half-way on domestic policy matters. They seldom openly opposed him and thereby muted partisan conflict. Their strategy was to cooperate and establish a reputation for the Democrats as a party of constructive government. Nixon brought no such skills of political accommodation to his Presidency as Eisenhower had. Rather, he saw the Washington professionals as his enemies who would do everything possible to thwart his programs. He developed a leadership strategy of direct appeal to his constituencies in the country. For example, he often uses radio for major speeches so that the television commentators cannot comment on his words after he speaks. He has held fewer press conferences than any of his predecessors. Another clear sign of his distrust of the Washington mores of political accommodation was seen in his preference for staffing the White House with essentially nonpolitical associates, men like H. R. Haldeman, his chief of staff, and John Ehrlichman, his chief domestic adviser.[32] After Haldeman and Ehrlichman left the White House in the spring of 1973 in the wake of the Watergate scandal Nixon turned to General Alexander Haig to replace Haldeman as his chief of staff and relied increasingly upon Ron Ziegler, his press secretary and a former advertising man, as a close confidant. The junior ranks of the White House were filled with aspiring young men from the ranks of business and advertising who were people with very little experience in the Washington politics of accommodation. White House aides like Bryce Harlow (who had served with President Eisenhower) and Melvin Laird (who had been a member of Congress, Secretary of Defense, and returned to government in 1973 to assist the President after the departure of Haldeman and Ehrlichman), who did have a feel for bargaining and compromise, were never taken fully into the President's confidence. He seemed not to want to hear any advice that would require him to compromise with the Washington professionals.

Three tendencies thus came together in the Nixon administration: the managerial impulse, the conservative rhetorical and symbolic appeals to the public, and the disdain and distrust for the Washington professionals. To some extent these tendencies were present in the situation of a Republican President in a Democratic city but they were intensified by Nixon's own distrust of others outside his immediate circle and his preference for going his own way in a semi-plebiscitary Presidency. Nixon most values order, ascendence over his opponents, and possesses, in Arthur Schlesinger's words, "an urgent psychological need for exemption from the democratic process."[33]

Because he wanted and expected less of Congress than a Democratic President, Nixon resolved upon a general policy of defiance of Congress, maximum use of the veto, action as much as possible by administrative means, and direct appeals to the public for support. He chose to have face-to-face contact with a limited number of trusted aides—chiefly Haldeman and Kissinger—who screened the information coming to him from others and exercised great influence over those who could see the President. He was not their captive; rather, they were doing his bidding. This is not to say that Nixon did not see his principal advisers in key cabinet posts, men like George Schultz, Secretary of the Treasury, Roy Ash, head of the Office of Management and the Budget, and Henry Kissinger, the Secretary of State. But the pattern of reliance upon a few within the cabinet and virtually ignoring the rest is much the same as resorting to a few White House aides. The President has failed to open himself up to continuous, face-to-face discussion either with the members of his own cabinet or with members of Congress. As Schlesinger puts it, he has sought to "banish challenge from the Presidential environment."[34]

This style is not well suited to reaching agreement with Congress on anything and this was not really Nixon's goal. He knew little about Congress and cared less. As a member of the House he had been primarily a lone wolf. Perhaps most important, he did not like the kind of face-to-face bargaining and persuasion in which Lyndon Johnson took so much enjoyment.[35] Neither Haldeman nor Ehrlichman had any knowledge of Congress and their general attitude toward it was one of thinly disguised contempt. They were devoted to serving Richard Nixon and never felt any loyalty to the long-established folkways of compromise and political accommodation that permeated life in Washington.

Nixon was badly served upon a number of occasions by this attitude of his staff. The White House congressional liaison staff were generally in favor of accommodation with Congress and a Presidential posture of openness and compromise. But it was commonly felt in Congress that they did not have Nixon's ear and his preference for a posture of little consultation, veto, and impoundment of funds authorized by Congress contrary to his wishes suggests this was the case.[36]

In his first term Nixon presented little domestic legislation to Congress and most of what he did present was rejected. His proposals for revenue sharing with the states were finally passed in 1972 in the form of fiscal relief for state and local government through return of federal revenues to those jurisdictions without strings. But hopes for special revenue sharing in which local governments are to be given the responsibility for programmatic action in vital social areas such as education and urban development, along with federal funds, and all without strings, have not been successful across the board. The Congress has been defensive of the categorical programs of the Great Society and its controls over them. It was out of this conflict that Nixon issued a challenge to Congress in early 1973 while still riding upon the crest of his reelection victory. He made clear in strong language that he would impound any funds appropriated by Congress that were over the spending limits set by his budget. The declared objective of such action was to have a non-inflationary budget. The political and governmental goal was to secure by administrative action what he was unable and unwilling to achieve through legislative compromise.[37]

Previous Presidents had used impoundment sparingly and almost always on the conviction that the money appropriated could not be well spent for the purposes intended or should be delayed for a time until it could be better used. Such Presidential actions, however, were usually worked out in a process of give and take with Congress. For example, President Kennedy failed to spend money appropriated by Congress for additional B-70 bombers but he did so only after he had persuaded the chairman of the House Armed Services Committee, Carl Vinson, to put flexible language in the bill that would grant Presidential latitude.[38] The constitutional right of a President to impound funds is vague and limited to the execution of his duties as commander-in-chief and to matters in which the President is authorized to withhold funds from local governments that are not enforcing the laws, such as school districts refusing to desegregate.

Nixon, however, asserted a broad prerogative to impound funds as he wished as a defense against congressional actions that would increase inflation through unbalanced budgets or require additional taxes to close such a gap. This was essentially a political stance by the President against Congress. He hoped to receive the political credit with the public as a defender of economy in government against a free spending Democratic Congress. He did not seem to care whether he had the constitutional power to impound, and even though the courts denied him that power in a number of cases in 1973 he continued his strategy. Large sums, running into the billions were impounded, in many policy areas but with the emphasis upon health, manpower, housing, educational, and environmental programs.[39] This was in essence a Presidential decision for selective enforcement of the law according to his policy goals regardless of the directives given by Congress and written into law.

Arthur Schlesinger interprets this and other attempts at Presidential aggrandizement to Nixon's intention to revolutionize the Presidency in the direction of a plebiscitary office in direct relation with a mass public opinion, which is thereby able to bypass Congress and divest it of its power. The buried assumption of course has been the President's belief that such public support would permit him to use his Executive powers to govern in important matters of both foreign and domestic policy without Congress.[40] Schlesinger questions whether this was a conscious goal for Nixon or simply the end result of a cluster of personal impulses. Michael Novack interprets this Nixon strategy as a design to bring about the redistribution of political power in America rather than as an effort to assert the ascendency of the Presidency in the national government.[41] Novack describes Nixon's appeals to his America of the South and the West, as evangelical America against the liberal, established America of the puritan Northeast. Examples are the remaking of the Supreme Court through the appointment of strict constructionists—in the President's phrase—including three southerners, two of whom were rejected by the Senate; the maintenance of two Presidential homes in Florida and California; the attacks on the national media and plans by the White House, that never quite materialized, to break up the national networks in favor of a scheme for regional organizations that would report the news with less of a liberal, cosmopolitan bias, which was assumed to be hostile to President Nixon.

Certainly this over-all strategy has been part of Nixon's desire to create a new political majority that could replace the Democratic majority, which emerged out of the New Deal era and which is presently shaky. Such a goal is not incompatible with a desire to increase the absolute power of the Presidency over the other organs of government. In fact Presidential power was the chief agency available to Nixon for such a strategy. But Schlesinger is probably right that all of this flowed less from a conscious design on Nixon's part than from a set of short-run impulses and visceral resentments. No President can avoid representing a coalition of part of America in the day-to-day choices he makes. And these choices about the budget and who gains and loses, about which laws to enforce with special effort, about what legislation to promote, will manifest the underlying view the President has of that portion of America with which he aligns himself. Given his view of himself and his coalition in the country it was predictable that Nixon would be a President of confrontation in Washington.

The question remains whether he might not have been a more

effective President in domestic affairs, in terms of his own goals, if he had elected the Eisenhower strategy of compromise with the Congress. He could have perhaps still have achieved his long-term political ends of realignment and redistribution of political power in the country by building a centrist to conservative coalition of support among both congressional parties. However this would have required a Presidential style that was not Nixon's and therefore by definition it could not and would not be done. A case study of success along such lines, which was atypical for the Administration, was the eventual enactment of manpower revenue sharing in December 1973 after a number of false starts over the preceding years. The story of this law and its predecessors illustrates the kinds of conflict between a conservative, managerial President and a liberal Congress, which emerge in a situation of divided power in the aftermath of a period of progressive reform.

In December 1970 President Nixon vetoed the Employment and Manpower Act because it contained a provision for public employment jobs for the unemployed of which he disapproved. The Administration had originally proposed, through the Department of Labor, legislation that would consolidate the many categorical manpower training programs directed to specific groups in the population into broad, general purpose programs to be administered by the states and localities. This ran afoul of the commitment of key Democratic members of the relevant congressional committees to past categorical programs for youth, agricultural workers, disadvantaged minorities, and so on. Eventually a compromise of sorts was worked out between officials of the Department of Labor, acting independently of the White House and the important congressional Democrats in this area such as Senator Gaylord Nelson of Wisconsin. The bill was something of a hybrid that collapsed some programs into general categories, retained other special favorites of some members of Congress, and provided for substantial delegation of initiation and administration of manpower training to local and state sponsoring organizations. The compromise fell apart when the Senate conferees succeeded in keeping their measure for public employment in the final bill. This ran counter to Administration philosophy and caused the President to veto the bill.[42] This story does not particularly reflect negatively upon the President. If anything it suggests that he was more prepared to try new approaches than were the Democrats in Congress. It also shows the kind of tension that was to be expected over the Great Society programs in a new Administration.

The sequel to the story is more significant. It illustrates what can be achieved in collaboration between President and Congress in such a situation. In December 1973 Congress enacted and the Presi-

dent signed the Comprehensive Employment and Training Act,
which was a modification of the previously vetoed bill and the first
breakthrough of the Administration's effort to get Congress to pass
a special revenue-sharing bill. Success was due to the fact that the
strategies dealing with Congress were not those habitually employed
by the Nixon White House. The law provided that the Labor Department would make direct grants to the 50 states and about 450 large
city and county governments to provide comprehensive manpower
training services and to provide public employment for unemployed
workers. Local contractors are granted federal funds to do the job
and have great latitude to develop programs as they wish within
broad federal guidelines set by the Department of Labor. The passage of the law superseded efforts of the Administration in preceding
years to implement much the same kind of program by administrative action and draw on its own interpretation of existing legislation
for the authority to do so. The White House had despaired of any
possibility of legislative agreement with Congress. The most important factor that broke the stand-off with Congress on the matter was
the resignation of John Ehrlichman as assistant to the President on
April 30, 1973. It was reported by participants in the story that
Ehrlichman had increased the tension between Congress and the
White House by his emphasis upon Executive power and his disdain
for the legislative process.[43] He was succeeded by Melvin Laird,
former congressman and secretary of defense, who publicly spoke his
intention to bring about new lines of dialogue and agreement between the White House and Congress. Laird's style was very much
that of a practitioner of the politics of accommodation of the Washington professionals. He was the principal force within the Administration who pushed for an effort to get a manpower bill by legislative
means. The leadership of the Labor Department was also congenial
to this goal and began to bargain with Senators Nelson and Javits and
key House members, both Republicans and Democrats, about the
shape of a new bill. It developed that congressional leaders in manpower matters were far more willing to go along with decategorized
revenue sharing programs than had been the case in 1970 and eventually a bill acceptable to all parties emerged from prolonged
negotiations. The President agreed and signed the bill with enthusiasm. The details of the compromise and bargaining are not so important as the point that a new style in the White House, personified by
Laird, was able to secure agreement with Congress on a matter of
considerable past contention. These initiatives on the part of Laird
and the Labor Department were possible because the President,
weakened by the Watergate scandal and the loss of his two most
important aides, Haldeman and Ehrlichman, was required to bring

a thoroughly political man like Laird onto his staff in order to increase his credibility with the Washington professionals.

This story suggests that Nixon might have been able to succeed with many of his legislative proposals with Congress in earlier years had he pursued such a policy of bargaining and accommodation, aided by politically knowledgeable staff assistants. But this was not his style and the impact of Laird upon the Administration in 1973 was so limited that he finally resigned. Nixon is not really a political man in the sense of wishing to get along with other professionals. He has spent his entire career making political capital by attacking professionals.

It must not be concluded that the Executive-legislative stand-off on rationalizing the Great Society programs or the pattern of federal-state relations were necessarily bad. In fact, the Administration had not fully thought through the implications of revenue sharing and Congress has done well to hold up legislation on it. It is a tenet of Nixon Administration ideology that government closer to the people in space is thereby more democratic. Much of the evidence we have is against this. Citizens have historically been more knowledgeable about, had more relationships with, and felt greater confidence in national government than they do in state and local governments. A unit of government over a large, heterogeneous constituency is likely to represent most groups within that area better than the government of a smaller, more homogeneous unit. In the latter case the dominant interest is more likely to prevail. Furthermore, the majority of the states and cities lack the policy-planning and bureaucratic delivery capabilities to take over many federal missions immediately on a carte blanche basis. A model of accommodation must be found for revenue-sharing and consolidation of programs that permits the continuation of a federal catalytic and supervisory role and ensures that governments at lower levels have the capabilities to deliver services and be politically responsive to the populations served. The Nixon proposals were not fully developed in this direction but gave too much away to the states too quickly without concern for the consequences.

Therefore, the kind of bargaining that has gone on over revenue-sharing between President and Congress is good. If both sides are willing to learn and compromise constructive solutions will eventually emerge as in the case of the manpower bill. The appearance of inaction on the part of Congress is often in fact incubation. Solutions will emerge in time to these dilemmas, and they will come through a mixed process of political competition and accommodation.

The entire cycle of three phases of Presidential leadership is in fact an incremental progression of innovation, enactment, and revision in which adjustments are made in programs on the basis of experience. Politics in the country and within Congress and the Executive is the means whereby these adjustments are agreed upon. It is a rational process in the sense that it draws on a great diversity of experience. But the process offends those who would have government operate rationalistically from a hierarchy of values and first principles. These different views of politics underlie the different prescriptions for congressional-executive relations to which we now turn.

PRESIDENT AND CONGRESS

In none of the three phases of the electoral cycle is the constructive, mutual collaboration of President and Congress in developing and enacting legislation the norm. This does occur in all three phases, but is not the dominant norm in any. Accommodation alternates with congressional initiative and Presidential acquiescence, stalemate, and Presidential dominance. The fifth logical possibility, consistent congressional dominance of the President across a range of issues, seems unlikely to occur again although it may have been the dominant pattern in the nineteenth century. It seems impossible to institutionalize an optimal relationship of mutuality and constructive collaboration between President and Congress because the patterns of politics do not always run in that direction. Rather, the relationship oscillates between the two extremes of a lack of social agreement that makes for stalemate and a sudden onrush of consensus and a burst of Presidential mastery. The instances of genuine collaboration come, in both slack and peak periods of activity, on issues on which there is general political agreement and on which Congress has a history of concern and a stockpile of expertise and can therefore make a positive contribution to Presidential initiatives.

There were a number of such cases during the Johnson years, for example, the enactment of medicare and aid to education. In fact the model of collaboration comes closest to being the norm when President and Congress are of the same majority party.[44] Johnson violated the spirit of collaboration on a number of occasions, particularly in the passage of the Equal Opportunity Act (the war on poverty), but he eventually paid a price in congressional paring down of the program. It is much better if Congress, or those relevant parts of Congress, feel there is a congressional stake in a piece of legislation. Then, once the legislation is enacted the slate is clean and the agenda is free for new controversies. A Presidential attempt to bulldoze Congress is therefore short-sighted and is likely to be self-defeating.

This is true of both the positive style of Johnson and the negative defiance by Nixon.

There are virtues in stalemate if it signifies either a time of issue incubation in which sufficiently strong political support for action has not yet developed or is a mark of widespread disagreement on policy purposes. This is not to deny that some stalemates are due to the deliberate veto of Presidential initiatives by strategically located members of Congress who are out of touch with majority opinion in the country. This kind of obstruction perhaps dominates the consciousness of many observers as a special problem because we still operate intellectually within the framework of post–New Deal politics that began in 1937 with the conservative coalition in Congress taking the measure of the President. This model ignores the political currents in the society that were permissive of such obstruction and takes no account of the continuous amount of policy initiative that comes from Congress itself because of the structure of dispersed power that also permits minority veto.

Congressional initiative is always present even during periods of Presidential dominance; the Wagner Labor Relations Act, for example, which extended the right of collective bargaining, originated in the Senate and was given only lukewarm support by President Roosevelt. Similarly, the postwar Taft-Hartley and Landrum-Griffin labor bills originated in Congress as did the Atomic Energy Act of 1946, the National Aeronautics and Space Act of 1958, the Communications Satellite Act of 1967, and the Water Quality Act of 1965.

These kinds of initiatives are based on the expertise and drive of individuals and are not the same thing as the routine kind of policy management of the interlocking alliances of congressional committee or subcommittee, Executive agency, and relevant interest groups. Such alliances seldom lead to innovation and Presidents are wary of invading these stable fields. This pattern has been dominant in agriculture, conservation, and public works, for example. These have not often been issues of high public visibility, and Presidents have limited political resources here. This is a kind of distributive politics that reflects the localism of congressional political incentives. However, many of these issues are opening up for Presidential leverage. For example, the simultaneous existence of the Environmental Protection Act and a new array of environmental action groups have given the President new political resources to use against the pork barrel public works system, and in fact President Nixon has correspondingly reduced the budget of the Army Corps of Engineers.

Aside from this kind of static alliance politics, parts of Congress take many direct legislative initiatives. These can be generated by an individual, for example, the authorship by Senator Henry Jackson, chairman of the Interior Committee, of legislation for national land-use planning. They can result from the mutual prompting of a committee and an Executive agency, perhaps aside from Presidential attention. The 1956 Civil Rights Act was passed through such an alliance of a Republican attorney general, Herbert Brownell, and Democratic committee chairmen with the President's passive approval. Sometimes Congress can prod the President to act, as was the case with President Eisenhower and the creation of the space agency.[45]

The great majority of initiators of new measures are Democrats, in part because the Democrats have controlled the committees, the locus of innovation, and in part because of their ideological orientation. The formal leaders of Congress play primarily coordinating roles. Policy entrepreneurs usually stand high on committees where they use their expertise. Such men are crucial in periods of both policy incubation and enactment. They are more likely to be in the Senate than the House because the looser structure and deference to individual autonomy in the former is more conducive to entrepreneurship.[46] Names like Kefauver, Humphrey, Muskie, Javits, and Edward Kennedy come to mind. This kind of innovativeness is made possible by the congressional subcommittee system, for it is in subcommittees that staff expertise exists, issues incubate, and a forum is provided for discussion and publicity.[47] Congressional policy innovation can coexist with Presidential leadership, but it seems to emerge most clearly when President and Congress are of different parties. However, as we have seen, Presidents can often use the veto power to overcome such initiatives; therefore, issue incubation is more likely than enactment.

This pattern of congressional initiative is not the dominant one when it comes to the passage of major legislation about which there has been great political controversy. The policy entrepreneurs of Congress can often prevail, but only on specialized issues in which their expertise is highly regarded. Nevertheless, it takes the President as catalyst to pull together all the supporting forces in Congress and the country for the most innovative actions.

We have drawn a picture of great institutional flexibility and dispersed initiatives in the relationships of President and Congress. This will displease those who feel that such a structure inevitably leads to policymaking processes that are incrementalist; that emphasize compromise, consensus and system stability; and that provide for decisions about crucial matters not all at once in terms of general recognition of the public interest but through limited discoveries, agreements, and adjustments over time. Such critics must ask themselves if there are any satisfactory alternatives of doing business in a complex, pluralistic, continental democracy. The fault is surely not in the institutions, which are highly permeable by social and political currents, but in the society that is difficult to organize and lead.[48]

THE PRESIDENCY AND LEADERSHIP

In Chapters 6 and 7 we have been examining a model of a three-stage cycle of government that seems to have repeated itself three times, with variations, in the twentieth century. No claim is made that such cycles occurred before that time or that the pattern will continue into the future. The dynamics of the cycle is seen to follow from the logic of political competition within one national ideological tradition, that of liberalism. Two elite subcultures, which change their social composition over time, exist in a permanent tension that grows out of the characteristics of a capitalist society. The division is between those who embrace capitalist values of achievement and individualism heartily and those who respond negatively to these impulses and affirm equality and community as goods to be enhanced. Neither group fundamentally challenges the structures and theory of capitalism however. Competition is always about incremental change with the initiatives being taken by the progressives.

Public opinion and electoral trends respond to changing social conditions and the initiatives of political leaders in ways that provide resources and set constraints for these competing elites. But any given government seldom has a clear public mandate to apply an ideology wholesale. It is not even clear whether public opinion becomes more or less ideological and divided along such lines during different stages of the governmental cycle. The evidence from 1952 to 1964 suggests that this did happen. The same heightening of consciousness and issues may have occurred during the Progressive era before World War I and during the New Deal. Ideological consciousness and divisions may have lapsed during the 1920s and 1950s. This does not seem to be true at the present time however. The 1972 election was certainly one in which ideological divisions were sharply drawn among voters, although the lines were most sharply etched by the losing camp of leaders and voters. But it is not clear that the Nixon era is a period of ideological and programmatic consolidation that will pave the way for a new era of reform. We may be living in a period of continuous turmoil in which national leaders are unable to resolve domestic problems. If this is so, neither the politics of reform nor of consolidation will be sufficient.

Congress as an institution of many parts is slower to act on national electoral rhythms than is the Presidency because of its fragmented electoral structure. Members of Congress bring bits and pieces of national social reality to their offices, but the institution lacks mechanisms to draw these together. An outside stimulus and lead are required from the President. This does not mean that a President can or should always get his way with Congress. There are many times when we would not wish him to succeed depending upon our values. There must be periods of waiting, stalemate, and incubation to permit a consensus to form in terms of which a President may lead Congress for positive action. Of course skillful Presidents can so lead public opinion and the legislature that they hasten the time for action. But the achievements of a President will not last unless such a consensus of the majority of citizens, the politically active members of the society, and the Congress supports them. This means that all major decisions must be taken in an open process of political accommodation between President and Congress. This decision process legitimizes political innovation in the society.

It follows from this that we should not expect all of our Presidents to be reforming heroes who will dominate Congress and push it toward action. The political resources for such achievement vary greatly over time. Rather, we need many different kinds of Presidents. John Kennedy was a President of preparation who was successful in terms of the problem he faced, which was to guide national opinion toward new ideas. His advocacy of tax cuts to stimulate the economy, civil rights legislation, arms control, and a diminution of the Cold War were his greatest achievements even though he lived to see none of them happen. Lyndon Johnson understood the requirements for a reform President to marshall his political resources and use them quickly and powerfully before they slip away from him. In this sense both he and Franklin Roosevelt saw their opportunities correctly. But Johnson overreached and tried to prolong a consensus that became artificial. Roosevelt had greater political sensitivity most of the time and in fact embodied the styles of caution and heroism of both Kennedy and Johnson during his long Presidency. He was several Presidents in one. Dwight Eisenhower also understood the frame of reference within which he had to work, and successfully acted out that role as a President of unity and consolidation. Richard Nixon did not choose to play the consolidating role of an Eisenhower. He sought to be an innovative President who would maximize the powers of the office and bring about a redistribution of political power. His basic problem and the reason for his failure has been that he did not use the normal devices of democratic politics to achieve his goals. He ignored his political party, made no effort to build a coalition of support in Congress, and relied primarily upon Presidential administrative powers and rhetorical appeals. The powers of his office were in fact employed with such ruthlessness by himself and his principal associates that the effort was exposed, backfired, and seriously weakened his Presidency. This was the story of Watergate. Appeals to publics are always fragile in their hold, and by 1974 the combination of economic malaise, including an energy shortage and declining public respect for the President as an individual, had destroyed any potential mass base for a new conservative majority. The President was put in the position of trying to hold onto his job in the face of possible impeachment by Congress even if it meant a political disaster for the Republican party in the 1974 fall elections. He told a press conference on February 26, 1974 that he would not resign from office, even if his party would be hurt by his continued tenure, because of the principle that the declining popularity of a President should not be permitted to shake the stability of the Presidency as an institution. He then cited a number of policies that were contingent upon Presidential stability such as détente with the Soviets and the settlement of the Middle Eastern conflict.[49] A careful analysis of the President's words reveals the implicit assumption that democracy should not be permitted to interfere with what a President wants to do. Of course he was trying to suggest that impeachment would in reality be an unjustified partisan political attack upon him, which, if successful, would hold future Presidents hostage to similar attacks and thereby weaken the independence and authority of the office. The flaw in the reasoning is that it is possible that impeachment of the individual might be justified on constitutional or legal grounds without affecting Presidential authority in the least. Nixon's outlook, however, is not simply a clever defense. It also reflects his enduring belief about the necessity of leadership being free of democratic, political restraints. In foreign affairs he has seen himself as accountable to history rather than to the immediate democracy. The same attitude is carried over into domestic policy matters. The problem is that it has not worked and in fact proved to be disastrous for the President because he tried to accomplish his goals through means other than politics.

One can conclude that solid, enduring policy achievement in American government depends upon the securing of widespread agreement about the necessity for action in given directions. This agreement can only be secured through Presidents who are practitioners of a democratic politics of persuasion. Successive Presidents are unwitting partners in the slow and incremental development of national responses to social problems. Even when they are on opposite sides of a question their efforts to persuade others contribute to a dialectical process of policy development that never stops. The kind of President we do not want is one who breaks the chain of persuasion by asserting his authority to rule alone. Politics usually catches up with such a leader, however, as the histories of both Johnson and Nixon reveal. All our Presidents need not be great heroes, but all should be democratic leaders.

8

The
President
and
Bureaucracy

The President is not made master in his own Executive house by the Constitution. The constitutional structure of separate institutions sharing powers gives Congress the authority to establish Executive departments and thereby to attempt to control them through the process of making appropriations and writing statutes. The departments must necessarily face two ways—upward to the White House and horizontally to Congress, or, more accurately, to particular sections of Congress, the committees and subcommittees.

Another constraint on Presidential authority within the Executive is the fact that many of the departments and agencies have developed symbiotic client relationships with organized interest groups, for example, the Department of Agriculture and farmers, or the Office of Education and school bureaucracies. These often become three-way alliance relationships between the department or agency, the interest group, and the relevant congressional committee or subcommittee, both legislative and appropriations. A web of horizontal relationships thus develops that can undercut Presidential vertical authority over his own Executive establishment.[1]

The evolution of the federal Executive departments from the original three to the present eleven came in a piecemeal fashion by ad hoc responses to the development of new functions by the federal government, for example, Interior and conservation, Agriculture and farm economy support, HEW and government action in education and welfare areas. Each of these creations was preceded by a long struggle by a coalition of interests that was eventually able to force the creation of a new department to serve that coalition. The department operates within the context of its supporting coalition.

237

This is apparent when a President appoints his cabinet. He does not really bring together a unified team with common policy goals but, rather, looks for people who will be acceptable to the coalition of constituents for each department. Often, he has not even met some of his future cabinet officers before his election.

Within the Executive, cabinet officers face two ways, upward to the President and Presidential government and downward to the permanent government. The Presidential government is that thin layer of Presidential appointees in the White House and Presidential agencies and at the top of each department. Their perspectives and loyalties are those of the President in great measure. The permanent government is composed of all those civil servants whose jobs are secure regardless of changes of Administration. They have strong commitments to departmental missions and close alliances with supporting groups in the social environment of the department and often with congressional figures on the key committees relevant to the department or agency.

Thus the President cannot rely upon the department heads he has appointed to serve his point of view completely. They must live with and speak for their departmental constituents and must answer to Congress. This often leads to relationships of tension with Presidents if they seem to be serving the permanent government more than the Presidential government.

The problems of Presidents and department heads in taking hold of the departments cannot just be attributed to the influences of Congress and the external society. As we saw in Chapter 4, a lively bureaucratic politics would exist in any event. Diverse perspectives follow from departmental and subdepartmental missions that are sometimes seemingly cast in iron by the culture of bureaucratic professionalism. Foreign Service officers, public health doctors, forest rangers, customs officials, education administrators, and of course the professional military all have strong ideas about organizational mission that comes not only from the objective role but from a blending of professional training and norms with organizational goals. Conflicts are common within departments. For example, within the Interior Department people who manage the public lands may come into conflict with fellow members of the department who are responsible for development and exploitation of oil and gas.

Not all departments are the same in their composition, internal politics, external alliances, and relationships with the President. There will be differences within each organization from bureau to bureau depending upon the issues and coalitions involved at a given time. A good initial typology, nonetheless, is the distinction Thomas Cronin draws between the "inner" and "outer" cabinet departments.[2] The inner cabinet, consisting of the departments of State, Defense, Treasury, and Justice, is more responsive to the President than the outer ring. They are less client-oriented departments; in fact, the President is their chief client. Any President must deal directly and frequently with the heads of these departments because their business is the highest on his list of concerns of national security and economic policy. In addition, legal questions cut across all policy areas, although they usually cluster around an issue whether it be civil rights or an Executive privilege question. The Department of Defense is different in some respects from the others in this category in that the professional military is a very strong pressure group with external allies in Congress and the public that can make life uncomfortable for a President. This is all the more reason why Presidents have closely tied secretaries of defense to themselves.

The outer cabinet is composed of the domestic policy departments, several of which are actually umbrellas over bureaus with long previous histories and often with conflicting missions: Health, Education, and Welfare; Housing and Urban Development; Agriculture; Interior; Commerce; Labor; and Transportation. The problems of command and control over such loose collections of bureaus exist at both the Presidential and secretarial levels.

In 1971 President Nixon sent to Congress a plan prepared by an advisory commission to consolidate these domestic departments into four on the principle of form following function. The four new goal-oriented departments of Natural Resources, Human Resources, Community Development, and Economic Affairs were intended to subsume all complementary functions under one roof and end contradictory tasks for the existing departments, such as the responsibility of Agriculture for the care of forests. They were also intended to bring complementary tasks closer together, such as urban development and transportation. The opposition of farmers and farmers' organizations to being submerged caused Nixon to give up on Agriculture, but he pressed on with the rest. The Presidential purpose was to straighten out the lines of governmental responsibility all down the chain of command and enhance his own control over the Executive. The example of Agriculture illustrates how difficult it might prove to be to cut apart the old alliances of bureaus and agencies, interest groups, and congressional committees.[3]

The plan was carefully designed so that the committee and subcommittee structure of Congress would not have to be changed. Each subcommittee would continue to attend to the segments of departments with which it had dealt in the past even though the new overall structure might be different. Any scheme requiring a rationalization of the committees would have been doomed from the start because it would have challenged personal prerogatives built up over the years. It would also have threatened long-established, and desirable, subcommittee knowledge of various parts of departments.

The principal reason that such reform measures do not pass however is that members of Congress perceive that the access and influ-ence of interest groups to departments and bureaus would be changed by Administrative reorganization. Farmers might not do nearly so well in a Department of Natural Resources as they are now doing in a department set up especially to serve them. From the Presidential viewpoint this is a strong argument for consolidation. A secretary responsible for natural resource questions could, at least theoretically, develop programs to integrate concerns for energy supply, land use, and the environment in a way that is now difficult to do across departments.

No reorganization plan along functional lines could hope to eliminate strong disputes within or between departments since conflicts are due not solely to organization but rather to the competing demands on government from society.[4] A classic case is the sharing of water resource responsibilities among the departments of Interior and Agriculture and the United States Army Corps of Engineers. The Interior committees have authority over the Bureau of Reclamation, the Agricultural committees over the Soil Conservation Service, and the Public Works committees over the Corps of Engineers. Each of the agencies and committees has limited and partially conflicting missions, yet there seems no politically feasible way to combine these missions under one roof because of organizational rivalry, impinging interests of groups, and competing congressional jurisdictions.

The real problem, however, is not so much government organization as the fact that several different and competing functions must be carried out: (1) improvement of rivers and harbors; (2) reclamation and irrigation; and (3) watershed protection. Conflicts often occur in the actual planning of river basins for multiple use, for example, but the organizational fights reflect the alternative uses and competing groups rather than organization per se. One can thus imagine that a new Department of Natural Resources would engender a great deal of bureaucratic infighting and would spawn new sets of subcommittees in Congress to watch over it. Inherent limits thus exist to the formal Presidential control of the Executive branch.

Similarly, no one department, even in the most rational of plans, could hope to have sole jurisdiction over its most important problems. Urban affairs, for example, cuts across human resources, community development, economic affairs, and natural resources in regard to pollution and land use. The President must have mechanisms at his level for policy development, resolution of disagreements between departments, and follow-through on program execution.

There is an irony about the managerially-minded Nixon Administration attempting to reorganize the domestic departments to give the President greater control over them. If each department were in fact run as a hierarchy with a unified mission, the political executives who run it would be very much at the mercy of the professional civil servants who carry out the department mission. There would be insufficient competition between diverse groups and missions within the department and all information and recommendations from below would be biased in the direction of the long-term interest of the professionals who can always outlast a President's appointees at the top. One of the best ways for a department head to control a department is to use the competition of groups within it to get conflicting information and perspectives. The experience of many Nixon appointees as corporation executives may not have served them in good stead. They had to act from the model of the private corporation, which is tightly controlled by executives from the top down. However, a corporation must meet the tests of market competition or fail, which is a great incentive for it to learn about its environment. Government departments lack any such market test; the need for competition is within them—a kind of internal organizational market competition. In any event such competition is inherent in government because of the conflicting and ambiguous tasks required. Any effort to reorganize conflict out of existence and replace it with hierarchy and control from the top by administrative rule will fail. Those at the top will learn less about the tasks of the organization rather than more because the tight controls they have imposed will cause distortion of the information coming up the ladder.

FOREIGN POLICY

Three models of a Presidential organizational system for making and implementing foreign policy are commonly discussed.[5] In the first the President and the White House national security staff dominate. In the second the President and the secretary of state, as his closest Presidential adviser, run things. The third is an intermediate system in which authority is dispersed between the White House staff, the State Department, and perhaps the Defense Department, but the President still remains in charge. Each model has costs and benefits and none is ideal.

President Eisenhower sought coherence in foreign policy through an elaborate system of interdepartmental committees. At the top the

National Security Council made decisions and at the lower levels the committees executed the policies. He did not build a strong analytic policy staff in the White House but relied on the secretary of state and other key department heads as well as his own experience and judgment in making decisions. There was coherence to this system and assurance that all organizational points of view would be discussed before decision. However, position papers coming up the chain of command were likely to reflect interdepartmental compromises of competing orthodoxies and policy directives going down were written in broad language agreeable to all but difficult to apply. Eisenhower's decision and execution mechanisms were almost too deeply rooted in the bureaucracy, although in actuality both he and John Foster Dulles, his secretary of state, often dealt with policy in personal ways, drawing on their great experience with a minimum of analysis.[6]

John Kennedy saw the Eisenhower system as a seemingly artificial separation of policy and administration and as an overbureaucratization of the decision process. He believed that policy developed out of concrete and specific decisions and therefore wanted to be actively and personally involved in choices before they were framed as options by a bureaucratic process. He initially expressed the hope that the secretary of state would be his principal adviser and the active implementor of policy across the government. However, in a short time he discovered that Dean Rusk had little interest in taking charge of policy execution and it became apparent that Kennedy intended to be his own secretary of state. The White House national security apparatus under McGeorge Bundy then became the chief mechanism for constructing a decision process to develop options, structure debate, and follow up on policy execution. Instead of the almost codified and structured process under Eisenhower, the Kennedy style was one of decision by ad hoc groups after intensive analysis and debate. Its failing was that there was little relation of one decision to another and somewhat less than full attention given to administrative follow-through. Innovativeness was enhanced but perhaps at the cost of coherence and the ability to fully implement policy, something White House staff could not really do.[7]

Kennedy found the State Department slow and unresponsive to his requests for new ideas and seemingly oblivious to his needs.[8] Rather than seek to reform the department, however, he developed an instrument in the Bundy staff to serve his purpose. This was more in keeping with Kennedy's personal style and reflected the requirement on any President to place immediate policy choices ahead of academic organizational change. Presidents seize the lever available.

Johnson was much less self-confident in foreign policy matters than

Kennedy and was anxious to establish continuity with past policy to legitimize his own government. For this reason he relied heavily on Rusk and McNamara, with both of whom he was compatible, and gave less free rein to the White House national security staff to expose policy options or to question prevailing policies and programs. He lacked the knowledge of how to use a staff for foreign policy nor was he adept at securing views from the upper levels of the bureaucracy. In his customary style he relied upon conversations at close quarters with Rusk, McNamara, and a few other officials and supplemented these with discussions across the top of government. Much of this effort was directed toward persuading others of the rightness of his policies. The decision process was symbolized by the "Tuesday Lunch" at which he and his top four or five associates made major decisions. But neither the close conversations at the top nor his wide persuasion efforts gave the government beneath much idea of what his policies were. Johnson's secretiveness and increasing defensiveness on Vietnam toward the end of his Presidency sealed him off from much of his government. His system had neither the coherence of the Eisenhower scheme nor the analytic capability of the Kennedy model.

Each President is likely to want to avoid what he sees as a deficient system of his predecessor, and Nixon was no exception. He did not wish to return to the inflexible Eisenhower system, having seen it firsthand, and he believed that the Kennedy freewheeling style was too ad hoc and pragmatic at the expense of a concern about how specific policies fit an overall pattern. Johnson had not really improved upon the Kennedy system because most policies had gone by default in the face of Vietnam. Nixon was determined to impose a new set of priorities on American foreign policy. Therefore he favored a decision system centered in the White House.

The main achievement of the Henry Kissinger White House national security staff was to impose an analytic responsibility on the departments. Kissinger directed the preparation of policy analyses in State, Defense, and occasionally other departments that would explicate the problem of policy choice; often the papers were sent back by Kissinger, more than once, for rewriting. His staff would usually rework these papers and add analyses of their own. The purpose was to permit Kissinger to go to the President and present a careful analysis of the widest possible number of options for decisions. This fit Nixon's preference for working with documents rather than people and for dealing with others through a key intermediary. But the primary purpose in designing the system in this way was to avoid the fixed, not analytically examined bureaucratic positions of the Eisenhower system and the loose, ad hoc procedures of the Kennedy period. In the latter case it was felt that coherence and even careful analysis were sometimes lost in the emotionally charged crisis atmosphere.

The Kissinger apparatus concentrated primarily on the major issues such as Vietnam, arms control, and relations with China and the U.S.S.R., with some conspicuous omissions such as the Arab-Israeli conflict, international economics, and weapons strategy and development. Weapons strategy was handled in the Pentagon and international economic questions, in which Kissinger was not expert, were dealt with by a number of White House and Treasury Department groups.[9]

The State Department role in this scheme was confined to the traditional one of diplomatic relations, although Kissinger's becoming the second man in the government on foreign policy, thus leaving the secretary of state in an embarrassing limbo, was perhaps not inevitable. The main reasons for this outcome were Nixon's preferred style of operating, Kissinger's strength of mind and personality, the nature of the questions of a Vietnam peace settlement, an overture to China, an agreement with the U.S.S.R., and the SALT arms control talks. All these required secrecy and the involvement of only a relatively few people at the top of government. It is doubtful that a tradition-bound State Department would have been a reliable mechanism for any of these innovations.

Nixon and Kissinger had restored the distinction between decision and operations that Kennedy had erased. Their efforts were focused on a few overriding policy choices, hoping to give the government new directions by imposing such a new intellectual framework. However, before long Kissinger saw that a separation of decision and implementation was artificial, and the staff began to work on policy follow-through as well as on analysis. At this point the fundamental institutional weaknesses in the model became apparent.[10] Kissinger was really trying to play two roles, that of policy adviser to the President and policy leader throughout the government, and the two proved to be incompatible for someone in the White House. He always sacrificed the second for the first when he had to. Closeness to the President and the immediate meeting of his demands formed the basis of Kissinger's influence. Often there was not time nor energy to do anything else.

A more serious problem was that Kissinger was not in an institutional position to lead in the implementation of policies throughout government. Although he could successfully chair high-level committees composed of department and agency heads on matters of policy choice, he did not direct an institutional chain of command and his staff had even less potential influence. Furthermore, no one else in government was doing what needed to be done for implementation. The secretary of state and his department were by and large cut off from the most important policy decisions, which made it difficult for them to know how to translate policy into implementation. They did not think along these lines but attended to their traditional business. A secretary of state with minimal Presidential authority behind him could not effectively be the chief agent for the implementation of policies. A related problem was that most policy matters not covered by the NSC system led to decision by default at lower levels in the departments in the process of day-to-day execution. This again shows the inability of a White House staff to do everything.

The Nixon-Kissinger system was suited to a time of emergency and secrecy but became less useful as the salient foreign policy questions changed and the number of government participants necessarily broadened. For example, it may have been necessary to keep Congress in the dark on the key policy changes of the Nixon first term, but by the beginning of the second term new questions of relations with Europe and Japan, international economics, future arms agreements with the Soviet Union, and energy supply problems required open discussion within the Executive and with Congress. In September 1973 Henry Kissinger was named secretary of state but continued as assistant to the President with an office and staff in the White House. The challenge was presented to forge new links between policy analysis, decision, and execution, with a secretary of state with the authority to do so. However, the stumbling block was the Department of State, its subculture, and its relationships with the rest of government.

Of the three models of foreign policymaking described at the beginning of this section—one centered on the White House, another on the State Department, and the third a mixture of the other two —only Nixon adhered to one of the models in pure form. Eisenhower came closest to the State-centered system but under no President since Harry Truman and the burst of creativity of postwar foreign policy has the State Department played the full role it might play as the center for foreign policy analysis advice and execution. Before we can assess the prospect for a viable State-centered system we have to ask what the problem has been and in so doing we will illustrate the difficulties a President has eliciting responsiveness from the national security bureaucracy.

Franklin Roosevelt loved to joke that a Foreign Service officer could get to be an ambassador if he met three requirements: (1) be loyal to the service, (2) do nothing to offend people, and (3) not be intoxicated at public functions.[11] Presidents have perhaps always had a certain disdain for the diplomat. In the immediate postwar period, however, the State Department was creative because of a conjunction of talented leaders and extraordinary problems. The department policy-planning staff invented the Marshall Plan of economic aid to Europe, devised the Truman Doctrine of aid to Greece and Turkey, and laid the intellectual basis for the containment doctrine in regard to the Soviet Union and for the development of systems of collective security around the world. The times required such creative responses and the cluster of personalities was able to meet the challenge. Harry Truman was very open to advice from his principal cabinet officers, whom he respected. Secretary of State George Marshall was a graduate of the army staff system and a strong manager of the department who charged the policy-planning staff with developing ideas which he used. George Kennan, director of that staff, was a brilliant and articulate expert on Soviet affairs.

The next two secretaries of state, Dean Acheson and John Foster Dulles, were lawyers used to dealing with issues and individuals and not to managing organizations. This factor was accompanied by a hardening of policy positions in an intensified Cold War, so that policy planning came to play less of a role. Policy responses increasingly became part of bureaucratic routine and secretaries of state advised Presidents and coordinated high diplomacy in relative disengagement from their own department. The external harassment of the department by anticommunist demagogues (especially Senator Joseph McCarthy) during this time, of which the so-called loss of China and the recrimination that followed was one example, contributed to the department's decline. This rigidity was not solely due to external causes. The Foreign Service Officers Corps and the State Department as an institution had developed habits of thinking and working that were uncongenial to either policy innovation or to a wide-ranging role within the government as a whole. These factors must be examined closely because they are the principal impediments to a State-centered foreign policy system today.

Foreign Service officers have a strong sense of collective identity and commonality of style that is protective of their traditional responsibilities but precludes their taking on new ones.[12] They see themselves as diplomats skilled in political negotiation and reporting and place important though secondary emphasis on economic matters. This leads to a general world view that might be called "classical realism," and it is perhaps characteristic of foreign office elites elsewhere too. The world of nations is seen as relatively unchanging in its importance of power relations despite surface manifestations of change. There is doubt about any effort to transform the world whether it be through foreign aid or counterinsurgency warfare.

Traditional societies or cultures are seen as difficult to change through American action. In short, there is a skepticism about activist foreign policies that go against these fundamental realities.[13]

Foreign Service officers are likely to think like historians in broad impressionistic terms and rely upon intuitive and empirical modes of observation and analysis in their reporting. For this reason the State Department has not been too receptive to academic research on world politics that has become increasingly abstract and quantitative. By the same token, they have been hostile to the technological approach to foreign policy problems derived from game theory and systems of weapons analysis, so much of which was involved in Vietnam planning and action, at least at the level of official rhetoric. They have also looked down upon the foreign aid and propaganda information agencies that are subordinate to State as strictly marginal to the important business. An effort in the mid-sixties to make ambassadors managers of "country programs" in which they would implement a program budgeting system in which different United States efforts in a country—such as aid, propaganda, and diplomacy—would be evaluated comparatively failed in part because it did not match the role perceptions of most ambassadors who saw themselves as diplomats rather than managers.[14]

This mode of thought probably corresponds to reality more closely than most world views do. Nonetheless, its adherents have been put at a disadvantage in a series of activist Administrations, beginning with that of John Kennedy, that wanted new ideas and innovations. Much of the thinking in State had become hardened around official positions of the past.

The "living system" of the State Department as an organization reinforces these predispositions.[15] One important dimension of the status system is that Foreign Service officers want to be ambassadors; as in the military, they therefore subordinate themselves to the requirements of rising in an organizational hierarchy. This means being circumspect, not provoking conflicts, pleasing superiors, and compiling a good record of evaluations. The emphasis is put upon safety and conformity and the system of initial selection, evaluation, and promotion ensures conformity to group norms—to get ahead you go along. This is further strengthened by the mystique of diplomacy as a special elite skill.

These informal group norms exist in a vast organizational system that must draw together information from all over the world and move it up through a hierarchy that becomes increasingly slender. Numerous studies have documented that the informal norms of careerism and conformity have put a premium upon agreement and consensus at the cost of boldness and originality in the transmission of information and recommendation across and up the ranks.[16] The dominant pattern is one of playing it safe and withdrawing from potential conflict before it occurs. This is the phenomenon of Group think on an organizational scale and it is the basic cause of the frustration of Presidents with the State Department. To them State seems to exist in a world of its own separate from Presidential business, and to a large extent they are right.

State has not been even potentially effective as an instrument for either policy analysis or implementation. The secretary of state has had no special office to provide analyses that would advise him but rather a series of successors to the policy-planning staff that has worked in a vacuum divorced from current policy. This has put the secretary at the mercy of line bureaus each with special interests to protect. The insularity of the Foreign Service officer's definition of his role has prevented any serious effort for State to become the chief implementor and coordinator of Presidential policy across the government. Such authority has not even been exercised within State's official domain in foreign aid, information, and international economic matters.

The greatest deficiency in the State Department is in military matters. Bureaucracies do not always seek to expand and often prefer a safe, limited role if it protects their prerogatives. In the years after World War II State worked out an implicit jurisdictional agreement with the Pentagon to the effect that it would not meddle in military matters if Defense would leave diplomacy to State. This was seen in the relationship of Rusk and McNamara. Rusk regarded Vietnam as a military matter and as a result McNamara became, by default and his own energy, the chief foreign policy adviser to the President. Because of State's restraint here and because of the tendency of Presidents and their associates to see foreign policy crises as military problems, the Pentagon has had far more influence over foreign policy than it might have had had State been vigorous. Still, the line between diplomacy and the use of military force is an unclear one, and the Pentagon crossed it by default on the part of State.

This has meant that Presidents have not been able to call on State for a fresh "political" perspective on national security matters vis-à-vis the Department of Defense. Nor have the diplomats in State been interested in riding herd on policy execution across the range of national security agencies.

An ideal system would give the President analytic help, provide for administrative follow-through and intergovernmental coordination for Presidential purposes, and achieve the primacy of the political perspective. I. M. Destler argues that the secretary of state is in a better position to help achieve such a set of balances than a White House assistant because he has an institutional position within the government as a basis for influence.[17] Destler would transfer the analytic expertise of the White House national security staff to the State Department and develop analytic capabilities there to develop policy options, challenge and evaluate the expertise of others, both within and outside the department, and take a broad political view of foreign policy problems. Such a staff would be linked to operations and budgets so that it would be immediately useful to a secretary in extracting alternatives for directing the department and in providing concrete policy options for the President. Such a system would be seen by the State Department bureaus as a threat to them, but it should be used as a catalyst to force them to open up and change their folkways away from artificial consensus and protected positions and toward genuine discussion. Assistant secretaries should have similar staffs with the goal of releasing a chain of reaction of contained adversary processes throughout the department.

A second necessary change, according to Destler, would be for department officials to be willing to take charge of implementing Presidential policy. This would never be easy, for it would have to have full public Presidential support and an interdepartmental committee mechanism would have to be devised. But the chief ingredient would be the will of the leadership of State and Foreign Service officer cadre to do it. Destler's model is that of lines of confidence running from the President down through State and out from State horizontally across the government. This is a huge undertaking involving restraint on the part of the secretary of defense and the willing subordination of officials in other departments to the leadership of State.

A number of obstacles arise to any such reformation. The role of the secretary of state is not structured to permit him to become a manager of either analysts or an organization. He is inevitably drawn into external diplomatic relationships. It will not be easy to find a secretary who knows how to use policy analysts. Even more important, it seems unrealistic to think that any President and secretary of state would give the highest priority to the reform of the internal bureaucratic culture of State to a degree sufficient to permit real change if it meant giving less attention to policy problems. The world will not stand still to wait for administrative reform and Presidents achieve fame for policy not administration. All Presidential incentives, including the shortness of time in office, seem to preclude a massive push toward reform, although only the President can give the push. The department cannot reform itself. Presidents do not take their styles of organization from administrative theory but rather follow their own personal predispositions, which seldom fit any ideal model.

It is highly unlikely that future Presidents will conform to any one model of White House-State Department relations. Each successive administration will be composed of different administrative styles and different problems. Organizational arrangements will change accordingly. Not all assistants to the President for National Security Affairs are going to be as assertive and self-confident as Henry Kissinger. Future secretaries of state may be very close to their Presidents but unable to lead the State Department—either from lack of interest or ability. Problems requiring a congressional role in their resolution are also likely to demand a more open, pluralistic kind of bargaining and discussion process within the Executive. Rather than adopt any ideal model in advance, a President about to take office should understand the general institutional and political costs and benefits to each way of organizing foreign policy affairs and then choose that mix of organizational strategies that will permit him to meet the kinds of policy problems ahead. An exclusive White House-centered system gives the President autonomy but may preclude a sufficiently wide diversity of views for discussion and poses problems for policy implementation. Reliance by a President upon the secretary of state and the department exclusively has the virtues cited above but runs up against the classic problems of drawing responsiveness from bureaucracy unless the secretary ignores his department, at which point the problems of the White House-centered system occur but without the virtues of the analytic strength of the White House scheme. A mixed system of some kind is probably the best, with the President relying upon both White House staff and secretary of state as well as the secretary of defense, the Treasury Department, and many other agencies such as the CIA. This model imposes a great burden upon the President to keep these forces in balance, usually without any clear sense of what balance means.

The chief requirements upon a President and the standards for judging the effectiveness of his administrative style in foreign policy-making are his ability to use imperfect instruments to do the following. He must ensure the primary of the political perspective over that of the military in foreign policy. That is as much a matter of world view as of organization but both are important. He must find a way to get analytic help to ensure scrutiny of fixed bureaucratic positions and the airing of diverse views guided by expertise. And finally, he must make sure that policy gets carried out. Presidents should be judged on these grounds and the strategies and instruments they use toward these ends judged secondary.

THE MILITARY

The relation of the White House to the Pentagon presents the most difficulties for Presidential authority because of the special problem of civilian control of the military. This problem takes a number of different forms. Civilians must find ways to direct weapons development in terms of long-term strategy in the face of measures of each service to secure hardware of its own. They must be able to assert political perspectives over the military impulse to perceive many foreign policy problems as susceptible to military resolution. The military machine must not be permitted to set its own strategies even in time of war since these strategies might contradict political objectives. Finally, there is the difficult task, requiring great subtlety, of reconciling civilian and military world views so that they are not fundamentally at odds. These problems are all organizational in part and will be considered in turn.

Strategy

A legally strong secretary of defense was created in 1958 by amendments to the National Security Act of 1947, which had originally set up the Defense Department as a holding company for military unification of the three services. In 1958 continuing interservice competition for the development and control of strategic weapons caused President Eisenhower to ask Congress for a strengthening of the role of secretary of defense. The three service secretaries were removed from the chain of command and unified multiservice commands responsible to the secretary of defense were created. The secretary's office was further strengthened by an increase in assistant secretaries and staff.

The man who later profited from these changes was Robert McNamara, for it was too late for the Eisenhower Administration to change its style. Eisenhower had relied on his own military knowledge and prestige to control the Pentagon and chose secretaries of defense who saw themselves as economic managers of a defense establishment rather than as strategists or policy makers. However, he lacked the tools to link a coherent defense strategy to budgets and service programs. The necessary kind of analytic staff work did not exist, either in the White House or the Defense Department. He functioned well with the Joint Chiefs of Staff by setting upper budgetary limits and relative service allocations and then allowing each service to set its own means toward strategic goals. The army resisted the new look, which favored air power and nuclear strength, but the

President prevailed. Still, he and his secretary of defense lacked the mechanisms to evaluate strategic programs and particular weapons systems in order to compare the utility of alternative strategic programs or weapons directed toward a given goal.[18] Toward the end of his tenure Eisenhower became worried about unceasing service pressure for the development of weapons, backed by pork barrel impulses in Congress and industry, and warned of a "military-industrial complex" in his farewell address.

Robert McNamara's impact upon the organization of the federal government was original and creative. He was instructed by President Kennedy to strengthen and diversify American military strategy so that a "flexible response" would be possible.[19] He did increase military capabilities in both nuclear and conventional directions, and because the cost of maintaining multiple strategic options was high he designed a system of relating alternative strategies to budgets. Through systems analysis his talented team of civilian staff, who had come from backgrounds in economics, statistics, and operations research, was able to assess new weapons that would achieve specified goals at the least possible cost. A second innovation was program budgeting in which strategic programs were organized across service lines; for example, nuclear strike capability, conventional forces, home defense, and alternative weapons systems within each category were compared for cost and effectiveness.

McNamara used analytic methods to sort out the claims of the services in a completely new way. Such analysis inevitably strengthens the hand of the central decision maker, and the services strongly resisted these innovations.

These techniques were not by themselves adequate guides to decisions about weapons. A systems analyst is not necessarily gifted at strategic thinking and may have too little regard for professional military experience. On the other hand, few of the high military had ever been trained to think in overall strategic terms. Rather, service goals had always been paramount.

There were, however, some ironies. McNamara could not fight the services on every issue, so he often had to compromise and give in on smaller matters in order to win on big ones. More importantly, the net effect of his system was to strengthen the impact of military arguments and influence in both the Kennedy and Johnson Administrations. This was due, in part, to the weakness of the State Department and to McNamara's intelligence and forcefulness. But it was also due to his having tamed the generals. He made military policymaking so centralized and efficient that the influence of the Pentagon—men speaking with one voice for the first time—was enhanced.

He also brought the military-industrial complex to its highest stage as the variety of weapons systems increased. In seeking to curb the military services, McNamara actually strengthened the role of the military in government with himself as its chief advocate. However, he was the only check on the military that the White House, lacking an analytic capability, had.

The Nixon Administration downgraded the analytic staff in the office of the secretary of defense. Secretary of Defense Melvin Laird kept a small staff that reviewed proposals from the Joint Chiefs of Staff, which by this time had joined the enemy and developed similar skills. The regression was probably part of an effort to stay on good terms with the military during a painful withdrawal from Vietnam. However, Secretary of Defense James Schlesinger, who took charge in 1973, had a background in systems analysis and used it. This is literally the only way that a President can protect himself against the fascination of the services with newer and better technology, whether it be a new airplane, submarine, or tank, which often becomes an end in itself regardless of overall strategy. The alternative is a return to the old days of interservice collusion, bargaining, and strategy set blindly by upper budgetary limits.

It would be a mistake to claim too much for systems analysis and program budgeting, however. Analytic procedures were brought to bear on the selection of specific weapons systems under McNamara. Some of the decisions guided by analysis, however, turned out to be blunders such as the choice of the F-111 fighter plane to be used jointly by the air force and navy in preference to separate service planes. The reason for the selection was the smaller cost of one plane —but it has never flown successfully. Effectiveness may have been sacrificed to cost concerns. One could find many opposite examples, however, in which particular services continue for years with unscrutinized weapons that never become effective regardless of great cost and waste (such as army efforts to develop tanks that are so mechanically and electronically sophisticated that they continually break down).[20] Analytic planning is useful, but it will not show policy makers what decisions to make. Analysis heightens the intellectual quality of decisions, but never supplies enough knowledge. Policy makers must pick their way among competing claims and cope with unknowns. For this reason interservice competition is a positive thing. It produces conflicting sets of facts and demands for decision makers and creates a competitive market system within the Department of Defense. Without such conflict there would be even less information for decision.

Policy

The very name "National Security Council" implies that the important foreign policy questions are also a matter of national security, and military membership is thus built into the council. This bias derives from the legacy of World War II when foreign and military policy were fused and was further strengthened by the Cold War. But this assumption ignores a prior question about whether the military should be so closely involved in high-level policymaking on a regular basis. The effect may be to cause policy makers to see world events in military terms. Organization of the NSC initially followed from a world view based on a fear of Soviet aggression, but it came in time to shape that world view. But, as we saw in Chapter 3, civilian leaders believed that they had to beat the drum of war to get popular and legislative support for foreign and domestic programs. Although this is clear in regard to foreign policy, national defense was also the justification for federal aid to education, the interstate highway program, and federal support of scholarly foreign area research.[21]

The high military has played an important role in United States foreign policy because civilian policy makers have been obsessed with the nation's military security, and the military has been able to extend its influence because of Pentagon organizational advantages over the State Department. The Pentagon has a larger budget than State, with a domestic constituency in and out of Congress. It is attuned to crisis and is ready with contingency plans for a President in a moment's notice. Furthermore, as we have seen, the side of the government that presents political options has been underdeveloped. Thus a President is more likely than otherwise to consider a military response in a crisis.[22] When the military participates in the day-to-day policy process it is bound to stress military danger ahead, for example, in estimating Soviet intentions.

The chief solution to this imbalance is a world view among civilian leaders that sees world problems in political terms and calls for military advice and help only when it is clearly needed. One can hope that in the aftermath of Vietnam and the spirit of détente this will occur. Nevertheless, the military has a long head start over the Foreign Service in the art of acquiring influence in government. Professional officers know how to analyze alternatives, prepare contingency plans, and manage programs in ways unknown to Foreign Service officers. Thus the Pentagon can outperform the State Department in staff work on foreign policy problems. This means that mere coordination of working groups in State, Defense, and the CIA by the State Department is not enough.[23]

Presidential Command and Control

It should not be assumed that methods of policy analysis at the decisionmaking level guarantee responsiveness to Presidential or secretarial operational directions. For example, despite the considerable talk in the Kennedy government about the need to develop a new capability in counterinsurgency warfare, none of the services were ready to fight such a war in Vietnam. The army was oriented to the massing of large formations of troops as in Korea and World War II. The air force simply bombed, as they did in World War II, and chose to ignore all the lessons of strategic bombing studies emerging from that war—about the limitations of saturation bombing. The navy was not prepared for river patrols but for deepwater work, and simply bombarded the shore from the rivers as if there were ships in the jungles. The consequence of all of this was that the massive power of the American military was no match for the small detachments of highly mobile Vietcong and North Vietnamese units who could out maneuver American forces at will. It is not clear that successive Presidents sought to force the military to change their strategies and tactics or just what really effective counterinsurgency capability would look like. Had Presidents made such an effort they surely would have failed, for the professional military have a monopoly over the means of implementing policy. A President cannot replace large sections of the military who refuse to adapt to new situations or orders. They have a monopoly upon the execution of policy. The same kind of conformity to received doctrine, smothering of dissent, and pursuit of advancement by catering to superiors that occurs in the State Department is also endemic in the military officer corps.[24]

A Professional Ethic

The main task of civilian officials in a democracy who direct military professional officers is to make sure that the professional ethic is supportive of democratic norms and values. There is always the danger of an absolutist cast of mind in an officer corps that sees politicians as either unaware of real external danger or as prepared to bargain away security in the long run for peace in the short run. The absolutist sees "no substitute for victory" and remembers the frustration of stalemate in Korea and Vietnam.[25] This is not to suggest that the military would ever stage a coup against a President or Congress, but a segment of the officer corps who have strong ideas and an aversion to softness or surrender can cause great turmoil in the society if aided by political allies. General MacArthur did this after Harry Truman fired him as commander in Korea in 1951.

Morris Janowitz calls for the inculcation of a "pragmatism" in the American officer corps that accepts that military violence is always necessarily bounded and limited by political objectives.[26] It is ironic that the pragmatists predominated in Vietnam, among both civilian and military, in that we deliberately fought a limited war. This was the case in both Korea and Vietnam. Top civilian and military policy makers rejected the absolutism of the MacArthur school of thought, which postulated in General MacArthur's phrase, "there is no substitute for victory." What went wrong in regard to Vietnam is that both civilian and military leaders had a distorted political view of the world in general and of Vietnam in particular. They overestimated the danger of a communist South Vietnam to the interest of the United States and underestimated the difficulties of the United States winning a limited war because of their blindness to the political dimension of the civil war there. Janowitz's pragmatism therefore, while certainly superior to the absolutism of an all-out victory credo, is incomplete as it does not postulate the political ends, which are to limit military claims.

The more general problem is one of reconciling the professional officer to democracy. In monarchical and aristocratic regimes of the past the officer corps had a stable identity as members of upper social classes; the military role was therefore somewhat relaxed and viewed as instrumental to the larger purposes of the state.[27] But in democratic regimes the officer corps are drawn from all ranks of society and must establish their sense of worth through the military role itself. Alexis de Tocqueville pointed out the irony that the leaders of armies in democracies are more likely to want to fight than the military elite of other regimes, for in this way they establish their value to the society.[28] Janowitz and Samuel Huntington see this as a particular problem in modern America. The so-called old army of the interwar period was a society apart with a highly developed professional ethic that concentrated upon the techniques of warfare without any overriding political ideology attached to it. The community offered social security and identity and little identification with politicians and their purposes.[29]

World War II and subsequent history had the effect of politicizing the military. The most civilian-like soldiers were chosen by President Roosevelt for high command, men like Marshall, Eisenhower, and Bradley. Political leaders distrusted MacArthur, Patton, and others who did not conform to civilian norms. Ironically the high military accepted civilian political ideologies, especially as the Cold War began. Several things were then joined: a fervent conception of service to the nation in an ideological conflict with communism; an identification of professional purpose with that mission; an important role in governmental decisionmaking about national security matters; a traditional skepticism about the commitment and staying power of politicians in a crisis; a bureaucratic professionalism that identified the achievement of the national goals of security and military superiority with the capabilities of particular services.

These all present a powerful package for civilian political leaders to handle, especially when it is joined to an ideological climate of combativeness and chauvinism in the country. The problem manifests itself in the pressure that the military is able to put upon the President and other political executives in regard to budgets, weaponry, and the conduct of military operations.

In the aftermath of Vietnam one can suggest several prescriptions for these problems: (1) The world view of both civilian and military leaders should be realistic and not dominated by ideological phantoms. (2) Political responses to international problems should predominate in the thinking of elite and public. (3) The political perspective should hold sway in the organization of government decisionmaking and execution. (4) Civilian leaders must work at the development of a professional ethic for the military officer that subordinates the use of violence to political purposes.

That is a large order for any President, presenting greater obstacles than the challenge of reforming the Foreign Service. And again, Presidents are likely to improvise when faced with impediments to their wishes within the military. They will select congenial service chiefs, try to balance political against military advice, and use systems analysis as best they can—acting through secretaries of defense who are responsive to their perspectives. There simply are no ideal organizational instruments for the making or carrying out of decisions. Realization of that fact is the beginning of wisdom for Presidents and those who would help them.

THE DOMESTIC DEPARTMENTS

Each of the domestic departments has a different relationship with the White House and these vary according to issues, personalities, and changes in Administration. Generalizations about the patterns of links with the Presidency for any one department, much less several, are therefore risky. A President may not have confidence in a department head and may instruct staff to work through an undersecretary, or he may so value the advice of a secretary that White House staff will then lack real influence with the President on matters dealing with that department. The White House may become involved in departmental matters salient to its purposes such as key legislation and leave all other business for routine department processes, or it may intervene in details of administration. There are many people along the chain who enrich the possible variations—those in the Office of Management and the Budget and other parts of the Executive Office as well as in the upper reaches of each department. Of course there are also complex interrelationships within the high levels of departments that change by issue, personality, and time. Any description of this web of human communication at one point in time would not hold for an earlier or later period, and there would have to be as many different models as there were issues. Thus, generalizations are not really possible.

Despite these factors some general statements can be made about problems and deficiencies in White House-department relations to which each successive Administration responds in an ad hoc way.

First, the Presidency is weak in policy analysis.[30] The White House is largely in the retail business when it comes to policy formulation. It receives ideas from elsewhere and reacts, responds, and makes modifications, whether the ideas be from departments or task forces. Strictly Presidential entities like task forces are usually one-shot affairs and are not organized for continuing evaluation of policy and its implementation.

President Johnson sponsored a secret study of this problem by a few close aides and former aides, who recommended the creation of an Office of Policy Development for the White House. The idea was shelved because of uncertainty about the relationship between such a body and the Bureau of the Budget, which helps develop and monitors all Presidential programs. President Nixon, in response to the same imperative, created the Domestic Council, which was to set program priorities and develop and implement programs in domestic policy. The Council has so far only been a clearing house for departmental ideas. It has not developed the kind of expert staff that would permit detailed policy analysis.

Second, the Presidency has a limited information system. The White House collects only scraps of information about the performance of agencies and their thousands of different programs and usually learns too late about program failures. Somehow an information retrieval system must be developed within the White House and the departments that will permit the President to evaluate programs.

Third, the President lacks administrative outreach beyond his own staff into the bureaucracy to oversee the coordination and implementation of plans and programs. Perhaps new kinds of systems managers are required in the White House who will act on the basis of systematic information gathered about program execution to monitor programs and spot problems quickly.[31]

To say all of this is not to advocate draining all initiatives and authority from other sources and giving them to the White House. One must not confuse analytic and coordinating roles with the actual running of programs, which must always be left to the departments. But the analytic weakness of the White House has led to clumsy ad hoc efforts by White House staff to guard the President's options in program development and execution.

William Carey, a former Bureau of the Budget official, describes how the Great Society was put together:

> What Johnson had to rely upon for digestion of task force studies and the development of a policy strategy based on them was the small group of White House staff generalists headed by Joseph Califano, together with the resources of the Bureau of the Budget. In marathon meetings held in Califano's office, interrupted by irascible jinglings of the telephone, task force proposals were combed and debated under conditions of pressure and human exhaustion hardly conducive to sensible outcome. The results were then worked over for review by the President on a highly summarized flip-chart basis which left little room to expose and discuss alternatives, much less minority opinion. Moreover, the use of the Bureau of the Budget encountered problems of policy dichotomies since the Budget Director was under explicit and colorful instruction from the President to hold expenditures below bare-lower totals, while the Califano staff was out to build the President's program in positive and politically profitable terms.[32]

The BOB actually had entered a period of decline by this point. It had come to influence under Roosevelt as a mechanism for him to oversee and coordinate the work of the various departments in his own interest, while at the same time keeping the purposes of his Presidency separate from those of the departments. But coordination and overview are not conducive to innovativeness in policy. The Bureau of the Budget became adept at striking balances and reconciling the President's directives with the missions of agencies and the perspectives of congressional Appropriations Committees. BOB functionaries were experts in the politics of incremental adjustment between forces pushing in opposite directions.

Johnson and Kennedy therefore lumped the BOB with the departments as a useless instrument for program development, although key individuals in BOB did participate in White House program development activities. However, these Presidents had little incentive to restructure the BOB because they did not challenge the incremental budgetary process by which new programs were added to old without any fundamental reevaluation of the old, a view in keeping with the expansionist attitudes of liberal Presidents. Programs were seen as a basis for political bargaining. To eliminate programs was to undercut Presidential political resources, especially with Congress. This point of view has been celebrated by political scientists who have joined liberal and incrementalist ideologies to argue that it is neither possible nor desirable to maintain a central overview over a complex budget. Rather, the process of decentralized bargaining and selective Presidential intervention was praised.[33] But this point of view is seriously outdated as a description of the budgeting process and a prescription for action.

In keeping with the commitment to rationalize and decategorize programs the Republican Administration scrutinized the budget intensively in terms of priorities, and the permanent officials of OMB enforce that policy and are now much less accommodating to either the agencies or Congress. This is another illustration of the emphasis upon autonomy of conservative Presidents discussed in Chapter 6. The doctrine of incrementalism had failed to keep pace with the fact that in a world of limited resources political executives must be able to impose a hierarchy of values upon a budget and eliminate old programs if they are to find the money for new ones.

One of the purposes in introducing the word "management" into the title of the Office of Management and the Budget was to build in greater White House capability for assessing how well the departments and agencies were actually implementing government programs. This was a reaction against the experience of the Great Society in which most of the energies at the top went into program preparation rather than into follow-through. It is, of course, congruent with Presidential political incentives to initiate programs and score legislative victories and reflects the general emphasis of liberals since at least the New Deal on enactment rather than administration.

Good policy analysis should have built into it anticipation about the organizational implementation of a policy, which should be part of the analysis of costs and benefits of alternative programs. But little of this has been done, in part because the knowledge of how to do it is limited but also because there has been no understanding of the need to do so.

The Presidency was a place of creative policy innovation in the 1960s. The challenge for the 1970s is for a decade of creative administrative innovation to ensure that federal programs work in ways that were intended. There are three prime tasks here. First department heads, acting as agents of the President, must find ways to take charge of their departments. Second, the Executive Office of the President must develop mechanisms and ideas about how to build the dimension of policy implementation into initial stages of policy decision. Third, the Presidency must learn how to monitor the administration of policy to ensure successful implementation. We will consider each problem in turn.

ORGANIZATION AND INNOVATION

A high-ranking official who was learning the ropes at Health, Education, and Welfare in 1969 was heard to mutter: "The place is unbelievable. It appears to run by itself."[34] HEW represents an extreme in its size and the degree to which it is a holding company of disparate agencies, but all of the outer cabinet departments share this characteristic of internal diversity of mission. Congress prefers it that way and has habitually written the fragmentation into law so that it can watch over the individual parts and thereby limit the power of a secretary over his own domain. For the same reason Congress has favored categorical legislation that gives specific grants of authority and money to particular agencies to perform certain functions so that the specialized congressional committees can watch over their bailiwicks closely and limit secretarial authority to reshuffle programs and funds. This, of course, means that departments get locked into responses to past problems and may lack the flexibility to move on their own to meet new ones.

Other constraints operate on a department head. Because of the fixed structure of most departments, as set by Congress, he has very limited authority to transfer funds from one program to another or to reorganize bureaus without congressional approval. Programs and bureaus are thereby insulated from his control in this respect. Therefore, he must persuade his subordinates to support him in terms of their own perspectives and incentives for he can seldom force them to do so. The autonomy of bureaus brings about a split between policy and operations, with the latter assuming more importance. A secretary can develop a policy and get a new program and budget, but that is no guarantee that anything will be done.

In addition, a department head has to worry about constraints set by the White House and OMB. Without Presidential support for legislative initiatives and on budgets with OMB a secretary is helpless. At the same time he must respond to constellations of interest group, agency, and congressional pressures that often run counter to Presidential demands.

There are also the seemingly insuperable problems of the ambiguity and often the conflicting nature of departmental goals that reflect diverse social goals and the great difficulties of estimating program effectiveness and goal attainment. It is difficult for a multipurpose department like HUD or Interior to have a coherent set of policy goals. Either the goals are apples and oranges, which are different in kind, or agency missions directly conflict. Interdepartment coordination thus becomes a hopeless task.

These many forces make it hard for a secretary to build stable coalitions of support for policies across his many constituencies. He cannot run a department in terms of some ideal hierarchy of goals that applies to all he does, even if he had such a vision, which is improbable. Rather, he must pick a few issues carefully and seek to build supporting coalitions for his positions. The temptation is great to concentrate on the passage of new programs for which he can secure Presidential help and allies in Congress and pay less heed to the administration of existing programs. The most effective way to encourage innovation in a department is to inject a new program into it. Democrats have taken this route more frequently than Republicans, who have worked for reduction of categorical programs to give department heads more latitude to recombine, withdraw funds, and respond to measures of program effectiveness. But this too Congress resists.

Secretaries have tried a variety of devices to assert control over their departments.[35] Two such methods that usually are paired are the extensive use of analytic staff and a program evaluation system.

A number of the domestic departments now have assistant secretaries for policy analysis and evaluation.[36] The titles vary as do the institutional strengths of the offices. For example, some have the responsibility for budget preparation which strengthens their position vis-à-vis the bureaus. Each assistant secretary has a staff of analysts who work on policy options, program evaluations, and, to a lesser extent, do actual research on problems. These are variations for the domestic departments on the original McNamara unit of "whiz kids" in the Pentagon and the Kissinger White House staff. One innovation is that new knowledge is developed by analysts to aid decisionmaking at the top but also a new role is introduced into the organization that affects other actors and general relationships. The chief function of such analysts is to give the secretary leverage over the bureaus and agencies by subjecting proposals and programs to intensive examination in terms of calculated costs and benefits and systematic program evaluation. A department head can use analysts to sharpen debate, challenge poor programs, widen his own options for choice, improve the evidence available for decision, and permit the actual evaluation of existing programs. Analysis is likely to be most effective if it is tied into budgetary decisions so that everyone can see the actual impact.[37]

The great risk in an apparatus of this kind is that it will create a set of adversary relationships with top officials and analysts on one side and program managers on the other in which communication and partnership actually suffer. This element was present in both the McNamara and Kissinger operations.

However, tension need not be the dominant tone. There is a basis for the optimism that analysts can be used by executives to open up an organization and increase the quality of discussion and coopera- tion. This support is found in research on the conditions for innova- tion in organization. One finds in this work the common view that an "innovative" organization has three essential characteristics: (1) executives with a style of authority that promotes openness of discus- sion and decision in a general atmosphere of informality; (2) special- ized professionals in staff roles who bring their professional styles of dialogue and discussion as well as their ties to sources of academic knowledge to the organizational ethos and thereby are agents of innovation; and (3) organizational structures and processes charac- terized by differentiation of roles, decentralization, a minimum of formalism, little stratification, and a greater concern with quality of performance than with production and efficiency seen in quantita- tive terms.[38] These three factors are said to be linked together in a kind of chain reaction in which democratic leaders, perceiving exter- nal challenges, alter organizational roles and decision processes in order to enhance processes of innovation. The literature is perhaps biased in the direction of innovation but it also contains disclaimers that not all organizations should seek to be innovative all the time and that the determination of the relative balance of adaptation to new conditions and organizational integration in terms of stable and accepted procedures is an important question.[39]

This organization theory is congruent with the literature on profes- sionals in government, which draws the same conclusions about the effects of introducing professionals such as lawyers, economists, and natural scientists into staff advisory positions in government. They are said to be less bound by organizational routine and established client ties than program managers and, as professionals, to be close to external sources of new knowledge and thus sensitive to possibili- ties for innovation. The literature makes clear that the effective utilization of such advisers can come only from political executives who wish to rely on them and know how to do so.[40]

However, the theory of innovation in organizations has been largely developed from the study of private entities, primarily corporations, rather than governmental bodies. This theory needs to be tested more in political settings in which organizational and role imperatives may be very different. In a governmental organization there is a possibility of appeal for help from external allies, whether interest groups or legislators or publics, against others within the organization. This complicates the uses and misuses of information, and the conflicts of bureaucratic politics may require organizational executives to place constraints upon those very factors that are said to promote innovativeness, such as openness and free wheeling discussion. Political executives may have to manipulate situations, structure decisionmaking, and exert sanctions even more consciously and deliberately than executives in private organizations. There is also a more difficult problem of measuring the effects of organizational processes upon policy in governmental organizations compared to corporations or hospitals or other private organizations. In the case of corporations or hospitals there is usually something to measure, whether productivity or successful adaptation to new markets or a decline in a given mortality rate. In government, however, it is not clear what one can measure to assess organizational effectiveness. For example, analysts may be very insightful about defective existing programs but lack political sensitivity to the risks of scuttling them. Program managers may be much more aware of political costs and benefits of action because of their close ties with legislators and client groups. But if the analysts carry the day how does one characterize a decision that may make substantive sense but that leads to a political uproar? This is a significant question about the consequences of giving relative weight to different modes of thought as carried by different roles.

However, analysts and information and evaluation systems do not overcome the most important constraints upon a secretary in administering a department as he wishes. These are the problems of conflicting and ambiguous goals; external constraints from Congress and the White House; interdepartmental conflicts; the difficulty of getting direct control over bureau operations; and the lack of continuity among political executives in his own department, and their likely uneven experience and ability both in the subject matter at hand and in guiding large organizations.[41]

Therefore, a secretary, like the President, must find help by enlisting the support of allies throughout his department, wherever he can find them. This means that the support of career civil servants must be elicited by persuasion from the top. This is institutional leadership not management. The former is the imparting of a series of shared purposes to those within an institution and it should never be confused with systems of management and control.[42] There is a great deal of slack energy and desire to serve beneath the surface of civil servant lives, and an executive with a gift for moral leadership can tap this resource.

This ultimately is the key to Presidential control of bureaucracy as well, especially in regard to the administration of programs. A President must be able to count on descending chains of like-minded associates, most of whom will work for department secretaries, who will do his business throughout the government.

These chains of Presidential associates must not only administer policy, they must initially build conditions of political support for it as well. A President needs department heads and others to work with Congress, interest groups, the press, key publics, and the agencies to develop support for ideas. Institutional leadership in government is thus inherently political, and to be effective, it may have to run counter to many of the canons of rational organization, planning, and analysis. Rationality in these forms cannot be substituted for politics, which has a logic of its own in the push for agreement.

In the final analysis Presidents and their associates have to live with very inadequate organizations and work through them. But skillful institutional leadership can break down many barriers and create alliances for action.

PROGRAM ANALYSIS AND EVALUATION

In most of the domestic policy departments there are units for program analysis and evaluation, usually located in the office of the secretary. The budget and program analysts scrutinize budgetary requests coming to the secretary from the bureaus, and challenge what appear to be unsubstantiated claims for increased funds or program success. This is a kind of rudimentary program assessment, which is adamant in placing the burden of proof upon program managers to show that their programs are in fact effective. Sometimes budget analysts are able to draw on evaluation studies of programs. For example, in the early 1970s researchers in the Department of Labor evaluation group concluded that the Neighborhood Youth Corps, a manpower training program, only slightly improved the earnings of graduates in comparison to a control group who had not had training. This kind of analysis gives political executives leverage to question whether bureau programs are doing the job intended. Career civil servant program-managers are not sympathetic to this kind of analysis in part because it challenges programs that they run and threatens the size of their budget and the relative influence of their bureau within the department. They are also likely to feel that the criteria for evaluation of such a program were too narrow, being those which the economist would pose. Neighborhood Youth Corps programs and other manpower training programs may have social value other than increased employment or earning power. They are income maintenance programs, which perhaps should be continued in the absence of any society-wide guaranteed minimal income. They also may have served to reduce alienation and inhibit violence especially among the young and black and have given many such people feelings of hope about the future. Such claims cannot be proven but they are felt very strongly by civil servants who manage such social welfare programs. Analysts, who are most often economists, have not found ways to build these kinds of considerations into their methodologies of evaluation and measurement criteria.[43]

The leverage of this kind of analysis in government is based upon the existence of the Office of Management and the Budget, which must ultimately pass upon departmental requests. If OMB examiners think that the department analysts are doing a good job monitoring and assessing bureau programs, they are more likely to favor department budgetary requests.

The Nixon Administration increased the emphasis upon evaluation of departmental management effectiveness when the Bureau of the Budget (BOB) was changed over into OMB. Program examiners used budgetary controls not only as manifestations of administration policy but as prods to improved management in the departments. In 1973, for example, the OMB officials who watch the Department of Labor were unhappy over the Unemployment Insurance program, which is a largely autonomous bureau within the Manpower administration. It seemed to have had no formula for allocation of funds to the state unemployment insurance offices, which administer the federal program. Comparable states were receiving different amounts of money and the UI could not explain why this was so to the satisfaction of OMB. The response was a substantial cut in the UI operating budget. This drove UI officials to work with department program analysts and to develop a cost basis model for determining payments to the states and the bureau received budget increases from OMB as a sign of approval.[44]

Notice that in the evaluation of the Neighborhood Youth Corps and the Unemployment Insurance program, both department and OMB analysts did not know why the programs were not working as they felt they should be. Their knowledge of programs was limited to statistical analysis of results measured along certain dimensions. This kind of analysis is therefore limited in its ability to prescribe ways to improve programs. That must be left up to the program managers and perhaps that is as it should be. Analysts who are quite distant from actual field situations might do a great deal of harm were they to attempt to prescribe in specifics how programs should be run. Yet the limitations of the kind of program analysis and evaluation described here are troubling. It may fail to catch much that is good about programs. Fortunately, such analysis is only one factor in the government-wide decision process and does not override the normal processes of political claims and bargaining.[45]

When it comes to program development, political executives in departments and departmental and OMB analysts are not often guided by systematic program appraisal. Rather, they take political and ideological cues about the proper direction of policy from the White House. Under the Nixon Administration the Department of Labor and OMB embraced the principle of revenue sharing and devolution of final responsibility for manpower training programs to state and city sponsors under Presidential direction without any expert analysis of how such a strategy would work. White House policy development people had made a judgment, in line with Presidential philosophy, that decategorization of manpower programs and consolidation of many separate training efforts under a small number of comprehensive programs organized at the local level would be superior to federally run programs. This was ideology laced with reflection upon experience. The OMB in the Nixon Administration has carried out such general policy views, distrusting a heavy federal administrative role in social programs, and favoring programs that directly transfer money to people without the intervention of bureaucracy.[46] It should be pointed out, however, that the ability of program analysts in either the departments or OMB to prescribe how programs might work under different administrative arrangements is severely limited. The kind of knowledge of program implementation that is needed has not yet been developed.

It is not likely that systematic program evaluation will ever be the key to the survival of programs in government. There are a number of obstacles. The chief political precondition for such evaluation is that the program have a clear and unambiguous objective.[47] Agreement is secured from the plurality of bargaining and compromise and the deliberate building of multiple appeals into social programs by participants in the Executive branch and Congress. The poverty program was not only going to cure poverty but improve education, health, community organization, provide employment, and much else. It would be difficult if not impossible to devise standards of measurement of success for systematic program evaluation.

Nor is it clear that program evaluation should ever be the sole basis for judgment of program success or failure on the part of the White

House. Many other perspectives must be included in such evaluations. The kinds of people chosen by a President to staff the high levels of the White House, the Office of Management and Budget, and political executives in the departments are crucial to the ability of a President to evaluate social programs. One undesirable extreme would be people with a solely political perspective who care only about the appearances of program success rather than the substance because that seems politically profitable for a President in the short run. This is a characteristic often seen in top department officials who know they will be in office a relatively short time (perhaps two years) and therefore place a premium on quick results that look good, or extravagant promises are made without the necessary funding required for effective program performance. The other extreme is a top cadre of Presidential assistants who are excessively managerial in their orientation, putting their faith in analysis and evaluation for the measurement of program success and failure. Their expectations are often too high and their confidence in the methods of evaluation are unjustified. Both types of executives lack a sense of government as an incremental, organic process in which one learns by trial and error, solutions to problems are never final, and remedies emerge out of efforts to cope without any clear sense in advance of what will work. Career civil servants who stay from administration to administration often have this organic sense and make use of historical memory of the conditions for program success and failure that political executives or analysts do not have. However, civil servants are also defenders of established organizational positions and are difficult to move from above. So the tension between innovation and bureaucratic regularity introduced by political executives and analysts is necessary. But it is most important that the top executives and chief analysts of any administration be characteristic of neither of these extremes but rather be people who know how to combine political and analytic perspectives in program formulation and evaluation and draw on the talents of diverse kinds of analysts and program managers as well as understand the thinking of congressmen, interest groups, and publics. Such people are rare.

Many businessmen and lawyers who come from private life have not developed such perspectives in advance and by the time they learn them their tenure in government is up. Most professional politicians serve in legislatures and also lack the experience of moving large organizations toward objectives. Among the more successful political executives in recent years in government have been former academics, like Henry Kissinger, George Schultz, and Daniel Patrick Moynihan. Academics bring expert knowledge of the substantive problems and need not learn from scratch. Also university life is not unlike government in the primacy of political conflict across the institution. Ability to operate in a university is good training for government work. Academics also understand how to conceptualize about policy problems and relate general ideas to details. And most of them, particularly in the social sciences, think of organizational life in terms of systems of input, output, and feedback, which makes them sensitive to the continual need to adjust policy on the basis of experience.[48] Of course only a few academics have these abilities and individuals in other professions have them as well. The point is, Presidents should select their top executives with an eye to such talents. One cannot be optimistic here because, as stated before, such talent is rare, difficult to recognize in advance, and Presidents select few of their associates directly. They must, therefore, pick the right people to do the selecting for them. The organizational style of a President's top appointees tells a great deal about the spirit of an administration, far more than the bureaucratic forms that are imposed upon government.

PROGRAM DEVELOPMENT AND IMPLEMENTATION

Policy makers are easily caught up in their own hopeful rhetoric about new programs and seldom see implementation problems at the time that policy and programs are formulated. Implementation is too often mistakenly viewed as a matter of technical detail that comes after policy decision. This is a great error, for ends and means are dependent upon each other. We are not likely to try to do something if the means necessary to do it are not available; our ambitions will be scaled down. Alternately, if new ways to carry out objectives are developed, we may raise our sights.[49]

White House and department policy analysts must learn to build a concern for alternative strategies of implementation into their work. When new programs are designed explicit attention should be paid to such areas as: the nature of the constituency being created and its likely impact upon program administration; which committees of Congress will have jurisdiction over the program and the effect this is likely to have upon the politics of program administration; and the organizational norms and values of the administering agency and their possible effect on a program—whether to enhance or distort policy objectives. Additional questions include: What are the levers of authority and power by which a President may ensure that the program meets the original goals and what program evaluation mechanisms can be instituted and how linked to the White

House? What mechanisms exist to ensure that field organizations administering the program will be effective and responsive to Presidential goals?[50]

This kind of knowledge can be pulled together now, to some extent, from practical experience and direct observation of concrete situations. But it will only carry policy makers and analysts part of the way toward the knowledge necessary for anticipation of implementation alternatives and problems. We will need considerable empirical research to develop a body of theory about implementation, which could then be applied to specific decisions. One can suggest the building blocks of such a theory and thereby raise the kinds of questions that policy makers should be asking now even if the answers are likely to be uncertain. The chief consideration should be to determine the range of available strategies and their applicability for given programs.

Administrative Action

The first kind of administrative action that might be attempted is direct regulation and control by federal officials. Officials apply rules that are intended to reflect the spirit of policy. Two examples would be wage and price controls and the work of the Federal Energy Office during the energy crisis of 1974. The advantage of this approach is that federal officials can keep control of administrative actions taken and compare them to goals. Very little power is delegated. The drawback is that the higher the administrative hierarchy the less knowledge about conditions throughout the society is likely to be available at the top. Spontaneous social forces will emerge and often take organized form in protest against administrative decisions because the original calculations on top were too limited. It may be that the effort to impose controls is misguided. It goes too strongly against the social and economic incentives of citizens. For example, wage and price controls do not seem able to be effectively enforced in any capitalist democracy since they run squarely up against the decentralized, self-interest incentives that guide businessmen, labor unions, and most organized producer groups in such societies.[51]

A more frequent variation on the first strategy is the delegation of authority by central government to state and local levels of government within general guidelines set from above. Examples include most federal social welfare programs such as public assistance, aid to education, and the United States Employment Service—all of which are administered through state agencies. The increased advantage over centralized administration is that administrative application of general rules can be adapted to varying local conditions. The debit comes from this very fact for local officials can distort federal purposes in the act of adapting, and federal officials thus often lose control of programs for which they are responsible. There is also the inherent limitation of any institutional mechanism to gear itself to the task at hand. Public school bureaucracies or social work professionals, for example, are not easily changed in their orientations to meet new trends in public policy. And even if such groups were more malleable the problems may be too difficult for their skills.[52]

Another variation of a theme is the delegation of governmental authority to private groups such as corporations and unions, for example, manpower training programs. This is often a very effective tactic because it short-circuits the necessity for government bureaucracy and draws upon the self-interest of private groups to perform public services because they are subsidized to do so. Even here, however, there is the risk of the implementing organization adapting the program to its own perspectives rather than those of government. For example, employers are likely to select those workers for manpower training who can be most easily trained so as to make the program look good to federal officials who will continue the grant and provide reliable future employees. But the most disadvantaged workers who are difficult to train can be left out completely.

Market Mechanisms

The major advantage of reliance upon the market is that one avoids bureaucracy altogether. This is the reason that federal officials seek to avoid gasoline rationing during times of energy shortage. Rationing requires a complex bureaucracy across the country and many official decisions. The market permits unplanned decisions by countless producers, suppliers, and consumers and is thus more efficient. However, the market may not be equitable in regard to distribution and this is the reason for a Federal Energy Office, which must take actions to ensure equity but seeks to do so within the operation of a market. If it works it is a good system but it does not always work.

A variation that is most effective is simple direct federal payments of money to individuals as a social welfare benefit and alternative to creating organizations and professions to minister to their needs. Social security is the prime example. A bureaucracy is required but its chief task is to keep accurate records and mail out the checks. Income maintenance schemes that have been proposed would have the same advantage. There are drawbacks. For example, the idea of the government granting housing allowances to people of low income with which they would find their own homes has the appeal of a direct payments system but it leaves aside the question of whether support services of counseling are necessary to permit such people to make the best choices they can.

There are political analogues to a market system. One is for the government to deliberately try to create a system of political bargaining by strengthening the hand of those groups that have theretofore been underrepresented in government. A classic example would be the Community Action agencies created under the Economic Opportunity Act in 1964. This encouraged groups representing the poor to organize against city hall and even against local federal agencies. A political bargaining mechanism is thus created, which operates like a market in that it requires little central overview. The drawback is that central government may still have to worry about the balances. In fact the Community Action program backfired because of the threat presented to local authorities. The federal response, under grass roots political pressure, was to deemphasize community action autonomy.[53]

An analogous strategy is for government officials to build competition into the bureaucracy itself. The chief spearhead of the poverty program, OEO, was an independent agency that was deliberately set up to compete with the old-line federal departments in the provision of services to the poor. It was a ginger group to keep the others on their toes. One problem is that such agencies should be located in the Executive Office of the President. It is practical to do this for only a few such efforts because a number of these groups would overload the White House with administrative business.[54] Also, new organizations of this kind eventually lose their vitality because an intense sense of mission cannot be sustained for long. They soon become much like the regular bureaucracy. The Peace Corps would be a good example.

Federal, State, and Local Government Relations

We really do not know enough about the political incentives that operate upon state and local governments to predict the effects of federal delegation of authority under general and specialized revenue sharing on policy implementation. An example would be manpower revenue sharing under a law passed in 1973.[55] The law calls for delegation of authority for manpower training to the 50 states and 450 other prime local government sponsors. One might predict that there will be political pressures on these sponsors to move the programs in certain ways that may or may not be in line with federal objectives and that the lower the level of government the greater the pressures will be. There may be a number of scandals in misuse of funds and an eventual call for tightening of federal controls. On the other hand the authors of the law are hoping that the political pressures will be constructive and create a political bargaining market much as in the case of community action with the poor and disadvantaged thus able to ensure that they are well served. One can see the difficult of knowing in advance which view is correct.

All such delegation raises difficult problems of coordination between federal agencies in Washington and in the field as well as within the different levels of government. Coordination is a political rather than an administrative problem because different viewpoints about program objectives are at stake as well as jurisdictional disputes. The stronger the state and local governments are the greater the problems of coordination. There is no organizational arrangement that will eliminate problems of clearance and disputes about objective and jurisdiction in a federal system.[56]

James Sundquist remarks that "a little chaos" in competition between levels of government is a good thing but that ultimately federal authority must resolve the disputes.[57] No cabinet department can coordinate or direct another department so the task goes to the White House. Sundquist suggests that the President have a unit within his domain that would advise him on how best to cope with problems of coordination of levels of government.[58] One could broaden that to ask for a group who would work exclusively upon implementation problems at both stages of policy decision and administration. This will probably require a new kind of Presidential assistant. Lawyers, economists, and even businessmen are not by profession expert in these matters. A new kind of expert in public administration is needed, one who will be able to apply a developing body of theory about implementation, based upon research, to concrete situations. This is a very different kind of person from the activists who usually work in the White House. Implementation experts are likely to understand how little we know about going about things and to urge caution and modesty in what Presidents try to achieve.

CONCLUSION

We do not select Presidents for their administrative ability and it is rare that we get one who has any. A premium is placed upon electoral political skills in the Presidential selection process. Few recent

Presidents, save Eisenhower, have had executive experience of any kind before becoming President. The last governor to be elected President was Franklin Roosevelt. He had developed executive skills as governor and as assistant secretary of the Navy during World War I, which he put to good use in the Presidency. This is not to say that Presidents should be good at management or administration in the narrow, technical sense of being able to impose and follow an organization chart or institute a system of statistical controls on organization. These are not the skills required. Government administration is intrinsically political and properly so. Conflicts about values, knowledge, and power are the stuff of government. The kind of executive ability required of Presidents is twofold. They should be able to structure decision processes so that they learn from as wide a variety of sources as possible. They must know how to build coalitions of support inside and outside government to get their ideas and policies carried out. These are political skills applied to the art of administration. They are different from the rhetorical and bargaining skills required of legislators. Such executive skills demand a kind of personal knowledge in a President that is much more subtle than ordinary management skills. They must understand how others think and feel and what it will take to move them in desired directions. Presidents should solicit advice from experts upon the costs and benefits of different ways of organizing government but they must also have the intuitive understanding of how to join disparate people and ideas in alliances for decision and execution.

Senators are not called upon to develop such abilities in their work to any great extent. We have turned to the Senate as our recruiting pool for Presidents because of the primacy of foreign policy and the presumed exposure to international affairs. The degree of exposure is actually overrated for most senators and certainly for the Senate as an institution.

If the Cold War erodes and the office of secretary of state is restored to influence, we might do well to once again look to governors for possible Presidents. Governors have the opportunity to develop the political-executive skills required of Presidents. One can probably predict a future President's executive style from his record as governor—as was the case with the two Roosevelts.[59] Eisenhower's style as President was clearly seen in his manner of military command. But it is much more difficult to predict with the Presidents who have not held executive positions like Kennedy, Johnson, and Nixon. Consideration of governors as potential Presidents would be one way to join our concerns about flaws and strengths in political personality with the desire to know about style of authority. Both are clearly revealed in executive posts. We do not want amateurs as Presidents, either in the political or the executive sense.

9
Prescriptions

Three groups of questions about Presidential power and purpose
have run throughout this volume. The first concerned the powers of
the President in foreign policy. It is not simply a matter of the President having or taking too much institutional leverage to act—
whether it be negotiating executive agreements with other nations
or sending armies to fight. Rather, the worry is that publics and
others leaders have learned to defer to Presidential authority and
have granted legitimacy to this power. Questions of reform then
become not only institutional but cultural and ideological. The second type of question asked about the proper degree of political and
institutional power and resources a President should have in regard
to domestic problems and policy. One point of view would have it
that the Presidency is too weak in domestic political resources. This
view sees the Presidency as the only governmental institution that
can provide integrated leadership on domestic policy. Congress and
the parties are seen as fragmented, representative bodies that must
respond and consent but not initiate. Yet the very fragmentation of
these groups is seen to limit the influence of a President over them.
The autonomy and institutional separateness of the Presidency in
foreign affairs strengthen Presidential power to act, but the same
position puts a President at a disadvantage in domestic policymaking.
The consent of other power holders is required more in domestic
matters. One reform response that would seek to link solutions to
both of these problems is the call for a strengthening of the role of
national political parties as instruments of party government which
would join together President, Congress, and a national party organization in terms of common ideas and policies and mutual respect and
constraints. Such a model, it is thought, would both restrain a Presi-

dent in foreign policy action and provide political resources for decisive governmental action, under Presidential leadership in domestic
policy. An alternative viewpoint would argue that party government
might actually strengthen the powers of the Presidency while weakening those of Congress and that the right direction in which to move
is to find ways to strengthen congressional independence of the Executive branch in both foreign and domestic affairs. This view holds
that it is no bad thing that a President must struggle through politics
to have his way. This view is compatible with ideas for reform of
American governmental institutions to make them work more effectively, all the way from the Presidency down to local government,
but it stresses the value of pluralistic conflict throughout government
and society and is less enamored of integrating models of government and party.

The third group of questions had to do with normative models of
Presidential character and style. What kind of President do we want?
The liberal model, which would have every President a hero—another Franklin Roosevelt—seems discredited. Do we need to find
ways to demythologize the Presidency so that the office is cast in less
heroic terms? Have the rich symbolic resources of the Presidency
been a source of bad as well as good, for example, in the great latitude
permitted the President in foreign policy? Do we need to recognize
that there is room and need for a variety of Presidential styles according to the times and that every President need not talk and act like
a Roosevelt? Are there not many other sources of policy innovation
in the political system and therefore is it not inaccurate to depict the
Presidency as the chief place for policy innovation? It must be asked,
however, if American political culture is congenial to a reduction of
Presidential mythology? We have a poverty of political symbols in
our republican society and the Presidency may be the one institution
that most successfully fills that vacuum. Moreover, we often value the
extra political resources that the Presidency accords to its incumbent
when we wish him to be able to act boldly on a given matter. There
is the risk in calling for more modest leadership style that we release
the President from the responsibility for moral leadership in regard
to the nation's problems.

A very difficult related question has to do with our understanding,
or perhaps our lack of knowledge, of Presidential personality and the
implications of character structure for behavior in the office. Can we
learn and predict what kind of a President an individual will be
before he takes office? If we can develop such understanding, is it
feasible and desirable to have public discussion on such questions? Is
personality a too remote entity to explore and therefore better left

alone? Should we develop ideal models of Presidential personality and compare candidates to them? What kinds of Presidents do we want?

Questions of reform encompass three interrelated dimensions: governmental institutions, patterns of politics, and political culture. Any reform proposal that considers one factor without taking account of the others is deficient and not likely to work in practice. Of course there is no guarantee that any reform will work in practice and we know very little about the conditions for success and failure of deliberate institutional reform.

It is not enough to change an institution if the patterns of politics are not supportive of the change. For example, suggested devices for Congress to restrain Presidential foreign policy action, such as new super-committees or legislative limits upon Presidential war powers, may depend far more upon the kind of political support a President can generate for his actions than upon new rules and structures for their effectiveness. We also should approach institutional reform from a view of American politics. For example, to what extent do we wish an increase of ideological debate in the competition of political parties, and what are the implications of the answer for the organization of parties and government itself? We must also ask if institutional and political changes recommended are compatible with the political culture. Can we seriously talk about Congress putting constraints on a President in foreign affairs when the Presidency has symbolic resources in the public mind that are simply not available to Congress? If this is so, can anything be done about it?

There are no neat institutional prescriptions for reducing or strengthening Presidential power. This means that all such discussions are ultimately unsatisfactory if there is a hope of a final solution that can be institutionalized. We are left dangling with sets of possibilities for change and reform that depend upon institutions, politics and culture, and the uncoordinated actions of wide numbers of people. But that is the nature of the reality.

Before turning to the three groups of questions it would be useful to conduct an academic inquiry to ask about the feasibility and desirability of the United States changing to a parliamentary system of the kind existing in Britain and Canada. This question was often raised for discussion during 1973, the year of Watergate. A political scientist found himself repeatedly asked if a parliamentary system would not have found a way to remove a prime minister much more easily than that in the cumbersome American process of impeachment? The larger appeal of the parliamentary model is that it would not have a chief executive with great powers to act as an individual, but rather a system of Cabinet government supported by a parliamentary party majority in which the Executive would be responsible to the legislature and public through the link of party. This model would seem to solve all the American problems at one time. The prime minister would be a much lesser figure than a President with few, if any, symbolic resources. He would be restrained not only by his Cabinet colleagues who would be politicians with reputations in their own right, but also by the parliamentary party rank and file. Yet, the device of party linking cabinet and parliament would permit government to act and eliminate the chronic American deadlock between executive and legislature that comes from separated institutions sharing powers.

An examination of British and Canadian parliamentary government and politics in terms of the American context might not only tell us something about how parliamentary government would work here but would cause us to realize that many reforms proposed for the American system are implicitly drawn from the parliamentary model, whether for good or ill.

A PARLIAMENTARY SYSTEM?

It is difficult to say how a parliamentary form of government would actually work in the United States because our politics and culture would shape it in unique ways. Nonetheless, we can examine Britain and Canada to see if the operation of the system at its best could solve our problems.

The British do not idealize their prime minister. He is a party politician who leads a government of politicians, and his virtues and frailties are not seen as crucial to the success or failure of the government. They do not suffer from a President fixation in this sense. The prime minister is responsible to his political colleagues in his cabinet and in Parliament but lacks autonomous bureaucratic power of his own. The evidence is mixed but it seems clear that the parliamentary party does exercise constraints and influences over its government, usually behind the scenes. The main link in the entire system is the party.

This seems particularly appealing to us today, and we often hear that the British would have handled a Watergate scandal by deposing the discredited leader. Perhaps so, but there would probably also have been the continuation of a cover-up. One prime minister would have given way to another and the governing party would have carried on as before with little increase in public knowledge of the facts, which is what happened after Suez in 1956. There would be no Senate Watergate committee to investigate, for parliamentary committees do not act so impolitely. An officially appointed inquiry could do the job but might also be very circumscribed in its charge.

Each system suffers from the defects of its virtues. British government has been vigorously criticized for some years by reformers because it lacks the virtues of American government. It has been pictured as too secretive and lacking in open, adversary processes for the discussion of policy in the formulation stage. Parliamentary debate has a certain mock combat quality without genuine discussion of issues and Parliament as an institution is very weak vis-à-vis the cabinet that runs the Executive. There has also been considerable criticism of the dependence of ministers upon civil servants for advice and the absence of the stimulus of new ideas and variety of expertise that American "in and outers" bring to administration.[1] The reforms of the sixties—specialized parliamentary committees, an increase in temporary expert advisers to ministers, and reform of the civil service in the direction of greater substantive and managerial expertise—have had difficulty taking root because they are contrary to the internal logic of the British parliamentary system as it is interpreted by the politicians.

In Canada one sees the same virtues as in Britain: collegiality, political sensitivity at the top, party accountability for government. But one also sees the same faults of a weak Parliament that cannot compare with Congress in its influence upon government. Party government is also marred by the splintering of parliamentary parties. This may be a consequence of the requirements of parliamentary party discipline in a society of great diversity. More unity is required than can be achieved and the result has been a fragmentation of parties into smaller, more coherent groups. This might occur in an American parliamentary system but it does not prevail now because party demands on members of Congress are minimal.[2] In addition, the Canadian prime minister lacks the symbolic resources of office available to an American President for popular leadership.

An American prime minister and government would be the children of what is now the Congress. It is uncertain what kinds of leaders would emerge, but it seems likely that seniority, provincialism, and extreme flexibility in style would be strong characteristics of such a government. Leaders would have to appeal to a variegated parliament, perhaps splintered into several parties in the Canadian fashion. The accountability of the Executive to a national electorate might be diminished, and most of the existing congressional institutional checks on the Executive would disappear.

The benefits of a parliamentary system in America are not clear enough to persuade sufficient people to support it. Such a system also runs against the grain of our political culture in which we venerate the Constitution as our chief national symbol and fuse the Presidency with our national mythology. It is not conceivable that we would abolish the office or turn it into a figurehead.

It is not necessary to belabor this point. The explosive volatility of the American system of government with its coexistence of separation of powers and checks and balances permits a great deal of constructive open conflict and collaboration as well as the forcing out of information and issues in ways uncongenial to a parliamentary system. On the other hand, it also provides great autonomy and the capacity for irresponsible acts for each branch of government, a possibility again unknown to British parliamentary government.

A change to a parliamentary system would be likely to be seriously considered in the United States only after a great shock such as an attempted totalitarian action by a President. Even then it is doubtful that parliamentary government would be the implicit model of reform should such an effort fail. Americans have the mechanical model of checks and balances as their omnipresent and implicit model for government organization. The consequence of such an attempt at a coup, if it failed, would probably be constitutional action to weaken the Presidency and make it subordinate to the Congress. In this sense the archetypes of our politics derive from the sixteenth- and seventeenth-century conflicts between monarchy and Parliament in Britain. It was not until the eighteenth century that British cabinet government developed to unite government and Parliament, leaving the principles of checks and balances behind. Our founding fathers did not see this reality but rather carried in their heads the picture of an earlier English politics with a balance between king and Parliament.

There are those who argue that the institutions of separate powers and checks and balances are more in keeping with the requirements of modern government than is the British or European parliamentary model.[3] Separated and fragmented institutions provide for permeability from the society, diverse centers of innovation within government, widespread movement of information and ideas, and the hammering of political conflict into political agreement. Parliamentary systems are said to be too subservient to executives, too secretive, too closed to social influences, and too responsive to the rituals and routines of government, party, and bureaucratic hierarchies. Such centralization of power was essential in the European democracies, including Britain, to achieve legislative action to create the positive state and accompanying measures of social and economic reforms in the first half of the twentieth century. Now it is claimed the American model, with its openness and permeability, has something to teach Europeans, although we do lag behind Europe in the achievement of social and economic reforms and the positive state. We also have the peculiar politics of the English sixteenth-century monarchy in the permanently unfinished quarrels of executive and legislature.

It is not really practical to think of a modern democracy changing in a deliberate way from one form of governmental system to another. Such changes have taken place in twentieth-century French and German history after revolutions and wars, but in each case the model adopted was drawn from an earlier version in the history of the country. One finds competing governmental traditions in these and other continental European countries which alternate over time as form of regime. The United States has a homogeneous political culture and it is therefore not feasible to think of resorting to institutions that do not reflect that culture. Nor would it be desirable because the political turmoil would probably be very great and the consequences unpredictable.

Change and reform of institutions must therefore take account of the parameters set by culture. One must cope with situations as they exist and not rely upon ideal models of things that might be. And so again, we return to the three areas of concern revolving around Presidential power and purpose.

PRESIDENTIAL POWERS IN FOREIGN POLICY

In the years after World War II American political leaders responded to the rivalry with the Soviet Union by developing a posture of competition and confrontation that became a firm ideology, fusing American power and virtue as the defender of freedom in the world. This is not to say that the United States was responsible for the origins of the Cold War or that there was no justification for the strong American response to the situation. The rivalry was inherent in the competition of two great powers for influence in the world. The key question is whether American leaders overreacted and turned a rivalry into a crusade. This does seem to have been the case, because of the necessity of carrying Congress and public opinion in support of the necessary first steps for the development of a response to the Soviets such as the Marshall Plan and the Truman Doctrine of military and economic aid to Greece and Turkey. One might also suggest that the crusading posture was the most congenial way for American leaders to look at the world. President Woodrow Wilson returned from Versailles in 1919 convinced that America had a mission to create and lead a League of Nations that would save the world from war just as the American purpose in fighting the war had been to save the world for democracy. Herbert Hoover, who had been a member of Wilson's delegation, returned with the conviction that the European nations were morally and politically corrupt and that America should refrain from an active international role and guard her unique virtue. Both attitudes are uniquely American and follow from a common premise of superior American morality in a world of fallen nations. This streak of moralism has run through American dealings with the world since the eighteenth century.[4]

These political and ideological developments came at a time of the conversion of American popular opinion away from isolationism and toward the belief in America playing an important role in the world. The defeat of Woodrow Wilson at the hands of the isolationists in 1919 was to be reversed. The Presidency was seen as the chief agent for this new international role. The lesson of the 1930s was that political leadership that vacillated in the face of dictatorship and aggression would only encourage aggression. The moral was drawn for future Presidents: there must be no appeasement. Truman's strong response to aggression in Korea was interpreted widely as the kind of action that should have been taken instead of the Munich agreement appeasement of Hitler by Britain and France. This was the best way to prevent a larger war—nip aggression in the bud. These ideas were particularly strong among American liberals.

The combination of firm Presidential leadership in a series of foreign policy crises by Truman, Eisenhower, and Kennedy created, confirmed, and periodically strengthened a popular world view and set of values that linked Presidential action and popular support for the President with the virtue of the American international role. This chain of events came to a culmination in Vietnam. A most intelligent, experienced, and liberal group of men in high office thought it necessary that the United States prevent the domination of South Vietnam by North Vietnam as one more example of drawing the line against world-wide communist aggression. The possibility that a Vietnamese civil war was taking place, which might have little effect upon the rest of the world regardless of the outcome, was not even raised.

Vietnam dramatized and brought to a head the assertions by Presidents of their prerogative to make war without the formal approval of Congress. At that point, the United States came to an impasse in which we either had to change the Constitution to give Presidents war powers they did not legally possess, or stop the Cold War as well as a hot war in order that the Constitution not be so strained by such claims to power. The secret and illegal bombing of Cambodia by the

Nixon government in 1969 and 1970 is a case in point.

The constitutional question became even more serious when President Nixon asserted that his inherent powers as protector of the national security abroad justified actions to curtail liberty at home. The national security state had finally spilled over into domestic matters and was now directed against American citizens.[5] The Huston plan for surveillance—wiretapping and burglary—that was first approved and then rescinded, the wiretapping of a number of White House aides and journalists, the plumbers unit that planned and executed the burglary of the office of the psychiatrist of Daniel Ellsberg were all examples of the powers of the state turned against its citizens in the name of national security.[6]

Three things had come together in a powerful way: Presidential institutional powers to wage war and conduct foreign policy without serious restraint; congressional and popular support for the full exercise of such powers in the name of national security; and Presidential powers of secret command in the area of domestic security. What remedies are available?

CURTAILMENT OF PRESIDENTIAL WAR POWERS

In 1973 Congress passed the War Powers resolution, which sets conditions under which the President can carry the nation into war.[7] President Nixon vetoed the bill as an unconstitutional challenge to Presidential prerogatives, but Congress passed it over his veto. This indicates the strength and depth of congressional feeling. According to the law the President may commit American combat troops to a military engagement for a sixty-day period unless Congress stops him by a joint resolution during that time. After the expiration of sixty days Congress must approve any further American military action. There are a number of criticisms of this law. Schlesinger argues that it grants the President constitutional powers to begin a war—which the Constitution does not give him.[8] Rather, no President can begin a war without the consent of Congress. This depends upon the constitutional interpretation of inherent Presidential powers to defend the nation and act in behalf of the national security, which has not been tested in court. Schlesinger's point may be well taken but is perhaps moot since it is likely that future Presidents will act to commit troops if they see it as desirable and justify their actions with constitutional language. Congress therefore was seeking some protection against this fact of life. The hope is that a President will think twice before acting in such a way if he must come to Congress and publicly justify his actions sixty days later if not before. Another basic difficulty with the law is that it fails to recognize that the congressional response to Presidential action in such cases has depended and will depend upon politics not legality. The rally round the flag factor will predominate. Both Congress and public are likely to stand behind a President in such a situation; perhaps not in the immediate future because the memory of Vietnam will still be strong, but in the distant future when it has weakened. There seems to be no foolproof institutional protection against this possibility.

INSTITUTIONAL REFORMS

It has been suggested that greater coordination and sharing of information and perspectives among members of the Foreign Affairs, Armed Services, and Appropriations Committees within each house of Congress could permit a more continuous and coherent overview and questioning of foreign policy as conducted by the Executive. The Appropriations Committees and subcommittees fund the programs of which policy is composed, but do not really perform systematic appraisals of program effectiveness or of the relation of programs to each other. On the other hand the substantive committees authorize appropriations of given amounts but do not link final budget allocations with program performance. Nor do the members of the Foreign Relations and Armed Services Committees meet to share perspectives in any formal way, perhaps largely because the perspectives of the two groups of members have been so different in the past. The first has been far less supportive of military responses to foreign policy problems than the latter. There has also been little consideration of questions of weapons development and strategy in terms of a larger political context of American foreign policy, which a joining of the perspectives of the two groups might make possible. An additional proposal that has often been made but not acted upon is that the Foreign Affairs and Armed Services Committees receive the regular estimates of international trends supplied by the CIA to the Administration. The cry that this would endanger necessary secrecy and security is not a serious one since the Administration itself often leaks such estimates when it feels its purposes would be served. Much of the work of the CIA is political and economic reporting and analysis of the kind found in the *New York Times*. Highly sensitive matters about personalities and predictions of events could perhaps be deleted. But the general body of writing would give members of Congress information in a coherent form that their own committee staffs cannot ever provide. If the procedure did lead to dangers of security then it would have to be stopped. This would provide the incentive for members of Congress to preserve confidences received.

These are not really institutional reforms so much as pleas that key members of Congress exert the will to use the powers they now possess to oversee Administration foreign policy. Members of Congress have understandably resisted being taken in as junior partners in the formulation of Executive foreign policy because the Executive receives all the credit if things go well, and they have no desire to share in the blame if there is failure. But the role of overseeing is different and is something that Congress can do well. The problem has been that until recent years members of these committees have been deferential to American foreign policy and have supported the Cold War cult of secrecy. Vietnam may have killed those attitudes and we can hope for more vigorous assertions of congressional prerogatives in the future.

A complementary reform would be for a President to make a serious effort to reform the State Department, and particularly the Foreign Service Officers Corps, so that the influence of the department would be enhanced within the councils of the Administration. By implication, that of the military and the Pentagon should be downgraded. This possibility was discussed in Chapter 5. The institutional problems are great and it might be a foolhardy thing for a new President to take on. In addition it is not clear that the interpretation of foreign policy crisis and confrontation in military terms in the postwar years has really been due to the bureaucratic influence of the military within the Executive. Rather, it may be that high Administration civilian officials have seen the problems in those terms themselves and have brought the military along as allies, with Congress and the public following. This is another instance of the rally round the flag phenomenon. A change in world outlook upon the part of civilian policy makers could be just as effective in restraining the military. However, the institutional weakness of the State Department within American government is an unsolved problem that will plague future Presidents unless something is done about it.

New Policies and Ideas

One can take heart that the Cold War with both the Soviet Union and China is eroding, although the competition for influence and power abroad with these nations will not disappear. Another encouraging sign is the character of foreign policy problems facing the United

States and the other industrial nations is changing from military and political crisis questions to the mundane yet serious matters of energy supplies and allocation, world food shortages, international economic inflation and instability, world overpopulation, poverty of the underdeveloped nations, and other like questions which will require foresight, planning, technical expertise, and diplomacy to resolve insofar as they can be resolved. These are also matters that are likely to be felt by citizens in their everyday lives and will therefore become part of domestic politics. Presidents will have to persuade Congress and publics of the rightness of their responses to such problems before effective national action can be taken. The great danger is not so much that Presidents will act unilaterally as that they will not know what to do because the problems are poorly understood and are difficult to solve or even cope with. This could lead to public negative reactions against Presidents who seem to fumble, and strengthen the hand of Presidents who promise strong, decisive action, at least in the short run. One can hope, however, that the injection of issues of this kind into domestic politics will be a powerful curb upon Presidential willfullness.

The best hope for a responsible, moderate, and constitutional use of Presidential powers in foreign policy is in a permanent rejection by leaders and publics of the messianic, militant world view of American power and virtue that took shape during the Cold War. It might be preferred that this view of things be replaced by the classical realism of George Kennan, which finds the world to be inherently a dangerous place in which nations inevitably come into conflict, but rejects moralism and claims of superior national virtue in favor of a realistic method of diplomacy, bargaining, and judicious but restrained employment of national powers in behalf of limited objectives.

The major problem with such a world view is that it may not be compatible with the deepest strains of American political culture and politics. Kennan himself was unable to get along with members of Congress whom, he felt, were injecting popular distrust of communist nations as inherently untrustworthy into policy formulation. There is also the fact that military threats to American security may recur in the future, at which time it may be necessary to mobilize public opinion by emotional appeals in order that government have latitude to act.

The problem is not now but twenty-five years from now when Vietnam is only a faint memory and we have the same Presidential institution, political culture, and uncertain world. The American ideology of our superior virtue is always latent to be triggered. Even those on the radical left who have rejected the use of American power abroad have assumed that we have a mission to save the world by demonstration of our superior virtue. The kinds of excesses in the use of national power that were seen in Vietnam could occur again in a situation of international crisis if a future President wishes to act. Congress and the public are likely to support him. In fact, they might be right. The best hope for the future is the development of new ideas about American foreign policy to replace those that were predominant during the Cold War. We need new alliances and agreements with other nations, both friends and rivals, that will involve us in international diplomacy. The resurrection of diplomacy as a means of resolving disputes is an absolute necessity. But in the final analysis there are few if any institutional protections against the abuses of Presidential powers in war and foreign policy. The effective restraints are in who we are and what we wish to achieve as a nation.

REFORM OF CONGRESS AND PARTIES

For many years, a model of reform of the national party system has been joined to the changes that would and should follow in Congress in a view of how American national government might be more responsible and accountable to the electorate and produce policy that was coherent in terms of general objectives and relations of means to ends more than has been the case in a system of fragmented decisionmaking.[9]

The package reform model assumes an ideological realignment of national parties so that the liberals and conservatives are in separate camps. This would follow a decline of regional political differences and an extension of party competition for congressional seats throughout all states and districts. Presidents would be even more closely tied to their national parties, as leaders of the party, and as the agents of party ideologies and program proposals. Members of Congress would be elected or defeated on the basis of national party performance in Congress. It follows that the positions of the majority and minority party leaders in the two houses of Congress should be strengthened vis à vis the relative autonomous committees and subcommittees to permit congressional government in behalf of the general principles and programs of the majority party with collective opposition from the minority. This model was originally put forward as an American adaptation of the principles of the parliamentary system, which would eliminate the habitual deadlock of President and Congress and provide for responsible party government. It was argued that the President's hand would be strengthened in Congress and that he would be able to get his legislative program passed just as if he were a prime minister in a parliamentary system.

The counter arguments against this model also reflect a model of American politics and government; one that practicing politicians and most political scientists have found more congenial.[10] It is first suggested that the changes proposed are not feasible and could not be engineered by a few structural changes in party and congressional organization. It is asserted as unlikely that the nationalization of politics and ideological realignment of parties in the South so that the liberals are Democrats and the conservatives are Republicans will actually produce ideological unity within each national party. The deep divisions within the Democratic national party between the bread and butter liberals of the labor movement and centrist liberals and the more radical social movement orientation of the representatives of minorities, militant women's groups, and activist social reformers are given as a case in point. By the same token it is argued that the ethos of Congress is entirely opposed to disciplined leadership from the top. There may have been such a system of rule in the nineteenth and early twentieth centuries (for example, under the iron hand of Speaker of the House Joseph Cannon) but the modern Congress, it is claimed, is a body of decentralization, fragmentation, and division of labor in which different fiefdoms show great respect for the territorial rights of others. The strongest assertion is that party government would weaken the great strengths of Congress, which are the capabilities at specialization, division of labor, and spontaneous policy initiatives. It is argued that such reforms would strengthen the hand of the President in undesirable ways and threaten the independence of Congress.

The bias of the author is in the direction of the second view. In Chapters 6 and 7 the domestic Presidency was not described as in crisis because either Congress or the party system imposed obstacles to legislative action. In fact it was suggested that a President should not always get his own way with Congress. I quite agree that we need liberal social programs but disagree that the real obstacles to their enactment are primarily institutional. Rather, in this view, the roadblocks have been political and ideological. American political culture as inculcated in Americans causes them to be distrustful of collective action, and the institutions manifest this fact rather than cause it. In addition, not all liberal reform proposals of Presidents have been based on good knowledge or been sufficiently thought out. It is not at all clear that will plus funds plus government bureaucracy can solve a social problem. This sense of frustration upon the part of liberals, however, has been exacerbated by the absence of any constructive response to social problems on the part of American conservatives, who have made few if any contributions to social policy since the time of the New Deal, unlike conservatives and conservative parties in Britain and Canada.[11] Liberals have felt that they were carrying the sole burden of getting things done. The Nixon Presidency of course has caused congressional and other liberals to look about for ways to strengthen the autonomy and independence of Congress vis à vis the Executive and many conservatives find themselves in the unfamiliar position of defending Presidential power and prerogatives. Should a Democrat return to the White House in 1976 congressional liberals will probably perform another about-face and begin to defer to their President again.

One would hope that Democrats have learned from the experience of Lyndon Johnson, and Republicans have learned a lesson from Richard Nixon. Whether liberal or conservative, Congress as an institution has a stake in congressional autonomy and independence that is more important than policy results and that matters for the health of the larger political system. Simply, it is that Presidents and the Executive branch should never be permitted to prevail without challenge. A decentralized Congress with much division of labor is best in a position to issue such challenges in the initial process of legislative decision as well as in subsequent process of monitoring and evaluating the Administration and performance of programs. Given this view, congressional reform in the direction of party government is unnecessary and perhaps undesirable.

The majority party leaders of each House have been primarily coordinators and facilitators of the collective business of the House in concert with the committee chairmen who have exercised independent powers. Even the strongest leaders like Lyndon Johnson in the Senate and Sam Rayburn in the House in the 1950s were not able to impose their policy views on their colleagues. Rather, their strength was based upon their ability to fashion coalitions for action out of many different bargains, but this meant a politics of compromise in the enactment of policy. It is doubtful that current proposals to strengthen the majority leaders' power would work or be well received in a Congress that is increasingly filled with young, ambitious people anxious to make their own mark. The chief proposals would give greater powers of appointment of committee chairmenships and other posts to the party leaders and develop policy research staffs for each house under the direction of the leadership.[12] The assumption is that this would curtail the power of the committee chairmen and make party government possible. Such changes would also probably increase the susceptibility of Congress to Presidential leadership because the President would have to persuade primarily the leadership rather than the committee and subcommittee chairmen. And by and large party leadership has been cooperative with the President, even a President of the opposite party.[13] It is a very real question whether it would be wise to surrender the independence of Congress in such a manner.

A rebuttal would cite the cases in which Congress is unable to check the actions of the President when its members might wish to do so because the institution lacks the capacity to take a common positive stand against outside forces.[14] This is particularly true on the budget, for Congress has not been able to pull its many parts together to take an overview of budget priorities and make decisions accordingly. Rather it has reacted to the President's budget through its many parts. President Nixon's challenge in 1973 to impound funds voted by Congress if they were above a specified budget ceiling was not met by a counter-strategy by the Congress. It was saved by a number of court decisions forbidding impoundment and the erosion of the President's political strength with the advent of the Watergate investigations. It seems unlikely that Congress could ever develop the capacity to develop its own budget because of the extensive degree of compromise required, the lack of program analysis and evaluation expertise, and the absence of leadership to force agreements. The main reason is that a more skillful President than Nixon will in the future be able to get his congressional party on his side in such matters and therefore split the body.[15]

A decentralized Congress is likely to be weak vis à vis the Executive in similar cases requiring integrative capabilities. Matters that require Presidential emergency powers are one example, and as we have seen at length, much of foreign policy provides numerous instances of the inability of Congress to develop independent positions. But in these matters Congress can play a strong role of watchdog and evaluator of what the Executive is doing.

Despite what has been said here there is perhaps a trend, which is not altogether bad, toward strengthening the integrative capabilities of the congressional parties if not of the Congress itself. The nationalization of politics is occurring with the decline of the one-party South, although it is not clear that political competition is increasing in congressional constituencies. But it seems to be the case that members of the same party in Congress more and more share common policy perspectives when compared to the opposition, even though each party will always have different ideological tendencies with it just as the highly disciplined and unified English parliamentary parties do. In recent years there have been a number of reforms at the behest of the congressional rank and file that should strengthen the leadership and rank and file at the expense of committee chairmen. Under rules adopted in 1971 and 1973, committee members of both parties now vote on the selection of chairmen and ranking minority members. No chairmen have lost their posts, but they are on warning that they could do so. Other rules changes adopted in 1973 require that chairmen convene the majority members of a committee prior to any meeting of the full committee and call for open committee meetings under most conditions. Such reforms that reduce the powers of chairmen would seem to increase that of the party leadership and put leaders in direct reciprocal relations with their party rank and file. However, the tasks of party leaders could be increased thereby for the subcommittees may have become even stronger and this could lead to 130 fiefdoms that no one can control.[16]

There are valid positive arguments for strengthening the leadership. Strong leadership might be able to lessen the influence of the enduring alliances of committees, Executive agencies and impinging interest groups and cause the consideration of policy from broader and more coherent viewpoints. Congressional overseeing of Executive programs might also be strengthened. Party leaders can sometimes take a longer and more comprehensive view of programs than can committees and subcommittees, which are closely tied to stable alliances in the bureaucracy and the society. However there is the danger that if the leaders are the handmaidens of the President they will not encourage oversight of Executive actions. What would Senate Democratic party leaders have done with Senator Fulbright's challenge to President Johnson's policies in Vietnam in which he used the Foreign Relations Committee?[17] Party leaders responsive to the President should have removed him as chairman. Failure to do so would have signaled open defiance of the President, a difficult step for congressional party leaders to take during a war or at any other time.

It is clear that the trends of internal congressional governance are mixed, but it is not clear what the new stable pattern will be and strengthening of the party leadership, while bringing some benefits, must be treated very skeptically because it might have the opposite effect of those who seek it. The President might be strengthened rather than restrained.

Congress should seek to strengthen itself as an institution in the things that it can really do well and will safeguard its independence, that is, to require open discussion and justification for policy action by the Executive and to monitor and evaluate the administration of programs. There is a clear need for reform here. In many cases congressional committees are not organized to consider policy options in a given subject in a coherent manner but, rather, different committees consider various parts of a program area that are seldom if ever looked at whole by anyone in Congress. An example would be transportation. Congress created a Department of Transportation during the second term of the Johnson Administration but it did not set up corresponding committees that could ensure comprehensive transportation policies were developed and administered. Responsibility for transportation concerns is still divided among Merchant Marine and Fisheries, Interstate and Foreign Commerce, Public Works, and Banking and Currency Committees of both houses.[18]

Two goals are necessary here. The first is the objective that Congress should be so organized in its subparts that these parts, the committees and subcommittees, can require the Executive departments and agencies to explain what they want to do in the way of policy as a coherent overall strategy and justify the actions they wish to take and for which they wish congressional support. Secondly, the same organizational structure should be able to follow the progress of program implementation and require the evaluation of program results, as measured against initial objectives, either by Congress, one of its arms, or by the Executive departments. Neither of these functions is fully performed at present because fragmentation of committee structure does not permit it.

Another important obstacle is that the political incentives of individual members of Congress do not run in these directions. When it comes to policy formulation they are entrepreneurs seeking reelection who fasten onto particular positions and constituencies to serve as a means of attaining visibility and political support. Serving constituent needs and working at legislation are priority matters that leave little time for anything else. It is also true that when it comes to the evaluation of programs members are more concerned with the effects upon particular groups of constituents than they are with how programs have worked in terms of some set of abstract goals. These facts are often forgotten when it is urged that members of Congress make more use of expert staff. Given the general atmosphere of political entrepreneurship they do not need staff except as support for their particular causes. Members do not use staff in a general policy analysis function because they seldom wish to consider the widest range of possible policies.

There is a difference between the institutional interests of Congress as a whole and the interests of individual members and committees. Congress as an institution is strengthened vis à vis the Executive if it can focus public attention upon issues from a national perspective such as energy, transportation, or poverty. But the narrower the jurisdiction of a committee the more it will attract those in Congress, the Executive, and outside groups who wish to serve particular interests. The structure of congressional committees encourages this kind of multiplication and fragmentation of programs, fragmentation of authority within the Executive, and a piecemeal approach to national problems. Therefore, Congress would have been wise to have responded in a constructive way to the proposals of the Ash Commission in 1971 for reorganization of the domestic departments along functional lines of human resources, natural resources, economic affairs, and community development.[19]

The Ash Commission proposals did not call for the reconstitution of congressional committees to correspond to the new organization of the departments on the assumption that such an effort would challenge too many vested leadership positions in Congress. But the real source of congressional disinterest in the plan was the realization that favorite congressional groups and constituencies would be affected in terms of access to and influence in the departments. No one on the Executive side attempted to put together a coalition majority in Congress of those who felt their side would win out by the changes. Perhaps none could have been created since the idea was to reduce the influence of interest groups in Executive politics.

The role of Congress as an institution will be enhanced by requiring the Executive to explain itself in as comprehensive a manner as possible. It is not necessary for congressional committees to mirror the organization of the Executive branch, which is often changed in response to short-run expediencies. If anything, Congress should decide upon the proper functional groupings and hold the Executive to account in its terms. There should always be congressional flexibility to dismantle committees and create new ones, sometimes for ad hoc purposes on particular problems.[20] And of course there would always be overlap between committee jurisdictions and desirably so. It is a matter of primary emphasis. For example, if energy questions were to be taken away from the Interior Committees and given to a new Energy Committee, the Interior Committees that deal with the public lands and offshore questions would have to still consider energy. But competition is healthy in forcing issues up for all to consider.

If Congress is to strengthen its monitoring and overseeing role it must give increased support to its research and program evaluation arms that do the work for the several committees. The Congressional Research Service of the Library of Congress has been strengthened in numbers and staff in recent years and is doing a great deal more genuine policy research for members and committees than in past years when it was primarily an information service. Such an organization could publish articles and books, prepared by its staff, which is now forbidden by Congress. They could also contract for studies on policy problems and thereby contribute to the process of informed policy discussion. Another congressional institution that has shown new vigor since the 1970 Legislative Reorganization Act gave it new scope to undertake program evaluation is the General Accounting Office. This organization once concerned itself primarily with auditing how the Executive spent money appropriated by Congress in terms of efficiency and probity standards. But in its new lease on life under a dynamic director it has undertaken to provide studies of program evaluation for members of Congress. Examples of work under way in 1973 included: examination of the efficacy of the research, pilot, and demonstration programs in water pollution control; the evaluation of vocational rehabilitation programs; an analysis of federal programs to improve the living conditions of migrant and seasonal farm workers; a study evaluating the space shuttle program; and a review of the effectiveness of programs for the elderly and of programs to aid educationally deprived children. These are a few instances of a large number of studies that are often requested by congressional committees and are made available to them upon completion.[21] This kind of work is essential if the committees of Congress are to match guns with the departments and agencies who come to committee hearings with phalanxes of experts only to be faced by a few congressmen who vary in their shrewdness and knowledge and supported by competent but very small staffs who cannot possibly compete with the Executive armies of specialists.[22]

Several additional changes are necessary for Congress to make even more effective use of the GAO. The staffs of each committee and subcommittee should develop regular working relationships with GAO counterparts so that the framing of legislation and the subsequent program evaluation become one continuous phase with feedback to the committee. Congress should be explicit in the legislation it writes about what it wants the administering agencies to do in the way of program evaluation, which is to be reported back to Congress, and the GAO should monitor this process and supplement it with studies of its own. At the present time the links of GAO with the committees are irregular and depend upon the wishes of key committee members. Ways must be found to institutionalize this process. A second required change is for the GAO and the congressional committees it serves to have increased access to information within the Executive. Legislation was introduced in 1973 that would give the GAO the right to subpoena records from the Executive and appeal to the courts if agencies do not comply, something it cannot now do.[23] Too few statutes require disclosure of information of specified kinds by the agencies to the legislature and there is nothing to prohibit Congress from writing legislation to ensure that it receives the information it wants.

We must make the same disclaimer about the limitations of program evaluation as a methodology that were made in regard to Executive use of these techniques. Members of Congress resist being tied down to any single source of information and will always supplement program analysis with the soundings of their own finely tuned antennae. The argument for Congress playing a central program evaluation role is that it will require the kinds of committee work and organization that will give the legislature handles on what the Executive is doing. Congress can always tie the hands of Presidents by law if it wishes, but more effective constraint in any area is continuous publicity and debate about Executive actions. If the Congress acts vigorously in behalf of its prerogatives to know and be consulted and to oversee programs, and of course keeps the final power of decision on legislation, it will be possible to reestablish the basic principle of American government that all the great decisions of government must be shared decisions.[24] This is the most effective way to control Presidents. It also presents political resources for Presidents who would use them to lead. The more open and fluid the policymaking process and the greater the demand upon Presidents to persuade others of the rightness of what they wish done, the more legitimate and sound policy is likely to be. Presidents who act in secrecy for fear of challenge actually deny themselves the resources of knowledge and support they might otherwise have.

IDEOLOGY AND POLITICS

We have suggested that a party government which links President and Congress might weaken Congress and strengthen the President, particularly in foreign affairs. A President might be less helped in domestic policymaking because national parties would have to veer and tack according to politics much as they do in parliamentary systems. In short, it is not clear that the political resources for domestic policy of the President would be strengthened by party government. Would a transformation of American national parties into more unified and organized parties of principle, instead of the loose coalitions that they have been, strengthen the President's political resources? Would such changes at the same time impose new political accountability to his party on a President? It is difficult to answer these questions without a more precise notion of the character of the future party system being evaluated. Three models span the list of possibilities. First, there is the type of national political party that until recently was accepted as the American norm. It was a party of national, state, and local office holders and party officials; supplemented at the time of Presidential elections by volunteers attracted to the national candidate and his views. This type of party was a confederation of state parties and the national party convention was a grand time for bargaining and compromise on a candidate and a platform that would hold the party together for another four years. The national executive arms of the parties, symbolized in the national chairmen, were coordinators and spokesmen but not real executives with influence in disposition of funds or selection of candidates. The congressional wings of these parties were part of these loose networks but kept their distance and autonomy. This loose, pluralistic kind of party put a high premium upon accommodation and compromise as evidenced in the Democratic national coalition brought together by Franklin D. Roosevelt. Southerners, the unions, working men and women, Americans of recent immigrant stock, blacks, intellectuals, and many middle-class heirs of the Progressive movement all came together in the most effective electoral instrument ever devised. The Republican party was more homogeneous in its largely Protestant, middle-class bases. Here the divisions were ideological—between progressives and conservatives—and therefore the fights were more serious than those of the Democrats. Presidential candidates and Presidents used this kind of party as a resource for the weaving together of a popular electoral coalition for election and governance. The party made few demands on the candidate and President. Rather, he gave it a sense of purpose and direction.

This kind of party began to fade with the candidacy of Senator Barry Goldwater for the Presidency in 1964. His nomination was secured by means of the takeover of the state party convention delegations by organizationally skillful conservative cadre. The liberals in the party have not yet staged a comeback and the Republican party since that time has become a relatively closed party of conservative cadre. The war in Vietnam broke apart the Democratic party in its traditional form and it has yet to reintegrate itself. A party of compromise cannot handle issues of intensity well because those who feel intensely about an issue, such as the war, will be unwilling to compromise. The party regulars on the other hand sought to blur and compromise the moral issues of the war in 1968 in order to nominate a candidate who could appeal to a majority of the voters. Thus Hubert Humphrey was nominated rather than Eugene McCarthy, who had done well in a number of primary elections, but whom the party regulars saw as an unpredictable and fundamentally anti-party figure. Humphrey had greater support among rank-and-file Democrats, however. Those militants who lost this fight charged that the party was too closed and dominated by unrepresentative cigar smoking, red faced men and that something must be done to open up the party. Reform finally came in two ways in the period between 1968 and 1972. The number of state Presidential primary elections increased greatly in response to the demand that state conventions were too closed and rigged and the rules of the national party about state delegation requirements were changed to strongly suggest, and some thought require, that each state delegation give appropriate representation to women and minorities. The ideology and tactics developed in America of the mid-sixties that grew out of the civil rights and poverty movements were now directed against the most democratic party in Western democracy as if it were an enemy to democracy.[25] The results have been to open the party up to severe conflicts that cannot easily be resolved because of their ideological intensity and to diminish the role of politicians in the decision processes of the Democratic party. The compromising and integrating functions that were once performed in the selection of Democratic Presidential candidates at national conventions are now to be performed with much greater difficulty because of the greater importance of the state primaries and the increased intensity of factionalism.

The three models of the national party are thus: (1) the broker party of diverse groups dominated by politicians, (2) the cadre party of homogeneity and ideological fervor; and (3) the mass-based party of fervent supporters organized primarily around ideological principles. Neither party is the first in pure form any more. The Republican party is close to the second. At present the Democratic party is an unstable combination of all three.

There are many who are active in attempting to transform the Democratic party into one much like European mass parties particularly the socialist parties, which speak with one chorus of voices and ideology about national problems; and propose policies to meet them. Such a party would be highly organized as a national entity, would meet in convention often, and would hold its candidates for office accountable for implementing its principles. It is thought that this kind of party would provide both ideological and political resources for a President and restrain him in terms of the party principles. It is not clear what the mechanisms of restraint would be since the President controls the government. Presumably such a party might deny renomination to a President who strayed from the path of virtue.

It seems highly unlikely that this type of party could ever exist in the United States. The effort to create such an entity will surely flounder upon the pluralistic nature of American politics and lead to ever widening breaches and recriminations within the party. Such

parties would be harmful to Presidential political resources because
they could not elect Presidents. And if they did do so, they would
perhaps make the President's task of securing national agreement
more difficult if the party members and leaders adhered to a blazing
ideology. Americans have never produced an ideological movement
that could last as a political party. The movement usually burns itself
out as it influences politics and policy. The enthusiasts go home after
the battle and have little taste for the hard work of maintaining an
organization. This has always left the care of parties to bread and
butter politicians who have sought concrete fruits like patronage,
position, and prestige. But these incentives are now less attractive
and the result is that leadership of the parties is going begging. It may
be that ideological activists who receive incentives from their very
activity in behalf of a cause are filling the vacuum.

One can hope for developments more favorable to national unity
and Presidential leadership. The two national parties could restore
a respect for the politics of compromise by achieving a balance between competing principles. Office holders and their political associates would be the principal leaders of the party at all levels. Provision
would be made for fair and open processes of admission to the party
so that a diversity of membership would be possible. It might even
be desirable to create suborganizations within the party for youth
and other categories of the population in which representation
would be guaranteed, as is the case in the Canadian parties.[26] The
number of state Presidential primary elections would be reduced
drastically and the choice of candidates would fall to the national
party convention thus restoring the convention function as inte-
grater of the party. However, this would not be the same party as that
dominated by the regulars of old. It would be a much more issue-
oriented party, organized in terms of national rules but with a respect for politics and an understanding that ideological warfare
within a party can destroy it. Such a national party would be very
similar to the present Canadian national parties, which are composed
of national, provincial, and local office holders, provincial and local
cadre, plus auxiliary groups like organizations for women and youth;
with requirements for representation set by national rules.[27] This
may be the direction in which both Democratic and Republican
national parties are moving in their search for new forms and purposes.[28] Mature parties of this kind would be political resources for
Presidents because they would be diverse coalitions organized in
terms of general principles but tolerant and open to disagreement.

Ideas in Politics

Presidents can draw on ideologies as guides to policy and as political resources with followers and the public as seen in Chapter 6. This is not a constant force in history however. The ideas must be developed and germane to the needs of a given time. They must also be able to arouse widespread response. None of these conditions seems present in the mid-1970s for liberal, conservative, or radical ideologies in America. This is not an end of ideology in a grand consensus as many prophets were predicting would happen to the Western democracies in the late 1950s. It is, instead, an exhaustion of ideologies that have been spent and broken by bitter experience in the 1960s.

Liberalism has exhausted itself. The internationalist messianism of postwar liberalism was completely discredited by the Vietnam War. The simple belief in positive government action with funds and organization to solve domestic reforms, inherited from the New Deal, was abused by the experience of the Great Society. A more rhetorical moralism of radical liberalism associated with the civil rights movement, antiwar movements, and the demands of minorities of all kinds for greater representation and equality has not been able to find a vehicle for entry into politics and has found the politics of confrontation increasingly fruitless. Liberals have developed different responses to this condition, perhaps the most common among practitioners of politics is to be more modest, claim less, and say that it is a mistake for Presidents to raise popular expectations if they cannot fulfill them. Such people call for a tough-minded, empirical approach to government action in which liberals would try to achieve only those goals that can be accomplished and recognize that much in the way of social change is beyond the capability of government to affect.[29] Another liberal response, perhaps most common among intellectuals, is to blame not liberalism but the basic structure and values of a capitalist society, which has created a culture of egoism and individualism in which it is virtually impossible to secure basic reform for either the disadvantaged or to affect and alter the basic values of the society more in the direction of community and the general welfare.[30] This view would predict that we are condemned to endure urban sprawl and ugliness in America because of our worship of private property, that we will continue to be slaves to the automobile because of our high premium upon individual mobility, that we will fail to develop adequate health care for all citizens because of our belief that doctors should work by the profit motive, and our fear of what is sometimes mis-called "socialized medicine."

These claims may or may not be correct, but they are uttered in frustration because America appears to lack a legitimate radical politics by means of which they might be tested. This has generally been the case in American history. We have had many instances of utopian political movements and of highly emotional movements of middle-class reformers seeking basically limited reforms but talking what seemed at the time to be radical language—like much of the Progressive movement and the McGovern campaign of 1972. But America has lacked a viable radical tradition comparable to English socialism. We have never quite had anything like the Fabian Society, an organization of British intellectuals—Beatrice and Sidney Webb and George Bernard Shaw—who supplied the young British Labor party with a core of ideas as the basis for a program in the early 1920s. The British Labor Party, the Fabian Society, and the Canadian New Democratic Party, which stems from both, all share an intellectual style of tough-minded empiricism in which reform measures are carefully researched and planned in advance. Thus the British Labor party was quite prepared to carry out the completion of the welfare state in its 1945 to 1950 government. Our radicalism has been rhetorical and moralistic and very nonempirical and it has lacked any kind of viable political party to carry it along. This may be because the basic liberal values of the American political culture are not compatible with thoroughgoing radicalism of any kind.[31] Marxism is an appealing organizing framework for radicals because it permits a break with the American liberal tradition of incrementalist reform. But Marxism has never taken root in American soil.

Conservatism in America is not in much better condition. Like radicalism, modern American conservative ideology has primarily been a rhetorical, moralistic, and anti-intellectual phenomenon.[32] It has lacked the elegance of British conservatism, clearly seen in the British Conservative party, which has carried along the aristocratic principle of the art of governing in behalf of a general welfare. American conservatism has been primarily a sociological phenomenon, an extension of the anti-government ideology of a business civilization having little constructive to offer in the way of governmental action. For these reasons conservatives in America have never fully developed skills at the art of governance nor substantive ideas about what to do about the nation's social problems. Their role has been primarily to oppose.

This puts the burdens of governmental action for innovation in both foreign and domestic affairs upon the liberals. We are in the same dilemma cited by Lionel Trilling after World War II in his study of liberalism where he concluded that there was only one American tradition, that of liberalism, and that since it was the whole, ways would have to be found for liberals to be critical of themselves and their ideas.[33] Some may feel that the test was failed. We have believed in the goodness of the American mission abroad and in our capacity, through the use of reason, to solve our social problems. We have looked on the Presidency as the chief agent of those ends. We may have been naive. The theologian and political theorist Reinhold Niebuhr, a strong liberal himself, wrote of the "irony" in history in which a hidden relationship is discovered through experience. Virtue becomes vice through some hidden defect in the virtue. Strength becomes weakness because of the vanity in strength. Wisdom becomes folly because we do not know its limits. The ironic situation is distinguished from the pathetic or the tragic because the individual bears some responsibility for it. Niebuhr saw American liberal culture as continually overtaken by irony in its pretensions about the relationships of virtue, wisdom, and power.[34] We are blind to the sin of pride in our sense of virtue. Perhaps our innocence has been both our greatest hope and chief flaw. This is a fundamental dilemma for American liberals in their hope to join power and progress.

This mood will surely pass in time to be succeeded by new hopes, enthusiasms, and self-confidence as new ideas are developed and directed toward political and social problems. In either the short or the long run a liberal has little alternative to a strategy of forward movement, using whatever ideals and tools are at hand. To give up is to deny that anything can be done to improve society at all. The liberal must dent the belief of the radical that the American capitalist society is locked into a framework of individual and collective selfishness that cannot be changed except by revolution. The liberal believes that history is open-ended and that no matter how little one can see ahead or how much there is an exaggeration of what will be achieved by reform, there is no question that progress toward a more just and humane society can take place. The failures of the 1960s should not so much discourage the liberal as cause him to resolve to begin anew.

The short-range prospect is not for heroic Presidential leadership in the direction of liberal reform or in any direction for that matter. Neither the core of ideas, the concrete programs, nor the popular support for a new surge of reform exists. One might predict, rather, that we are entering an "era of governance" in which the ends of government will be debated less than the means.[35] What will count is competence at governing in three dimensions. First, there will be a premium upon the development of concrete plans to solve social problems without large political or social enthusiasm or dislocation being created. Programs of housing allowances, basic income maintenance payments, new ideas for improving land use planning, public education, and the general delivery of services to citizens will be developed. Second, there will be increasing emphasis upon reforming the structures of state and local government so that citizens may be better served and the load of responsibility may be taken off the federal government in many areas. This involves giving these governments new capabilities at planning and coordinating and requires a revolution in the expertise of those who staff the bureaucracies. Third, the accomplishment either of the first two sets of goals will require high levels of competence at governing and administering organizations of government. It is not clear whether the various professions now provide the kind of education that prepares people for government. New schools of public policy and the broadening of schools of management to encompass questions of administration in government are steps toward the new requirements.

Any attempt at a heroic Presidency now or in the near future would be a futile one. For the moment we need less moralism and more intelligence in policy. We should strive for an adventerous government in the future only when we know what to do with it. A period of germination and preparation must come first in which new ideas and plans are developed. There is little sign that such a period has even begun. The kind of incubation of reform proposals which took place in the Congress of the 1950s is not occurring in the mid-1970s. The parties and their organizations are not sources of new ideas.[36] Until the new ideas begin to evolve we cannot use a Presidency that calls us to great achievements.

NEW AND OLD MODELS OF THE PRESIDENCY

The ideal that runs through this book is that Presidents should lead by persuasion. Implicit in the ideal are normative models of the Presidency as an institution in relation to the other institutions of government and of skill and style for individual Presidents. The model for Presidents follows from the principles of the institutional operation of the Presidency.

A normative model of an institution puts forth an ideal set of possibilities as better than alternative patterns. It serves as a standard of judgment and aspiration. Such models shape the way we view institutions and so have consequences for the way government actually works if they become widely held throughout the society. We have seen numerous examples of how this has been the case with the heroic model of Presidential leadership, which was so prominent in scholarship, journalism, and in public attitudes toward the Presidency from the time of Franklin Roosevelt to the mid-sixties. The superior virtue of the Presidency as an agency for governmental action in contrast with the Congress and the other levels of government was asserted. These beliefs assumed a parochial Congress dominated by the coalition of Republicans and southern Democrats, a network of alliances between Congressional committees, executive agencies and interest groups (which made for stasis in policy innovation and implementation), and the general incompetence of most state and local governments to deal with policy problems. The Presidency, consequently, was seen as the sole hope for policy innovation. This was not true for conservatives who were not anxious for government to play a vigorous role in society. Liberals had to have the Presidency; there was no alternative.

We may have come to a point in history in which both liberals and conservatives can cooperate in the fuller development of the other institutions of government. We are less likely to romanticize the Presidency than at any time in recent history. A deliberate effort to demythologize the Presidency would not be practical however. The Presidency has great symbolic power in the minds of Americans because of our history and constitutional system. These cannot suddenly be erased by rewriting school texts, nor do we want to promote a diminishing respect for the Presidential office. The best way to get the office into correct perspective is to find ways to strengthen the other parts of government. Americans have symbolic traditions for the other institutions. Great senators like Henry Clay and Daniel Webster, Robert La Follette and Robert Taft, and important Supreme Court justices such as John Marshall, Oliver Wendell Holmes, Benjamin Cardozo, and Earl Warren are part of American myths of government.

The normative model of the Presidency that might in time replace the President as dominant hero idea would set aside the goal of Presidential victory over others and stress accomplishment through agreement. It would be accepted that all major policy decisions would be taken openly as shared decisions across President and Congress and that decisions reached through open process of conflict, bargaining, and compromise are likely to be better in quality and more long lasting in their acceptance than those reached in secrecy. This could be a model for democratic leadership throughout the society.[37] The governance of corporations, labor unions, universities, and the patterns of rule within the large public bureaucracies are by and large semiauthoritarian. And yet Americans do not rest easy with authority in the sense of having an authoritarian political culture. There seems to be a dichotomy in the culture in which we grant great institutional powers to individuals and then express ambivalence about their power. Yet we do little to invent institutional mechanisms by which they might be required to lead through persuasion. Political executives may have the greatest demands placed upon them of any executives in our society in this regard. Perhaps if democracy were extended to the governance of nonpublic institutions there would be greater public understanding of the need for democratic character and styles of leadership in the Presidency. This brings us to the question of the skills and styles we need in a President.

Model of Presidential Leadership

The most widely quoted and discussed model of Presidential leadership style is that developed by Richard Neustadt in 1960.[38] In his book Neustadt calls upon the President to acquire as much personal power as he can in the office in order to compensate for his lack of institutional powers. According to Neustadt, the key to Presidential influence is to find ways to extract support out of the self-interest of other power holders. He must persuade them that what he wants them to do is in their interest as they see it from the vantage points of their institutional positions. The basis of such influence for a President is his strategic sense of how his choices for action shape his influence over others. Members of Congress watch the pattern of his actions in order to predict what he will do should they defy him. If he exacts a penalty on them they will be loathe to do it again. They try to estimate his degree of public support so that they may know the political risks of asserting their independence. The President must also know how to educate public thinking on issues by joining his words and acts to events in ways that will be clear to people. The popular support that accrues for his interpretations of events becomes a political resource to be used with the Washington professionals. Neustadt portrays a picture of a President and many other Washington actors in Congress and the bureaucracy each of whom has powers the others need to perform their roles. Persuasion is the lubricant of government in such a situation. For Neustadt the skill of Presidents at winning others over to their support is the necessary energizing factor to get the institutions of the federal government into action. He supplies the agenda for others. The chief psychological basis of skill in this sense is his sensitivity to personal power and to the power dimension of human relationships. Franklin Roosevelt is presented as the President with the greatest sense of personal and Presidential power and Dwight Eisenhower, as President, is presented as lacking in either the skill or will to power. President Truman is pictured as less skillful in personal terms than Roosevelt but as having a Rooseveltian respect for Presidential prerogatives and power. Neustadt calls upon the next President, who was to be John Kennedy, to revive the principle of Presidential power.

As Peter Sperlich has pointed out, Neustadt's ideal President has too limited a set of tools in his kit.[39] The bases of Presidential power are much broader than appeal to the self-interest of others. Neustadt leaves out any possible dimension of common agreement upon values and purposes among power holders. His political world is an atomistic one in which the different actors are united temporarily only by coalitions of egoism. He thus sells the Presidents he admires short. Surely Franklin Roosevelt's ability to inspire was far more important to his success than his strategic and tactical skills. By the same token, Roosevelt's style of administrative leadership was of course based upon the Neustadtian ability to create many sources of information throughout the government in order to learn how things were going and where the key leverage points were. But the main basis for Roosevelt's influence over those who worked for him was his capacity to inspire them. "After an hour with the President I could eat nails for lunch," one associate commented.[40] This is what Philip Selznick calls "institutional leadership," that which inspires those in bureaucracy to serve the leader because he is able to communicate a sense of institutional purpose in value terms that is far more than management ability.[41]

If one broadly interprets Neustadt to include this kind of value leadership then his description of the requirements of Presidential skill is accurate. Any President must understand the perspectives of others and know how to appeal to them in order to win support. He cannot simply work from within the confines of his own thoughts and feelings. Sensitivity to the thoughts of others and ability to create solutions that draw together the positions of many different people are what distinguish a good political leader from a nonpolitician. Most of us are not good politicians but rather are rationalists and moralists who do not understand why others do not see things as we do.

We do not need to reject Neustadt's model of leadership but simply to bring the moral dimension out to greater fullness and join it with the idea of strategic and tactical skill. In the expanded version of Neustadt's model of leadership there must be moral leadership in which common values are invoked—but this must be done through politics, not through undemocratic efforts to override others through claims to special authority or to act in secrecy through the belief that the leader knows best. Political cleverness divorced from morality is self-defeating and morality that is not joined to politics becomes ineffectual or, even worse, can become moralism that claims a superiority over politics and so becomes dangerous to democratic processes.

Max Weber distinguishes between two concepts of leadership, "the ethic of responsibility" and "the ethic of ultimate ends."[42] The latter is adherence to a supreme cause and higher morality. The former is the understanding that political choices usually involve the selection of the lesser evil and the joining of competing principles in a compromise, all of which recognizes the moral ambiguity of political choice. The supreme task of political leadership is to weave the two together. James MacGregor Burns calls this the ability to transcend lower level claims on government into higher level ones.[43] The leader must be able to persuade others to part with parochial goals in support of more general values that unite the community and refer to ultimate moral standards of some kind, no matter how imperfectly. And of course political skills are required to do this. There is no guarantee that the moral principles to which a leader appeals will be the ones we would wish. The term morality in this sense refers not to one's own view of right and wrong but to a dimension of reality that is inherently a part of politics.

Neustadt recalls FDR saying that Lincoln "was a sad man because he couldn't get it all at once. And nobody can."[44] Thus the President, Neustadt says, must be a person "whose source of confidence must make him capable of bearing Lincoln's sadness with good grace. The power seeker whose self-confidence requires quick returns and sure success might make a mess of everything including his own power. Grace calls for humor and perspective. Political experience does not assure those qualities. Indeed, it may diminish them in the degree it brings a taste for power. The office holder who combines them with an insight into presidential influence and hunger for it is no ordinary politician."[45]

Neustadt concludes that Presidents must be chosen from a very small class of extraordinary politicians. But this brings us back to the dilemma posed in Chapter 2. Can the attributes of a political man, who seeks power to fulfill personal needs and who is skillful in its exercise, be combined in one person with the qualities of democratic character that are also essential for leadership in a constitutional government? Was Franklin Roosevelt unique, or virtually so, in being both a political man and a democratic character? Certainly few of our Presidents are likely to be so endowed. We would do better therefore to expect second-best leaders for our Presidents, not political geniuses, like Roosevelt or Churchill, although the mythology of the Presidency makes us long for such men. We must learn to expect and want democratic personalities who will have learned political skills. The Presidency is not a place for politically inexperienced amateurs. We must understand, however, that driving political ambition quite often carries unpleasant and destructive personality traits with it, as the recent instances of Johnson and Nixon show. The ability of these two men to manipulate others proved to be self-defeating because it eventually generated mistrust. Their identification of Presidential authority with their personal power position caused them to close off dissenting views from their immediate circle. As a result of these experiences we are much more sensitive to the effects of Presidential style of authority upon discussion processes throughout government, particularly in the Executive.

The greatest contribution of the next President to American government would not be to attempt to dominate everyone in sight but to deliberately act to restore openness to the national government by showing respect for Congress: indicating that he values independence in Cabinet members and department heads, scaling down the numbers and influence of anonymous White House staff, showing regard for the civil service, and making certain that policy and administrative decisions are in no way unduly influenced by interest groups in the society. Neustadt does not talk about these kinds of characteristics because he was writing in a different historical context and thinking of different goals. Similarly, writers on the office today are advancing the view that more than anything else we need a decent man of high personal character.[46] In time, this emphasis will pass as the dominant one and there will be a call for a high degree of political skill. But these criteria will vary over time. For example, if it is true that one of the great challenges for the next generation is to create new organizations and processes for implementing policy at all levels of government, we may wish that our Presidents be persons of great executive experience and ability. We must change our criteria of expectation and judgment as problems and situations change. Research on leaders in other kinds of organizations shows that any leadership style varies in its effectiveness depending upon the needs of the situation and the character of the group being led.[47] One should not seek to impose a fixed model of leadership on all situations across time. This is not to say, however, that we will not demand certain minimal but essential characteristics of our Presidents. They must be democratic personalities, with a feel for politics and a high degree of self-respect that permit them to relax and not take themselves overseriously. But this leaves great leeway for varieties of skill and properly so. In 1974 we have wearied of activist leaders and seek respite in a man of character. Presidential candidates should be evaluated both in terms of the possession of the essential minimal qualities and the specific abilities they bring to the problems of a particular time in history.

Not only do the times and problems change but the Presidency as an institution itself changes and new qualities are required in Presidents as a result. New dimensions of power in office have emerged in fullest form in regard to Vietnam and the crisis of the Nixon Presidency, which is blanketed under the term Watergate. Neustadt stresses that international conflict in the atomic age increases the isolation of the President because he alone must make decisions about peace and war.[48] He insists that only the President can know his policy problems in all their fullness and that advisers only bring partial views that the President must fit into his larger synthesis.

Neustadt does not take account of the risk of idealizing the lonely Presidential pinnacle. The fact that Presidents have a unique perspective on the world has far too often been used by the Presidents since Neustadt wrote to justify action in secret or contempt for the democratic process of consultation on the theory that only the President, as is often claimed, "has all the facts." Today we face a situation in which Presidents may feel they can act unilaterally without persuading and somehow they must be convinced that their style must be open and democratic for the good of the polity. If a President attempts to bludgeon others into supporting him, he will probably fail in the long run. Both Johnson, on Vietnam, and Nixon, on Watergate, have been brought low by the slow but thorough process of democratic politics. But as both cases illustrate it is very hard to bring Presidents to brook in the short run.

Our dilemma is that the system of government can become paralyzed if a President does not act as the persuader Neustadt wishes him to be. Negative checks by Congress and bureaucracy and unfavorable public attitudes cannot force him to do so, at least in the short run. This brings us to ask if anything can be done to ensure that we admit only democratic personalities to the White House?

Assessing and Predicting Presidential Character

The search for an ideal leader by means of personality analysis to separate the healthy from the unhealthy is as much an illusion as is the hope for an ideal set of institutional checks that will contain Presidents and require them to perform well. Both approaches mistakenly assume that uncertainty can be eliminated from politics. One still might ask whether crucially important positive and negative factors in the personalities of politicians who would be President can be detected by the use of psychology and, if it can be done, whether such methods could be successfully introduced into the selection process?

It is important in answering this question to distinguish between scholarship that seeks to use personality theory in explaining the actions of past Presidents through biography from an attempt to predict the behavior of future Presidents or Presidents in office. The former is gradually becoming a respectable technique among historians and political scientists because the work of Alexander and Juliette George and others has shown that psychology can be introduced as a competing factor in historical explanation and subjected to the same tests of plausibility that historians and biographers apply to any hypothesis.[49] James D. Barber, Fred Greenstein, and the present author have carried this approach further in suggesting the retrospective analysis and comparison of several leaders within a common theoretical framework.[50] This effort to develop general typologies is incomplete for two main reasons. Personality theory has not been sufficiently developed to permit very many cause and effect statements to be made about general relationships between factors in personality and political actions. The typologies themselves have to date proved incapable of capturing more than one dimension of personality. There is a great deal more to personality than basic character structure, but any attempt to build a comprehensive typology to encompass all Presidents that took into account a full model of personality joining character structure, cognitive style, and belief system would flounder on the fact that individuals who were alike on one dimension would not resemble each other on a different plane. For these reasons, personality theory is best applied to the study of individual leaders with comparisons and generalizations drawn from marginal comparisons between individuals. We may not develop much theory that way but we will be surer of the validity of what we say. This is not to preclude a theoretical breakthrough at some future date, which builds upon advances in psychology to develop a comprehensive typology and set of predictive propositions about leadership behavior.

Even if we had such a theory drawn from the study of past cases, it is not clear that it could be validly applied to the prediction of the future behavior possibilities of Presidential candidates or incumbent Presidents.[51] If leading candidates for the Presidency were required to take not only a physical but a psychiatric examination they would all surely pass the latter. Mental illness is not a quality found in many successful politicians. However, many have character disorders of one kind or another, but a psychiatric test would not be subtle enough to detect these. The fact that Richard Nixon has always nursed grudges against "enemies" does not make him a paranoid. It merely suggests that he is particularly rigid in the effect he brings to his interpersonal relationships. One cannot imagine that any panel of psychiatrists could agree upon the implications of this finding for the actions of Nixon as President or that the general public would know what to make of such a report. It is only after the emotional context of the Watergate investigations when we learn that the Nixon White House had an "enemies" list that we realize the full effect of this way of thinking upon the inner circle of Nixon staff. The talents of a leader are often the opposite side of the coin from his flaws. For example, Nixon's penchant for isolation and privacy may be one source of his great resilience and doggedness, which has brought policy achievements. The price that has been paid by remoteness however is obvious. Yet, an initial analysis of Nixon the candidate in these terms would permit quite different interpretations upon the implications of the style according to the political coloration of the person judging. It would be very difficult to separate such judgments from partisanship. In fact, it is really quite difficult to be precise about just what a given individual is really like. Personality has so many component parts, all of which work simultaneously, that any attempt to size up an individual once and for all will surely suffer from being too simple. Does Nixon really love confrontation as much as he claims? One can find examples when he pressed a conflict to the logical end and won—as in his bombing pressure upon North Vietnam in 1972. But there are also instances when he talked tough and backed down. Realizing that he had miscalculated the negative response of public opinion on the Cambodian invasion in May 1970 he hastily retreated and withdrew American troops from Cambodia as soon as possible. He vented his anger at the Senate for the rejection of the nomination of Harold Carswell, of Florida, to be a justice of the Supreme Court in a public statement of the greatest harshness. Yet he backed down and changed the pattern of his nominees to the court to men who could be confirmed. Which was the real Richard Nixon? Perhaps even he did not know.

Even if personality theory was practicable and could be applied to the prediction of the behavior of politicians, one can imagine the obstacles to the use of such knowledge in the nomination and election process. Our experience with the utilization of expert knowledge in government policymaking shows that the effort generates experts and counter-experts and a process of competing claims of interpretation as to what the data mean. The issues are finally resolved by political processes with varying degrees of scientific expertise influencing the outcome. The attempt to use personality theory in candidate selection might do more harm than good by creating confusion and contradictory claims that voters would be unable to sort out. It might also distract attention from the important issues that are the basis for a campaign.

Yet Barber is right that our failure to pay attention to the importance of personality as a vital factor in the behavior of Presidents has exacted a price. If there can be no direct application of personality analysis to candidate selection, what can be done to ensure that we at least screen out destructive personalities and can intelligently discuss what kind of a President a given person is likely to be? Three possibilities come to mind. First, we could follow Barber's cue and look hard for signs of active-negative personality characteristics in specific individuals. Journalists and others who write about candidates could provide evidence for rigid or destructive behavior. This kind of evidence will interest politicians who help to nominate candidates as they place high reliance upon predictability, flexibility, and integrity in Presidents. A politician must keep his word if he is to have credibility. For this reason most politicians are skeptical of finely tuned, introspective personalities. This was one basis for the distrust of Democratic politicians for Senator Eugene McCarthy in 1968. Hubert Humphrey seemed so much more predictable and congenial. Perhaps they were right. Of course, such thoughts did not prevent Republican politicians from nominating Richard Nixon in 1968. Second, we could have a much more sophisticated discourse among journalists about the likely style of authority of a given individual in the White House based upon his performance to date. David Broder is almost unique among journalists in his sensitivity to this kind of reporting.[52] He has pointed to the problem of having a Presidential candidate pool largely based upon the United States Senate because that body provides a limited range of experience for developing skills needed in the White House. It does not provide the opportunity for becoming an effective executive as exists for governors. Broder, therefore, believes that journalists who play such a crucial role in building up and tearing down candidates should work to broaden the potential national candidate pool by introducing governors, mayors, and other talented people to public view. One could go a step further and suggest that it would be proper journalism and good political science to compare the styles of authority of many such individuals so that we might have some notion of what their general approach to Presidential roles would be. Third, we could increase the general acceptance of the model of a democratic style of authority set forth earlier so that candidates would be implicitly screened in terms of the criteria of democratic style. This would not involve analysis of the dynamics of personality, but rather, the perception of flexibility, tolerance, openness, persuasiveness, and so on. If we genuinely want and seek democratic leaders in all the institutions of our society, we will get them. It is not clear that this is the case today.

Perhaps the best way to find leaders with democratic authority styles is in the nomination process when other politicians pass upon a fellow professional. This is not guaranteed of course. But one wonders what kinds of candidates will throw themselves into a two-year race for the Presidency as required by the present marathon system of primary elections. Are we likely to get the tightly, driven kind of leader who confuses his own ambition with the welfare of the republic? Perhaps the emotional investment in this arduous process is so great that the kinds of people who emerge will not be what we seek in our Presidents. The weakening of the importance of political professionals in our national parties and the decline of the convention in the decision process may not be a good thing. Ways must be found to both broaden the candidate pool and strengthen the role of professionals in the choice of party nominees.

Biographical scholarship about past Presidents can be very useful for our understanding of the interplay of personality and power in the office. It can make us sensitive to the importance of Presidential personality in decision processes for example, as we saw in Chapter 5. This in turn can lead to suggestions about how to introduce factors in that process or in the relationships between Congress and the Executive that will counteract the negative effects of Presidential personality. This is the principal value of this kind of scholarship. As this book is being written, the nation is faced with this question carried to the extreme degree. Can we find ways to fairly judge and, if necessary, remove a President charged with unconstitutional and perhaps criminal actions?

WATERGATE

At the writing of this book, the series of scandals collectively known as Watergate came into full public view. It was difficult to incorporate successive revelations as they emerged from Senate hearings, criminal confessions and indictments, and journalistic investigation into the book because no one could say for sure where it was all going or what the full dimensions of Presidential personal involvement were. By the early spring of 1974 it appeared that President Nixon would be impeached by the House of Representatives. Whether he would remain in office for a trial by the Senate or whether the Senate would vote to convict him should such a trial take place could not be foretold. The courts will establish guilt or innocence in time in regard to the former Administration officials who have been indicted in matters relating to Watergate.

The criticisms of the Nixon Administration contained in this book, whether connected with Watergate or not, do not depend upon criminal convictions of the President and his aides for their validity. The essential sin of the Nixon group was the violation of the spirit of democratic politics in their conduct of government. This was widely felt among their critics before any knowledge of Watergate scandals was known. A book by Rowland Evans and Robert Novack, two perceptive journalists, on the first Nixon Administration documents the contempt that the President and his chief White House aides, such as H. R. Haldeman and John Ehrlichman, felt for Congress, the bureaucracy, the press, and the norms of accommodation and mutual trust that are essential for the proper functioning of the national government.[53] The revelations of Watergate simply compound the story and suggest how the original basic attitudes may have led such men to commit the crimes charged.

The charges include allegations of Presidential knowledge of the cover-up, knowledge of the operations of the unit that burglarized the headquarters of the Democratic national committee in June 1972, and charges that the President took active steps to limit the FBI investigation and impede the first special prosecutor in his inquiries into these charges to the point of discharging him. There was also the charge that the President created special units within the White House in 1971, which engaged in illegal burglary and wiretapping. In 1970 it is charged that the President approved an intelligence plan (drafted by an aide), known as the Huston Plan, which included authorization for burglaries, wiretapping, surveillance, and the opening of mail. The President was seen as having withheld knowledge of the burglary of the office of Ellsberg's psychiatrist from the judge in the trial in which Ellsberg was charged with making the Pentagon Papers public. Nixon was also said to have attempted to bribe the judge by dangling the directorship of the FBI before him during the trial. Other possible charges included granting favors to milk producers and the gigantic ITT corporation in return for large campaign gifts, and drawing up a list of White House "enemies" who were to be investigated by the Internal Revenue Service after the 1972 election. There were also allegations about the personal finances of the President; the large federal expenditures upon his two homes and the fact that he paid minimal federal income taxes over several years on the basis of a possibly illegal claim of a tax deduction for giving his Vice Presidential papers to the National Archives after the repealing of the law permitting deductions. The final questions deal with the exercise of constitutional powers. It was asserted that the President ordered, without congressional authorization and without announcing it publicly, a bombing campaign in Cambodia in 1969 and 1970 and permitted military operations in Laos in 1970 after Congress had passed legislation prohibiting ground combat there. It was also charged that the President had impounded or refused to spend $40 billion that had been appropriated by Congress, mostly for social programs.[54] Presidential defense in many of these cases was either to claim lack of personal knowledge, deny any lack of propriety (as in matters of personal finances), or claim inherent constitutional powers to protect the national security by authorizing actions against subversives, and the power to defend the national interest through the use of military power abroad.

Were these kinds of actions, many of which clearly took place whether with Presidential knowledge or not, unique to the Nixon Administration or were they a logical result of the imperial Presidency? Can one find such occurrences in previous administrations? It was under the Johnson Administration that army units began to secretly spy on anti-war protesters and to collect data upon supposed critics of the war, including United States senators. The FBI practiced electronic surveillance of Martin Luther King, the civil rights leader, during the administrations of Presidents Kennedy and Johnson, and in the administration of the latter there was a massive and still not fully uncovered secret effort by government to infiltrate and spy upon black militant and anti-war movements.[55] These are only a few examples of the dangerous identification in the minds of Presidents of domestic dissent with the threat to national security. Watergate in many of its ramifications was clearly an outgrowth of Vietnam and the rise of dissenting confrontation politics over the war that caused both Presidents Johnson and Nixon to feel threatened and insecure in the face of such violent dissent. The Ellsberg burglary matter and the authorization of the Huston Plan follow directly from these concerns.

It is the personal view of the author that the excesses of the Nixon Administration were greater in both degree and kind than those that had come before, but this is a matter for trial and conviction rather than assertion. Such a view does not, however, answer the question of how such illegal actions by lawful government can be prevented in the future. Conviction of Presidential aides and impeachment of a President may not be sufficient to prevent such actions by future people in these offices unless something is done to ensure that the secretive White House government that makes such actions possible is dismantled. It is important to recognize that exercise of these kinds of powers is only possible in large part because much of it can be done in secrecy within the White House. The principal aides of the President are neither subject to congressional confirmation at the time of their appointment, nor required to testify before Congress during their tenure. Even though many of them wield greater power than Cabinet officers the Congress cannot find out what they do, for they are protected under the doctrine of Executive privilege. We do not really know what kinds of White House interventions with the Justice Department and the regulatory commissions take place on behalf of economic interest groups for Presidential political reasons. The fragmentary evidence suggests that the possibilities for corruption are too great to have been ignored. The only answer to this danger of abuse of power is for Congress to open up the White House by changing the law to require confirmation and testimony before Congress of the President's principal associates in the White House. The budgets and actions of their various operations could thereby also be openly scrutinized by Congress. They could invoke claims of Executive privilege to not speak of confidential conversations with the President, just as Cabinet members may. But this leaves a great deal of room for legitimate public inquiry about their activities. This is only to point a general direction for reform without specifying details that should be thought through carefully. It is only fundamental structural changes of this kind that can prevent future Watergates and like abuses.

IMPEACHMENT

It is inconceivable that a prime minister of the parliamentary systems of Britain and Canada could stand accused of the charges made against President Nixon and have remained in office. He would have been cashiered by his party at the very least because they would have held him responsible for the actions of his subordinates. A Presidential system does not have this kind of protection and, moreover, a President is supplied with considerable authority to protect himself against impeachment. By early 1974 President Nixon had a large number of lawyers on the White House payroll who were acting as his attorneys—at public expense—in trying to prevent impeachment action. He invoked doctrines of Executive privilege to deny Presidential documents and tapes to the special prosecutor and the House Judiciary Committee that they felt they needed for their responsibilities. What appeared to be deliberate destruction of evidence in the tape of one Presidential conversation that had an eighteen-minute gap had no effect one way or the other because it could not be proved that the President was responsible for the erasure. In short, we may suspect that a President has broken the law but it is very difficult to prove the fact if he has much of the evidence necessary to do so.

The problem would then appear to be that the American constitutional system has no device for removing a President from office between elections short of impeachment—and impeachment is not only a most difficult process to get under way but is a very limited instrument. It seems it can only really be invoked against a President who appears to have committed criminal acts. It seems to have been the case that the authors of the Constitution intended broader bases than criminal charges in their recital of the grounds for impeachment: "Treason, Bribery, or other high Crimes and Misdemeanors." According to Raoul Berger, the leading authority on impeachment, the founding fathers saw high crimes and misdemeanors in the context of English parliamentary practice as meaning crimes against the state, that is, unconstitutional actions by ministers or violations of the public trust by members of the Executive that might fall short of criminality.[56] This interpretation of the Constitution may be valid, but it does not follow that an impeachment and conviction would occur from a constitutional conflict. In fact the evidence would seem to be against it. The trial of President Andrew Johnson, which was based upon constitutional and policy conflicts between President and Congress, gave a bad name in history to impeachment as a way to curb Presidents. To many citizens the conflict seemed to be political rather than constitutional.[57] There is so much room for argument over interpretations of the Constitution that President Nixon and his critics could argue endlessly and never resolve whether he had the inherent authority to bomb Cambodia under his war powers or to authorize wiretapping on grounds of national security. The best protection against Presidential actions of this kind therefore is not impeachment but publicity, exposure, and political opposition. Congress and the press are the vital checking institutions here.

The charges against President Nixon or any future President that would be brought to bear in an impeachment trial would have to do with personal criminal activity on the part of the President. It is clear that this is not an easy kind of charge to prove because of the difficulty of those who must impeach in securing the evidence. But events in early 1974 suggest that these are not insuperable obstacles and that once a large enough number of Americans begin to suspect that a President has broken the law the issue will be joined in an impeachment proceeding.

The question remains as to whether there should be some constitutional way to remove a President from office short of impeachment on the grounds that he has lost the confidence of the nation. One proposal is that Congress might pass a resolution supported by two-thirds of its members calling upon him to resign. One wonders, however, if a President who was so disliked would be affected by congressional opinion.[58] A variation on this idea would be a general election for both Congress and the Presidency 30 to 60 days after such a vote so that the people might decide whom to support in the controversy. This is appealing and should be considered carefully, but the obvious flaws make one wonder whether any such devices that are borrowed from the parliamentary model can be grafted onto a Presidential government. Members of Congress would be very reluctant to place their own offices on the line in an election in order to attack a President. The same motivations hold in Britain and Canada and dissolutions from actual votes of no confidence have been very rare in this century. Parties stand behind their leaders even when they are in the process of changing them by a behind the scenes process. It is quite possible that in such an appeal to the voters both the President and the bulk of the members of Congress would be returned and the dispute would not be resolved. The fact of party accountability to the electorate for the conduct of both executive and legislature, which holds in a parliamentary system, is not likely to occur in a Presidential system unless at some future time there was a perfect meshing of electoral support for Presidents and for their parties in Congress. If this was in fact the case, such open warfare between a President and the majority party in Congress—his party —would be unlikely and the device of dissolution would not be used, as in the case in Britain and Canada. This small example only goes to warn the reader against deceptively simple and appealing institutional reforms that are often peddled in times like the present. As mentioned earlier, such changes are not appropriate because they do not match the pattern of politics. However, the patterns of Americans politics do permit the institutional strengthening of Congress to provide for much greater holding of Presidents and their appointees accountable for their actions before the Congress and the public. This is probably the only effective way to curb a lawless President.

VIETNAM, WATERGATE, AND THE CRISIS OF THE CONTEMPORARY PRESIDENCY

In a modern, industrial society the functional morality and rationality dictated by the logic of the organizations we serve often block out concern with ultimate morality or rationality. We serve the immediate aims of institutions whether they are compatible with the higher principles of the society and our ultimate systems of morality or not. Automobile companies must manufacture and sell cars without asking themselves whether such quantities of automobiles are good for the nation. Highway engineers seek to build roads for the same reason. The trucking industry wants the roads built for its own reasons. Any thought of a general public interest on the part of such groups is either identified with the interests of the organization or is ignored. Fortunately, in a democracy, other groups will disagree from the logic of their own organizational functions and bargaining and compromise take place. There surely is a public good over and above these competing interests but few refer to it except in rhetorical debate. The means to growth and influence of organizational missions have substituted for ultimate moral ends in many areas of industrial society, whether capitalist or socialist. This situation creates moral dilemmas for many individuals who find their personal morality opposed by the logic of organizational activity in which they find themselves.

This disease has infected American government. In the Pentagon Papers there was no mention of ultimate moral principles or of whether American ideals were best served by the growing American role in Vietnam.[59] Rather, one saw that American national power had become a justifiable end in itself for these men. They were intoxicated with what could be achieved by violence. The same limited perspective and arrogance was displayed by the Nixon men who prevented full public disclosure of the facts about the Watergate bugging for fear that disclosures of related incidents such as the Ellsberg burglary might adversely affect the reelection of President Nixon. This was the ultimate end—not the preservation of the democratic process. The same phenomenon was seen in the everyday conduct of government when men huddled together in closed organizational groups and justified deliberate destruction of villages in South Vietnam as "pacification." All of this appears to be exacerbated by the national cult of success and celebration of power whether it be in sports or politics.

There may be less myopia of this kind at the top of the smaller democracies because leaders and publics are not obsessed with a power that is nonexistent. The geographic and organizational scale is usually much smaller than in the United States and therefore leaders acknowlege publics as persons rather than as distant objects to be manipulated through propaganda. Organizational life in closed groups generates a certainty and smugness of feeling that those outside the charmed circle lack the understanding of the world that is given to those within it. Power and purpose become confused in such a situation and men give way to the sin of pride. This is the ultimate lesson of Vietnam and Watergate. They were manifestations of a power-intoxicated society that were compounded by the conditions of secrecy and closed decisionmaking within government. Functional morality and rationality thereby superseded awareness of ultimate standards of moral law and reason. Reality was mistaken for what was accepted as truth within the walls of the institution.

Probably the best antidote to such subversion of true morality and rationality is to be found in open politics that push men to admit they do not know the answers to questions, that they need to consult with others, that there are many possible points of view on a subject, and that no set of men can intelligently make decisions affecting the lives of others under conditions of secrecy. Another lesson of Vietnam and Watergate is that secret decisions lead to misgovernment and that open government gives us a chance to solve our problems. Not only do we develop more knowledge and points of view but we are able to shake loose of a narrow organizational morality and rationality and appeal to higher principles. The admission that one's viewpoint is a partial one permits the search for a larger principle by which to act.

This book cannot provide all answers to the crisis of the modern Presidency. In part that is because there are many different problems involved that all seem to have come together in our awareness at once. It is important to separate these and consider remedies appropriate for the nature of the problem. We should try to select good persons as our Presidents. New institutional devices must be found for both checking power and permitting bureaucracy to function more effectively. Our values and purposes should be fundamental to the exercise of power. The taming of the American Presidency is a task for many people in many different positions and places. It is to all of these people and the citizens who are dependent upon them for intelligent action that the message of this book is ultimately directed. We must learn to practice democratic politics among ourselves in all of our institutions in a spirit of mutual respect and trust. If we cannot do this, then we deserve to be ruled by an authoritarian Presidency.

Notes

Preface

1. Harold D. Lasswell, *Power and Personality* (New York: Norton, 1948); Alexander and Juliette George, *Woodrow Wilson and Colonel House; a Personality Study* (New York: John Day, 1956); James David Barber, *The Presidential Character, Predicting Performance in the White House* (Englewood Cliffs, N.J.: Prentice-Hall, 1972).
2. Alexander L. George, "The Case for Multiple Advocacy in Making Foreign Policy," *The American Political Science Review*, September 1972, vol. 66, pp. 751–785; Irving L. Janis, *Victims of Group Think* (Boston: Houghton Mifflin, 1972).
3. Graham J. Allison, *The Essence of Decision: Explaining the Cuban Missile Crisis* (Boston: Little, Brown 1971); Richard E. Neustadt, *Alliance Politics* (New York: Columbia University Press, 1970).
4. Louis Hartz, *The Liberal Tradition in America* (New York: Harcourt, Brace and World, 1955); Angus Campbell et al., *The American Voter* (New York: Wiley, 1960). James L. Sandquist, *Politics and Policy: The Eisenhower, Kennedy and Johnson Years* (Washington, D.C.: The Brookings Institution, 1968).

Chapter 1

1. Arthur M. Schlesinger, "Our Presidents: A Rating by 75 Historians," *The New York Times Magazine*, July 29, 1962, p. 12; "The U.S. President," *Life Magazine*, 25 (Nov. 1, 1954) p. 66.
2. Thomas A. Bailey, *Presidential Greatness: The Image and the Man from George Washington to the Present* (New York: Appleton-Century-Crofts, 1966), p. 25.
3. James MacGregor Burns, *Presidential Government: The Crucible of Leadership* (Boston: Houghton Mifflin, 1966), pp. 83–98.
4. Frank Parkin, *Middle Class Radicalism: The Social Bases of the British Campaign for Nuclear Disarmament* (New York: Praeger, 1968), p. 207.
5. Ralph K. Huitt and Robert L. Peabody, eds., *Congress: 2 Decades of Analysis* (New York: Harper, 1969), passim.
6. Richard E. Neustadt, *Presidential Power: The Politics of Leadership* (New York: Wiley, 1960); Clinton Rossiter, *The American Presidency* (New York: Harcourt, Brace, & World, 1956); Louis Koenig, *The Chief Executive* (New York: Harcourt, Brace, & World, 1968).
7. Reinhold Niebuhr, *The Irony of American History* (New York: Scribner, 1952), passim.
8. Fred Greenstein, *Children and Politics* (New Haven: Yale University Press, 1965), passim.
9. John E. Mueller, "Presidential Popularity from Truman to Johnson,"

320

American Political Science Review, 61 (March 1970) pp. 18–34.

10. Robert E. Lane, *Political Ideology: Why the American Common Man Believes What He Does* (New York: Free Press, 1967), p. 148.

11. Roberta Sigel, "Image of the American Presidency: Part II of an Exploration Into Popular Views of Presidential Power," in Aaron Wildavsky, ed., *The Presidency* (Boston: Little, Brown, 1969), pp. 296–309; *Midwest Journal of Political Science*, 10 (Feb. 1966), pp. 123–127.

12. Burns, op. cit., p. 100.

13. Ibid., pp. 101–105.

14. Sebastian DeGrazia, *The Political Community: A Study of Anomie* (Chicago: University of Chicago Press, 1948), p. 113.

15. Bradley Greenberg and Edwin B. Parker, eds., *The Kennedy Assassination and the American Public: Social Communication in Crisis* (Stanford, Calif.: Stanford University Press, 1965), passim.

16. Arthur H. Miller, Thad A. Brown, and Alden S. Raine, "Social Conflict and Political Estrangement, 1958–1972," Paper delivered at the 1973 Midwest Political Science Association Convention, Chicago, May 3–5, 1973, p. 6.

17. William Chapman, "66% Feel Distrust in Government," *Washington Post*, Jan. 8, 1974, p. A7.

18. Louis Harris, "U.S. Institutions Fall in Popular Esteem," *Iowa City Press-Citizen*, October 25, 1971, cited in Jack Dennis, "Public Support for American National Political Institutions," August 1973, unpublished manuscript.

19. Survey results given in Robert G. Lebner, "Public View of State Governors," in Thad Beyle and J. Oliver Williams, eds., *The American Governor in Behavioral Perspective* (New York: Harper & Row, 1973), pp. 258–269.

20. Fred I. Greenstein, "What the President Means to Americans: Presidential Choice Between Elections," in James D. Barber, ed., *Choosing the President* (Englewood Cliffs, N.J.: Prentice-Hall, 1974), p. 127.

21. Dennis, op. cit., pp. 8, 16.

22. Donald J. Devine, *The Political Culture of the United States* (Boston: Little, Brown, 1972), pp. 158–163.

23. Chapman, op. cit.

24. *The Washington Post*, March 21, 1974, p. A10.

25. Greenstein, "What the President Means to Americans," pp. 138–139.

26. Jules Witcover, "Public Unhappy with Nixon, Uneasy on Impeachment," *The Washington Post*, Jan. 13, 1974, p. A1.

27. Chapman, op. cit.

28. Greenstein, op. cit., pp. 134–140.

29. *The Pentagon Papers* as published by *The New York Times*, based on investigative reporting by Neil Sheehan (New York: Bantam Books, 1971), passim.

30. George F. Kennan, *Memoirs: Nineteen Fifty to Nineteen Sixty Three* (Boston: Little, Brown, 1972), passim.

31. James L. Sandquist, *Politics and Policy: The Eisenhower, Kennedy, and Johnson Years* (Washington, D.C.: Brookings, 1968), passim.

32. Aaron Wildavsky and Jeffrey Pressman, *Implementation* (Berkeley: University of California Press, 1973), passim.

33. Thomas E. Cronin, "The Textbook Presidency," in Charles Peters and John Rothschild, eds., *Inside the System* (New York: Praeger, 1973), pp. 6–19.

34. Burns, op. cit., p. 112.

35. George Reedy, *The Twilight of the Presidency* (New York: World Publishing, 1970), passim.

Chapter 2

1. Reinhold Niebuhr, *The Irony of American History* (New York: Scribner, 1952), passim.

2. Erwin C. Hargrove, *Presidential Leadership, Personality and Political Style* (New York: Macmillan, 1966), passim.

3. Richard Neustadt, *Presidential Power: The Politics of Leadership* (New York: Wiley, 1960), passim.

4. Harold D. Lasswell, *Psychopathology and Politics* (Chicago: University of Chicago Press, 1930); *Power and Personality* (New York: Norton, 1948); "Democratic Character," in *Political Writings of Harold D. Lasswell* (Glencoe, Ill.: Free Press, 1951), passim.

5. Rowland Evans and Robert D. Novack, *Lyndon B. Johnson: The Exercise of Power* (New York: Signet Books, 1968), pp. 118–122.

6. Ibid., p. 312.

7. Philip E. Converse, et al., "Electoral Myth and Reality: the 1964 Elections," *American Political Science Review*, 59 (June 1965), p. 331.

8. Evans and Novack, op. cit., chapter 23.

9. Chester Cooper, *The Last Crusade: America in Vietnam* (New York: Dodd Mead, 1970), p. 416.

10. Eric F. Goldman, *The Tragedy of Lyndon Johnson* (New York: Dell, 1968), p. 590.

11. James David Barber, *The Presidential Character: Predicting Performance in the White House* (Englewood Cliffs, N.J.: Prentice-Hall, 1972), Part 5; Bruce Mazlish, *In Search of Nixon* (New York: Basic Books, 1972).

12. *Life Magazine*, pp. 54A–54B, 1971.

13. Ibid., p. 58.

14. Ibid., p. 61.

15. Barber, op. cit., p. 10. The idea of the first independent political success becoming the basis for the development of a subsequent political style was conceived by Barber.

16. Richard M. Nixon, *Six Crises* (New York: Pocket Books, 1962), pp. 20–21.

17. Ibid., p. 103.

18. Ibid., p. 108.

19. Ibid., p. 128.

20. Barber, op. cit., p. 436.

21. Saul Pett, "The Worst Thing You Can Do in This Job Is Relax," *The Providence Journal*, Jan. 14, 1973., pp. 1–3.

22. Barber, op. cit., pp. 11–14. The reader should know that Barber and I disagree on Eisenhower. He depicts him as a passive-negative whereas I see him as an active-positive. This chapter does not deal with Barber's two passive types, passive-positive (Taft and Harding) and passive-negative (Coolidge and Eisenhower). They are treated at length by Barber in his book. Two criticisms of the Barber typology are, Erwin C. Hargrove, "Presidential Personality and Revisionist Views of the Presidency," *The American Journal of Political Science*, 17 (Nov. 1973) pp. 819–835; Alexander L. George, "Assessing Presidential Character," *World Politics*, 26 (Jan. 1974) pp. 234–282.

23. Neustadt, op. cit., p. 155.

24. Frank Freidel, *Franklin D. Roosevelt: The Apprenticeship* (Boston: Little, Brown, 1952), p. 65.

25. Frances Perkins, *The Roosevelt I Knew* (New York: Viking, 1946), p. 21.

26. Arthur M. Schlesinger, Jr., *The Crisis of the Old Order* (Boston: Houghton Mifflin, 1957), p. 407.

27. John Gunther, *Roosevelt in Retrospect* (New York: Harper & Row, 1950), p. 4.

28. Perkins, op. cit., p. 27.

29. Arthur M. Schlesinger, Jr., *The Coming of the New Deal* (Boston: Houghton Mifflin, 1959), p. 548.

30. Rexford G. Tugwell, *The Democratic Roosevelt* (New York: Doubleday, 1957), p. 332.

31. James MacGregor Burns, *Roosevelt: The Lion and the Fox* (New York: Harcourt, Brace, 1956), p. 348.

32. Schlesinger, *Coming of the New Deal*, p. 557.

33. Joseph Alsop and Robert Kitner, *The 168 Days: The Story Behind the Story of the Supreme Court Fight* (New York: Doubleday, 1938).

34. Richard E. Neustadt, "Approaches to Staffing the Presidency: Notes on FDR and JFK," *American Political Science Review*, 57 (Dec. 1963) pp. 855–863.

35. Louis Brownlow, "A Letter from Louis Brownlow," *American Political Science Review* 57 (Dec. 1963) pp. 864.

36. Perkins, op. cit., p. 97.

37. Ibid., p. 277.

38. Robert Sherwood, *Roosevelt and Hopkins* (New York: Harper, 1948) p. 882.

39. Hargrove, op. cit., chapter 1. Barber does not deal with Theodore Roosevelt, but I see him as an active-positive in Barber's terms.

40. Alexander L. George, "The Case for Multiple Advocacy in Making Foreign Policy," *American Political Science Review*, 66 (Sept. 1972) pp. 762–763.

41. Peter W. Sperlich, "Bargaining and Overload: An Essay on Presidential Power," in Aaron Wildavsky, ed., *The Presidency* (Boston: Little, Brown, 1969), pp. 168–192.

42. Wilfred E. Binkley, *President and Congress* (New York: Random House, 1962), p. 354.

43. Kenneth S. Davis, *Soldier of Democracy* (New York: Doubleday, 1945), p. 166.

44. Erwin C. Hargrove, "Popular Leadership in the Anglo-American Democracies," in Lewis J. Edinger, ed., *Political Leadership in Industrialized Societies* (New York: Wiley, 1967), p. 193.

45. Bradley Greenberg and Edwin B. Parker, eds., *The Kennedy Assassination and the American Public: Social Communication in Crisis* (Stanford, Calif.: Stanford University Press, 1965), passim.

46. Henry Fairlie, *The Kennedy Promise: The Politics of Expectation* (Garden City, N.Y.: Doubleday, 1973), passim.

47. Barber, op cit., p. 337.

48. Richard J. Walton, *Cold War and Counter-Revolution: The Foreign Policy of John F. Kennedy* (Baltimore, Md.: Penguin Books, 1972), chapter 7.

49. Arthur M. Schlesinger, Jr., *A Thousand Days: John F. Kennedy in the White House* (Boston: Houghton Mifflin, 1965), pp. 973–978.

50. Alexander L. George and Juliette L. George, *Woodrow Wilson and Colonel House: A Personality Study* (New York: John Day, 1956).

51. Walton, op. cit., passim.

Chapter 3

1. Arthur M. Schlesinger, Jr., *The Imperial Presidency* (Boston: Houghton Mifflin, 1973), p. 221.

2. Library of Congress, "Development of the White House Staff," *Congressional Record*, June 20, 1972, H5818–H5820; Thomas E. Cronin, "The Swelling of the Presidency," *Saturday Review of the Society*, February 1973.

3. Richard E. Neustadt, "Approaches to Staffing the Presidency: Notes on FDR and JFK," *American Political Science Review*, 57 (Dec. 1963) pp. 855–863.

4. Ibid.

5. Richard E. Neustadt, "Presidency and Legislation: The Growth of Central Clearance," in Aaron Wildavsky, ed., *The Presidency* (Boston: Little, Brown, 1969), p. 609.

6. Ibid., p. 611.

7. Ibid., p. 532.

8. Ibid., p. 622.

9. Lester G. Seligman, "Presidential Leadership: The Inner Circle and Institutionalization," *Journal of Politics*, 18 (Aug. 1956) p. 416; Elmer E. Cornwell, Jr., "The Truman Presidency," in Richard S. Kirkendall, ed., *The Truman Period as a Research Field* (Columbia, Mo.: University of Missouri Press, 1967).

10. Edward S. Flash, Jr., *Economic Advice and Presidential Leadership, the*

Council of Economic Advisors (New York: Columbia University Press, 1965).

11. Erwin C. Hargrove, *Presidential Leadership, Personality and Political Style* (New York: Macmillan, 1966), chapter 6.

12. Patrick Anderson, *The President's Men* (Garden City, N.Y.: Doubleday, 1969), chapter 5.

13. Op. cit., chapter 6.

14. Norman C. Thomas, "Presidential Advice and Information: Policy and Program Formulation," in Norman C. Thomas and Hans W. Baade, eds., *The Institutionalized Presidency* (Dobbs Ferry, N.Y.: Oceana Publications, 1972).

15. Thomas E. Cronin, "Everybody Believes in Democracy Until He Gets to the White House," in Thomas and Baade, op. cit.

16. George Reedy, *Twilight of the Presidency* (New York: World Publishing, 1970).

17. Albert Speer, *Inside the Third Reich* (New York: Macmillan, 1970), p. 472.

18. Robert F. Kennedy, *Thirteen Days: A Memoir of the Cuban Missile Crisis* (New York: Norton, 1971), p. 112.

19. Chester Cooper, *The Last Crusade: America in Vietnam* (New York: Dodd Mead, 1970), p. 223.

20. Jerald Hage and Michael Aiken, *Social Change in Complex Organizations* (New York: Random House, 1970), passim.

21. Dom Bonafede, "White House Report/Staff, Style Changes Slow in Coming Despite President's Post-Watergate Reforms," *National Journal*, 5 (July 21, 1973) pp. 1057–1062.

Chapter 4

1. Walter Lippmann, *The Public Philosophy* (Boston: Little, Brown, 1950), passim.

2. Gabriel Almond, *The American People and Foreign Policy* (New York: Praeger, 1960), 2nd ed., passim.

3. Ibid., Introduction.

4. Kenneth N. Waltz, *Foreign Policy and Democratic Politics, the American and British Experience* (Boston: Little, Brown, 1967), p. 273; William R. Caspary, "The 'Mood Theory': A Study of Public Opinion and Foreign Policy," *American Political Science Review*, 64 (June 1970) pp. 536–547.

5. V. O. Key, Jr., *Public Opinion and American Democracy* (New York: Knopf, 1961), p. 552.

6. Richard E. Neustadt, *Presidential Power* (New York: Wiley, 1960), chapter 5.

7. Bernard C. Cohen, *The Public's Impact on Foreign Policy* (Boston: Little, Brown, 1973), pp. 17–18.

8. Louis Hartz, *The Liberal Tradition in America* (New York: Harcourt, Brace, & World, 1955).
9. Cohen, op. cit., pp. 172–176.
10. John E. Mueller, "Presidential Popularity from Truman to Johnson," *American Political Science Review*, 64 (March 1970), p. 21.
11. Roberta S. Sigel, "Image of the American Presidency: Part II of an Exploration into Popular Views of Presidential Power," in Aaron Wildavsky, ed., *The Presidency* (Boston: Little, Brown, 1969), p. 301.
12. Ibid., p. 301.
13. John E. Mueller, *War, Presidents and Public Opinion* (New York: Wiley, 1973), pp. 69–70.
14. Ibid., p. 70.
15. Ibid., pp. 122–123.
16. Mueller, *American Political Science Review*, op. cit., pp. 21–22.
17. Waltz, op. cit., p. 289.
18. Richard Boyd, "Popular Control of Public Policy: A Normal Vote Analysis of the 1968 Election," *American Political Science Review*, 66 (June 1972) pp. 442–443.
19. Philip E. Converse and Howard Schumann, "The Silent Majority and the Vietnam War," *Scientific American*, 222 (June 1970) p. 20.
20. Ibid.
21. Graham Allison, *The Essence of Decision, Explaining the Cuban Missile Crisis* (Boston: Little, Brown, 1971), p. 193.
22. David Halberstam, *The Best and the Brightest* (New York: Random House, 1972), p. 425; Townsend Hoopes, *The Limits of Intervention* (New York: David McKay, 1969), p. 115; Harry McPherson, *A Political Education* (Boston: Atlantic, Little, Brown, 1972), pp. 109, 390–391.
23. Cohen, op. cit., p. 71.
24. Richard A. Brody and Benjamin I. Page, "Policy Voting and the Electoral Process: The Vietnam War Issue," *American Political Science Review*, 66 (Sept. 1972) p. 994.
25. John E. Mueller, *War, Presidents and Public Opinion*, pp. 100–101; "Trends in Popular Support for the Wars in Korea and Vietnam," *American Political Science Review*, 65 (June 1971) p. 365; Waltz, op. cit., p. 274.
26. Mueller, "Trends in Popular Support," pp. 363–367; Waltz, op. cit., p. 276; Converse and Schumann, op. cit., p. 20.
27. Waltz, op. cit., p. 280.
28. Irving L. Janis, *Victims of Group Think* (Boston: Houghton Mifflin, 1973), chapter 3.
29. Waltz, op. cit., pp. 284–285.
30. Sidney Verba et al., "Public Opinion and the War in Vietnam," *American Political Science Review*, 61 (June 1967) p. 320.
31. Ibid., p. 332.
32. Cohen, op. cit., pp. 205–208.
33. Leon D. Epstein, "Democracy and Foreign Policy," in William N. Chambers and Robert Salisbury, eds., *Democracy in the Mid-Twentieth Century* (St. Louis: Washington University Press, 1960).

Chapter 5

1. Graham T. Allison, *The Essence of Decision: Explaining the Cuban Missile Crisis* (Boston: Little, Brown, 1971), chapter 3.
2. David Halberstam, *The Best and the Brightest* (New York: Random House, 1972), pp. 186–188.
3. Ibid., pp. 204–205.
4. Francis E. Rourke, *Bureaucracy and Foreign Policy* (Baltimore: Johns Hopkins University Press, 1972), p. 20.
5. Chester I. Cooper, "The CIA and Decision-Making," *Foreign Affairs*, 50 (Jan. 1972) pp. 223–236.
6. Ibid., p. 231.
7. Frederick C. Mosher and John Harr, *Programming Systems and Foreign Affairs Leadership* (New York: Oxford University Press, 1970), passim.
8. Theodore Geiger and Roger D. Hansen, "The Role of Information in Decision Making on Foreign Aid," in Raymond A. Bauer and Kenneth J. Gergen, eds., *The Study of Policy Formation* (New York: Free Press, 1968), chapter 9.
9. Allison, op. cit., p. 267.
10. Rourke, op. cit., pp. 68–69.
11. Ibid., p. 16.
12. Allison, op. cit., chapter 5.
13. Alexander L. George, "The Case for Multiple Advocacy in Making Foreign Policy," *The American Political Science Review*, 66 (Sept. 1972) pp. 751–785.
14. Roger Hilsman, *To Move a Nation: The Politics of Foreign Policy in the Administration of John F. Kennedy* (Garden City, N.Y.: Doubleday, 1967), pp. 425–426.
15. Chester L. Cooper, *The Last Crusade: America in Vietnam* (New York: Dodd, Mead, 1970), pp. 215–216.
16. Ibid., p. 374.
17. I. M. Destler, *Presidents, Bureaucrats and Foreign Policy: The Politics of Organizational Reform* (Princeton: Princeton University Press, 1972), p. 60.
18. Halberstam, op. cit., pp. 507–508.
19. Charles E. Lindblom and David Braybrooke, *A Strategy of Decision: Policy Evaluation as a Social Process* (New York: Free Press, 1963), passim.
20. Halberstam, op. cit., pp. 347–349, 354.
21. Ibid., p. 257.
22. Glen D. Paige, *The Korean Decision, June 24–30, 1950* (New York: Free Press, 1968).
23. Irving L. Janis, *Victims of Group Think* (Boston: Houghton Mifflin, 1972), chapter 2.
24. Allison, op. cit., chapter 6.

25. Joseph De Rivera, *The Psychological Dimension of Foreign Policy* (Columbus, Ohio: Charles E. Merrill, 1968), chapter 6.
26. Janis, op. cit., chapter 1.
27. Ibid., chapter 3.
28. Hilsman, op. cit., chapter 35.
29. George, op. cit., p. 783.
30. Lindblom and Braybrooke, op. cit.
31. George, op. cit.
32. Barbara Tuchman, *Stilwell and the American Experience in China, 1911–1945* (New York: Macmillan, 1970), passim.
33. *The Pentagon Papers* (New York: Bantam, 1971), p. 422.
34. Hugh Sidey, "Escalation in Vietnam," *Life Magazine,* 72 (May 19, 1972) pp. 38–41.
35. Henry A. Kissinger, *American Foreign Policy* (New York: Norton, 1969), p. 30.
36. Richard E. Neustadt, *Alliance Politics* (New York: Columbia University Press, 1970), passim.
37. George F. Kennan, *Memoirs, 1950–1963* (Boston: Little, Brown, 1972).
38. Harry McPherson, *A Political Education* (Boston: Atlantic-Little, Brown, 1972), pp. 112–114.
39. Robert F. Kennedy, *Thirteen Days* (New York: Norton, 1971), pp. 53–55.
40. "War Powers Resolution," Public Law 93–148, 93rd Congress, 1st session, Nov. 7, 1973.
41. Aaron B. Wildavsky, "The Two Presidencies," in Aaron B. Wildavsky, ed., *The Presidency* (Boston: Little, Brown, 1969), Table 1, p. 231.
42. Raymond A. Bauer, Ithiel De Sola Pool, and Lewis Anthony Dexter, *American Business and Public Policy: The Politics of Foreign Trade* (Chicago: Aldine-Atherton, 1972), chapters 2–5.
43. Holbert Carroll, *The House of Representatives and Foreign Affairs* (Pittsburgh: University of Pittsburgh Press, 1958), pp. 58, 73, 88, 192–193, 207–208.
44. Richard F. Fenno, Jr., *The Power of the Purse: Appropriations Politics in Congress* (Boston: Little, Brown, 1966), passim.
45. Francis Wilcox, *Congress, the Executive and Foreign Policy* (New York: Harper & Row, 1971), pp. 135–136.
46. Halberstam, op. cit., pp. 412–417.
47. Ibid., p. 146.
48. Adam Yarmolinski, *The Military Establishment: Its Impacts on American Society* (New York: Harper & Row, 1971), p. 130.
49. Halberstam, op. cit., pp. 528–529.
50. Wilcox, op. cit., p. 22.
51. Schlesinger, op. cit., chapter 6.
52. Leon D. Epstein, *British Politics in the Suez Crisis* (Urbana: University of Illinois Press, 1964), passim.
53. Kenneth N. Waltz, *Democracy and Foreign Policy: The American and British Experience* (Boston: Little, Brown, 1967), passim.
54. Bauer, Pool, and Dexter, op. cit., Part 5.
55. Schlesinger, op. cit., pp. 58–60.

56. Ibid., pp. 106–108.
57. Ibid., p. 256.
58. Ibid., chapters 1 and 6.
59. Ibid., pp. 141–150.

Chapter 6

1. Aaron B. Wildavsky, "The Two Presidencies," in Aaron B. Wildavsky, ed., *The Presidency* (Boston: Little, Brown, 1969), pp. 230–243.
2. Louis Hartz, *The Liberal Tradition in America* (New York: Harcourt, Brace and World, 1955), passim; Donald J. Devine, *The Political Culture of the United States* (Boston: Little, Brown, 1972), passim.
3. Clinton Rossiter, *Conservatism in America*, 2nd ed. (New York: Alfred A. Knopf, 1962), pp. 84–96.
4. G. Horowitz, "Conservatism, Liberalism and Socialism in Canada: An Interpretation," *Canadian Journal of Economics and Political Science*, 32 (May 1966) pp. 143–171.
5. Philip Converse, "The Nature of Belief Systems in Mass Publics," in David Apter, ed., *Ideology and Discontent* (New York: Free Press, 1964), chapter 6.
6. Lloyd A. Free and Hadley Cantril, *The Political Beliefs of Americans: A Study of Public Opinion* (New York: Simon and Schuster, 1968), pp. 5–6; Devine, op. cit., cites a number of surveys throughout his book, which confirm the general findings of Free and Cantril that American ideology is "liberal" in the sense postulated by Louis Hartz.
7. Free and Cantril, op. cit., pp. 11–12, 16.
8. Ibid., pp. 24–32.
9. Ibid., pp. 39–40.
10. Ibid., pp. 122–123.
11. Ibid., pp. 180–181.
12. William Chambers and Walter Dean Burnham, eds., *The American Party System: Stages of Political Development* (London: Oxford University Press, 1967), passim.
13. Walter Dean Burnham, *Critical Elections and the Mainsprings of American Politics* (New York: Norton, 1970), p. 282.
14. Richard W. Boyd, "Electoral Trends in Postwar Politics," in James David Barber, ed., *Choosing the President* (Englewood Cliffs, N.J.: Prentice-Hall, 1974), chapter 7.
15. Everett C. Ladd, Jr., *American Political Parties, Social Change and Political Response* (New York: Norton, 1970), p. 310.
16. Angus Campbell, Philip E. Converse, Warren E. Miller, and Donald E. Stokes, *The American Voter* (New York: Wiley, 1960), pp. 182–184, 249, 544, chapter 9.
17. Gerald M. Pomper, "From Confusion to Clarity: Issues and American Voters, 1956–1968," *The American Political Science Review*, 66 (June 1972) pp. 418–419.
18. Ibid., p. 419.

19. Ibid., pp. 421, 424–428.
20. James L. Sundquist, *Politics and Policy: The Eisenhower, Kennedy and Johnson Years* (Washington, D.C.: The Brookings Institution, 1969), pp. 484–489, 496.
21. Ibid., chap. 2.
22. Ibid., pp. 448–450, 468.
23. Ibid., pp. 456–470.
24. Ibid., pp. 442–452, 484–489.
25. Theodore R. Marmor, "The Congress: Medicare Politics and Policy," in Alan Sindler, ed., *American Political Institutions and Public Policy: Five Contemporary Studies* (Boston: Little, Brown, 1969), chapter 1.
26. Philip E. Converse, W. E. Miller, J. G. Rusk, and A. C. Wolfe, "Continuity and Change in American Politics: Parties and Issues in the 1968 Election," *The American Political Science Review*, 63 (Dec. 1969) pp. 1085–1087.
27. Ibid., pp. 1100.
28. Arthur H. Miller, Warren E. Miller, Alden S. Raine, and Thad A. Brown, "A Majority Party in Disarray: Policy Polarization in the 1972 Election" (Paper prepared for delivery at the 1973 Annual Meeting of the American Political Science Association, New Orleans, La., Sept. 4–8, 1973), pp. 16–17.
29. Walter Dean Burnham, "What Started the Landslide?" *The National Observer* (Nov. 18, 1972) p. 30.
30. Gerald M. Pomper, "Toward a More Responsible Two Party System? What Again?" *Journal of Politics*, 33 (Nov. 1971) pp. 916–940.
31. Arthur H. Miller, et al., op. cit., pp. 16–17.
32. Ladd, op. cit., pp. 309–310.
33. Burnham, *Critical Elections*, p. 169.

Chapter 7

1. Richard W. Boyd, "Electoral Trends in Postwar Politics," in James D. Barber, ed., *Choosing the President* (Englewood Cliffs, N.J.: Prentice-Hall, 1974), p. 176.
2. Ibid., pp. 184–185.
3. Ibid., pp. 186–187.
4. John C. Donovan, *The Policymakers* (New York: Pegasus, 1970), p. 61.
5. Gerald M. Pomper, "Nixon and the End of Presidential Politics," *Society*, 10 (Mar./Apr. 1973) pp. 14–16.
6. Fred I. Greenstein, *The American Party System and the American People*, 2nd ed. (Englewood Cliffs, N.J.: Prentice-Hall, 1970), p. 99.
7. Grant McConnell, *Private Power and American Democracy* (New York: Knopf, 1966), pp. 108–110.
8. Raymond A. Bauer, Ithiel De Sola Pool, and Lewis Anthony Dexter, *American Business and Public Policy: The Politics of Foreign Trade* (Chicago: Aldine-Atherton, 1972), Part V.

9. Harry McPherson, *A Political Education* (Boston: Little, Brown, 1972), pp. 368–369.

10. John S. Saloma III, *Congress and the New Politics* (Boston: Little, Brown, 1969), pp. 97–107.

11. Arthur M. Schlesinger, Jr., *A Thousand Days: John F. Kennedy in the White House* (Boston: Houghton Mifflin, 1965), p. 17.

12. Randall B. Ripley, *Majority Party Leadership in Congress* (Boston: Little, Brown, 1969), p. 17.

13. Ibid., p. 12.

14. Hugh Douglas Price, "Schools, Scholarships and Congressmen: The Kennedy Aid-to-Education Program," in Alan F. Westin, ed., *The Centers of Power: Three Cases in American National Government* (New York: Harcourt, Brace and World, 1964), chapter 2.

15. Theodore H. White, *The Making of the President, 1968* (New York: Atheneum, 1969), p. 115.

16. Eric F. Goldman, *The Tragedy of Lyndon Johnson* (New York: Dell, 1968), p. 65.

17. Ibid., p. 66.

18. Ibid., p. 196.

19. Graham T. Allison, *The Essence of Decision: Explaining the Cuban Missile Crisis* (Boston: Little, Brown, 1971), pp. 265–269.

20. Rowland Evans and Robert D. Novack, *Lyndon B. Johnson: The Exercise of Power* (New York: Signet Books, 1968), p. 427.

21. Tom Wicker, *JFK and LBJ: The Influence of Personality Upon Politics* (New York: William Morrow, 1968), p. 169.

22. Goldman, op. cit., p. 377.

23. Ibid., p. 381.

24. Evans and Novack, *Lyndon B. Johnson*, p. 516.

25. Theodore R. Marmor, "The Congress: Medicare Politics and Policy," in Alan Sindler, ed., *American Political Institutions and Public Policy: Five Contemporary Studies* (Boston: Little, Brown, 1969), chapter 1.

26. Goldman, op. cit., p. 348.

27. Evans and Novack, *Lyndon B. Johnson*, pp. 453–457.

28. David Broder, *The Party's Over: The Failure of Politics in America* (New York: Harper & Row, 1971), pp. 55–57.

29. White, op. cit., pp. 22–23.

30. Broder, op. cit., p. 76.

31. Richard E. Neustadt, *Presidential Power: The Politics of Leadership* (New York: Wiley, 1960), chapter 4.

32. Rowland Evans and Robert D. Novack, *Nixon in the White House: The Frustration of Power* (New York: Random House, 1971), p. 51.

33. Arthur M Schlesinger, Jr., *The Imperial Presidency* (Boston: Houghton Mifflin, 1973), p. 216.

34. Ibid., p. 219.

35. Evans and Novack, *Nixon*, pp. 106–107.

36. Ibid., pp. 110–129; John Osborne, *The Third Year of the Nixon Watch* (New York: Liveright, 1972), pp. 190–192; Broder, op. cit., pp. 100–101.

37. Schlesinger, *Imperial Presidency*, pp. 233–241.

38. Ibid., p. 237.
39. Ibid., p. 238.
40. Ibid., pp. 252–255.
41. Michael Novack, "The Presidency and Professor Schlesinger," *Commentary*, 57 (Feb. 1974) pp. 74–78.
42. Roger H. Davidson, *The Politics of Comprehensive Manpower Legislation* (Baltimore: Johns Hopkins University Press, 1972), passim.
43. Charles Culhane, "Manpower Report/Revenue Sharing Shift Set for Worker Training Programs," *National Journal Reports*, 6 (Jan. 1974) pp. 51–58.
44. Ripley, *Majority Party Leadership*, pp. 168, 182.
45. Ronald C. Moe and Steven C. Teel, "Congress as Policymaker: A Necessary Reappraisal," in Ronald C. Moe, ed., *Congress and the President: Allies and Adversaries* (Pacific Palisades, Calif.: Goodyear Publishing, 1971), chapter 2.
46. John R. Johannes, *Policy Innovation in Congress* (Morristown, N.J.: General Learning Press,), pp. 5–13.
47. Ibid., pp. 17–18.
48. Alfred De Grazia, *Republic in Crisis: Congress Against the Executive Force* (New York: Federal Legal Publications, 1965), chapter 5; Laurence H. Chamberlain, *The President, Congress and Legislation* (New York: Columbia University Press, 1946), p. 464.
49. Carroll Kilpatrick, "Nixon Promises 'to Stand and Fight' for Presidency," *The Washington Post*, Mar. 20, 1974, p. Al.

Chapter 8

1. Richard F. Fenno, Jr., *The President's Cabinet* (New York: Vintage Books, 1959), chapter 1.
2. Thomas E. Cronin, "Everybody Believes in Democracy Until He Gets to the White House," in Norman C. Thomas and Hans W. Baade, eds., *The Institutionalized Presidency* (Dobbs Ferry, N.Y.: Oceana Publications, 1972).
3. "The President's Message to the Congress Proposing the Establishment of a Department of Natural Resources, a Department of Community Development, a Department of Human Resources and a Department of Economic Affairs," March 25, 1971. *Weekly Compilation of Presidential Documents* (Mar. 29, 1971) pp. 545–561.
4. Harold Seidman, *Politics, Position and Power: The Dynamics of Federal Organization* (New York: Oxford University Press, 1970), passim.
5. Keith C. Clark and Laurence J. Legere, *The President and the Management of National Security* (New York: Praeger, 1969), pp. 15–16.
6. Ibid., pp. 58–98.
7. Ibid., pp. 70–78.
8. I. M. Destler, *Presidents, Bureaucrats and Foreign Policy: The Politics of Organizational Reform* (Princeton: Princeton University Press, 1972), chapter 5.

9. John P. Leacacos, "Kissinger's Aparat," *Foreign Policy*, 5 (Winter, 1971–72) passim.
10. Destler, op. cit., pp. 121–153.
11. Ibid., p. 310.
12. Chris Argyris, "Some Causes of Organizational Ineffectiveness Within the Department of State," Center for International Systems Research Occasional Paper Number 2 (Jan. 1967); John Franklin Campbell, *Foreign Affairs Fudge Factory* (New York: Basic Books, 1971); Charles Frankel, *High on Foggy Bottom* (New York: Harper & Row, 1968); John E. Harr, *The Professional Diplomat* (Princeton: Princeton University Press, 1969).
13. Campbell, op. cit., pp. 26–31.
14. Frederick C. Mosher and John E. Harr, *Programming Systems and Foreign Affairs Leadership* (New York: Foreign Affairs Leadership, 1970), passim.
15. Argyris, op. cit.
16. Ibid.
17. Destler, op. cit., chapters 8 and 9.
18. Samuel P. Huntington, *The Common Defense: Strategic Programs in National Politics* (New York: Columbia University Press, 1961).
19. Alain C. Enthoven and K. Wayne Smith, *How Much is Enough: Shaping the Defense Program, 1961–1969* (New York: Harper & Row, 1971).
20. Robert Levine, *Public Planning: Failure and Redirection* (New York: Basic Books, 1972), pp. 144–145, 154–155.
21. Adam Yarmolinski, *The Military Establishment: Its Impacts on American Society* (New York: Harper & Row, 1971), p. 95.
22. Ibid., pp. 126–127.
23. Ibid., p. 132.
24. Ibid., p. 391; Levine, op. cit., pp. 125–127.
25. Morris Janowitz, *The Professional Soldier: A Social and Political Portrait* (New York: Free Press, 1960), chapters 14–16.
26. Ibid. chapter 20.
27. Samuel P. Huntington, *The Soldier and the State* (Cambridge: Harvard University Press, 1957), chapter 2.
28. Alexis de Tocqueville, *Democracy in America*, Book III, No. 49 (New York: New American Library, 1956), pp. 274–280.
29. op. cit., chap. 11.
30. William D. Carey, "Presidential Staffing in the Sixties and Seventies," *Public Administration Review*, 29 (Sept.–Oct. 1969) pp. 450–458.
31. Cronin, op. cit.
32. Carey, op. cit., p. 451.
33. Aaron B. Wildavsky, *The Politics of the Budgetary Process* (Boston: Little, Brown, 1964), passim.
34. George D. Greenberg, *"Governing HEW: Problems of Management and Control at the Department of Health, Education and Welfare"* (Ph.D. dissertation, Harvard University, 1972), p. 1.
35. Ibid., chapter 4.
36. HEW, HUD, Interior, Labor, Transportation, Commerce.
37. John K. Inglehart, "Budget Report/HEW Department, Largest Fed-

eral Spender, Seeks to Funnel More Money to Poor," *National Journal*, 4 (Jan. 29, 1972) pp. 168–180.

38. Tom Burns and G. M. Stalker, *Management and Innovation* (London: Tavistock Publications, 1968); Victor A. Thompson, *Bureaucracy and Innovation* (University, Ala.: University of Alabama Press, 1969), passim; Jerald Hage and Michael Aiken, *Social Change in Complex Organizations* (New York: Random House, 1970); Warren G. Bennis and Philip E. Slater, *The Temporary Society* (New York: Harper & Row, 1968), passim; Frederick C. Mosher, "The Public Service in the Temporary Society," in Dwight Waldo, ed., *Public Administration in a Time of Turbulence* (Scranton: Chandler, 1971).

39. Louis Gawthrop, *Bureaucratic Behavior in the Executive Branch* (New York: Free Press, 1969), passim.

40. Edward S. Flash, Jr., *Economic Advice and Presidential Leadership: The Council of Economic Advisers* (New York: Columbia University Press, 1965), passim.

41. Greenberg, op. cit., pp. 169–172.

42. Philip Selznick, *Leadership in Administration: A Sociological Interpretation* (New York: Harper & Row, 1957), passim.

43. Erwin C. Hargrove, Interviews in the Department of Labor, 1973–1974.

44. Ibid.

45. Charles L. Schultz, *The Politics and Economics of Public Spending* (Washington, D.C.: The Brookings Institution, 1968), passim.

46. John Hebers, "The Other Presidency," *New York Times Magazine*, Mar. 3, 1974, p. 16.

47. Pamela Horst, Joe N. Nay, John W. Scanlon, and Joseph S. Wholey, "Program Management and the Federal Evaluator" (Washington, D.C.: The Urban Institute, 1974).

48. Joseph Kraft, "Government by Professor," *The Washington Post*, Feb. 7, 1974, p. A19.

49. Aaron B. Wildavsky and Jeffrey L. Pressman, *Implementation* (Berkeley: University of California Press, 1973), pp. 137, 143.

50. Seidman, op. cit., pp. 283–285.

51. Levine, op. cit., pp. 51–58.

52. Ibid., pp. 61, 65, 81–86.

53. Ibid., pp. 95–102.

54. Wildavsky and Pressman, op. cit., p. 128.

55. "The Comprehensive Employment and Training Act of 1973," Public Law 93–203, 93rd Congress, 1st session, December 28, 1973.

56. Wildavsky and Pressman, op. cit., pp. 134, 161–162.

57. James L. Sundquist, *Making Federalism Work: A Study of Program Coordination at the Community Level* (Washington, D.C.: The Brookings Institution, 1969), p. 27.

58. Ibid., pp. 244–246.

59. Erwin C. Hargrove, *Presidential Leadership, Personality, and Political Style* (New York: Macmillan, 1966), chapters 1 and 3.

Chapter 9

1. Erwin C. Hargrove, *Professional Roles in Society and Government: The English Case* (Beverly Hills, Calif.: Sage, 1972), passim.

2. Leon D. Epstein, "A Comparative Study of Canadian Parties," *American Political Science Review,* 58 (Mar. 1964) pp. 46–59.

3. Kenneth N. Waltz, *Foreign Policy and Democratic Politics: The American and British Experience* (Boston: Little, Brown, 1967), passim.

4. George F. Kennan, *American Diplomacy, 1900–1950* (Chicago: University of Chicago Press, 1950), passim.

5. Arthur M. Schlesinger, Jr., *The Imperial Presidency* (Boston: Houghton Mifflin, 1973), pp. 260–269.

6. J. Anthony Lukas, "The Story So Far," *The New York Times Magazine,* July 23, 1973; "The Story Continued," *The New York Times Magazine,* Jan. 13, 1974. Both issues are devoted to Watergate; the first to a summary of Watergate testimony, the second to events in the fall and winter of 1973–1974.

7. "War Powers Resolution," Public Law 93–148, 93rd Congress, 1st Session, Nov. 7, 1973.

8. Schlesinger, op. cit., pp. 301–307.

9. James MacGregor Burns, *Deadlock of Democracy: Four Party Politics in America* (Englewood Cliffs, N.J.: Prentice-Hall, 1963), passim; Robert A. Dahl, *Congress and Foreign Policy* (New York: Harcourt, Brace, 1950), passim.

10. Austen Ranney and Willmore Kendall, *Democracy and the American Party System* (New York: Harcourt, Brace, 1956), passim.

11. Clinton Rossiter, *Conservatism in America* (New York: Alfred A. Knopf, 1962), passim.

12. Charles O. Jones, "Congressional Committees and the Two-Party System," *Working Papers on House Committee Organization and Operation,* Select Committee on Committees, 93rd Congress, House of Representatives, June 1973, pp. 7–8.

13. John F. Bibby, "Reforming the Committees While Retaining the Unique Role of the House," *Working Papers on House Committee Organization and Operation,* Select Committee on Committees, House of Representatives, 93rd Congress, June 1973, p. 3.

14. Jones, op. cit., p. 3; Joseph Cooper and David W. Brady, "The House and Its Committees: Some Organizational Perspectives," *Working Papers on House Committee Organization and Operation,* Select Committee on Committees, House of Representatives, 93rd Congress, June 1973, pp. 6–11.

15. Schlesinger, op. cit., p. 399.

16. Robert L. Peabody, "House Leadership, Party Caucuses and the Committee Structure," *Working Papers on House Committee Organization and Operation,* Select Committee on Committees, House of Representatives, 93rd Congress, June 1973, pp. 4–5.

17. Randall B. Ripley, "Party Leaders and Standing Committees in the

House of Representatives," *Working Papers on House Committee Organization and Operation*, Select Committee on Committees, House of Representatives, 93rd Congress, June 1973, pp. 8–9,11.

18. Harold B. Seidman, Panel Discussions before the Select Committee on Committees, House of Representatives, 93rd Congress, 1st Session, Vol. 2 of 3, Part 2 of 3 (June 26–29, July 12–13, 1973), p. 390.

19. Ibid., pp. 389–391.

20. Arnold R. Weber, Ibid., p. 397.

21. Elmer B. Staats, Panel Discussions before the Select Committee on Committees, House of Representatives, 93rd Congress, 1st Session, Vol. 2 of 3, Part 1 of 3 (June 13–15, 20–22, July 11–13, 1973), pp. 223–224.

22. Weber, op. cit., p. 396.

23. Staats, op. cit., p. 225.

24. Schlesinger, op. cit., pp. 406–407.

25. Theodore H. White, *The Making of the President, 1972* (New York: Bantam Books, 1973), chapter 2; Austen Ranney, "Changing the Rules of the Nominating Game," in James D. Barber, ed., *Choosing the President* (Englewood Cliffs, N.J.: Prentice-Hall, 1974).

26. Carl Baar and Ellen Baar, "Party and Convention Organization and Leadership in Canada and the United States," in Donald R. Matthews, ed., *Perspectives on Presidential Selection* (Washington, D.C.: Brookings Institution, 1973), pp. 55–65.

27. Ibid.

28. *Choosing the President.* (Report of the Forty-fourth American Assembly, Columbia University, Dec. 16–19, 1973), pp. 4–9.

29. Daniel Patrick Moynihan, *Coping: On the Practice of Government* (New York: Random House, 1973), passim.

30. Richard N. Goodwin, *The American Condition* (New York: Doubleday, 1974), passim.

31. Donald J. Devine, *The Political Culture of the United States* (Boston: Little, Brown, 1972), passim.

32. Erwin C. Hargrove, "On Canadian and American Political Culture," *Canadian Journal of Economics and Political Science*, 33 (Feb. 1967) pp. 107–111; G. Horowitz, "Conservatism, Liberalism and Socialism in Canada: An Interpretation," *Canadian Journal of Economics and Political Science*, 32 (May 1966) pp. 143–171.

33. Lionel Trilling, *The Liberal Imagination: Essays on Literature and Society* (New York: Doubleday, 1950), pp. 9–15.

34. Reinhold Niebuhr, *The Irony of American History* (New York: Scribner, 1952), passim.

35. I am indebted to my colleague Michael Springer for this phrase.

36. David Broder, "The Democrats' Dilemma," *The Atlantic*, 223 (Mar. 1974) pp. 31–40.

37. Waltz, op. cit.; Schlesinger, op. cit. Each of these books rests on a theory of openness and persuasion as the key to democratic processes. The justification is both ethical and prudential.

38. Richard E. Neustadt, *Presidential Power: The Politics of Leadership* (New York: Signet Books, 1964), passim.

39. Peter Sperlich, "Bargaining and Overload: An Essay on Presidential Power," in Aaron Wildavsky, ed., *The Presidency* (Boston: Little, Brown, 1969), passim.

40. James MacGregor Burns, *Roosevelt: The Lion and the Fox* (New York: Harcourt, Brace and World, 1956), p. 174.

41. Philip Selznick, *Leadership in Administration: A Sociological Interpretation* (New York: Harper & Row, 1957), passim.

42. Max Weber, "Politics as a Vocation," in H. H. Gerth and C. Wright Mills, eds., *From Max Weber: Essays in Sociology* (New York: Oxford University Press, 1958), pp. 77–128.

43. James MacGregor Burns, "Toward the Conceptualization of Political Leadership," unpublished paper, Sept. 1973, p. 21.

44. Neustadt, op. cit., p. 172.

45. Ibid.

46. David Broder, "A Politician for President," *Providence Journal*, July 18, 1973, p. 20.

47. Fred E. Friedler, *Leadership* (Morristown, N.J.: General Learning Press, 1971), passim.

48. Neustadt, op. cit., pp. 188–189.

49. Alexander L. George and Juliette L. George, *Woodrow Wilson and Colonel House: A Personality Study* (New York: John Day, 1956), passim.

50. Fred I. Greenstein, *Personality and Politics: Problems of Evidence, Inference and Conceptualization* (Chicago: Markham Publishing, 1969); Erwin C. Hargrove, *Presidential Leadership, Personality and Political Style* (New York: Macmillan, 1966); James D. Barber, *The Presidential Character: Predicting Performance in the White House* (Englewood Cliffs, N.J.: Prentice-Hall, 1972).

51. Erwin C. Hargrove, "Presidential Personality and Revisionist Views of the Presidency," *American Journal of Political Science*, 17 (Nov. 1973) pp. 819–835; Alexander L. George, "Assessing Presidential Character," *World Politics*, 26 (Jan. 1974) pp. 234–282.

52. Broder, op. cit.

53. Rowland Evans and Robert D. Novack, *Nixon in the White House: The Frustration of Power* (New York: Random House, 1971), passim.

54. "A Catalogue of Matters Involving the President," *The New York Times*, Feb. 10, 1974, section 4, p. 3.

55. William Grieder, "Impeaching Politics Past," *The Washington Post*, Dec. 2, 1973, p. B1.

56. Raoul Berger, "Impeachment for 'High Crimes and Misdemeanors,' " in *Impeachment: Selected Materials*, Committee on the Judiciary, House of Representatives, 93rd Congress, 1st Session, Oct. 1973, pp. 617–662.

57. Schlesinger, op. cit., p. 379.

58. Ibid., p. 412.

59. *The Pentagon Papers as published by The New York Times* (New York: Bantam Books, 1971), passim.

Bibliography

General Interpretive Books

Bailey, Thomas A. *Presidential Greatness: The Image and the Man From George Washington to the Present.* New York: Appleton-Century-Crofts, 1966.

Burns, James MacGregor. *Presidential Government: The Crucible of Leadership.* Boston: Houghton Mifflin, 1966.

DeGrazia, Alfred. *Republic in Crisis: Congress Against the Executive Force.* New York: Federal Legal Publications, 1965.

Neustadt, Richard E. *Presidential Power: The Politics of Leadership.* New York: Wiley, 1960.

Watergate: Its Implications for Responsible Government. A report prepared by a panel of the National Academy of Public Administration at the request of the Senate Select Committee on Presidential Campaign Activities (Mar. 1974), Washington, D.C.

American Culture and Ideology

Devine, Donald J. *The Political Culture of the United States.* Boston: Little, Brown, 1972.

Free, Lloyd A., and Cantril, Hadley. *The Political Beliefs of Americans: A Study of Public Opinion.* New York: Simon and Schuster, 1968.

Hartz, Louis. *The Liberal Tradition in America.* New York: Harcourt, Brace and World, 1955.

Lane, Robert E. *Political Ideology: Why the American Common Man Believes What He Does.* New York: Free Press, 1967.

Niebuhr, Reinhold. *The Irony of American History.* New York: Scribner, 1952.

Rossiter, Clinton. *Conservatism in America.* New York: Vintage Books, 1962.

President and Public

Barber, James P., ed. *Choosing the President.* Englewood Cliffs, N.J.: Prentice-Hall, 1974.

Cohen, Bernard C. *The Public's Impact on Foreign Policy.* Boston: Little, Brown, 1973.

Greenberg, Bradley, and Parker, Edwin D., eds. *The Kennedy Assassination and the American Public: Social Communication in Crisis.* Stanford: Stanford University Press, 1965.

Greenstein, Fred I. *Children and Politics.* New Haven: Yale University Press, 1965.

Lippmann, Walter. *The Public Philosophy.* Boston: Little, Brown, 1950.

Mueller, John E. *War, Presidents and Public Opinion.* New York: Wiley, 1973.

Parties and Elections

Barber, James P., ed. *Choosing the President.* Englewood Cliffs, N.J.: Prentice-Hall, 1974.

Burnham, Walter Dean. *Critical Elections and the Mainsprings of American Politics.* New York: Norton, 1970.

Burns, James MacGregor. *Deadlock of Democracy: Four Party Politics in America.* Englewood Cliffs, N.J.: Prentice-Hall, 1963.

Campbell, Angus et al. *The American Voter.* New York: Wiley, 1960.

Chambers, William, and Burnham, Walter Dean, eds. *The American Party System: Stages of Political Development.* London: Oxford University Press, 1967.

Presidential Personality

Barber, James David. *The Presidential Character: Predicting Performance in the White House.* Englewood Cliffs, N.J.: Prentice-Hall, 1972.

Burns, James MacGregor. *Roosevelt: The Lion and the Fox.* New York: Harcourt, Brace and World, 1956.

———. *Roosevelt, The Soldier of Freedom.* New York: Harcourt, Brace and World, 1973.

George, Alexander L., and Juliette L. *Woodrow Wilson and Colonel House: A Personality Study.* New York: John Day, 1956.

Greenstein, Fred I. *Personality and Politics: Problems of Evidence, Inference and Conceptualization.* Chicago: Markham, 1969.

Hargrove, Erwin C. *Presidential Leadership, Personality and Political Style.* New York: Macmillan, 1966.

Latham, Earl, ed. *John F. Kennedy and Presidential Power.* Lexington, Mass.: D. C. Heath, 1972.

Nixon, Richard M. *Six Crises.* New York: Pocket, 1962.

Osborne, John. *The First Two Years of the Nixon Watch.* New York: Liveright, 1971.

———. *The Third Year of the Nixon Watch.* New York: Liveright, 1972.

———. *The Fourth Year of the Nixon Watch.* New York: Liveright, 1973.

Wills, Gary. *Nixon Agonistes.* Boston: Houghton Mifflin, 1970.

The Institutionalized Presidency

Anderson, Patrick. *The President's Men.* Garden City, N.Y.: Doubleday, 1969.

Cronin, Thomas E., and Greenberg, Sanford D., eds. *The Presidential Advisory System.* New York: Harper & Row, 1969.

Flash, Edward S., Jr. *Economic Advice and Presidential Leadership: The Council of Economic Advisers.* New York: Columbia University Press, 1965.

Reedy, George E. *The Twilight of the Presidency.* New York: World Publishing, 1970.

Thomas, Norman C., and Baade, Hans W., eds. *The Institutionalized Presidency.* Dobbs Ferry, N.Y.: Oceana, 1972.

The White House Transcripts. The full text of the Submission of Recorded Presidential Conversations to the Committee on the Judiciary of the House of Representatives by President Richard M. Nixon. Introduction by R. W. Apple, Jr. New York: Bantam, 1974.

Foreign Policymaking

Allison, Graham T. *The Essence of Decision: Explaining the Cuban Missile Crisis.* Boston: Little, Brown, 1971.

Chamberlain, Laurence H. *The President, Congress and Legislation.* New York: Columbia University Press, 1946.

Cooper, Chester L. *The Last Crusade: America in Vietnam.* New York: Dodd, Mead, 1970.

DeRivera, Joseph. *The Psychological Dimension of Foreign Policy.* Columbus, Ohio: Charles E. Merrill, 1968.

Evans, Rowland, and Novack, Robert D. *Lyndon B. Johnson: The Exercise of Power.* New York: Signet Books, 1968.

———. *Nixon in the White House: The Frustration of Power.* New York: Random House, 1971.

Goldman, Eric F. *The Tragedy of Lyndon Johnson.* New York: Dell, 1968.

Halberstam, David. *The Best and the Brightest.* New York: Random House, 1972.

Hilsman, Roger. *To Move a Nation: The Politics of Foreign Policy in the Administration of John F. Kennedy.* Garden City, N.Y.: Doubleday, 1967.

Hoopes, Townsend. *The Limits of Intervention.* New York: David McKay, 1969.

Janis, Irving L. *Victims of Group Think.* Boston: Houghton Mifflin, 1973.

Kennan, George F. *Memoirs: Nineteen Fifty to Nineteen Sixty-Three.* Boston: Little, Brown, 1972.

Kennedy, Robert F. *Thirteen Days: A Memoir of the Cuban Missile Crisis.* New York: Norton, 1971.

Moe, Ronald C., ed. *Congress and the President: Allies and Adversaries.* Pacific Palisades, Calif.: Goodyear Publishing, 1971.

Neustadt, Richard E. *Alliance Politics.* New York: Columbia University Press, 1970.

Paige, Glen P. *The Korean Decision: June 24–30, 1950.* New York: Free Press, 1968.

The Pentagon Papers as Published by the New York Times. New York: Bantam Books, 1971.

Ripley, Randall B. *Majority Party Leadership in Congress.* Boston: Little, Brown, 1969.

Schlesinger, Arthur M., Jr. *A Thousand Days: John F. Kennedy in the White House.* Boston: Houghton Mifflin, 1965.

———. *The Imperial Presidency.* Boston: Houghton Mifflin, 1973.

Walton, Richard J. *Cold War and Counterrevolution: The Foreign Policy of John F. Kennedy.* Baltimore: Penguin, 1972.

Waltz, Kenneth N. *Foreign Policy and Democratic Politics: The American and British Experience.* Boston: Little, Brown, 1967.

Wilcox, Francis. *Congress, The Executive and Foreign Policy.* New York: Harper & Row, 1971.

Domestic Policymaking

Chamberlain, Laurence H. *The President, Congress and Legislation.* New York: Columbia University Press, 1946.

Evans, Rowland, and Novack, Robert D. *Lyndon B. Johnson: The Exercise of Power.* New York: Signet Books, 1968.

———. *Nixon in the White House: The Frustration of Power.* New York: Random House, 1971.

Goldman, Eric F. *The Tragedy of Lyndon Johnson.* New York: Dell, 1968.

Holtzman, Abraham. *Legislative Liaison: Executive Leadership in Congress.* Chicago: Rand McNally, 1970.

McConnell, Grant. *Private Power and American Democracy.* New York: Knopf, 1966.

Moe, Ronald C., ed. *Congress and the President: Allies and Adversaries,* Pacific Palisades, Calif.: Goodyear Publishing, 1971.

Ripley, Randall B. *Majority Party Leadership in Congress.* Boston: Little, Brown, 1969.

Schlesinger, Arthur M., Jr. *A Thousand Days: John F. Kennedy in the White House.* Boston: Houghton Mifflin, 1965.

Sundquist, James L. *Politics and Policy: The Eisenhower, Kennedy, and Johnson Years.* Washington, D.C.: Brookings Institution, 1969.

President and Bureaucracy

Campbell, John Franklin. *Foreign Affairs Fudge Factory.* New York: Basic Books, 1971.

Clark, Keith C., and Legere, Laurence J. *The President and the Management of National Security.* New York: Praeger, 1969.

Destler, I. M. *Presidents, Bureaucrats and Foreign Policy.* Princeton: Princeton University Press, 1972.

Fenno, Richard F. *The President's Cabinet.* New York: Vintage Books, 1959.

Levine, Robert. *Public Planning: Failure and Redirection.* New York: Basic Books, 1972.

Mosher, Frederick C., and Harr, John E. *Programming Systems and Foreign Affairs Leadership.* New York: Oxford University Press, 1970.

Rourke, Francis E. *Bureaucracy and Foreign Policy.* Baltimore: Johns Hopkins University Press, 1972.

Seidman, Harold. *Politics, Position and Power: The Dynamics of Federal Organization.* New York: Oxford University Press, 1970.

Wildavsky, Aaron B., and Pressman, Jeffrey L. *Implementation.* Berkeley: University of California Press, 1973.

Yarmolinski, Adam. *The Military Establishment: Its Impact on American Society.* New York: Harper & Row, 1971.

POSTSCRIPT:
August 9, 1974

The immediate crisis of the Presidency has ended. Today, Richard M. Nixon resigned his office and was succeeded by Gerald R. Ford. Nixon left under the pressure of events that he himself had unloosed by disclosing the text of a tape recorded conversation of June 23, 1972 in which he had directed the curtailing of the FBI investigation of the Watergate burglary. This event destroyed any hope the President might have had of avoiding impeachment and conviction. He was persuaded by Republican congressional leaders to resign.

It seems likely that he would have been impeached and convicted in any event. The House Judiciary committee the week before had recommended impeachment on three counts of obstruction of justice, abuse of power, and defiance of Congress. The key to the actions of the committee was the development of a center group of southern Democrats and moderate Republicans who felt that their constitutional obligations required them to join the majority of Democrats on the committee in supporting impeachment.

It was clear the impeachment process was working in the way the Founders had hoped. A President was held accountable for crimes against both law and the Constitution. Neither petty criminality nor broad political disagreement was thought germane. A process of public education and persuasion was set in motion by the public debates of the Judiciary committee, whose continuation would have strengthened a broad agreement among citizens and the Congress on the bitter necessity of impeachment and conviction.

Several forces were simultaneously at work here. First, the folkways of Congress require a honing of issues to permit maximum breadth of agreement across both parties on such major questions. Congress can be criticized for searching for the least common denominator in legislative disagreements, but national opinions and divisions are strong, and various and important action that will bind all can only be taken through such a process of reaching out and bringing together. Second, political partisanship, while always a factor, was beginning to give way in Congress to a larger awareness of constitutional morality. There was a growing realization that if Richard Nixon were not impeached the constitutional morality of America would appear to be seriously flawed. Finally, one could see the seeds of affirmation fully emerge in the spirit of national unity and consecration expressed as President Ford was inaugurated.

An atmosphere prevailed, similar to that in the aftermath of the death of John F. Kennedy. A violent blow against the republic was healed by the words and actions of Lyndon Johnson, calling the nation to unity behind our national ideals. President Ford and the leading political figures of the nation made the same affirmations and seem to have received the same genuine public response.

A parliamentary system would have easily removed a chief minister who had violated the constitution and the law. In either Britain or Canada there would have been little deference or awe accorded to such a man because of his position. But Americans cannot treat the President and the Presidency in such a manner. The dominant mood among people and Congress was one of sadness at the necessity, and awe at the responsibility, of acting to remove a Chief Executive from office. The legacy of constitutional monarchy as a lingering archetype behind the Presidency is perhaps a factor explaining this feeling. The very transfer of office has a medieval, sacremental quality in that at a given moment in time one man ceases to be President and another is simultaneously annointed. These feelings, however, are probably not nearly as strong as is the mystique of the Presidency as the prime office of national popular election. To remove a President is to set aside the expressed decision of the electorate. The symbolic authority of the office as the focal point of national unity increases this reluctance. But the Constitution is an even greater symbol as events have shown.

This deference to office and incumbent is both a strength and weakness for American democracy. It permits tolerance of the abuse of power and impedes accountability. But these same sentiments give us the Presidency as a symbol of national unity and purpose. One searches in vain for an institution that could fulfill the same function under an American parliamentary system.

We cannot therefore escape our legacy but must direct it within the rule of law of the Constitution. The Presidency will not be demythologized and it will not be long before liberals will once again be advocating a strong Presidency and conservatives expressing skepticism. Those traditional postures were reversed by Vietnam and Watergate. A politics of extreme language and action caused by social turmoil and war is vanishing as these past events recede. President Ford and the leaders of Congress are likely to bring us back to a politics of openness, trust, and mutual accomodation. Whether these leaders and those who follow will have the intelligence and wisdom to cope successfully with the extraordinary policy problems that remain and are to come, is another question that cannot now be answered.

The events of August 1974 permit the ending of this book on a constructive, optimistic note. We have come through a time of troubles since 1963—a civil rights revolution that has not yet ended, massive social reform that has raised popular expectations but not solved the underlying problems, deep divisions of the generations and social groups over a wretched war, the disclosure of abuse of power in the highest place, and the resignation of a President under threat of removal. And yet our national ideals and constitutional processes are stronger than ever because these conflicts have been resolved in constitutional ways through normal political processes. We have resisted the impulse to tear our neighbors throat because of disagreement. Constitutional democracy is a slow and cumbersome instrument for the achievement of civilized life, but every success in its use strengthens it for the trials ahead.

Index

Accountability, Presidential, 28
Acheson, Dean, 85
Active-positive leaders
    destructive behavior by, 77–78
    evaluation of, 57–58
Adams, Sherman, 63
Almond, Gabriel, on public involvement in foreign policy, 104–105
American government, power *vs* morality in, 307–319
American history, progressive interpretation of, 11–12
American politics, and liberal ideology, 177–178
Anticommunism, and foreign policy, 115, 116
Ash Commission, 293
Authority style, democratic, 78

Baker, Newton D., 51
Ball, George, 148
Barber, James David, and typology of Presidents, 50
Bargaining, in decision process, 143–144
Bay of Pigs invasion (1961), 67, 87
Berger, Raoul, on impeachment, 316
Berlin crisis, 67
BOB. *See* Bureau of Budget
Book, focuses of, 32
Boyd, Richard, on voter party identification, 203
Bundy, McGeorge, 86, 92, 242
Bureaucratic organizations
    and biased information, 125–127
    importance of, 127–128
    internal culture in, 124–125
    limited repertoire of, 127
    presidential control of, 264–265
    and Vietnam policy mishap, 149–150. *See also* High bureaucratic politics
Bureau of Budget
    and domestic policy, 259–260
    and legislative development, 82, 83
Burnham, Walter Dean, on McGovern failures, 195–196

Burns, James MacGregor, 8
    on Hamiltonian Presidency, 29
    on orientation toward history, 6
    on political leadership, 306
    on Roosevelt's leadership ability, 54

Cabinet departments
    conflicts between, 240–241
    evolution of, 237–238
    relationship with President, 238–239
    reorganization by Nixon of, 239–240, 241. *See also* Outer cabinet departments
Califano, Joseph, 92
Cantril, Halley, on liberal ideology, 183–184
Carey, William, on Great Society program, 259
"Checkers" speech (1952), 44
Civil rights, Kennedy commitment to, 68
Civil Rights Act (1964), 68
Closed politics, defined, 123
Cold War
    and executive power in foreign policy, 98–99
    foreign policy posture in, 281–282
    and Presidential power, 282–283
    and Vietnam policy making, 147
Committee to Reelect the President (Nixon), 185
Comprehensive Employment and Training Act (1973), 228
Congress
    and cabinet departments, 237
    composition of, 203–205
    and consent for Presidential policy, 158–163
    decentralization of, 289, 290
    and deference to Presidents, 163–165
    Democratic domination of, 202
    and extra-constitutional action by President, 171
    in foreign policy making, 167, 168, 169–170
    and foreign policy option debates, 162–163

343

ABOUT THE AUTHOR

Erwin C. Hargrove is a professor of political science at Brown University specializing in the Presidency, policymaking, and the bureaucracy of American government, and leadership and policymaking in British government. He received both his B.A. (1953) and Ph.D. (1963) from Yale University and has been Faculty Research Fellow of the Social Science Research Council (1967–1968) and Senior Fellow at the Urban Institute (1973–1975). Dr. Hargrove has written *Presidential Leadership, Personality and Political Style* (1966) and *Professional Roles in Society and Government: The English Case* (Sage: 1972). He has contributed articles to *Comparative Politics, Political Studies,* and the *American Journal of Politics.*

A Note on the Type

The text of this book was set by computer. The type is based on the original Caledonia, a Linotype face designed by W. A. Dwiggins. It belongs to the family of printing types called "modern face" by printers—a term used to mark the change in style of type-letters that occurred about 1800. Caledonia borders on the general design of Scotch Modern, but is more freely drawn than that letter.
The book was composed by The Haddon Craftsman Inc., Scranton, Pa., printed and bound by Halliday Lithograph Inc., West Hanover, Mass.